Global Trends, Practices, and Challenges in Contemporary Tourism and Hospitality Management

Debasish Batabyal
Amity University Kolkata, India

Dillip Kumar Das
University of Burdwan, India

A volume in the Advances in
Hospitality, Tourism, and the
Services Industry (AHTSI) Book
Series

Published in the United States of America by
> IGI Global
> Business Science Reference (an imprint of IGI Global)
> 701 E. Chocolate Avenue
> Hershey PA, USA 17033
> Tel: 717-533-8845
> Fax: 717-533-8661
> E-mail: cust@igi-global.com
> Web site: http://www.igi-global.com

Library of Congress Cataloging-in-Publication Data

Names: Batabyal, Debasish, 1978- editor. | Das, Dilip Kumar, 1974- editor.
Title: Global trends, practices, and challenges in contemporary tourism and
   hospitality management / Debasish Batabyal and Dillip Kumar Das, Editors.
Description: Hershey PA : Business Science Reference, an imprint of IGI
   Global, [2020]
Identifiers: LCCN 2018054600| ISBN 9781522584940 (hardcover) | ISBN
   9781522585138 (softcover) | ISBN 9781522584957 (ebk.)
Subjects: LCSH: Tourism--Management. | Hospitality industry--Management.
Classification: LCC G155.A1 G496 2020 | DDC 910.68--dc23 LC record available at https://lccn.
loc.gov/2018054600

This book is published in the IGI Global book series Advances in Hospitality, Tourism, and the Services Industry (AHTSI) (ISSN: 2475-6547; eISSN: 2475-6555)

British Cataloguing in Publication Data
A Cataloguing in Publication record for this book is available from the British Library.

All work contributed to this book is new, previously-unpublished material.
The views expressed in this book are those of the authors, but not necessarily of the publisher.

For electronic access to this publication, please contact: eresources@igi-global.com.

Advances in Hospitality, Tourism, and the Services Industry (AHTSI) Book Series

ISSN:2475-6547
EISSN:2475-6555

Editor-in-Chief: Maximiliano Korstanje, University of Palermo, Argentina

MISSION

Globally, the hospitality, travel, tourism, and services industries generate a significant percentage of revenue and represent a large portion of the business world. Even in tough economic times, these industries thrive as individuals continue to spend on leisure and recreation activities as well as services.

The Advances in Hospitality, Tourism, and the Services Industry (AHTSI) book series offers diverse publications relating to the management, promotion, and profitability of the leisure, recreation, and services industries. Highlighting current research pertaining to various topics within the realm of hospitality, travel, tourism, and services management, the titles found within the AHTSI book series are pertinent to the research and professional needs of managers, business practitioners, researchers, and upper-level students studying in the field.

COVERAGE

- Travel Agency Management
- Tourism and the Environment
- Service Training
- Sustainable Tourism
- Leisure & Business Travel
- Customer Service Issues
- International Tourism
- Destination Marketing and Management
- Service Design
- Service Management

IGI Global is currently accepting manuscripts for publication within this series. To submit a proposal for a volume in this series, please contact our Acquisition Editors at Acquisitions@igi-global.com or visit: http://www.igi-global.com/publish/.

Titles in this Series

For a list of additional titles in this series, please visit:
https://www.igi-global.com/book-series/advances-hospitality-tourism-services-industry/121014

Positioning and Branding Tourism Destinations for Global Competitiveness
Rahmat Hashim (Taylor's University, Malaysia) Mohd Hafiz Mohd Hanafiah (Universiti Teknologi MARA, Malaysia) and Mohd Raziff Jamaluddin (University Teknologi MARA, Maaysia)
Business Science Reference • ©2019 • 332pp • H/C (ISBN: 9781522572534) • US $205.00

Tourism-Oriented Policing and Protective Services
Peter E. Tarlow (Texas A&M University, USA)
Business Science Reference • ©2019 • 310pp • H/C (ISBN: 9781522575795) • US $195.00

Neoliberalism in the Tourism and Hospitality Sector
Vipin Nadda (University of Sunderland, UK) Sahidi Bilan (University of Sunderland, UK) Muhammad Azam (University of Sunderland, UK) and Dirisa Mulindwa (University of Sunderland, UK)
Business Science Reference • ©2019 • 241pp • H/C (ISBN: 9781522569831) • US $185.00

Conservation and Promotion of Heritage Tourism
Surabhi Srivastava (University of Kota, India)
Business Science Reference • ©2019 • 260pp • H/C (ISBN: 9781522562832) • US $195.00

Environmental Impacts of Tourism in Developing Nations
Ravi Sharma (Symbiosis Institute of International Business, India) and Prakash Rao (Symbiosis Institute of International Business, India)
Engineering Science Reference • ©2019 • 348pp • H/C (ISBN: 9781522558439) • US $225.00

Handbook of Research on Socio-Economic Impacts of Religious Tourism and Pilgrimage
José Álvarez-García (University of Extremadura, Spain) María de la Cruz del Río Rama (University of Vigo, Spain) and Martín Gómez-Ullate (University of Extremadura, Spain)
Business Science Reference • ©2019 • 455pp • H/C (ISBN: 9781522557302) • US $285.00

For an entire list of titles in this series, please visit:
https://www.igi-global.com/book-series/advances-hospitality-tourism-services-industry/121014

701 East Chocolate Avenue, Hershey, PA 17033, USA
Tel: 717-533-8845 x100 • Fax: 717-533-8661
E-Mail: cust@igi-global.com • www.igi-global.com

Editorial Advisory Board

Table of Contents

Detailed Table of Contents

Chapter 1

 Ravi Sharma, Symbiosis International University, India

A study of the water quality assessment of the Betwa River stretch was conducted
in order to explore the detrimental effects of assorted anthropogenic and visitors'
activities on the river. The religious tourism activities are the main type of tourism
activities explored under the study in context to India. Samples were collected
during May 2014 (pre-monsoon) to December 2015 (post-monsoon) period. Twelve
different physicochemical parameters were collected through primary data and
field investigations, while the bacteriological parameters like total coliform and
fecal coliform levels were analyzed through secondary data, except biochemical
oxygen demand. The results suggest that the seasonal and spatial variations are
significantly different. The results also conclude that the chloride, nitrite, phosphate,
COD, nitrate, and BOD as evaluated using PCA extraction method shows a higher
degree of positive correlation in a component which indicates anthropogenic and
industrial impacts on water quality.

Chapter 2

 Carlos Balsas, University at Albany (SUNY), USA

Solar salinas in Portugal are progressively changing from places of work to places
of tourism. The research question is the extent to which these special landscapes
have been understood, marketed, and enhanced to the benefit of mostly tourists and

visitors or also local constituencies. This research question arises from a sense of stigmatization, perceived lack of potential, and outmoded technological development associated with traditional cultural heritage and sun and sea tourism paradigms. The purpose of this chapter is to analyze how two Portuguese municipalities (i.e., Aveiro and Figueira da Foz) have engaged in the rehabilitation of their solar salinas. The argument is that given the considerable natural areas of wetlands in the case studies, solar salinas, and their potentialities from ecotourism and environmental education ought to perform a more central role in the municipalities' territorial development strategies. The key finding is the identification of a set of lessons learned useful to the partial rehabilitation of solar salinas.

Chapter 3

Partho Pratim Seal, Manipal Academy of Higher Education, India

The technology development in hospitality is continuing at a relentless pace which is challenging for the hospitality professional for both present and the future generations. The hotel front office is moving towards automation with less human interface. Reservations are mostly being made with help of booking engines and guest interaction with hotels are by apps and chatbots. Artificial intelligence (AI) also occupies a major role to facilitate and enhance guest experience. The trends now include use of augmented reality, predictive analysis, beacons, robotics, block chain technology, and biophilic designs in the hotel. The research is to study about how various hotel chains are adopting new technology and incorporating it in their establishment. The research is based upon data collected from hotel websites and other secondary sources to determine the acceptance of new trends by the hotel chains. The result suggests that though some international hotel chains have started accepting the new trends, the major Indian chains specially are lacking behind.

Chapter 4

Emel Memis Kocaman, Tokat Gaziosmanpasa University, Turkey
Mehmet Kocaman, Tokat Gaziosmanpasa University, Turkey

Customers expect a high standard and fast service from enterprises. In addition, competition among enterprises necessitates that enterprises renew themselves, meet customer expectations at maximum level, and raise the standard of products and services. Traditional restaurant management is inadequate to provide all this. This situation led to search, and restaurant management systems (RMS) have been developed. RMS, which emerged in the 1970s, are now much more developed, facilitating both the operation and management process and offering a professional management opportunity. RMS has made it possible for the restaurants to institutionalize and establish chain enterprises. Moreover, income and expense control can be made more effective via RMS. This chapter explains RMS and the operation of RMS via a sample program.

Chapter 5
Debasish Batabyal, Amity University Kolkata, India
Dillip Kumar Das, University of Burdwan, India

Bolpur is a district town in Birbhum, West Bengal. This place is famous for Viswabharti in Shanti Niketan where a new school of thought was initiated by Rabindranath Tagore. Later on, the place became an epicenter for Bengali education and culture. Though the place has other noteworthy academic and cultural records, this place has immense scope for urban and rural ecotourism. With the blend of rural Bengal and its rich artistic and spiritual exuberance, Birbhum offers a lot. Now, as a mean of entrepreneurship and employment, ecotourism can provide the local people with new alternative scope and opportunities. This chapter is an attempt to revisit and reorganize destination Bolpur with a sustainable marketing orientation for ecotourism. Further attempt is also made to support industry leaders and tourism academicians interested to invest or study for business and commerce. Familiarization trip has been conducted along with a survey for the tourists to better understand their expectations and perceptions.

Chapter 6
Abhijit Pandit, Amity University, India

This chapter focuses on how people of Kallakurichi, Tamil Nadu, India can become conscious of ecotourism, bio-cultural diversity, and sustainable development, vital for both present and future. It utilized a sustainable development framework for considering biological and cultural perspectives. The primary target audience of this research was 100 local people of this lesser known and sparsely populated area, and 31 questionnaires were found to be useful. Simple random sampling was used in this regard. The collected data were analyzed using mean, t-test, Pearson's product moment correlation, and regression analysis. The researcher concluded with findings that point to the need for shared community authority, management, and decision making; mutual benefits; recognition of the rights, values, norms, power structures, and dynamics of local populations; respect for belief systems as well as traditional and local ecological knowledge; and the importance of contextual adaptation.

Chapter 7

Cristi Spulbar, University of Craiova, Romania
Birău Ramona, Constantin Brâncusi University of Targu Jiu, Romania
Jatin Trivedi, Amity University Mumbai, India

This chapter aims to provide an exhaustive overview of the importance of banking system in Romanian tourism and hospitality industry. Romania is a member of the European Union since 1 January 2007, but is not a member of the Schengen area and haven't adopted the euro currency yet. The banking system plays an essential role in financial intermediation being a major factor in raising productivity of Romanian tourism and hospitality industry. From a long-term perspective, a global perspective on the banking system can lead to the development of tourism and hospitality business. The interdependence between banking system and the tourism and hospitality industry in Romania is an increasing challenge for public and private investment. However, Romania's tourist attractions are still not capitalized due to the lack of financial investments. The Romanian tourism potential is significant, but the relatively low number of foreign tourists and even indigenous tourists reflects the lack of relevant financial investments and effective promotion.

Chapter 8

Natisha Saqib, University of Kashmir, India

The tourism industry certainly has been a formidable pillar as an unfailing and reliable source of revenue and capital for many nations. Many countries have been elevated from poor to appreciable economic statuses as a result of the invaluable contributions their tourism sectors have succeeded in adding to their overall economic growth. Tourism is a major engine of economic growth and an important source of foreign exchange earnings in India. Over the last decade, India has been the fastest growing tourism region in the world. This chapter primarily aims and seeks to identify and examine the paradigm shifts in the tourism industry over the seeming years and how the trends have behaved in India. It seeks to study the current trends in the tourism industry and evaluates the role of tourism in economic development. The future outlook is bright for the tourism sector, and the region is expected to maintain a high rate of growth well into the next century. The chapter contributes to an improved understanding of economic growth of a country because of tourism development.

Pricing an alpine tourism is unlike pricing a tangible product. As a part of overall marketing strategy pricing a destination has lot of intricate issues that starts from the basic characteristics of the destination elements to the changing demand aspects. At the time of packaging, an alpine destination by a tour operator or destination promotion organization (DPO), a simplified model, is used that is not essentially limited to an absurd analysis of attraction features through FAM trips a priori. In almost all Indian leisure destinations, tourists are found to be price sensitive and per capita spending is not so high. So, an Indian alpine destination-specific model, based on simple linear regression equation, largely explaining the spending of tourists and thereby implying a modified landscape value has been explained here.

This chapter seeks to make an approach to the financial instrument called REIT, Real Estate Investment Trust, specifically in the hotel industry in Mexico. This tool has allowed many investors to make business in the real estate sector, and it has provided a wider range of hosting services. This research takes us into the strategies the REIT leader in the hotel industry has implemented to position themselves as such. In large part this is explained by network theory and agent – principal theory. The study method is based on a literature review of several theories, as well as the study of a successful case. The analysis of results presents and describes the features that have contributed to business success.

Most of the spiritual programs organized by mega Pentecostal and charismatic churches in Nigeria constitute serious touristic attractions, which over the years, have immensely been contributing to socio-economic development in the country. These programs pull a multitude of national and international expectant tourists, who in the course of satisfying their various spiritual pursuits, often get involved in many other cultural and recreational activities. Hinging on empirical understandings, this chapter examines the extent to which these religious programs contribute—or may contribute—to tourism and socio-cultural development in Nigeria, particularly in host communities. The chapter equally explores some of the challenges of religious tourism in Nigeria. It is specifically anchored on the three following questions: (1) Which are the major religious activities attracting tourists in Nigeria? (2) To what extent foreign tourists' attendance at these programs does not only benefit the churches? and (3) How could these programs further contribute to tourism development in Nigeria?

Chapter 12

An effective internal control system will help achieve performance and profitability targets within the core objectives of the business, help to prevent the need for loss of resources, and ensure that financial reporting is realistic and reliable. The purpose of this chapter is to identify the components of the internal control system in the enterprise and to show whether these factors affect the firm performance. When the results of the study are evaluated in general, it has been determined that the elements of the internal control system of the companies have an effect on the firm performance. According to this, the control environment 1, the control environment 2, the risk evaluation, the control activities, the information and the communication, the monitoring variables are effective on the positive side and the control variables on the firm performance have positive effect on the firm performance of the operation bed capacity, the operation period, and the existence of the internal control unit.

Chapter 13

This chapter aims to present the academic tourism segment as a rising trend that can improve indicators, both academic and marketing, of tourist destinations. On the one hand, economistic arguments were presented; on the other, the academic tourist can be highlighted as a source of reliable information about the destination. That is, returning to their place of origin, the individual will share their experience with other people, including students, commenting on their experiences at the university, and of course, on the receiving destination. At this time, both the power of attraction of their listeners to the place will increase and will act as a paradiplomacy. However, both financial aspects (impacts of academic tourism) and marketing (influence on the image of the destination) are strong arguments for betting on this segment, both from the academic literature, as well as destinations with good universities.

Foreword

This book is a spectacular collection of essays on contemporary issues and trends in tourism management and practices in wider perspective. There are thirteen chapters in this collection and all the authors claim responsibility of handling their subjects in a remarkable manner. I'm happy to introduce this collection to the series of books on Advances in Hospitality & Service Industry, IGI Global, USA. Through the book, readers will have chance to find crucial and different insights for assessment and management of tourism industry and academics. In this work all the authors have investigated on contemporary trends and issues of tourism management and practices around the world.

This book is composed of thirteen chapters with a wide range of diversified contemporary tourism trends and issues with managerial and strategic implications. The first chapter of this book, deals with the impacts of anthropogenic and tourism activities on river water quality in Betwa river stretch, Madhya Pradesh, India. Here, the author has addressed both anthropogenic as well as industrial dependency on water and how tourism and agricultural activities are influencing the water body as a whole. The second chapter is on revaluating saltscapes in Portuga with respect to ecotourism, eco-museums and environmental education. The author in the third chapter has investigated the retention of guests through automation. It is an analytical study with emerging trends in hotels in Indian Sub-continent. While the forth chapter is dealing with digital conversion in restaurants with its management systems the fifth one is an attempt to analyze the urban and rural ecotourism marketing and destination development in and around Bolpur, Shantiniketan of the noble laureate poet and philosopher Rabindranath Tagore. In the sixth chapter the author has discussed the sustainable development framework and ecotourism consciousness, bio-cultural diversity in a lesser known hilly area of Kallakurichi in Villupuram district of Tamil Nadu, India. The seventh chapter highlights the importance of banking system in tourism and hospitality industry in Rumania with new issues and challenges. Eighth chapter is a new descriptive study with current trends and future outlook of Indian tourism industry with nice presentation of empirical evidences.

Another unique attempt is made in the chapter nine with a new linear pricing model for the Himalayan hill stations in India with special reference to Sikkim. The tenth chapter has outlined the investment diversification in hotel sector in Mexico through the case model of Fibras. The next eleventh chapter is dealing with the relationship between Christianity and tourism development in Nigeria with respect to socio-economic discourses. Last but not the least, the twelfth chapter is an assessment of the internal control system in the accommodation firm with its relationship with performance in future. The last chapter analyses how academic tourism is a segment with its rising trend that can improve indicators, both academic and marketing of tourist destinations.

Therefore, I congratulate the editor and the contributors who had put in a lot of effort and time in bringing out this book to address many vital concerns for a better understanding of the issues of tourism industry and environment in larger perspectives.

Sarat Kumar Lenka
Indian Institute of Tourism and Travel Management Bhubneswar, India

Preface

As tourism is one of the largest service industries serving millions of international and domestic tourists yearly, it is important to understand its current trends, practices and challenges. Advent of new types and forms of tourism, changes in existing tourism practices, challenging competitions and market trends, influence and use of technology are the focusing areas for business studies and future academic development as well. This book is a unique set of modern trends, issues and challenges with regard to tourism management and its practices in wider perspective. There are thirteen selected chapters in this collection and all the authors claim responsibility of handling their subjects in a remarkable manner. We are happy to introduce this collection to the series of books on Advances in Hospitality & Service Industry, IGI Global, USA. Through the book, readers will have chance to find crucial and different insights for a better understanding on contemporary issues, trends and management practices from different parts of the world.

The first chapter of this book, 'Impacts of Anthropogenic and Tourism Activities on River Water Quality', presented by Sharma R., aims to analyze the study of the water quality assessment of the Betwa River stretch in order to explore the detrimental effects of assorted anthropogenic and visitors' activities on the river. The religious tourism activities are the main type of tourism activities explored under the study in context to India for a recent time period from May- 2014 (Pre- Monsoon) to December- 2015 (Post-Monsoon).

In his chapter 'Revaluing Saltscapes in Portugal: Ecotourism, Ecomuseums, and Environmental Education', Carlos Balsas C. of the University of Albany describes how the natural areas of wetlands in the study have been understood, marketed, and enhanced to the benefit of mostly tourists and visitors or also local constituencies. The key finding in the study is the identification of a set of lessons learned useful to the partial rehabilitation of solar Salinas and suitable sustainable tourism practices. In the third chapter, ' Guest Retention through Automation: An Analysis of Emerging Trends in Hotels in Indian Sub-continent', Seal P.P., has outlined the modern technological development in hospitality at a relentless pace which is challenging for the hospitality professional for both present and the future generation. The author has described the hotel front office is moving towards automation with less human interface and reservations are mostly being made with help of booking engines and guest interaction with hotels are by apps and chatbots. Seal has also depicted the use of Artificial Intelligence (AI) with its major role to facilitate and enhance guest experience. The research in the study is about how various hotel chains are adopting new technology and incorporating it in their establishment. The forth chapter, 'Restaurant Management System (RMS) and Digital Conversion: A Descriptive Study for the New Era', Kocaman, E.M. and Kocaman, M. have discussed how modern customers expect a high-standard and fast service from enterprises. They also added how competition among enterprises meet customer expectations at maximum level, and raise the standard of products and services. Traditional restaurant management is found inadequate and this situation has led to a search and restaurant management systems (RMS) have been developed.

In the fifth chapter, 'Urban and Rural Ecotourism in and Around Bolpur: A Study of Destination Marketing and Challenges – Ecotourism Practices in West Bengal, India', Batabyal D. and Das D.K. have put forward an attempt to revisit and reorganize destination Bolpur with a sustainable marketing orientation for ecotourism and sustainable destination development. Further attempt is also made to support industry leaders and tourism academicians with destination specific issues and challenges. The article has described a changes in expectation and perception of tourists with sustainable issues for all the stakeholders.

Another chapter is on 'Sustainable Development and Ecotourism Consciousness: An Empirical Analysis for Kallakurichi, Tamil Nadu, India'. Here the author Pandit A. focuses on how people of Kallakurichi, Tamil Nadu, India can become conscious of ecotourism, bio-cultural diversity and sustainable development, vital for both present and future. The concerned chapter has introduced a new sustainable development framework for considering biological and cultural perspectives.

The seventh chapter of this book, 'Understanding the Importance of Banking System in Romanian Tourism and Hospitality Industry', contributed by Spulbar C., Ramona, B. and Trivedi J. have provided an exhaustive overview of the importance of banking system in Romanian tourism and hospitality industry. The interdependence between banking system and the tourism and hospitality industry and challenges have been addressed with regard to the public and private investment.

In the eighth chapter, Saquib, N. attempts to extract the ways and means of how tourism has become a pillar for elevating from poor to appreciable economic status. According to her, tourism is a major engine of economic growth and an important source of foreign exchange earnings in India. Over the last decade, the India has been the fastest growing tourism region in the world. Her chapter aims and seeks to identify and examine the paradigm shifts in the tourism industry over the seeming years and how the trends have behaved in India. It seeks to study the current trends in the tourism industry and evaluates the role of tourism in economic development. The future outlook is bright for the tourism sector, and the region is expected to maintain a high rate of growth well into the next century.

In the ninth chapter, 'Pricing for Hill Tourism Destination: An Empirical Analysis of Sikkim Himalaya, India: Linear Price Model for Himalayan Hill Station', Batabyal D. has introduced a linear pricing model for the Himalayan hill stations. The model is explaining the spending of tourists and thereby implying a modified landscape value in the area.

In his contributed tenth chapter, 'FIBRAs as a Tool for Investment Diversification in Mexican Hotel Sector: The Case of FIBRA Inn', Hernández, J.G.V., Altamirano, H.D.G. have focused on financial instrument called REIT, Real Estate Investment Trust, specifically in the hotel industry in Mexico. They explained how the tool has allowed many investors to make business in the real estate sector, and it has provided a wider range of hosting services. This research takes us into the strategies the REIT leader in the hotel industry has implemented to position themselves as such.

The eleventh chapter, 'Christianity and Tourism Development in Nigeria: A Socio-Economic Discourse' is dealing with the spiritual programs organized by mega Pentecostal and charismatic churches in Nigeria. Hinging on empirical understandings, this chapter examines the extent to which these religious programs contribute – or may contribute – to tourism and socio-cultural development in Nigeria, particularly in host communities. The chapter equally explores some of the challenges of religious tourism in Nigeria.

The twelfth chapter titled 'Assessment of the Internal Control System in the Accommodation Firm and Its Relation to Performance' exhibited an effective internal control system that will help achieve performance and profitability targets within the core objectives of the business. Here, the author Erdoğan M. identified the components of the internal control system in the enterprise and to show whether these factors affect the firm performance. When the results of the study are evaluated in general, it has been determined that the elements of the internal control system of the companies have an effect on the firm performance.

The thirteenth chapter, 'Academic Tourism: A Segment on the Rise', aims to preset the academic tourism segment as a rising trend that can improve indicators, both academic and marketing, of tourist destinations. The author Soares J.R.R. raises arguments on the academic tourist and their knowledge on destinations. The author positively conceptualized how the tourists share knowledge of the places of origin, destinations, including students, commenting on their experiences at the university, and of course, on the receiving destination. He claimes that the power of attraction of their listeners to the place will increase, and will act as a paradiplomacy. However, both financial aspects (impacts of academic tourism) and marketing (influence on the image of the destination) are strong arguments for betting on this segment, both from the academic literature, as well as destinations with good universities.

We sincerely think that these issues are of paramount importance and have been pretty well researched and commented in the form of research papers in the book. At the same time, the authors also seek for greater analysis and further study in all these areas of diverse tourism resource analysis in different economies in the world.

We hope you'll like this book as much as we do.

Debasish Batabyal
Amity University Kolkata, India

Dillip Kumar Das
University of Burdwan, India

Acknowledgment

First and foremost we would like to thank our parents for their unending inspiration and for standing beside us throughout our career and particularly while we were editing this book. It would not have been possible to achieve the objectives of the project without the encouraging response from the distinguished contributors in the beginning and subsequently contributing scholarly chapters in their respective domain of scholarship. Their timely cooperation at every stage in the progress of the project has immensely contributed in making this volume worth reading for the targeted audience. We do hereby acknowledge all the experts and staff at IGI Global USA. In particular, I wish to put on record the timely guidance and cooperation I received from Ms. Jordan Tepper.

We, finally, acknowledge the role our family members because they have shared a large part of our responsibility, even if it was indirect in nature. In fact, we have taken a more than fair share of our times due to them, especially of the children. Dr. Debasish fondly remembers his inspiring mother Ava and wife Proma who have shouldered a great responsibility of taking care of the family. Dr. Dillip wishes to express his gratitude to his mother and wife Tripti who are amazingly accommodative in nature. Together we acknowledge the contribution of our children Gayetree, Pratyush and Nachikate while editing this book.

Debasish Batabyal
Amity University Kolkata, India

Dillip Kumar Das
University of Burdwan, India

Chapter 1
Impacts of Anthropogenic and Tourism Activities on River Water Quality:
A Case Study of Betwa River Stretch, Madhya Pradesh, India

Ravi Sharma
Symbiosis International University, India

ABSTRACT

A study of the water quality assessment of the Betwa River stretch was conducted in order to explore the detrimental effects of assorted anthropogenic and visitors' activities on the river. The religious tourism activities are the main type of tourism activities explored under the study in context to India. Samples were collected during May 2014 (pre-monsoon) to December 2015 (post-monsoon) period. Twelve different physicochemical parameters were collected through primary data and field investigations, while the bacteriological parameters like total coliform and fecal coliform levels were analyzed through secondary data, except biochemical oxygen demand. The results suggest that the seasonal and spatial variations are significantly different. The results also conclude that the chloride, nitrite, phosphate, COD, nitrate, and BOD as evaluated using PCA extraction method shows a higher degree of positive correlation in a component which indicates anthropogenic and industrial impacts on water quality.

DOI: 10.4018/978-1-5225-8494-0.ch001

INTRODUCTION

The contamination of the river water is a highly growing prodigy resulting into depurating of aquatic systems (Zhou, Zhang, Fu, Shi, & Jiang, 2008). The problem related to lack of deterioration of water quality is a debated issue for the recent decade and under the sustainable development goals of world nations. There is much water intensive and dependent activities which are anthropogenic in nature considered to important criteria for the development of the country. Irrigation for agriculture (Bates, Kundzewicz, Wu, & Palutikof, 2008) and industrial consumption is one such high water- consumption activities. The decline in water resources due to pollution including groundwater, degradation of surrounding environment, reduction in precipitation, climate change consequences are among the few phenomenon which are responsible for day- by- day growth in water demand (Ipcc, 2007; Parry et al., 2009). The lakes, rivers and wetlands are important attributes for tourism attraction and recreational activities along with other landscapes visited by tourists (Stefan Gössling et al., 2012). Apart from it there are many other forms of tourism existing in different forms on the bases of nature and typology of activities like agri- tourism, water sports, theme parks, rural tourism, coastal tourism etc. In a nutshell, both anthropogenic and industrial dependency on water including tourism and agricultural activities have increased pressure on water resources as well as made the quality of surface water more prone towards degradation and contamination (Rashid & Romshoo, 2013; Simeonov et al., 2003).

The main cause of contamination of water bodies due to tourism and other anthropogenic activities from different origin in vicinity to the destination site having aquatic ecosystem is nutrient loading through enrichment (Garcia-Esteves, Ludwig, Kerhervé, Probst, & Lespinas, 2007; Harrison et al., 2004) and chemicals discharge into the reservoirs(Jin and Hu, 2003 (M. Singh, Ansari, Müller, & Singh, 1997). The contamination through alteration of landscape for infrastructure development required for tourism and urban development is another main cause reported by different researchers (Benedict & McMahon, 2000; S. Gössling, 2002). The externalities associated with them are other factors for contribution to the strain on water resources. Human settlements and industries have long been concentrated along rivers, estuaries, and other water resources due to predominance water trade. These alterations results into the direct physical disturbance to sediments and vegetations (Hadwen, Arthington, & Mosisch, 2003; Liddle & Scorgie, 1980) causing the entrants of pollutants and heavy metals through leaching- precipitation, run- offs and storm water into the water bodies. The direct visitor's activities like bathing, swimming, washing and cleaning in the water are other responsible causes of nutrient enrichment and contamination. In country like India, where the rivers are considered to be sacred and a symbol of divinity bears the loads of mass religious tourism activities. The religious tourism activities in India include many rituals and ceremonies resulting into the pollution load into the water bodies. The immersion of idols by different communities, mass bathing, performing of rituals are some of the examples quite common in India. The situation of rivers becomes grimmer in case the rivers are used as a dumping sources of garbage, sewage and industrial effluents without any treatment.

There are many studies by the researchers done in the past highlighting the environmental impacts of tourism representing broad scenario of impacts (Davies, Davies, & Cahill, 2000; Ding et al., 2015; Jahan & Strezov, 2017; Jiang, 2009; Pereira, Soares, Ribeiro, & Goncalves, 2005; Sun & Walsh, 1998), but very few emphasis has been given to study the anthropogenic and tourism impact on river bodies (Rashid & Romshoo, 2013). This study intends to measure the present quality of river water and the degree of impact of anthropogenic- tourism activities on the river water quality. We are interested in studying how far the anthropogenic activities has affected the nature and quality of interaction with 'tourist- anthropogenic- industrial ecosystem' and to what extent the correlation between the different physicochemical variables stands. To explore this kind of issue, we draw upon the literature on influence of different activities, physicochemical parameters required approach, source of pollution and anthropogenic activity linkages has been explored to provide the insight into how to approach the problem of 'river quality assessment'. Moreover, in this study, secondary data collected for fecal coliform (FC), Total coliform (TC), and fauna indicators from Central Pollution Control Board (CPCB) India, which determines the current condition of the river water quality as well as the level of pollution. The study also aims to review the spatio- temporal variations of parameters at different sites and examining its relation with the recreational activities at the Betwa River stretch.

BACKGROUND STUDY

The pollution issue of the surface water is the most serious problem faced by the developing countries (Banerjee, Maiti, & Kumar, 2015; Suthar, Sharma, Chabukdhara, & Nema, 2009). The urban rivers of the developing nations have been treated as end point effluent discharge point by the industries (Phiri, Mumba, Moyo, & Kadewa, 2005). The quality of river and the causes which impairs or influences the drinking water quality has been advocated by many scholars in past (Jarvie, Whitton, & Neal, 1998; Pandey, Kass, Soupir, Biswas, & Singh, 2014; Razmkhah, Abrishamchi, & Torkian, 2010; Silva, Srinivasalu, Roy, & Jonathan, 2014). The rivers are considered to be loaded when the enrichment, both chemical and natural weathering processes, is dominated by the loading due to anthropogenic influences. Hence, in order to prepare a strategic management plan to conserve these valuable resources, a systematic study and monitoring programme is very important (Kaushik et al., 2009) to timely predict the status of pollution and trend in fluctuating parameters which are indicators of water quality. The influence of urban activities on water quality due to urban sprawl has strong positive relation with Nitrogen- Phosphorous parameters and chemical oxygen demand (COD), (S. Li, Gu, Tan, & Zhang, 2009; J. Tong & Chen, 2009; Zhao et al., 2014) which represents human interference at urban communal level badly (C. Li et al., 2015). The development of infrastructure, amenities, recreation activities in and around water, paved surfaces causes alteration of hydrology resulting into loading of nutrients (Lee, Miller, & Hancock, 2000; Rose, 2002) and other contaminants into the water (Callender* & Rice, 1999; Mallin, Williams, Esham, & Lowe, 2000). The contamination primarily enters from fecal waste and other recreational activities like swimming, bathing etc (Cole, 2000).

There is strong evidence that recreation use of water bodies and watershed managed areas can unfavorably impact the quality of surface drinking water sources and contains fecal and other bacterial forms (Cole, 2000; Suk, Sorenson, & Dileanis, 1987). Solid waste in the form of litter and debris are other curse for water body degradation as they accrue at the bottom of the streams (William E. Hammitt, Cole, & Monz, 2015). There is a proven linkage of nutrient concentration, autotrophic community production and decomposition with the dissolved oxygen (DO) in aquatic ecosystems. In the warm streams due to this intricate relationship and other recreational use, there is an excessive growth rates which is associated with the alteration in oxygen supply and species composition of the aquatic community (W.E. Hammitt, Cole, & Monz, 2015). The loading of phosphorous due to trampling (Dickman & Dorais, 1977) and vehicular traffic are the obvious reasons of nutrient enrichment, especially due to uncontrolled mass tourism during peak seasons.

The contaminations of water resources, which are the main attraction for the visitors, have a rebound impact on the recreational activities and therefore the tourism business. Example, the recreational boating is important use activities of visitors, which rely on the water depths (Bergmann-Baker, Brotton, & Wall, 1995) and experience of the visitors by the use of the facilities rely on the water quality itself. Hence, the degradation of water resources results in impairment of both water services in terms of quantity and quality resulting in scarcity for recreational activities as well as for local people who depends on the source itself. In India, the population density is higher on the banks of the rivers. The collective sewage overflow both from municipal, urban local bodies (ULB) and tourism activities are the principle cause of nutrients in the water bodies. The phenomenon of storm run- offs, erosion, and leaching are the major reasons for nutrient transport (Ding et al., 2015).

The nitrate concentration is attributed due to over fertilizer use and excessive tilling which results in erosion and making conditions perfect for surface run- offs resulting into algal blooms growth and eutrophication (Carpenter, 2008; S. T. Y. Tong & Chen, 2002). Therefore, for safeguarding the public health and protection of degrading water resources the monitoring program is required (Chow et al., 2016; Kannel, Lee, Kanel, & Khan, 2007; Varol & Şen, 2012).

The estimation of the water quality is done on the bases of various multiple parameters which are collected and analyzed over different monitoring sites during spatio- temporal differences. This exercise results into a complex datasets and which are crucial to evaluate the water quality overall and changes occurring within the sites (Boyacioglu, Boyacioglu, & Gunduz, 2005; Deborah Chapman, 1992; Palma et al., 2010). There are empirical evidences from different researches which advocated the use of physical and chemical parameters of water to historically determine the quality (Alobaidy, Abid, & Maulood, 2010) and the sources of the apportionment. The other frequent issue in the monitoring for the river quality is to determine and differentiate whether a variation in the concentration of measured parameters should be attributed to pollution which is manmade, spatial or to natural showing temporal changes in the river system (Alberto et al., 2001; Juang, Lee, & Hsueh, 2009; Vutukuru, 2003). Besides these channels, the seasonal variation also plays a crucial role on the concentration of pollutants in rivers (Jha, Waidbacher, Sharma, & Straif, 2010; Karbassi, Nouri, Mehrdadi, & Ayaz, 2008; Ouyang, Nkedi-Kizza, Wu, Shinde, & Huang, 2006). In a nutshell, the river water system and pollutant interaction and activities are the linkages of natural and anthropogenic sources and are multivariate and complex systems. Therefore, river water quality assessment requires a fundamental understanding of spatial and temporal variations of the water physicochemical properties both seasonally and site specific locations (Chow et al., 2016; Haque et al., 2016; Harun, Dambul, Abdullah, & Mohamed, 2014; Phung et al., 2015; K. P. Singh, Malik, Mohan, & Sinha, 2004). Different multivariate statistical methods such as regression analysis, Discriminant Analysis (DA), Cluster analysis (CA), Factorial Analysis (FA) and Principal Component Analysis (PCA) have been performed. These are considered to be widely accepted statistical techniques to typify water quality and study temporal and spatial differences caused due to natural and anthropogenic factors linked to seasonality (Garizi, Sheikh, & Sadoddin, 2011; Helena et al., 2000; Juahir et al., 2011; Kannel et al., 2007; Krishna, Satyanarayanan, & Govil, 2009; K. P. Singh, Malik, & Sinha, 2005).

Methodology

Study Area

The origination of River Betwa is from the Kaliasot and other smaller upstream of Mandideep (Bhopal, Madhya Pradesh). The river is part of Yamuna River basin and joins it at the downstream of Hamirpur (U.P). River originates from Barkheda village in Raisen district, M.P. rising at an elevation of about 576m. Raisen district is situated in the central part of Madhya Pradesh and lies mostly on the plateau and partly in the Narmada valley. From the origin of the Betwa River to its meeting with the Yamuna river is 590 kilometers, out of which 232 kilometers lies in Madhya Pradesh and the balance of 358 kilometers in Uttar Pradesh (National Water Development Agency, 2006). The total catchment area that lies in Madhya Pradesh is 30,238 Sq. km. (National Water Development Agency, 2006).

The stretch of Betwa River from Mandideep is taken into account till it passes through the Raisen district. For this particular case study as it passes through the most important industrialized belts of Mandideep- Obedullagunj area. As per the Madhya Pradesh Audyogik Kendra Vikas Nigam -MPAKVN (2016), there are 755 small scale and large industries situated in Mandideep in running condition. Though the number of industries is high, invent new technologies for cleaner production and effluent/ sewage treatment plant installed under the guidance and monitored by rules and regulations of State Pollution Control Board (SPCB) can explain the stability of these contaminants and remediation practices over a period of time. In the year 2014, MPPCB inspected 104 companies and asked them to treat effluents before discharging into the streams.

The different clusters as per the industrial- anthropogenic scenes are divided and selected for achieving the objectives of the study. The tourism related activities are only prevalent at sampling point 1 (Bhojpur Ghat), SP2 (Near Gokulakundi village) and SP10 (Berkhedi Ghat). Amongst these, the SP1 and SP10 are mostly religious activity driven sites while the SP2 is used for recreational purpose by visitors. The main religious activities that site delves with are religious rituals of worship during festivals and days of religious importance. These days witnesses the high peak visitor's inflow to the area and are unregulated. No authentic influx data of visitors are available with the authorities for the destination site under study. It is assumed that the annual average influx of the visitor's to the site is 2.5- 3 lakh approximately with lots of visitors at the time of fair and festival periods. The recreation activities includes the usage of water by the visitors for leisure purpose, like, bathing in the river, cleaning utensils, picnicking, washing clothes, boating (non- diesel). Most of the populations in and around the study area are farmers- agriculturist or laborers.

Very few local populations are dependent on the tourism related activities occurring at the destination area. The kind of opportunities that tourism has provided to the local communities is parking owners, stall and shop keepers (includes artifacts, religious and worship material vendors, etc.). The type of industries present

Methods and Materials

Physicochemical Analyses of Water

In the present study, total six sampling stations for pre-monsoon and post-monsoon sampling were selected (Figure 1). For each station total two sampling sites/ points were selected therefore comprising of total 12 sampling points (SP1, SP2, SP3, SP4, SP5, SP6, SP7, SP8, SP9, SP10, SP11, SP12) on the Betwa River stretch the limits of Raisen District of State Madhya Pradesh, which was considered into account for the objective of the present investigation. The sites were categorized on the bases of its anthropogenic activity dominance. The all the sites are described into Industrial, religious- recreational, and rural habitation site as per the type of activity prominent in the area. The religious- recreation sites (Station 1 and 5) are the main area where the religious rituals, religious festivals and visitors recreational use is performed on the river. The Bhojpur temple which is a main attraction of tourism on this stretch attracts more than 50,000 visitors in a single month during peak seasons (unofficial data sources). The same sampling stations were considered for the collection of parameters during the winter season. The sampling stations were fixed and located exactly with the GPS (Garmin) locator in order to maintain the constancy of the sampling stations. For the convenience of analysis of results, the same sampling stations/points were labeled as SP13, SP14, SP15, SP16, SP17, SP18, SP19, SP20, SP21, SP22, SP23, SP24, which represents the sampling points for winter (Post- Monsoon period) at the same sampling sites as stated earlier. The descriptions of sampling stations are provided in table 1.

Sampling and Analytical Procedures for Quality Assessment

Water samples were collected from six stations (12 sampling points) during May-2014 (Pre- Monsoon) to December- 2015 (Post-Monsoon) periods. Sampling points within the sampling stations were selected based on certain factors taken into account like accessibility, convenience in the collection of samples. The processing and transportation of samples were as per the standard protocol (APHA/AWWA/WEF, 2012). The samples were analyzed for twelve physicochemical variables to monitor from 12 sampling points. These were temperature (^{o}C), pH, total dissolved solids

Table 1. Description of sampling points and locations on Betwa River stretch

Name/ Location (Station Number)	Sampling Points in each station	Category of Sampling station on the bases of anthropogenic activities
Bhojpur (Station-1)	SP1(Bhojpur Ghat) SP2 (Near Gokulakundi Village)	Industrial-Religious- Recreation Site Recreational – Rural
Rasuliya village (Station-2)	SP3 (Rauliya Village) SP4 (Rasuliya Village ahead 1Km)	Rural
Kanora Village (Station-3)	SP5 (Kanora before bridge 300 m) SP6 (Near Chandla Khedi))	Rural
Silpuri village (Station- 4)	SP7 (Mendori Village) SP8 (Silpuri Bridge ahead 300 m)	Rural Rural - Urban Sprawl
Berkhedi Ghat (Station- 5)	SP9 (Near Barla before Berkhedi village) S10 (Berkhedi Ghat)	Rural habitation Religious- Recreation Site
Pagneshwar village (Station- 6)	SP11 (Gram Phagneshwar Bridge) SP12 (Ahead Bridge 700 m)	Semi- Urban Sprawl Rural- Industrial Site

Figure 1. Sampling station and location map on Betwa River stretch

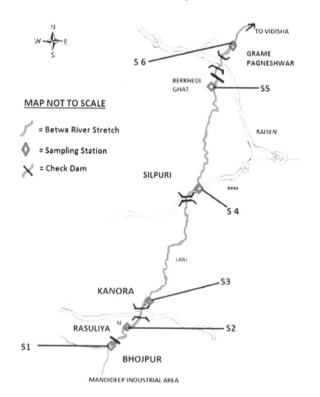

(TDS, mg/L), phosphate (PO_4-3, mg/L), nitrate- nitrogen (NO_3-N, mg/L), Nitrite-Nitrogen (NO_2-N, mg/L), chloride (mg/L), Alkalinity (mg/L), total hardness (mg/L), biochemical oxygen demand (BOD, mg/L), Chemical oxygen demand (COD, mg/L) and dissolved oxygen (DO, mg/L). The parameters such as temperature, pH, total dissolved solids (TDS) were determined at the collection point while the remaining parameters were determined in the laboratory within 1- day of sampling by adopting standard protocols (APHA/AWWA/WEF, 2012). The parameters analyzed in the laboratory namely BOD (5-day incubation), COD (Dichromate reflex method), DO (Winkler Method), NO_3-N (Cadmium reduction method), Alkalinity (Titrimetric), Phosphate and Nitrite (spectrophotometric).

The Fecal coliform (FC) and Total coliform (TC) levels of the Betwa river stretch were based on secondary data collected from the monitoring agency, CPCB reports (Central Pollution Control Board, 2010, 2013). The reports were published for the sampling locations on Kaliasot river (which confluences into river Betwa in Mandideep), Betwa river near road bridge of Bhojpur (between our sampling point SP1 and SP2), Intake point Raisen (near Sampling point 11 and 12). The results were discussed separately in the discussion section of this chapter.

Statistical Analysis

Data for physicochemical variables of water samples were described as mean values and analyzed using descriptive analysis. Association between the variables were determined using the Pearson's coefficient with statistical significance set at $p<0.05$. Before proceeding to investigate the seasonal effect on water quality parameters, the whole observation period was divided into two fixed seasons (summer and winter) and assigned a numerical value in the data file. The measured data were initially arranged according to the stations and normality test were performed using IBM SPSS® statistics 21 software using the Shapiro- Wilk test. As per the Shapiro-Wilk test, except pH, TDS, and BOD all the variables were log-normally distributed with 95% or higher level of confidence. After the normalization test, in order to examine the suitability of the data for PCA and FA, Kaiser-Meyer-Olkin (KMO) and Bartlett's Sphericity tests were performed (Haque et al., 2016; Shrestha & Kazama, 2007; Varol & Şen, 2009, 2012). The value of 0.6 is a suggested minimum to check the measure of sampling adequacy using KMO. A high value close to 1generally indicates that PCA/ FA may be useful. A summary of CA, DA and PCA is described in the following sections.

Cluster analysis is a pattern recognition technique, and groups the cases into smaller groups or clusters on the basis of relatively similar cases which are dissimilar to other groups (Vega, Pardo, Barrado, & Debán, 1998). Hierarchical agglomerative clustering analysis (HCA) was performed on the normalized data set by means of Ward's method using squared Euclidean distances. This gives us a measure of similarity (Helena et al., 2000; Sahu et al., 2013; K. P. Singh et al., 2005). CA was performed to the water quality datasets with an objective to do the grouping of similar sampling sites. This grouping will help in understanding the spatial similarity or dissimilarities over the stretch of the river and is presented in the dendrogram (McKenna, 2003).

Principal component analysis (PCA) is a data reduction technique, where the normalized variables are extracted without losing original information into significant principal components (PCs). PCs were computed from covariance or cross- product matrixes, which describe the dispersion of the multiple measured parameter, from which the eigen values are obtained (Alberto et al., 2001). After the PCA, the FA further reduces the contribution of less significant variables (Chow et al., 2016). The PCs were subject to varimax rotation generating a new group of variables known as varifactors (VF) (Chow et al., 2016; Sârbu & Pop, 2005; K. P. Singh et al., 2004). Corresponding to VFs, variable loadings and the variance explained were calculated which classifies the factor loadings (FL) as "strong", "moderate" or "weak" based on the loading values. VF coefficient with a correlation of > 0.75 are explained as strong significant FL, while correlation ranges from 0.75- 0.50 and 0.50- 0.30 were considered as moderate and weak FL respectively (Liu, Lin, & Kuo, 2003).

RESULTS AND DISCUSSION

The water mentoring applications are considered to be a very useful tool as it provides the water quality datasets. These datasets can be explored at different temporal conveniences to forecast the relationship models of the change and identifying causative factors of change. The statistical approach for developed using the spatio-temporal characteristics provides useful answers to the objectives in hand for water quality analysis.

In this case study, the summary statistics of the physicochemical parameters measured during the period of one year (May 2014 – March 2015) from different sampling sites in Betwa river stretch under study is summarized in Table 2. The variables nitrate, nitrite, and chloride were recorded highest level of mean at sampling point 2 (S2) of station 1 during summer and winter season both. The BOD and DO value were recorded highest (BOD= 14.6; DO=8.4 mg/l) during summer season only, while COD value was highest during winter as well as summer season (72.1 mg/l and 82.8 mg/l respectively) at station 4. The TDS value was found to be highest at upstream sites while lower at lowest downstream sites across the stretch (ranges from minimum 320 mg/l to maximum 467 mg/l). The BOD and DO values showed a decreasing trend from summer to winter's i.e., higher values in summer. Based on the water quality variables recorded from the study, it is found that Bhojpur site (station 1) which is a religious recreational site as well as first site where industrial effects are visible at the confluence shows greater variation in annual mean concentration for TDS (M= 395.47, SD 39.26), Chloride (M= 88.39, SD= 30.17), Alkalinity (M= 151.52, SD= 38.89), Total Hardness (M= 187.11, SD= 20.13), BOD (M= 8.88, SD= 3.34), COD (M= 49.41, SD= 27.5) and DO (M= 5.28, SD= 1.92) values. The BOD level was found to be higher during the summers (M= 10.23; SD= 3.75) compared to winters (M= 7.53; SD= 2.3) at all sites. Overall, we observed the significant degree of spatial and temporal variations in the concentration of water quality variables using ANOVA ($p<0.005$) and t-test ($p<0.01$) analysis.

Spatial Correlation of Physicochemical Parameters

To study the association between the spatial water quality parameters, the coefficient of correlation was used. The results of Pearson correlation analysis in the present investigation resulted are displayed in Table 3. The nitrate, nitrite, phosphate and alkalinity at $p<0.05$ and $p<0.01$, shows a strong correlation among themselves. The strong correlation suggests the loading of the organic matter due to waste disposal, agricultural run-offs, and fertilizers along with domestic usage of water. In addition to domestic and agricultural run- offs, industrial effluents and urban waste water along with natural weathering are possible contributing factors to the pollution of river water. The strong positive correlation of chloride with COD and phosphate, strong negative correlation of COD with alkalinity illustrates the high level of organic pollutants in river water. Towards downward stretch (Station 3, 4 and 5) of the river, the addition of agricultural waste and fertilizers along with the detergents are the major cause of higher association of BOD with other organic pollutant indicators. These stations have only rural habitation or semi- urban sprawls near to the river. The loading of phosphorous and increase in BOD are results of over- fertilizer used for agricultural practices.

In order to interpret the impact of human activities on the river quality, the bacteriological parameters were also studied on the basis of secondary data collected from CPCB (Table 4). The two bacteriological parameters- fecal coliform (FC) and total coliform (TC) were collected for the year 2009 and 2011 (Central Pollution

Table 2. Recorded physico-chemical seasonal variables of water of Betwa River stretch

Summer Season

Sampling Station	Station 1		Station 2		Station 3		Station 4		Station 5		Station 6	
Sampling Site / Variables	SP1	SP2	SP3	SP4	SP5	SP6	SP7	SP8	SP9	SP10	SP11	SP12
Temp. (°C)	39	39.2	39.1	39.4	39.5	39.8	40	39.9	**40.2**	40	39.6	40.1
pH	**8.6**	7.6	7.9	8	8.2	8	8.3	8.2	7.5	6.8	7.3	7.2
TDS (mg/l)	438	380	**467**	428	320	342	328	330	375	378	372	375
Phosphate (mg/l)	0.34	**0.56**	0.39	0.43	0.26	0.23	0.24	0.24	0.09	0.119	0.2	0.136
Nitrate (mg/l)	3.8	**4.22**	4	4.01	1.3	2.22	2.21	1.91	2.4	2.2	1.9	2.17
Nitrite (mg/l)	0.13	**0.19**	0.16	0.13	0.084	0.06	0.055	0.07	0.06	0.03	0.06	0.05
Chloride (mg/l)	**138**	104	123	121.6	92.99	93.1	92.4	92.8	54.2	59.2	55.1	56.2
Alkalinity (mg/l)	122	120.8	142	128.3	134	131	193	152.6	**220**	209	215	214.6
Total Hardness (mg/l)	180	**180.8**	180.2	180.3	160	161.2	161	160.7	178	178.9	179	178.6
BOD (mg/l)	12.1	10.9	12.3	11.76	14.2	10.4	**14.6**	13.06	2.9	4.9	9.8	5.86
COD (mg/l)	64.8	60.1	78.9	67.9	72.5	68.9	**82.8**	74.73	12.5	12.7	12.5	12.56
DO (mg/l)	3.2	4	3.4	3.5	7.8	8.1	**8.4**	8.1	7.2	7.5	8	7.56

Winter Season

Sampling Station	Station 1		Station 2		Station 3		Station 4		Station 5		Station 6	
Sampling Site / Variables	SP1	SP2	SP3	SP4	SP5	SP6	SP7	SP8	SP9	SP10	SP11	SP12
Temp. (°C)	23.1	23	23.3	23.2	23.4	23.7	23	23.2	23	23.9	**24**	23.5
pH	7.3	7.4	7.4	7.35	7.1	**7.8**	7.7	7.4	7.2	7.1	7.2	7.2
TDS (mg/l)	**442**	438	439	440.5	407	401	398	402.5	395	398	400	397.5
Phosphate (mg/l)	0.29	0.21	**0.31**	0.3	0.17	0.16	0.2	0.185	0.16	0.21	0.19	0.175
Nitrate (mg/l)	2.3	**2.7**	**2.7**	2.5	1.8	2.1	2.19	1.995	2.2	2.2	2.1	2.15
Nitrite (mg/l)	**0.14**	0.09	0.13	0.135	0.063	0.034	0.12	0.0915	0.03	0.06	0.04	0.035
Chloride (mg/l)	124	**129.9**	119	121.5	86	91.1	89.2	87.6	46.46	45.8	50.1	48.28
Alkalinity (mg/l)	120	119	121	120.5	112	111	112	112	181	**182.1**	182	181.5
Total Hardness (mg/l)	204	202	205	204.5	166	184	189	177.5	**224**	214	220	222
BOD (mg/l)	**9.5**	8.9	8.9	9.2	9.2	8.9	9	9.1	4.8	4.8	3.8	4.3
COD (mg/l)	56.9	60.4	64.1	60.5	69.1	64.2	**72.1**	70.6	12.2	11.5	11.6	11.9
DO (mg/l)	3.9	3.1	3.4	3.65	**5.1**	4.4	4.8	4.95	4.1	4.8	3.9	4

Table 3. Pearson Correlation analysis comprising physicochemical parameters

	Temp.	pH	TDS	Phosphate	Nitrate	Nitrite	Chloride	Alkalinity	Total Hardness	BOD	COD	DO
Temp.	1.000											
pH	0.493	1.000										
TDS	-0.48	-0.23	1.000									
Phosphate	0.241	0.424	0.292	1.000								
Nitrate	0.278	0.300	0.535	0.791	1.000							
Nitrite	0.071	0.311	0.498	0.858	0.716	1.000						
Chloride	0.031	0.539	0.470	0.655	0.547	0.766	1.000					
Alkalinity	0.386	-0.33	-0.41	-0.488	-0.266	-0.59	-0.762	1.000				
Total hardness	-0.71	-0.560	0.529	-0.092	0.035	-0.066	-0.232	0.083	1.000			
BOD	0.389	0.782	-0.15	0.582	0.240	0.497	0.698	-0.502	-0.643	1.000		
COD	0.064	0.677	0.067	0.503	0.247	0.557	0.808	-0.781	-0.530	0.856	1.000	
DO	0.613	0.139	-0.87	-0.417	-0.544	-0.49	-0.428	0.542	-0.654	0.134	-0.11	1.000

*Correlation is significant at the 0.05 level ** Correlation is significant at the 0.01 level.

Table 4. Fecal coliform, total coliform, and BOD levels in Betwa River stretch

Biological Parameter	Recorded levels(in MPN/100ml)		Standard Limits
	2009	2011	
Total Coliform (TC)	17×10^3	16×10^4	5000 MPN/100ml
Fecal Coliform (FC)	700	11×10^4	2500 MPN/100ml
BOD (mg/L)	6-10	5.4 - 104	> 30 mg/L

Source: Central Pollution Control Board, India (CPCB, 2010; CPCB, 2013)

Control Board, 2010, 2013). These results were interpreted in association with BOD, key physicochemical variable.

The data for the bio- mapping of the Betwa river stretch was also collected secondarily in order to understand the biota of the study and interpreting status of the pollution based on the type of benthic macro- invertebrates present in the water. The Betwa, which is a tributary of Yamuna basin is place in Class 'D' having orange indicator color category (CPCB-ENVIS, 2013). This category is considered to be as heavily polluted and having a range of saprobic score (Biological Monitoring Working party- BMWP) of 2-5. The range of diversity score for this saprobic score is 0.4 and less with the taxonomic families from group Mollusca, Hemptera, Coleoptera, Oligochaeta and Dipterean families because of their tolerance to wide variety of pollutants. The results as depicted in table 4 indicates that there is a significant increase in the TC, FC and BOD levels of the water in the past years. The results presented here through primary and secondary data both, are clear indicators that the water quality of Betwa river stretch under study has humongous impact of anthropogenic activities. The similarities or differences among the sampling sites and correlation among different variables within the sites are explored through statistical applications as explained in next sections.

Site Grouping and Similarity

The objective of CA as explained in methodology section is to arrange variables into groups such that the degree of association is strong between members of the same cluster. Similarly on other hand, the group variables should have a weak association between members of different clusters, therefore, solves the classification problem (Bhat & Pandit, 2014). Cluster analysis performed to analyze the spatial similarity of sampling sites under the study. The classification is shown by a dendrogram (Figure 2), groups all the sampling sites on the river stretch into three statistically significant clusters. The dendrogram illustrates strong spatial and temporal association on the basis of variations of different variables. It also indicates the grouping of sites to

Figure 2. Dendrogram showing sampling site clusters on Betwa River stretch

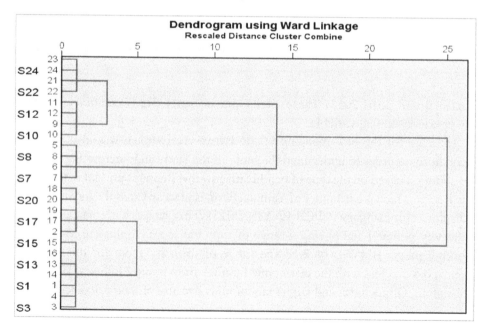

the highest level of satisfaction. The dendrogram attempts to show the status of the pollution variables as well as the effect of anthropogenic activities on various site clusters indicating the effect of contamination at different sampling sites. The CA using spatial data generated three groups (clusters): Station 5 & 6 consisting of SP9, SP10, SP11, SP12, SP21, SP22, SP23, SP24 (Group 1); Station 3 & 4 consisting of sites SP5, SP6, SP7, SP8 (Group 2). The third group shows transition similarity with the station 2 and 5 and includes SP1, SP2, SP3, SP4, SP13, SP14, SP15, SP16, SP17, SP18, SP19 SP20 (Group 3). The dendrogram shows that stations 5 and 6 shows more close association and similarity with respect to the pollution factors and variations in the parameters. Similarly, stations 3, 4, and station 1 and 2 shows close similarities among each other.

The sampling stations so grouped after the spatial cluster analysis reveals that there is some association in a variation on the location. The sampling site 1, 2, 3 and 4 are located near to the origin of the Betwa River and is a major tourist spot also along with the agglomeration of various industries (Mandideep industrial area) situated near to the river. The site 5, 6, 7 and 8 are located in the areas with no industrial unit and having rural habitats' and villages situated along the banks of the river flow thereby under the stress of domestic usage of water and loads of domestic waste into the river due to various anthropogenic use including run water storm and agricultural run-offs (non- point sources of pollution). The remaining sites are on the downstream of the stretch and include few point sources of pollution and mainly the urban and rural mix of settlements along the river stretch. The sampling station 6 is almost the last sampling station of the river in Raisen district, which is a near to Vidisha district having again different conglomerates of industries. It is clearly seen that sampling station 1 and station 2 are more polluted as compared to station other stations. These are the stations which have a great mix of heavy industrial conglomeration, urban settlements, semi- urban establishments and religious activities happening on the large scale. Hence, the impact of human activities at station 1 and 2 is relatively high as compared to others and is significant. Using the analysis we could categorize sampling sites into three groups viz., high polluted site (Station 1 and 2); moderately polluted sites (site 5 and 6) and low polluted sites (station 3 and 4). The site 3 and 4 receives pollution mostly from non-point resources like agricultural run-off, natural processes, and domestic use of water.

Based on the seasonal analysis of water quality parameters, box and whisker plots of the investigated parameters are plotted for selected parameters to compare the seasonal variations in variables (Figure 3). The average concentration of Nitrate, alkalinity, phosphate, BOD, COD, and DO is comparatively higher in summer compared to the winter season, while TDS level is higher in winter season as compared to summer. The alkalinity in summers shows clear higher trend and

Figure 3. Box- whisker's plot of water quality parameters for Betwa River

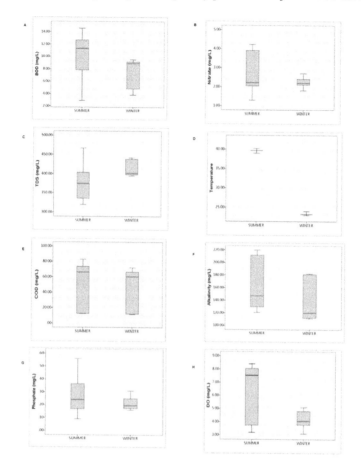

decline in winters and this may be resulted due to augmented weathering process during the monsoons in between the two seasons thereby resulting in declination of COD and BOD due to excessive dilution and increase in flow during winters.

PCA was performed to extort the physicochemical patterns between the water samples and to identify the factors influencing each one. The PCA results in 3-factor components, which the eigen values greater than 1 and explains 88.36% of the total variability.

The first factor corresponding to the largest eigen value (5.473) which accounts for accounts for 45.6% of the total variance and was positively correlated with phosphate, nitrate, nitrite, chloride, BOD and COD (Table 5). PC2 in this study shows positive strong correlation with DO and temperature variations while the negative strong correlation with total hardness and TDS. The PC3 shows correlation >0.70 with none of the parameters. The second and third factor corresponds to 30.41%

Table 5. Variable loading of the parameters using principal component analysis

Parameters	Factor 1	Factor 2	Factor 3	Communality
Temperature	0.134	**0.769**	0.597	0.966
pH	0.631	0.567	-0.028	0.719
TDS	0.388	**-0.823**	0.083	0.834
Phosphate	**0.837**	-0.072	0.382	0.852
Nitrate	0.679	-0.254	0.637	0.932
Nitrite	**0.861**	-0.214	0.225	0.838
Chloride	**0.928**	-0.062	-0.141	0.886
Alkalinity	**-0.764**	0.241	0.523	0.916
Total Hardness	-0.288	**-0.871**	0.063	0.846
BOD	**0.769**	0.532	-0.176	0.905
COD	**0.835**	0.280	-0.430	0.960
DO	-0.430	**0.872**	-0.003	0.946
Variance	5.473	3.649	1.479	10.601
Var. (%)	45.605	30.407	12.324	88.336

Table 6. Variables factor loading with varimax rotation

Parameters	VF1	VF2	VF3	Communality
Temperature	-0.070	**0.921**	0.336	0.966
pH	0.635	0.506	0.247	0.719
TDS	0.053	**-0.758**	0.507	0.834
Phosphate	0.398	0.037	**0.832**	0.852
Nitrate	0.082	-0.044	**0.961**	0.932
Nitrite	0.476	-0.151	**0.767**	0.838
Chloride	**0.782**	-0.133	0.507	0.886
Alkalinity	**-0.841**	0.425	-0.167	0.916
Total Hardness	-0.465	**-0.790**	0.072	0.846
BOD	**0.821**	0.419	0.236	0.905
COD	**0.963**	0.094	0.154	0.960
DO	-0.122	**0.832**	-0.489	0.946
Variance	3.953	3.404	3.244	10.601
Var. (%)	32.939	28.368	27.030	88.336

and 12.32% respectively of the total variance. The remaining variables so identified in the study have eigen values less than 1 and therefore doesn't considered to be significant. An equal number of varifactors (VFs) obtained for parameters through factorial analysis (FA) performed on the PCs. A correlation matrix of these variables computed and variable loadings and the variance explained presented in Table 6.

Among the varifactors (VFs), VF1 explains 3.95% of total variance, had strong loadings (>0.70) on chloride (0.782), Alkalinity (-0.841), BOD (0.821) and COD (0.963), while moderate loading (0.75-0.50) for pH and for other parameters shows very weak loadings (<0.50). The VF2 described 3.4% of the total variance and had strong loadings on temperature (0.921), TDS (-0.758), total hardness (-0.790) and DO (0.832), while the VF3 (3.24% of the total variance) shows strong loadings on phosphate (0.832), Nitrate (0.961), Nitrite (0.767) while moderate loadings on total dissolved solids and chloride (0.507).

The VF1 explains BOD, COD, alkalinity, and chloride variable with strong factor loadings. This strong loading represent the anthropogenic input typically organic pollution, detergents, dissolved organic matter from solid and domestic waste disposal along with the other agricultural run-off activities (Vega et al., 1998; Yeung, 1999). Apart from that the bathing and swimming activities also results in addition of nutrients. The VF2 explaining strong negative loadings on TDS and total hardness, positive strong loading for DO while, moderate positive loading on pH and temperature basically points to common source of natural processes of soil constituents, weathering of minerals during its natural flow, and indicates towards the origin in run-off from the fields with high load of solids and waste disposal activities. The moderate positive loading in this cluster on pH could explain the loading of industrial waste water containing mineral acids or other metals and waste water from metallurgical and electroplating industries. The positive loading on DO at VF2 depicts the urban domestic source of pollution due to the fact that domestic discharge might be discharged into the river (Geiser, Ingersoll, Bytnerowicz, & Copeland, 2008). At VF3, the strongest loading on phosphate, nitrate, and nitrite explains the common source of origin and suggests the discharge of wastewaters (domestic or industrial) and agricultural run-off. The higher level of these parameters and strong correlation with each other can also be attributed due to reason that the flow of water at these cluster sites is slow and is located near to the urban, industrial and rural agglomerations besides the banks of the river stretch. Also, the check dam causes sudden reduction of flow in river water at most of the sites thereby resulting in stagnation of water and natural degradation and accumulation of organic waste in water resulting in increased variation in water quality and other mineral contents in water (Darwish, 2013). The strong loadings of nitrate and nitrite along with phosphate at this cluster also illustrate the abundance of detergents, domestic organic waste deposited in the river at the stretches. The visual sight of algal blooms (eutrophication process) also accolades the statement (Berna, Moreno, & Ferrer, 1991).

From the PCA and FA loadings, it is apparent that for all the three clusters the major group of parameters with strong loadings emerged are phosphate, nitrate, and nitrite along with BOD, COD, TDS, and alkalinity. These parameters depict organic pollution group representing influences from point sources such as domestic and industrial effluents and nutrient parameter groups influencing from agricultural run-off, urban runoff, and atmospheric depositions as a non-point source of pollution. Alkalinity, total hardness, TDS due to soil leaching, erosion process, and mineral weathering processes (K. P. Singh et al., 2005). The VF3 expresses the non-point source of pollution mainly from NPK fertilizers and other organic matters.

CONCLUSION

In this study, HACA grouped the sampling sites into three clusters. These sites stand of similar characteristics revealing the water quality parameters. The results suggest that the current state of water related anthropogenic influence and religious activities at the Betwa River is not sustainable. Although the anthropogenic and industrial activities are major factor responsible for altering the water quality parameter but the results of religious centered activities on the Betwa River has shown significant cumulative impacts on water quality and association with other sampling sites in terms of water quality parameters.

PCA/ FA identified three latent factors that explained 88.36% of the total variance of 12 parameters, standing for chloride, nitrite, phosphate, COD, nitrate, and BOD for component 1 as evaluated using PCA extraction method that shows a higher degree of positive correlation in a component. The higher trend for alkalinity, TDS, and total hardness attributed to enhanced weathering process between the two seasons. FA also demonstrated the role and contribution of weathering and anthropogenic activities. The results suggested that most of the variations in water quality variables are explained by the weathering process (seasonal variations), non- point sources (agriculture and storm water run- offs) and other anthropogenic organic pollutants (recreation activities, domestic use, detergents, and waste discharge). The sampling point 1 (Bhojpur ghat) and 2 (Near Rasuliya Village) being the most polluted thereby concluding station 1 as the most polluted among the other stations considered in the study. The results also showed that there is transitional spatio- temporal similarity between the SP1 and SP10 sites. These both are points are dominating in religious and recreational concentration sites. Prior studies has proved that the water quality related issues are mainly due to the nutrient enrichments such as phosphorus and nitrogen which gets added to the main stream through human skin, urine, cleansing substances (Binder, 1994; Schulz, 1981). It has been empirically calculated that an average of 0.094 gm per day of phosphorus is added to the water body by the bathers or swimmers (Schulz, 1981). The fecal concentration is an another indicator of visitors recreational impact on water (Kay, Wyer, Crowther, & Fewtrell, 1998). Therefore, it can be concluded that the tourism activities and religious activities are also major factor contributing to the nutrient enrichment to the river water apart from the other anthropogenic impacts.

This result carries significance in terms of rapid assessment of river water quality for future monitoring and planning programs. In a sense that only, one site in each cluster may serve and selected as a good spatial assessment of water quality as a whole network and can offer useful and reliable information on surface waters in the whole region. Thereby, also reducing the cost and without losing the significance of the outcome (Alberto et al., 2001; Simeonov et al., 2003; K. P. Singh et al., 2005).

Recommendations and Future Scope

The study delve with the empirical evidences provided to support that the anthropogenic activities including recreation purposes have direct implications and addition pressure on the water resources. The pressure on the water resources leads to the water scarcity due to unavailability of the water for consumption purpose. This scarcity directly affects the experience of visitors and overall tourism business in nutshell. The increase level of coliform and other bacteriological parameters in water has other health related and aesthetic issues associated for visitors and local habitants. The study is an attempt to showcase how the religious and other recreational activities have contributed to the contamination of the water bodies. This is significant in the case of developing countries like India, where the monsoon and water are important driving force for the economy. The other issue that has to be resolved for the destination areas is proper sustainable visitors' management strategies. The religious tourism in India is uncontrolled and unregulated without any concrete data of visitors' arrivals with the officials so as to help them in planning and mitigating for impacts resulting due to over- tourism. The tourism projects should be so focused to and designed by the planners to have a minimal negative impacts and potentially positive impacts. The study needs to be validated with more robust methodology through which the impact of tourism alone can be delineated from other cumulative impacts. To maintain the current pace of tourism development and projected increase in tourist and related tourism amenities, the development must be considered to complement with the environmental surroundings and socio-cultural acceptability. The study demands more robust studies in the field of tourism, especially the unregulated religious tourism.

ACKNOWLEDGMENT

The authors express their gratitude and thank Symbiosis Center for Research and Innovation (SCRI), Symbiosis International University Pune for financial support (vide SIU/SCRI/Minor Research Approval/ 2014/06/SIIB3/1489/ dt. 20/03/2015) to carry out research work is deeply acknowledged. The authors declare that there is no conflict of interests.

REFERENCES

Alberto, W. D., María del Pilar, D., María Valeria, A., Fabiana, P. S., Cecilia, H. A., & María de los Ángeles, B. (2001). Pattern Recognition Techniques for the Evaluation of Spatial and Temporal Variations in Water Quality. A Case Study. *Water Research*, *35*(12), 2881–2894. doi:10.1016/S0043-1354(00)00592-3 PMID:11471688

Alobaidy, A. H. M. J., Abid, H. S., & Maulood, B. K. (2010). Application of Water Quality Index for Assessment of Dokan Lake Ecosystem, Kurdistan Region, Iraq. *Journal of Water Resource and Protection*, *2*(9), 792–798. doi:10.4236/jwarp.2010.29093

APHA/AWWA/WEF. (2012). Standard Methods for the Examination of Water and Wastewater. *Standard Methods, 541*.

Banerjee, S., Maiti, S. K., & Kumar, A. (2015). Metal contamination in water and bioaccumulation of metals in the planktons, molluscs and fishes in Jamshedpur stretch of Subarnarekha River of Chotanagpur plateau, India. *Water and Environment Journal: the Journal / the Chartered Institution of Water and Environmental Management*, *29*(2), 207–213. doi:10.1111/wej.12108

Bates, B. C., Kundzewicz, Z. W., Wu, S., & Palutikof, J. P. (2008). *Climate Change and Water*. doi:10.1016/j.jmb.2010.08.039

Benedict, M. A., & McMahon, E. T. (2000). Green Infrastructure: Smart Conservation for the 21st Century. *Recreation*, (37), 4–7. doi:10.4135/9781412973816.n70

Bergmann-Baker, U., Brotton, J., & Wall, G. (1995). Socio-economic impacts of fluctuating water levels on recreational boating in the great lakes. *Canadian Water Resources Journal*, *20*(3), 185–194. doi:10.4296/cwrj2003185

Berna, J. L., Moreno, A., & Ferrer, J. (1991). The behaviour of LAS in the environment. *Journal of Chemical Technology and Biotechnology (Oxford, Oxfordshire)*, *50*(3), 387–398. doi:10.1002/jctb.280500310

Bhat, S. A., & Pandit, A. K. (2014). Surface Water Quality Assessment of Wular Lake, A Ramsar Site in Kashmir Himalaya, Using Discriminant Analysis and WQI. *Journal of Ecosystem, 18.* doi:10.1155/2014/724728

Binder, W. (1994). Schutz der Binnengewässer [in German]. *Economía, 5,* 183.

Boyacioglu, H., Boyacioglu, H., & Gunduz, O. (2005). Application of Factor Analysis in the Assessment of Surface Water Quality in Buyuk Menderes River Basin - EW_2005_9-10_05.pdf. *European Water,* 43–49. Retrieved from http://www.ewra.net/ew/pdf/EW_2005_9-10_05.pdf

Callender, E., & Rice, K. C. (1999). *The Urban Environmental Gradient: Anthropogenic Influences on the Spatial and Temporal Distributions of Lead and Zinc in Sediments.* doi:10.1021/ES990380S

Carpenter, S. R. (2008). Phosphorus control is critical to mitigating eutrophication. *Proceedings of the National Academy of Sciences of the United States of America, 105*(32), 11039–11040. doi:10.1073/pnas.0806112105 PMID:18685114

Central Pollution Control Board. (2010). Status of Water Quality in India- 2009. *Central Pollution Control Board, Monitoring Series: MINARS/ /2009-10.*

Central Pollution Control Board. (2013). *Status of Water Quality in India- 2011.* Central Pollution Control Board.

Chapman. (1992). Water Quality Assessments -A Guide to Use of Biota, Sediments and Water in Environmental Monitoring - Second Edition. Unesco/Who/Unep, 6(5), 419.

Chow, M. F., Shiah, F. K., Lai, C. C., Kuo, H. Y., Wang, K. W., Lin, C. H., ... Ko, C. Y. (2016). Evaluation of surface water quality using multivariate statistical techniques: A case study of Fei-Tsui Reservoir basin, Taiwan. *Environmental Earth Sciences, 75*(1), 1–15. doi:10.100712665-015-4922-5

Cole, D. N. (2000). *Dispersed Recreation.* Retrieved from http://winapps.umt.edu/winapps/media2/leopold/pubs/421.pdf

CPCB-ENVIS. (2013). *Inclusion of Biological Parameters for Bio-Mapping CPCB Initiative for Bio-Mapping of River Basins in India.* Retrieved from http://cpcbenvis.nic.in/newsletter/bio-mapping-march1999/march1999.htm

Darwish, M. A. G. (2013). Geochemistry of the High Dam Lake sediments, south Egypt: Implications for environmental significance. *International Journal of Sediment Research, 28*(4), 544–559. doi:10.1016/S1001-6279(14)60012-3

Davies, T., Davies, T., & Cahill, S. (2000). *Environmental Implications of the Tourism Industry*. Academic Press.

Dickman, M., & Dorais, M. (1977). The impact of human trampling on phosphorus loading to a small lake in Gatineau Park, Quebec, Canada. *Journal of Environmental Management*, *5*(4), 335–344. Retrieved from https://www.cabdirect.org/cabdirect/abstract/19781940757

Ding, J., Jiang, Y., Fu, L., Liu, Q., Peng, Q., & Kang, M. (2015). Impacts of Land Use on Surface Water Quality in a Subtropical River Basin: A Case Study of the Dongjiang River Basin, Southeastern China. *Water (Basel)*, *7*(12), 4427–4445. doi:10.3390/w7084427

Garcia-Esteves, J., Ludwig, W., Kerhervé, P., Probst, J. L., & Lespinas, F. (2007). Predicting the impact of land use on the major element and nutrient fluxes in coastal Mediterranean rivers: The case of the Têt River (Southern France). *Applied Geochemistry*, *22*(1), 230–248. doi:10.1016/j.apgeochem.2006.09.013

Garizi, Z., Sheikh, V., & Sadoddin, A. (2011). Assessment of seasonal variations of chemical characteristics in surface water using multivariate statistical methods. *International Journal of Environmental Science and Technology*, *8*(3), 581–592. doi:10.1007/BF03326244

Geiser, L. H., Ingersoll, A. R., Bytnerowicz, A., & Copeland, S. A. (2008). Evidence of Enhanced Atmospheric Ammoniacal Nitrogen in Hells Canyon National Recreation Area: Implications for Natural and Cultural Resources. *Journal of the Air & Waste Management Association*, *58*(9), 1223–1234. doi:10.3155/1047-3289.58.9.1223 PMID:18817115

Gössling, S. (2002). Global environmental consequences of tourism. *Global Environmental Change*, *12*(4), 283–302. doi:10.1016/S0959-3780(02)00044-4

Gössling, S., Peeters, P., Hall, C. M., Ceron, J. P., Dubois, G., Lehmann, L. V., & Scott, D. (2012). Tourism and water use: Supply, demand, and security. An international review. *Tourism Management*, *33*(1), 1–15. doi:10.1016/j.tourman.2011.03.015

Hadwen, W. L., Arthington, A. H., & Mosisch, T. D. (2003). The impact of tourism on dune lakes on Fraser Island, Australia. *Lakes and Reservoirs: Research and Management*, *8*(1), 15–26. doi:10.1046/j.1440-1770.2003.00205.x

Hammitt, W. E., Cole, D., & Monz, C. (2015). Recreation Ecology. In Recreation Ecology (pp. 121–180). Academic Press.

Hammitt, W. E., Cole, D. N., & Monz, C. (2015). *Wildland Recreation: Ecology and Management.* John Wiley & Sons, Inc. Retrieved from http://download.e-bookshelf. de/download/0003/2464/78/L-G-0003246478-0006240746.pdf

Haque, M. Z., Rahim, S. A., Abdullah, M. P., Embi, A. F., Elfithri, R., Lihan, T., ... Mokhtar, M. (2016). Multivariate chemometric approach on the surface water quality in langat upstream tributaries, peninsular Malaysia. *Journal of Environmental Science and Technology*, *9*(3), 277–284. doi:10.3923/jest.2016.277.284

Harrison, S. S. C., Pretty, J. L., Shepherd, D., Hildrew, A. G., Smith, C., Hey, R. D., & Harrison, S. (2004). The effect of instream rehabilitation structures on macroinvertebrates in lowland rivers. *Journal of Applied Ecology Journal of Applied Ecology Journal of Applied Ecology*, *41*(6), 1140–1154. Retrieved from https:// besjournals.onlinelibrary.wiley.com/doi/pdf/10.1111/j.0021-8901.2004.00958.x

Harun, S., Dambul, R., Abdullah, M. H., & Mohamed, M. (2014). Spatial and seasonal variations in surface water quality of the Lower Kinabatangan River Catchment, Sabah, Malaysia. Academic Press.

Helena, B., Pardo, R., Vega, M., Barrado, E., Fernandez, J. M., & Fernandez, L. (2000). Temporal evolution of groundwater composition in an alluvial aquifer (Pisuerga River, Spain) by principal component analysis. *Water Research*, *34*(3), 807–816. doi:10.1016/S0043-1354(99)00225-0

IPCC. (2007). *Climate Change 2007: impacts, adaptation and vulnerability: contribution of Working Group II to the fourth assessment report of the Intergovernmental Panel.* IPCC. doi:10.1256/004316502320517344

Jahan, S., & Strezov, V. (2017). Water quality assessment of Australian ports using water quality evaluation indices. *PLoS One*, *12*(12), 1–16. doi:10.1371/journal. pone.0189284 PMID:29244876

Jarvie, H. P., Whitton, B. A., & Neal, C. (1998). Nitrogen and phosphorus in east coast British rivers: Speciation, sources and biological significance. *The Science of the Total Environment*, *210–211*, 79–109. doi:10.1016/S0048-9697(98)00109-0

Jha, B. R., Waidbacher, H., Sharma, S., & Straif, M. (2010). Study of agricultural impacts through fish base variables in different rivers. *International Journal of Environmental Science and Technology*, *7*(3), 609–615. doi:10.1007/BF03326170

Jiang, Y. (2009). Evaluating eco-sustainability and its spatial variability in tourism areas: A case study in Lijiang County, China. *International Journal of Sustainable Development and World Ecology, 16*(2), 117–126. doi:10.1080/13504500902808628

Juahir, H., Zain, S. M., Yusoff, M. K., Hanidza, T. I. T., Armi, A. S. M., Toriman, M. E., & Mokhtar, M. (2011). Spatial water quality assessment of Langat River Basin (Malaysia) using environmetric techniques. *Environmental Monitoring and Assessment, 173*(1–4), 625–641. doi:10.100710661-010-1411-x PMID:20339961

Juang, D. F., Lee, C. H., & Hsueh, S. C. (2009). Chlorinated volatile organic compounds found near the water surface of heavily polluted rivers. *International Journal of Environmental Science and Technology, 6*(4), 545–556. doi:10.1007/BF03326094

Kannel, P. R., Lee, S., Kanel, S. R., & Khan, S. P. (2007). Chemometric application in classification and assessment of monitoring locations of an urban river system. *Analytica Chimica Acta, 582*(2), 390–399. doi:10.1016/j.aca.2006.09.006 PMID:17386518

Karbassi, A. R., Nouri, J., Mehrdadi, N., & Ayaz, G. O. (2008). Flocculation of heavy metals during mixing of freshwater with Caspian Sea water. *Environmental Geology, 53*(8), 1811–1816. doi:10.100700254-007-0786-7

Kaushik, A., Kansal, A., Santosh, Meena, Kumari, S., & Kaushik, C. P. (2009). Heavy metal contamination of river Yamuna, Haryana, India: Assessment by Metal Enrichment Factor of the Sediments. *Journal of Hazardous Materials, 164*(1), 265–270. doi:10.1016/j.jhazmat.2008.08.031 PMID:18809251

Kay, D., Wyer, M. D., Crowther, J., & Fewtrell, L. (1998). Faecal indicator impacts on recreational waters: Budget studies and diffuse source modelling. *Journal of Applied Microbiology, 85*(S1), 70S–82S. doi:10.1111/j.1365-2672.1998.tb05285.x PMID:21182695

Krishna, A. K., Satyanarayanan, M., & Govil, P. K. (2009). Assessment of heavy metal pollution in water using multivariate statistical techniques in an industrial area: A case study from Patancheru, Medak District, Andhra Pradesh, India. *Journal of Hazardous Materials, 167*(1–3), 366–373. doi:10.1016/j.jhazmat.2008.12.131 PMID:19304387

Lee, C.-M., Miller, W. F., & Hancock, M. G. (2000). *The Silicon Valley Edge: A Habitat for Innovation and Entrepreneurship | Stanford Graduate School of Business.* Stanford University Press. Retrieved from https://www.gsb.stanford.edu/faculty-research/books/silicon-valley-edge-habitat-innovation-entrepreneurship

Li, C., Yang, J., Wang, X., Wang, E., Li, B., He, R., & Yuan, H. (2015). Removal of nitrogen by heterotrophic nitrification-aerobic denitrification of a phosphate accumulating bacterium Pseudomonas stutzeri YG-24. *Bioresource Technology, 182*, 18–25. doi:10.1016/j.biortech.2015.01.100 PMID:25668754

Li, S., Gu, S., Tan, X., & Zhang, Q. (2009). Water quality in the upper Han River basin, China: The impacts of land use/land cover in riparian buffer zone. *Journal of Hazardous Materials, 165*(1–3), 317–324. doi:10.1016/j.jhazmat.2008.09.123 PMID:19019532

Liddle, M. J., & Scorgie, H. R. A. (1980). The effects of recreation on freshwater plants and animals: A review. *Biological Conservation, 17*(3), 183–206. doi:10.1016/0006-3207(80)90055-5

Liu, C.-W., Lin, K.-H., & Kuo, Y.-M. (2003). Application of factor analysis in the assessment of groundwater quality in a blackfoot disease area in Taiwan. *The Science of the Total Environment, 313*(1–3), 77–89. doi:10.1016/S0048-9697(02)00683-6 PMID:12922062

Mallin, M. A., Williams, K. E., Esham, E. C., & Lowe, R. P. (2000). Effect of human development on bacteriological water quality in coastal watersheds. *Ecological Applications, 10*(4), 1047–1056. doi:10.1890/1051-0761(2000)010[1047:EOHDOB]2.0.CO;2

McKenna, J. E. (2003). An enhanced cluster analysis program with bootstrap significance testing for ecological community analysis. *Environmental Modelling & Software, 18*(3), 205–220. doi:10.1016/S1364-8152(02)00094-4

National Water Development Agency. (2006). *Feasibility Report of Ken Betwa Link Project DPRs Phase I and II Completed.* Retrieved March 26, 2018, from http://www.nwda.gov.in/content/innerpage/FRof-DPR-Phase-I-and-II-Completed.php

Ouyang, Y., Nkedi-Kizza, P., Wu, Q. T., Shinde, D., & Huang, C. H. (2006). Assessment of seasonal variations in surface water quality. *Water Research, 40*(20), 3800–3810. doi:10.1016/j.watres.2006.08.030 PMID:17069873

Palma, P., Alvarenga, P., Palma, V. L., Fernandes, R. M., Soares, A. M. V. M., & Barbosa, I. R. (2010). Assessment of anthropogenic sources of water pollution using multivariate statistical techniques: A case study of the Alqueva's reservoir, Portugal. *Environmental Monitoring and Assessment, 165*(1–4), 539–552. doi:10.100710661-009-0965-y PMID:19444629

Pandey, P. K., Kass, P. H., Soupir, M. L., Biswas, S., & Singh, V. P. (2014). Contamination of water resources by pathogenic bacteria. *AMB Express, 4*(1), 51. doi:10.118613568-014-0051-x PMID:25006540

Parry, M., Arnell, N., Berry, P., Dodman, D., Fankhauser, S., Hope, C., ... Wheeler, T. (2009). Assessing the costs of adaptation to climate change: A review of the UNFCCC and other recent estimates. *IIED, 3*. doi:10.1641/0006-3568(2001)051[0723:CCAFD]2.0.CO;2

Pereira, R., Soares, A. M. V. M., Ribeiro, R., & Goncalves, F. (2005). Public attitudes towards the restoration and management of Lake Vela (Central Portugal). *Fresenius Environmental Bulletin, 14*(4), 273–281.

Phiri, O., Mumba, P., Moyo, B. H. Z., & Kadewa, W. (2005). Assessment of the impact of industrial effluents on water quality of receiving rivers in urban areas of Malawi. *International Journal of Environmental Science and Technology, 2*(3), 237–244. doi:10.1007/BF03325882

Phung, D., Huang, C., Rutherford, S., Dwirahmadi, F., Chu, C., Wang, X., ... Dinh, T. A. D. (2015). Temporal and spatial assessment of river surface water quality using multivariate statistical techniques: A study in Can Tho City, a Mekong Delta area, Vietnam. *Environmental Monitoring and Assessment, 187*(5), 229. doi:10.100710661-015-4474-x PMID:25847419

Rashid, I., & Romshoo, S. A. (2013). Impact of anthropogenic activities on water quality of Lidder River in Kashmir Himalayas. *Environmental Monitoring and Assessment, 185*(6), 4705–4719. doi:10.100710661-012-2898-0 PMID:23001554

Razmkhah, H., Abrishamchi, A., & Torkian, A. (2010). Evaluation of spatial and temporal variation in water quality by pattern recognition techniques: A case study on Jajrood River (Tehran, Iran). *Journal of Environmental Management, 91*(4), 852–860. doi:10.1016/j.jenvman.2009.11.001 PMID:20056527

Rose, S. (2002). Comparative major ion geochemistry of Piedmont streams in the Atlanta, Georgia region: Possible effects of urbanization. *Environmental Geology*, *42*(1), 102–113. doi:10.100700254-002-0545-8

Sahu, B. K., Begum, M., Khadanga, M. K., Jha, D. K., Vinithkumar, N. V., & Kirubagaran, R. (2013). Evaluation of significant sources influencing the variation of physico-chemical parameters in Port Blair Bay, South Andaman, India by using multivariate statistics. *Marine Pollution Bulletin*, *66*(1–2), 246–251. doi:10.1016/j.marpolbul.2012.09.021 PMID:23107366

Sârbu, C., & Pop, H. F. (2005). Principal component analysis versus fuzzy principal component analysis: A case study: The quality of danube water (1985-1996). *Talanta*, *65*(5), 1215–1220. doi:10.1016/j.talanta.2004.08.047 PMID:18969934

Schulz, L. (1981). Nährstoffeintrag in Seen durch Badegäste. (in German). *Zbl. Bakt. Hyg. I. Abt. Orig.B.*, *173*, 528–548.

Shrestha, S., & Kazama, F. (2007). Assessment of surface water quality using multivariate statistical techniques: A case study of the Fuji river basin, Japan. *Environmental Modelling & Software*, *22*(4), 464–475. doi:10.1016/j.envsoft.2006.02.001

Silva, J. D., Srinivasalu, S., Roy, P. D., & Jonathan, M. P. (2014). Environmental conditions inferred from multi-element concentrations in sediments off Cauvery delta, Southeast India. *Environmental Earth Sciences*, *71*(5), 2043–2058. doi:10.100712665-013-2606-6

Simeonov, V., Stratis, J. A., Samara, C., Zachariadis, G., Voutsa, D., Anthemidis, A., ... Kouimtzis, T. (2003). Assessment of the surface water quality in Northern Greece. *Water Research*, *37*(17), 4119–4124. doi:10.1016/S0043-1354(03)00398-1 PMID:12946893

Singh, K. P., Malik, A., Mohan, D., & Sinha, S. (2004). Multivariate statistical techniques for the evaluation of spatial and temporal variations in water quality of Gomti River (India)—A case study. *Water Research*, *38*(18), 3980–3992. doi:10.1016/j.watres.2004.06.011 PMID:15380988

Singh, K. P., Malik, A., & Sinha, S. (2005). Water quality assessment and apportionment of pollution sources of Gomti river (India) using multivariate statistical techniques - A case study. *Analytica Chimica Acta*, *538*(1–2), 355–374. doi:10.1016/j.aca.2005.02.006

Singh, M., Ansari, A. A., Müller, G., & Singh, I. B. (1997). Heavy metals in freshly deposited sediments of the Gomati River (a tributary of the Ganga River): Effects of human activities. *Environmental Geology, 29*(3–4), 246–252. doi:10.1007002540050123

Suk, T. J., Sorenson, S. K., & Dileanis, P. D. (1987). The relation between human presence and occurrence of Giardia cysts in streams in the Sierra Nevada, California. *Journal of Freshwater Ecology, 4*(1), 71–75. doi:10.1080/02705060.1987.9665163

Sun, D., & Walsh, D. (1998). Review of studies on environmental impacts of recreation and tourism in Australia. *Journal of Environmental Management, 53*(4), 323–338. doi:10.1006/jema.1998.0200

Suthar, S., Sharma, J., Chabukdhara, M., & Nema, A. K. (2009). Water quality assessment of river Hindon at Ghaziabad, India: Impact of industrial and urban wastewater. *Environmental Monitoring and Assessment.* doi:10.100710661-009-0930-9 PMID:19418235

Tong, J., & Chen, Y. (2009). Recovery of nitrogen and phosphorus from alkaline fermentation liquid of waste activated sludge and application of the fermentation liquid to promote biological municipal wastewater treatment. *Water Research, 43*(12), 2969–2976. doi:10.1016/j.watres.2009.04.015 PMID:19443007

Tong, S. T. Y., & Chen, W. (2002). Modeling the relationship between land use and surface water quality. *Journal of Environmental Management, 66*(4), 377–393. doi:10.1006/jema.2002.0593 PMID:12503494

Varol, M., & Şen, B. (2009). Assessment of surface water quality using multivariate statistical techniques: A case study of Behrimaz Stream, Turkey. *Environmental Monitoring and Assessment, 159*(1–4), 543–553. doi:10.100710661-008-0650-6 PMID:19051048

Varol, M., & Şen, B. (2012). Assessment of nutrient and heavy metal contamination in surface water and sediments of the upper Tigris River, Turkey. *Catena, 92*, 1–10. doi:10.1016/j.catena.2011.11.011

Vega, M., Pardo, R., Barrado, E., & Debán, L. (1998). Assessment of seasonal and polluting effects on the quality of river water by exploratory data analysis. *Water Research, 32*(12), 3581–3592. doi:10.1016/S0043-1354(98)00138-9

Vutukuru, S. S. (2003). Chromium induced alterations in some biochemical profiles of the Indian major carp, Labeo rohita (Hamilton). *Bulletin of Environmental Contamination and Toxicology*, *70*(1), 118–123. doi:10.100700128-002-0164-9 PMID:12478433

Yeung, I. M. H. (1999). Multivariate analysis of the Hong Kong Victoria Harbour water quality data. *Environmental Monitoring and Assessment*, *59*(3), 331–342. doi:10.1023/A:1006177824327

Zhao, W., Wang, Y., Lin, X., Zhou, D., Pan, M., & Yang, J. (2014). Identification of the salinity effect on N2O production pathway during nitrification: Using stepwise inhibition and15N isotope labeling methods. *Chemical Engineering Journal*, *253*, 418–426. doi:10.1016/j.cej.2014.05.052

Zhou, Q., Zhang, J., Fu, J., Shi, J., & Jiang, G. (2008). Biomonitoring : An appealing tool for assessment of metal pollution in the aquatic ecosystem. *Analytica Chimica Acta*, *606*(2), 135–150. doi:10.1016/j.aca.2007.11.018 PMID:18082645

Chapter 2
Revaluing Saltscapes in Portugal:
Ecotourism, Ecomuseums, and Environmental Education

Carlos Balsas
University at Albany (SUNY), USA

ABSTRACT

Solar salinas in Portugal are progressively changing from places of work to places of tourism. The research question is the extent to which these special landscapes have been understood, marketed, and enhanced to the benefit of mostly tourists and visitors or also local constituencies. This research question arises from a sense of stigmatization, perceived lack of potential, and outmoded technological development associated with traditional cultural heritage and sun and sea tourism paradigms. The purpose of this chapter is to analyze how two Portuguese municipalities (i.e., Aveiro and Figueira da Foz) have engaged in the rehabilitation of their solar salinas. The argument is that given the considerable natural areas of wetlands in the case studies, solar salinas, and their potentialities from ecotourism and environmental education ought to perform a more central role in the municipalities' territorial development strategies. The key finding is the identification of a set of lessons learned useful to the partial rehabilitation of solar salinas.

DOI: 10.4018/978-1-5225-8494-0.ch002

INTRODUCTION

Portugal is currently experiencing a tourism boom. However, most of the tourism activity takes place in the very central locations of Lisbon, Porto and Algarve. The country is perceived as being very affordable, safe and with a distinct identity. However, tourism-based conflicts between tourists and residents are starting to emerge in the historic districts of Lisbon with the rise of too many *alojamentos locais* establishments (local accommodations in traditionally residential city-center neighborhoods), traffic and rickshaw congestion, and displacement of residents (Urry, 1990; Ribeiro & Fidalgo, 2015).

Simultaneously, many solar salinas in Portugal are progressively changing from places of work to places of ecotourism. Traditionally, salterns were places utilized to produce salt. Nowadays that industrial salt production has replaced traditional artisanal salt making, saltscapes are being utilized for other purposes including, cultural and wellness tourism, environmental education, and nature preserves. Ecomuseums and artisanal salt making demonstration projects are central to the rehabilitation of salterns. The rehabilitation of solar salinas can be understood as an example of environmental daylighting, since many salterns have been completely abandoned and destroyed, while others have been performing below their full potential. A strong awareness of saltscapes' cultural, ecological and biodiversity potential is helping to rehabilitate many of them for both artisanal, cultural and educational purposes.

Furthermore, since many of the cities with some of the greatest concentrations of solar saltscapes are not necessarily within the two largest metropolitan areas of Lisbon and Porto (Balsas, 2012), they have remained below their full potential as alternative ecotourism sites. The research question is the extent to which these special landscapes have been understood, marketed, and enhanced to the benefit of mostly tourists and visitors or also local constituencies. This research question arises from a sense of stigmatization, perceived lack of potential and outmoded technological development associated with traditional cultural heritage and sun and sea tourism paradigms.

The purpose of this chapter is to analyze how two Portuguese municipalities (i.e. Aveiro and Figueira da Foz) have engaged in the rehabilitation of their solar salinas. The argument is that given the considerable natural areas of wetlands in the case studies, solar salinas and their potentialities from ecotourism and environmental education ought to perform a more central role in the municipalities' territorial development strategies. The methodology is threefold: (1) to analyze these municipalities' recent tourism strategies, (2) to review the specialized literature on ecotourism, ecomuseums and environmental education, and (3) to critically reflect on the field work conducted in both municipalities during recent years. The key finding is the identification of a set of lessons learned useful to the partial rehabilitation of solar salinas. The theory of landscape and ecosystem services is partially utilized to analyze solar salinas' current transition phase from abandonment to new alternative uses such as wellness and ecotourism and environmental education, among others (Termorshuizen & Opdam, 2009; O'Connell, 2003).

This chapter is in four parts. Following this introduction, Part one is the analytical mechanism centered on: (1) Revaluing saltscapes, (2) ecotourism, (3) ecomuseums, and (4) environmental education. Part two is an overview of the evolution of Portuguese saltpans and tourism. Part three is an introduction to the case studies of Aveiro and Figueira da Foz in central Portugal. Part four is the comparative discussion of the case studies. And Part five is the conclusion and identification of some public policy implications.

Analytical Mechanism

This analytical mechanism is in four parts. Its goal is to identify important postulates to analyze and discuss the case studies in Part four of the chapter. The relationships among saltscapes, ecotourism, ecomuseums and environmental education are quite complementary and increasingly stronger as tourists and visitors become culturally and environmentally savvier, and develop more genuine preferences for authentic and unique destinations, likely to provide them with more rewarding knowledge-based experiences.

In fact, Zhang & Lei (2012, p. 924) have confirmed the relationships between "residents' environmental knowledge, attitudes towards ecotourism and intention to participate in ecotourism, as well as the mediating effect of landscape likeability between attitudes and intention" in contexts of saltscape tourism. On the other hand, Wu, Xie, & Tsai (2015, p. 204) have also recently identified three main themes for salt-related tourism: "(1) Production processes, where salt culture is revealed, (2) products offered at salt destinations to tourists, and (3) abandoned salt fields without interventions [and] interpretation programs."

Many ecomuseums are increasingly complementing their offerings with dynamic experiences for visitors (O'Dell, 2005), which go beyond simply passively acquiring knowledge to actually engaging with more dynamic salt livelihoods. Environmental education consists of structured and semi-structured learning opportunities about the environment for individuals engaged in compulsory educational programs and or optional continuing education endeavors.

Revaluing Saltscapes

Solar salinas are an ancient technology aimed at producing salt by natural solar evaporation. Saltmaking by solar evaporation comprises not only the salterns, channels, evaporation basins, crystallization ponds, pumps, windmills, salterns' homes, storage warehouses, scraping and collection tools, but also the individuals who make a living of this professional activity and their traditions, beliefs and local knowledge. Coastal salinas tend to be located in estuaries of rivers, which are by themselves important wetlands for various bird species, such as flamingos, storks, and other waders (Rufino, 2004a). Many of these wetlands have been abandoned, filled with construction debris and converted to other uses due to growing urbanization pressures or decline in salt making activity (Saurí-Pujol & Llurdés-Coit, 1995; Pacitto & Jacquemin, 2017).

This millenary activity has declined in many estuaries due to fierce industrial competition created by the mechanization and the exploration of very large seaside locations in other parts of the world (Kurlansky, 2003), such as Perugia in Italy, north-Africa and the Caribbean. The farming of large salinas through the use of heavy machinery and industrial practices has lowered the cost of salt and enabled the economies of scale, which also contributed to the decline of traditional artisanal salt making. Nonetheless, traditional salterns still constitute a very important cultural heritage, rich in social traditions, history, biodiversity, and human imprints in the landscapes of many estuaries and coastal regions (Beatley, 2014). Many saltscapes are recognized by the RAMSAR Convention of 1971, which initially recognized the conservation value of wetlands, such as lakes, marshes and other estuarine and riverine environments.

Even though this ancient activity tended to employ individuals with low qualification skills, salt making has always had a strong place attachment, and for many centuries, it remained a very productive business with well-defined labor practices and adhesion rules (Thompson, 1999). The science of making salt by solar evaporation is complex and requires an understanding of many variables, procedures, measurements and operational techniques, such as the quantity and salinity of the water in different pools of the saltern complex as it progresses to more shallow pools and higher salinity levels. Therefore, salt making activity has left a strong material and social mark in the cultural heritage of many coastal regions (López, Aguilera, Schmitz, Castro, & Pineda, 2010).

Salinas' cultural and patrimonial value has received international recognition from professional and academic networks, such as the *SALT (Interreg 2001)*, ALAS – *All about salt in the Mediterranean (2002)*, and the *ECOSAL Atlantis* (2007–2013). Many of these networks were created to promote the rehabilitation of salterns complexes throughout Europe, and especially the Mediterranean region. For instance, the ALAS project included principal partners from Greece, Portugal, Slovenia and Bulgaria, while the *ECOSAL Atlantis* project consisted of 13 partners from four countries (i.e. Portugal, Spain, France and the United Kingdom).

The overall goal of the *ECOSAL Atlantis* project was the delineation of "a route easily recognized by the general public in the Atlantis area" (Martins, Albuquerque, & Silva, 2013, p. 2). Many of these networks were started by local champions, and then grew in scope and ambition due to regional and national endorsements. Funding from the European Union (EU) was critical to the development and implementation of some of these networks' projects. EU funding also facilitated the full development of the networks, enabled more effective communication and knowledge exchanges, and the widespread dissemination of findings at congresses and through publications.

Some of the activities which helped to revalue saltscapes included the purchase and ownership of salterns by municipalities and universities. Some of those salterns were then adapted as pilot projects aimed at maintaining this artisanal activity alive and to remind the new generations of the importance of ancient salt production techniques. Other salterns are increasingly utilized as demonstrative sites of this once bourgeoning coastal activity. In many estuaries, saltpans have become important ecotourism sites endowed with ecomuseums, which constitute the ideal settings for environmental education programs. Examples of internationally well-known saltpans complexes in Europe are the *Margherita di Savoia* in southern Italy, and the *Marais Salants de Guérande* in Loire-Atlantique in France. Outside of Europe, the *Songor Keta Lagoon* in Ghana, the *Yucatan* in Mexico, and the *Rajasthan* in India constitute important salt making locations.

Ecotourism

Ecotourism is an idiosyncratic form of tourism that combines leisure with a strong environmental component. Although ecotourism gained notoriety in the 1990s, in the 21st century it has developed a broader scope and distinctive depth. Ecotourism is exemplified by its emphasis on environmental citizenship and more recently by involving tourists in active and rewarding participatory activities. This transformation has also led to a major change in the turists' role from mere spectators to active participants in the ecotourism experiences (Dolnicar, Crouch, & Long, 2008). One central motivation of ecotourism in the 21st century is its attempt at reducing harmful human impacts on planet earth while conciliating an inevitable ecological footprint with societal development (Hall & Lew, 2009). Finally, ecotourism involves not only natural environments but also the community, social justice opportunities, heritage conservation, cultural rituals and the celebration of many social traditions, increasingly in contexts of climate change (Hall, Baird, James, & Ram, 2016). Published research on tourism and saltscapes remains scarce (Petanidou & Vayanni, 2004). Nonetheless, these three scholarly pieces are particularly relevant. Kortekaas (2004) reviewed sustainable tourism initiatives in European saltscapes. Zhang & Lei (2012) developed a structural model of residents' intention to participate in ecotourism activities in Taiwan. And finally, Wu, Xie, & Tsai (2015) analyzed perceptions of attractiveness for salt heritage tourism from a tourist perspective, also in Taiwan. Wu, Xie, & Tsai (2015, p. 208) have also identified "theme, product, and design" as the three most important attributes potentiating the attractiveness of salt destinations and fostering tourists' choices to salt heritage areas.

Ecotourism appears to be an alternative developmental strategy in saltscapes. It includes many ecological activities including bird watching, gastronomy and educational trips. Many of those trips and guided tours include the active participation of visitors in the practice of salt making. Active workers and or knowledgeable tour guides are able to provide explanations about the whole cycle of producing salt by solar evaporation, including the cleaning and preparation of salterns, the control of water flows, the crystallization processes, the impact of the weather in the production processes and the scheduling of various seasonal activities from cleaning and irrigation to the collection of crystals and storage of salt. To a certain extent this is similar to picking strawberries or apples and or participating in grape harvesting campaigns in wine producing regions of the world.

According to Kortekaas (2004, p. 202–203) there are different types of specialized tourism that can be found in salterns: Cultural, agritourism, ecotourism, educational tourism, health tourism, and gastronomic tourism, among others. The gastronomic tourism includes the preparation of dishes with *"flôr de sal"*, a type of salt quite valued by *haute-cuisine* chefs. Ecotourism can also comprise two types of activities on river banks and on the water. The former includes walking and trekking guided tours, and the latter comprises sightseeing boat cruises. Moreira & Santos (2010) have analyzed the growing opportunities of tourism in Portuguese riverine environments. Saltworks tourism can be considered a sub-set of river tourism mostly confined to river estuaries, where waters are traditionally calmer and enable boat tours of the river estuary, contrarily to river rafting in more upstream locations. Short cruises and boat excursions are common in estuaries with high concentrations of saltscapes.

Zhang & Lei (2012, p. 916) have concluded that "residents' environmental knowledge positively affects attitudes towards ecotourism, which in turn directly and indirectly determine the intention to participate in ecotourism through their individual landscape affinity." Furthermore, the same authors have also concluded that "residents' involvement in ecotourism may be stimulated through appropriate management strategies aimed at increasing their environmental knowledge, encouraging positive ecotourism attitudes, and environmental planning that promotes residents' affinity for local attractions." In conclusion, ecotourism attitudes consist of three main dimensions: "Encouraging environmental awareness, low impact activities, and environmental protection management" (Zhang & Lei, 2012, p. 923).

Ecomuseums

Ecomuseums are specialized types of museums (Kirshenblatt-Gimblett, 1998). Particularly, salt museums can be considered a branch of either maritime or rural interpretation museums, although with a slightly more confined mission and scope. The particular activity in this case is salt making by solar evaporation and the typical recreational activity at salt museums consists in learning the technological fundamentals of this ancient production technique through contact with a variety of raw materials (i.e. water, wood, mud, and crystalized salt) and tools. Salt museums are variously designed as salt interpretation centers and ecomuseums (Dahm, 2004). Independently of their designations, they aim at preserving and restoring the biological, human and cultural traditions associated with man-made saltscapes (Vieira & Bio, 2004).

Usually, these museums have written information about the salt making processes, the tools utilized in those activities, the mercantile networks of salt established with other regions of the world, and samples of various types of salt on display. The main goal is to preserve the living memory of those engaged in the activity and enable new generations to learn about this millenary production technique. Increasingly, ecomuseums have distinct activities for various publics and age groups (Davis, 1999). The active participation at ecomuseums include the traditional visits to the museums' grounds and to the salterns themselves, guided walking tours, hikes of nature preserve trails, boat tours and an active engagement with salt production. Besides the traditional museum store where visitors can acquire souvenirs and samples of various types of salt (e.g. culinary salt and its more refined and gourmet version *"flôr de sal"*), many ecomuseums are adopting a universal design paradigm of accessibility for all, especially for mobility and visually impaired individuals.

Recent efforts to revalue solar salinas have also included the restoration of tide watermills in various parts of river estuaries. Tide watermills are also important ancient cultural heritage on the water-land edge. Their location, construction and technology represent ancient knowledge applied to the harvesting of renewable energy for various purposes, including grinding grain in order to obtain flour. The rise and fall of the water tide enables the movement of an engine that is used to move the grinding stones. The rehabilitation of these mills has helped tourists learn about the history, functioning principles and patrimonial heritage of such built-up structures. Some watermills also include display exhibits and others have even received new uses such as restaurants, which serve to increase gastronomic tourism and augment the number of regional touristic attractions. The *Musée des Marais Salants* in *Guérande* was founded as an eco-museum devoted to the natural values of salinas and birdlife as early as 1887 (Kortekaas, 2004). Nowadays, this museum attracts about 100,000 visitors a year (Martins, Albuquerque, & Silva, 2014, p. 381).

Environmental Education

Environmental education has evolved from fighting for environmental causes, such as eradication of various forms of pollution, to learning and applying findings to change human behaviors and to reduce their negative environmental consequences. According to Schmidt, Nave, O'riordan, & Guerra (2011, p. 162) environmental education has emerged as "a response to environmental degradation and its relationship with technical and scientific progress, and as a reaction to the tendency to increase the unsustainable use of natural processes and natural resources."

If initially environmental education was centered on alerting and mobilizing individuals to various environmental issues, now it tends to encompass civic responsibility, citizenship, health, human rights, social justice and equity, and the avoidance and depletion of non-renewable resources, among others. This evolution has led to major curricular upgrades in order to reflect the broader depth of the subjects being studied. Increasingly, formal classroom learning is complemented with visits to *in situ* locales to fully grasp the proportion, extent, significance, impacts and potential solutions to resolving environmental and cultural problems.

It is a fact that learning needs to be tailored to the existing background and grade level of the students in their progression from kindergarten, elementary, middle and high-school to college. The ultimate goal of environmental education is to impact changes in people's lifestyles in order to alter behavior and facilitate the achievement of more sustainable living patterns. There is also a relationship between ecotourism and environmental education.

Zhang & Lei (2012, p. 923) have argued that "knowledge about the local environmental resources and the characteristics and management principles of ecotourism can all be incorporated into educational programs... to encourage positive attitudes in residents and to advance their involvement in local tourism." Saltpans are increasingly sought after by tourists because of their peaceful scenery, high quality moments of leisure and wellbeing, and serenity opportunities (Albuquerque, Silva, Martins, & Costa, 2018). One of the latest trends in the rehabilitation of saltscapes consists in taking advantage of the minerals in the mud and brine waters of the solar salinas for thermal and SPA treatments.

On the other hand, wetlands enable biological diversity for plants, birds, reptiles and fish, and saltpans, in particular, also help to prevent flooding and improve water quality (Coelho, Hilário, Silva, & Silva, 2014). Since saltpans are fragile ecosystems; environmental education tends to privilege cultural traditions and issues of biodiversity. The presence of salt requires physiological adaptations to fauna and flora. Therefore, biodiversity in and around solar salinas maybe slightly lower than in other parts of river estuaries. Nonetheless, the relative isolation from human interference propels numerous habitats, nidification places and sources of food for migratory birds and other animal species in complex nodes of biotic connectivity networks (Herbert et al., 2018). Many species live, feed and reproduce in salt marshes since the topographic position of solar salinas constitute an asset in terms of natural protection against wind and tides.

The conversion of solar salinas to aquaculture and industrial fish farming has also enabled the development and administration of environmental education programs centered on the production of fish for human consumption, nutrition and even the impacts of mono-species in natural habitats. One important observation is the fact that halophilic microorganisms are outcompeted by generalist species when solar salinas are converted to other uses and optimal saline conditions disappear.

PORTUGUESE SALTPANS AND TOURISM

The Portuguese solar salinas have a great affinity with their Mediterranean and Atlantic counterparts (Walmsley, 1999; Crisman, 1999; Crisman et al., 2009). The Portuguese evaporation salinas comprise estuarine solar salinas and inland explorations. They are concentrated mostly in the center region of the Atlantic coast, just south of the greater Lisbon metropolitan area, and in Algarve. In fact, this last region is known for possessing the best weather conditions and for producing the largest quantities of marine salt in the country (Evaristo & Botequilha-Leitão, 2008; Sainz-López, 2017). Some Mediterranean regions have also traditionally produced salt in naturally occurring holes on the land-water interface (Grove & Rackham, 2001). According to Sciolino (2009, p. A12),

The history of Portugal and salt is long and romantic. The first known document related to Portuguese salt works dates back from the 10th century, when a countess donated salt marshes to a monastery that she founded. A century later, the Algarve region was shipping salt across Europe; in the 15th and 16th centuries, salt help make Portugal a global power.

In fact, salt was a very valuable commodity in the preservation of food before the discovery of modern refrigeration. After the European discoveries in the 16th and 17th centuries subsided in intensity, mercantile salt routes were created to export salt to countries in central and northern Europe. Portugal has eight major river deltas

Table 1. Evolution of solar salinas in Portugal 1960s–2000s

	Active Salinas 1960s	**Active Salinas 2000s**
Aveiro	270	c.15
Figueira da Foz	229	c.50 (a)
Leiria	1	(b)
Rio Maior	Active	Active
Óbidos	3	(b)
Tejo	230	1
Sado	300	6
Vila Nova de Milfontes	1	(b)
Algarve	136	c.15
Estimated total	1,170	c.87

Source: Neves (2005, p. 132). (a) active *cómodos,* (b) disappeared.\

(i.e. Minho, Lima, Douro, Vouga, Mondego, Tejo, Sado, and Guadiana). Perhaps, with the exception of the Douro River estuary, all others have had very important solar salinas at some point in the history of the country. Some saltern complexes are located closer to the Atlantic Ocean (e.g. *salgado de Aveiro* and *salgado da Figueira da Foz)* and others are located farther inland (e.g. Sado's Alcácer do Sal and Guadiana's Castro Marim (Balsas, 2016)).

Salt production in traditional solar salinas experienced a major halt in the 1930s–1940s, which led to the abandonment and decline of many of the country's saltscapes and their numbers have continued to decrease abruptly until the early 2000s. The reduction in salt production peaked when Portugal became a EU member and subsidies were attributed to stimulate other economic sectors such as agriculture and aquaculture (Rodrigues, Bio, Amat, & Vieira, 2011). Table 1. shows the evolution of solar salinas in Portugal 1960s–2000s. The disappearance of more than a thousand salinas in that period is quite troublesome and reflects the poor state of affairs involving traditional saltmaking not only in Portugal, but also in many Mediterranean countries (Neves, 2005).

Nonetheless, a strong effort has been implemented to rehabilitate some of the most emblematic regional salinas, especially from the 1990s onwards. Among the new uses devised for saltscapes one finds aquaculture, ecotourism and wellness tourism, birdwatching programs, and environmental education activities. The importance of wellness tourism for the country has been recognized as Portugal appears in the top 20 wellness tourism market rankings with 3.6 million trips taken and almost 74,500 jobs directly generated by its activities (Albuquerque, Silva, Martins, & Costa, 2018,

p. 63). It is also estimated that the number of tourists in Portugal will reach 18.3 million in 2020. This is likely to be a direct consequence of an increase in disposable income, travel motivations, the growth of emerging markets and diversification of traditional destinations, major technological changes, and also the growth of the ecotourism segment (Coelho, Hilário, Silva, & Silva, 2014, p. 148).

CASE STUDIES

The case studies analyzed in this chapter are those of the municipalities of Aveiro and Figueira da Foz, both located in central Portugal (see Figure 1.). With a population of about 78,000 people in 2011, the city of Aveiro is bordered by the Vouga River estuary and home to the *Universidade de Aveiro*. On the other hand, with about 62,000 residents in 2011 Figueira da Foz is a well-known summer resort city on the Atlantic coast currently without a university. Nonetheless, the Mondego estuary of Figueira da Foz has been studied quite comprehensively by many scholars from the *Universidade de Coimbra,* which is located approximately 50 kilometers inland from the coast.

Figure 1. Case studies' location in Portugal

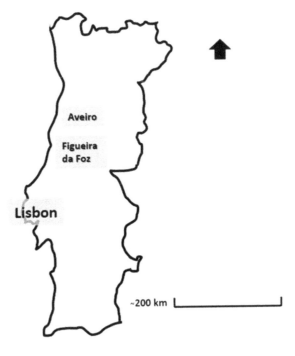

Aveiro has a large and shallow lagoon *(i.e. Ria de Aveiro)* and a history of collecting algae from the water for use as fertilizer in agriculture, while Figueira's Mondego estuary is an important rice producer. Figueira da Foz was once a popular beach destination for domestic and foreign tourists, especially Spaniards. For that reason, Figueira da Foz was known as the "queen of the Portuguese beaches" (see Figure 2.).

On the other hand, Aveiro is sometimes nicknamed the Portuguese Venice given its numerous and long water canals and the unobstructed solar luminosity reflected on the expansive surface of the adjacent mirror-like lagoon punctuated by mosaic salinas (see Figure 3). These two case studies offer a very powerful analysis of the evolution, decline and rehabilitation of saltscapes in southern Europe. The solar salinas rehabilitation strategies of these two municipalities are relatively similar with the main caveat that the *Universidade de Aveiro* owns a large solar salina (i.e. Marinha de Santiago da Fonte) physically adjacent to its main campus and some of its scholars (i.e. faculty and students) have been highly involved in its reactivation and academic scholarship.

The case studies are discussed according to some of the following parameters: Location and river estuary; evolution, number and area occupied by saltspaces; economic impact and present economic situation; reasons for the economic decline; recent rehabilitation activities (e.g. ecomuseum, alternative uses such as a SPA in Aveiro, and guided visits, participation in international networks, and salinas' ownership); tourism and recreational practices; and environmental education activities.

Figure 2. Bird's eye view of coastal Figueira da Foz
Credit: Photo by Carlos Balsas.

COMPARATIVE DISCUSSION

Both saltscapes complexes are located in central Portugal, on relatively well-protected ocean-front estuaries. The Vouga River feeds into the lagoon *Ria de Aveiro* and the Aveiro salinas complex is known as the *salgado de Aveiro*. The Vouga estuary occupies an area of approximately 2,600 hectares, while the *salgado de Aveiro* occupies a considerably smaller area of the municipalities of Aveiro and Ilhavo (approximately 1,500 hectares). The Ria de Aveiro has two stretches, one expanding north towards Ovar and the other expanding south towards Mira in a linear distance of about 45 kilometers.

The *salgado da Figueira da Foz* is located in the Mondego River estuary. The Mondego estuary occupies an extension of approximately 3,500 hectares. The two arms of the Mondego River form the *Ilha da Morraceira* of marsh lands and salinas with an area of approximately 600 hectares. The *salgado da Figueira da Foz* occupies an area of approximately 845.2 hectares distributed through three distinct zones: *Morraceira Island*, *Lavos* (south margin of the Mondego River estuary), and *Vila Verde* (north margin) (Teixeira, Marques, Mota, & Garcia, 2018, p. 233).

In both estuaries, salt production was a very important economic activity for many centuries. The much closer physical proximity of the solar salinas to the city of Aveiro, perhaps, led to a stronger imprint in the city's identity, well observed

Figure 3. Art nouveau buildings and moliceiro boats in Aveiro
Credit: Photo by Carlos Balsas.

by the presence of salt architecture of wooden warehouses (i.e. *palheiros*) in the neighborhood of Sá-Barrocas, and public art and murals in highly visible public spaces of the downtown area (see Figure 4.) than in Figueira da Foz, where summer tourism of "sun and sea" has always constituted a very important socio-economic activity.

The first reference to solar salinas in Figueira da Foz dates back to 1217 (Gomes & Veiga, 2002). The evolution of solar salinas in the two estuaries is relatively similar with the difference that when the Ria de Aveiro lagoon temporarily lost its connection to the ocean in 1575, the city's economy declined considerably. However, the opening up of the navigation canal (i.e. *barra de Aveiro)* enabled commerce to be reactivated and the city to recover some of its maritime functions. Both cities have experienced an abandonment of their saltpans due to the collapse of the cod fisheries – a major consumer of salt, and in the case of Aveiro also due to the silting up and degradation of the Ria de Aveiro canals, which contributed to an increased difficulty in transporting materials for the reconstruction of walls as well as the harvest and transport of salt itself (Coelho, 2008).

In Aveiro there were approximately 270 salinas in operation in 1956 and now there are fewer than 10 salinas (Martins, Albuquerque, & Silva, 2014, p. 383). In terms of occupied area, there were about 1,661 hectares of salinas in the 1970s (Rodrigues, Bio, Amat, & Vieira, 2011). However, many salinas were abandoned and or converted to other uses, especially aquaculture farms. Teixeira, Marques, Mota, & Garcia (2018, p. 232) concluded that "during the 80's and 90's fish farms replaced salt exploration at a rate of 13 salinas per year." Intensive aquaculture is also making land for salt works a lot more expensive. According to Rodrigues, Bio, Amat, & Vieira (2011, p. 3), in 2007 3.3% of Aveiro's salinas were still used as active and or semi-active salinas, 5.2% were inactive salinas, 16.1% were occupied with aquaculture and 72% were completely abandoned. On the other hand, in Figueira da Foz there are now approximately 45 salinas when in the 1950s that total comprised about 300 active salinas (Henriques, 2017). Also, in Figueira da Foz, the local authority has been "encouraging the implementation of aquaculture facilities as a mean to [promote] local economic development" (Teixeira, Marques, Mota, & Garcia, 2018, p. 232). And Marques, Marques, Mota, Pinto, & Garcia (2017) have just recently finalized a market study for the intensification of aquaculture exploration in the city's *salgado*.

Both estuaries are designated as Important Bird Areas (IBA); they are also classified as ZPE – *Zonas de Proteção Especial* (or special protection areas – SPA) within the Nature 2000 network under the EU Birds Directive 79/409 CEE, and they also belong to the National Ecological Reserve (REN). Furthermore, both areas are also RAMSAR Convention sites. The Mondego River estuary is considered one of the most important Portuguese areas for nidification in the country (Cruz, Neves, Pacheco, Fonseca, & Martins, 2014, p. 26). Both areas are currently experiencing

Figure 4. Mural celebrating saltwork in Aveiro
Credit: Photo by Carlos Balsas.

strong environmental gradients and anthropogenic pressures (Rufino, 2004b; Lu et al., 2018).

The first attempts at rehabilitating saltscapes in Aveiro were implemented by regional non-profit organizations (Balsas, Kotval, & Mullin, 2001). In the early 1990s, the municipality of Aveiro purchased the solar salina of Troncalhada and the University of Aveiro purchased the Santiago da Fonte salina. The city of Aveiro then created a salt museum (i.e. *Museu da Troncalhada)* in 2000 in the Troncalhada saltpan. The goal was to help transmit knowledge about this ancient artisanal technique and provide interpretation opportunities in the saltpans themselves. However, the saltscapes of Aveiro only started to receive increased municipal attention from the mid-2000s onwards, when the city benefited from the national urban and environmental regeneration program POLIS, which led to the rehabilitation of waterfront public spaces in Aveiro (Gomes & Marques, 2008), including a bicycle trail connecting the Troncalhadas salinas to the museum by the same name.

Figueira da Foz became a very important pioneer in the rehabilitation of saltpans in southern Europe when the municipality purchased the *Corredor da Cobra* salina in the locality of Lavos in 2000, and the city became a partner in the EU-funded international project *ALAS – All about salt* (Neves, 2004a; 2004b; 2004c). Mayor Eng. António Duarte Silva (1941–2011), with experience in running shipyards, was

Figure 5. Pedestrian salinas trail in the Mondego River estuary, Figueira da Foz
Credit: Photo by Carlos Balsas.

an important champion of the rehabilitation of the Figueira da Foz' saltpans. He incentivized the participation of the city in the international ALAS network and promoted the knowledge exchanges on the cultural and ecological preservation of the city's saltscapes, which resulted in the rehabilitation of that particular pilot-salina.

That rehabilitation also involved the renovation of a salt warehouse, the construction of a *Núcleo Museológico do Sal* (a salt ecomuseum) in 2007, and the development of pedestrian (i.e. *Rota Pedestre)* and riverine trails (i.e. *Rota Fluvial)*, the latter sailed by a boat *"Sal do Mondego"* with capacity to carry 10 tons of salt (see Figure 5.). The Figueira's salt ecomuseum provides information about the salt making process, how this activity evolved over the centuries in Figueira da Foz, and background about other salt making locations in Portugal, as well a basic understanding about whomever worked in the saltpans, and the tools they utilized in this artisanal activity.

As Hueso & Petanidou (2011, p. 222) demonstrate, the tangible and intangible values of salinas make them "a perfect educational setting to teach and learn about history, geography, economy, architecture, religion, ethnology, botany, zoology, ecology, and geology." According to Gomes & Marques (2008), attendance at the museum of Troncalhada and salinas has increased from approximately 3,000 in 2000 to 12,359 in 2005 and more than 18,000 visits in 2017 (Lusa, 2018). Also in Aveiro, the *Marinha Santiago da Fonte* promotes scientific visits of its own solar salina, and the *Ilha dos Puxadoiros,* only accessible by boat, promotes individual ecotourism and environmental education activities (Martins, Albuquerque, & Silva, 2014).

In the last decade or so, the two cities embarked on major attempts at strengthening their ecotourism and environmental educational activities. The city of Aveiro conducted a major prospective market study in 2007 (Branco, 2007). And the University of Aveiro became a partner in the international research network *ECOSAL Atlantis* (2007–2013) with other partners from Portugal, Spain, France and the United Kingdom. As it was mentioned in the analytical mechanism above, the overall goal was the delineation of a salt route in the Atlantis-project area.

Aveiro's attempts at helping to rehabilitate some of its own saltpans took place in three phases. The rehabilitation and environmental educational activities involved workshops with special publics in order to test a guided visit for a pilot-group of teachers and students from the city's elementary and high schools. Some of those students identified and collected samples of invertebrates and sediments for further analysis in the laboratory. Another goal of the project was to help disabled individuals with mobility and visual impairments access the solar salinas under a philosophy of universal design and accessible tourism (Martins, Albuquerque, & Silva, 2014). This resulted in the production of braille language materials and smoother accessibility and mobility conditions for individuals on wheelchairs between the salt warehouse and the saltern itself.

The Aveiro team also produced videos about the salt of Aveiro and other informational materials and brochures with the intent of disseminating information among school groups and the general public. This was hoped to strengthen environmental education opportunities substantially. Specific pedagogical materials were also prepared to expand curricula and to increase awareness among teachers and students. Furthermore, specialized and scientific activities were also conducted in order to study conservation of aquatic avifauna feeding and reproduction patterns of various bird species and birdwatching (Martins, Albuquerque, & Silva, 2013; Cruz, Neves, Pacheco, Fonseca, & Martins, 2014). Finally, the third phase of the project consisted mostly in engaging with tourism operators, planners, and agents in order to increase their participation in the planning and management of tourism activities of saltpans (Nedelec, 2008; Martins, Albuquerque, & Silva, 2013). In conclusion, the standard guide visitor model was developed to guarantee the route's perpetuation.

In Figueira da Foz, the latest efforts at rehabilitating the city's saltscapes were part of institutionalized attempts at devising a Local Agenda 21 (LA21) process – implemented in conjunction with the revision of the municipality's master plan (known as PDM). Although the LA21 covered the whole jurisdictional territory (not only the city's wetlands) and comprised four important thematic areas (i.e. environment, economy, society and culture), the rehabilitation of the river estuary and the saltscapes was given special attention under the philosophy of a *local educational project* (LEP), which had the *Ilha da Morraceira* at its core.

The plan for the promotion of the *Ilha da Morraceira* had three main axis comprising: (1) the launching and requalification of infrastructure (i.e. new trails, boat piers, rehabilitation of the *Moinho de Maré das Doze Pedras* (tidal mill with 12 engines very unique in Portugal), (2) the conception and development of touristic products (e.g. cycle-routes, accessible tourism, a parking lot for individuals with special mobility needs), and (3) destination marketing (e.g. brochures, webpages, tourism guides and a *local educational project*) (Cordeiro & Paredes, 2013). These planning efforts resulted from a collaborative protocol between the municipality of Figueira da Foz and the University of Coimbra, which was centered on the following collaborative principles: Participation, equality of opportunities, solidarity, autonomy, continuing education, transgenerational and sustainable development (Paredes, Rochette, & Marques, 2013, p. 1124).

The LA21 in Figueira da Foz was part of a broad environmental planning effort which resulted in four main actions: (1) an environmental urban atlas (specialized cartography to map environmentally sensitive areas in the city), (2) a municipal environmental lab (aimed at monitoring pollution levels and to devise strategies to eradicate pollution), (3) the conceptualization of a research and interpretative center in the Morraceira island (aimed at promoting the *salgado da Figueira,* and to help interpret its ecological and saltscape cultural and ecological values), and (4) a touristic promotional plan for Morraceira (in order to strengthen the touristic appeal of the saltscapes based on the sound computation of touristic carrying capacity of the island and the creation of touristic trails with emphasis on accessible tourism for individuals with various types of disabilities) (Paredes, Rochette, & Marques, 2013, p. 1123).

This institutionalized planning effort also aimed at strengthening the "sea cluster" in Figueira da Foz – a cluster which has always had a very important role in the destines of the city. However, under the LA21 and the LEP, this cluster was to be approached from a smart city, entrepreneurial and intelligent perspective in hopes to further protect and strengthen the natural and touristic vocation of the municipality. In fact, Pinto, Patrício, Neto, Salas, & Marques (2010, p. 395) have argued that traditional saltworks offer a wide range of opportunities for leisure, bird watching and museum activities in Figueira da Foz and that "the ecosystem represents one of the key green spaces for outdoor activities in the region, contributing to 75% of visitors that are interested in ecotourism activities."

On the other hand, Costa, Azeiteiro, & Pardal (2013a, p. 235) reported that tourism recreational activities in Figueira da Foz, which are most significant during the summer, have quite relevant social and economic importance representing about 8.1–12.8 million Euros a year. Furthermore, the same authors have also reported that "over the years, a progressive increase in the number of tourists visiting the Mondego estuary and adjacent areas has occurred." In fact, tourists and visitors seem to find knowledge acquisition about the Mondego River estuary and the solar salinas quite positive and rewarding, because Morais (2012, p. 68) has concluded that interpretative activities of saltscapes in Figueira da Foz are successfully impacting the pro-environmental behaviors of visitors in their purchase and consumption habits of more ecological products after visiting the city's saltscapes.

Furthermore, Costa, Pardal, & Azeiteiro (2013b, p. 243) have claimed that the Mondego estuary has great potential to be used for "educational purposes related to ecology, conservation biology, and sustainability," given the current existence of interpretative routes, scientific texts, and teachers' training programs. The same authors have also reported two activities involving a Biology class of 10th graders and an 8th grade class of Natural Sciences, which combined field visits with experimental nature using intertidal habitat as a support for those educational activities (Costa, Pardal, & Azeiteiro, 2013b, p. 245). On the same vein, Paredes, Rochette, & Marques (2013) have argued that schools ought to assume a crucial role in learning processes contributing to a better understanding of sustainability, ethics, humanism, citizenship, and competitiveness.

CONCLUSION

There is little doubt that "Mediterranean societies have undergone profound social changes at all levels, particularly in relation to systems and means of production" (Gauci, Schembri, & Inkpen, 2017, p. 14). Salscapes are important cultural and environmental heritage in need of further rehabilitation. Traditional saltworks are "a mixture of culture, nature, agriculture, industry, history, architecture, archeology, geology, and medicine" (Kortekaas, 2014, p. 205). Their abandonment has resulted in natural, cultural and historic heritage losses throughout southern Europe and the Mediterranean region. Saltscapes are examples of labor intensive, seasonal, and weather dependent artisanal activities. They are also very important settings for educational and cultural activities, which can offer "high quality products for gastronomic, therapeutic, industrial and biotechnological use" and attract specialized ecotourism publics (Hueso & Petanidou, 2011, p. 213).

The examples discussed in this chapter demonstrate how saltscapes in Aveiro and Figueira da Foz are being rehabilitated for alternative forms of ecotourism and environmental education activities. Their acceptance by ecotourists (i.e. visitors interested in experiencing authentic artisanal activities) and by area regulators and community stakeholders (e.g. business leaders, environmental advocates, elected officials, schools' principals, and academics and scholars) appears central to their success (Coelho, Hilário, Silva, & Silva, 2014). Tourism in saltscapes ought to go beyond simple visits. It seems that there is further interest in active participation for instance in salt production, wellness treatments, tasting of salt recipes and active learning of the local and regional history of the saltpans. The stimulation of environmental and cultural aspects of salt making as well as the emotional significance of saltscapes, among alternative publics – including those with various types of disabilities – has been key to many of the Portuguese projects discussed in this chapter.

Traditional education based mostly on the transmission of knowledge and facts seems to have left space for the creation of interpretative centers and applied learning opportunities outside of the classroom (Brundiers, 2010). Saltscapes are highly suitable for the creation and implementation of didactic-pedagogical activities. However, it is also important to note that new curricular proposals oriented towards education for sustainability and civic engagement with cultural heritage tend to place new demands on teachers and museum curators. Both the Vouga and the Mondego Rivers' estuaries (and their saltscapes) present excellent opportunities to help motivate not only students, the general public, tourists and visitors in learning about saltpans but also teachers and scholars in the development of new curricular and investigative materials (Costa et al., 2013b; Martins, Albuquerque, & Silva, 2013).

The tourism market has changed considerably in the last decades and tourists are increasingly looking for complementarity in travel options, authenticity, and new tourism destinations, while also expanding their knowledge through experiential tourism (Coelho, Hilário, Silva, & Silva, 2014). The same authors have also recognized that new demonstration projects based on ecotourism, biological products, landscape rehabilitation and environmental education may even help to revamp the profitability of traditional salt production and as well as help promote sustainable development in perspectives of territorial competitiveness. Moreover, wellness tourism is likely to also contribute to reverse the decline and abandonment of traditional saltpans (Albuquerque, Silva, Martins, & Costa, 2018). However, some caution is needed, because an increase in the number of tourists and visitors at particular destinations may result in increased human pressure over these sensitive natural and cultural ecosystems.

REFERENCES

Albuquerque, H., da Silva, A. M., Martins, F., & Costa, C. (2018). Wellness tourism as a complementary activity in saltpans regeneration. In I. Azara, E. Michopoulou, F. Niccolini, B. Taff, & A. Clarke (Eds.), *Tourism, Health, Wellbeing and Protected Areas* (pp. 56–67). Wallingford, UK: CAB International. doi:10.1079/9781786391315.0056

Balsas, C. (2012). Sustainable development in Portugal: An analysis of Lisbon and Porto. I. Vojnovic (Ed.), Building Sustainable Communities: A Global Urban Perspective (pp.633–651). East Lansing, MI: Michigan State University Press.

Balsas, C. (2016). Mediterranean Saltscapes: The need to enhance fragile ecological and cultural resources in Portugal. ZARCH: Journal of Interdisciplinary Studies in Architecture and Urbanism, 7, 133 160. doi.org/. doi:10.26754/ojs_zarch/zarch.201671519

Balsas, C., Kotval, Z., & Mullin, J. (2001). Historic Preservation in Waterfront Communities in Portugal and the USA. *Portuguese Studies Review*, *8*(1), 40–61.

Beatley, T. (2014). *Blue Urbanism: Exploring Connections between Cities and Oceans*. Washington, DC: Island Press. doi:10.5822/978-1-61091-564-9

Branco, M. (2007). *Revitalização e valorização económica do salgado de Aveiro – relatório final*. Aveiro: MultiAveiro.

Brundiers, K., Wiek, A., & Redman, C. L. (2010). Real-world learning opportunities in sustainability: From classroom into the real world. *International Journal of Sustainability in Higher Education*, *11*(4), 308–324. doi:10.1108/14676371011077540

Coelho, C. (2008). Os muros (motas) das marinhas de sal de Aveiro. In I. Amorim (Ed.), *A Articulação do Sal Português aos Circuitos Mundiais: Antigos e novos Consumos* (pp. 279–289). Porto: Instituto de História Moderna – Universidade do Porto.

Coelho, R., Hilário, M., Silva, F., & Silva, S. (2014). Peixe Rei Solar Salt Works Project: Ecotourism and tourism experience as complementary activities. In European Salt Producers Association (EuSalt) (Eds.), *Solar Salt Works & The Economic Value of Biodiversity – Proceedings of the International Conference* (pp.155–186). Trapani, Sicily: EuSalt.

Cordeiro, A. R., & Paredes, L. C. (2013). Valorização turística da ilha da Morraceira (Município da Figueira da Foz): Novas utilizações do potencial endógeno do estuário do Mondego. *Caderno de Geografia, 32*, 229–238. doi:10.14195/0871-1623_32_18

Costa, S., Azeiteiro, U., & Pardal, M. (2013a). The contribution of scientific research for integrated coastal management: The mondego estuary as a study case. *Journal of Integrated Coastal Zone Management, 13*(2), 229–241. doi:10.5894/rgci391

Costa, S., Pardal, M., & Azeiteiro, U. (2013b). The use of an estuarine system (Mondego estuary, Portugal) as a didactic tool to incorporate education for sustainable development into school curricula. *Journal of Integrated Coastal Zone Management, 13*(2), 243–251. doi:10.5894/rgci417

Crisman, T. L. (1999). Conservation of Mediterranean coastal saline ecosystems: The private sector role in maintaining ecological function. In: N. A. Korovessis & T. D. Lekkas (Eds.), *Proceedings of the Post Conference Symposium Salworks: Preserving Saline Coastal Ecosystems* (pp.39–47). Academic Press.

Crisman, T. L., Takavakoglou, V., Alexandridis, T., Antonopoulos, V., & Zalidis, G. (2009). Rehabilitation of abandoned saltworks to maximize conservation, ecotourism and water treatment potential. *Global NEST Journal, 11*(1), 24–31. doi:10.30955/gnj.000614

Cruz, T., Neves, R., Pacheco, C., Fonseca, C., & Martins, F. (2014). A avifauna aquática das salinas estuarinas da Ria de Aveiro e da Foz do Rio Mondego. *Revista Captar: Ciência e Ambiente para Todos, 3*(2). Retrieved July 27, 2017 from <http://revistas.ua.pt/index.php/captar/article/view/2900>

Dahm, H. (2004). Salt museums. In R. Neves, T. Petanidou, R. Rufino & P. Pinto (Eds.), ALAS – All About Salt: Salt and salinas in the Mediterranean (pp. 104–107). Figueira da Foz: Intermezzo.

Davis, P. (1999). *Ecomuseum, A sense of place*. London: Leicester University Press.

Dolnicar, S., Crouch, G. I., & Long, P. (2008). Environment-friendly tourists: What do we really know about them? *Journal of Sustainable Tourism, 16*(2), 197–210. doi:10.2167/jost738.0

Evaristo, V., & Botequilha-Leitão, A. (2008). *Multifunctional planning and design for the Castro Marim and Vila Real de Santo António Salt-Marshes Natural Reserve*. In *1st WSEAS International Conference on Landscape Architecture (LA '08)*, Algarve, Portugal.

Gauci, R., Schembri, J. A., & Inkpen, R. (2017). Traditional use of shore platforms: A study of the artisanal management of salinas on the Maltese Islands (Central Mediterranean). *SAGE Open*, *7*(2), 2158244017706597. doi:10.1177/2158244017706597

Gomes, A., & Marques, G. (2008). Ecomuseu Marinha da Troncalhada – Centro Interpretativo: Impulsionador das Salinas de Aveiro. In I. Amorim (Ed.), *A Articulação do Sal Português aos Circuitos Mundiais: Antigos e novos Consumos* (pp. 329–338). Porto: Instituto de História Moderna – Universidade do Porto.

Gomes, P., & Veiga, A. (2002). *Figueira da Foz – Memória, Conhecimento, e Inovação...* Paços de Ferreira: Néstia Editores.

Grove, A., & Rackham, O. (2001). *The Nature of Mediterranean Europe: An ecological history*. New Haven, CT: Yale University Press.

Hall, C. M., Baird, T., James, M., & Ram, Y. (2016). Climate change and cultural heritage: Conservation and heritage tourism in the Anthropocene. *Journal of Heritage Tourism*, *11*(1), 10–24. doi:10.1080/1743873X.2015.1082573

Hall, C. M., & Lew, A. (2009). *Understanding and Managing Tourism Impacts: An Integrated Approach*. London: Routledge. doi:10.4324/9780203875872

Henriques, F. (2017, July 1). Vidas de sal. *Público*.

Herbert, R. J., Broderick, L. G., Ross, K., Moody, C., Cruz, T., Clarke, L., & Stillman, R. A. (2018). Artificial coastal lagoons at solar salt-working sites: A network of habitats for specialised, protected and alien biodiversity. *Estuarine, Coastal and Shelf Science*, *203*, 1–16. doi:10.1016/j.ecss.2018.01.015

Hueso, K., & Petanidou, T. (2011). Cultural aspects of Mediterranean salinas. In T. Papayannis & D. Pritchard (Eds.), *Culture and wetlands in the Mediterranean: An evolving story* (pp. 213–226). Athens: Med-INA.

Kirshenblatt-Gimblett, B. (1998). *Destination Culture – Tourism, Museums and Heritage*. Berkeley, CA: University of California Press.

Kortekaas, K. H. (2004). Sustainable tourism initiatives in European saltscapes. In F. Pineda, C. A. Brebbia, & M. Mugica (Eds.), *Sustainable Tourism: First International conference on sustainable tourism* (pp. 199–207). Southampton, UK: WIT Press.

Kurlansky, M. (2003). *Salt: A world history*. New York: Penguin Books.

López, E., Aguilera, P. A., Schmitz, M. F., Castro, H., & Pineda, F. D. (2010). Selection of ecological indicators for the conservation, management and monitoring of Mediterranean coastal salinas. *Environmental Monitoring and Assessment*, *166*(1–4), 241–256. doi:10.100710661-009-0998-2 PMID:19479329

Lu, Y., Yuan, J., Lu, X., Su, C., Zhang, Y., Wang, C. C. X., ... Garbutt, R. A. (2018). Major threats of pollution and climate change to global coastal ecosystems and enhanced management for sustainability. *Environmental Pollution*, *239*, 670–680. doi:10.1016/j.envpol.2018.04.016 PMID:29709838

Lusa. (2018, February 21). Museus de Aveiro ultrapassaram os 100 mil visitants. *Diário de Noticias*.

Marques, J., Marques, C., Mota, J., Pinto, S., & Garcia, A. (2017). *Avaliação integrada, ecológica e sociocultural – o salgado da Figueira da Foz na perspectiva do desenvolvimento sustentável*. Figueira da Foz: Câmara Municipal da Figueira da Foz.

Martins, F., Albuquerque, H., & Silva, A. M. (2014). Salinas acessíveis – um projeto para todos: O caso da Marinha Santiago da Fonte em Aveiro, Portugal. *Revista Turismo & Desenvolvimento*, *4*(21–22), 377–392.

Martins, F., Albuquerque, H., & Silva, M. (2013). Learning about natural places – Santiago da Fonte saltpan visitor model. In *Proceedings of the 7th WEEC*. Fondation Mohammed VI Pour La Protection de L'Environnement.

Morais, J. P. (2012). La eficacia de las actividades de educacion e interpretacion ambiental en contextos de ecoturismo. El caso de la Ruta de las Salinas de Figueira da Foz, Portugal. In L. Muñoz, M. Pubill, J. Álamo, & P. Cartea (Eds.), *Nuevas Investigaciones Iberoamericanas en Educación Ambiental* (pp. 68–85). Madrid: Ministerio de Agricultura, Alimentación y Medio Ambiente.

Moreira, C., & Santos, N. (2010). New opportunities for water environments. River tourism and water leisure activities. In E. Brito-Henriques, J. Sarmento, & M. Lousada (Eds.), *Water and Tourism – resources management, planning and sustainability* (pp. 147–168). Lisbon: CEG.

Nedelec, L. (2008). Les Marais Salants Portugais, Vers Une Gestion Intégrée? In I. Amorim (Ed.), *A Articulação do Sal Português aos Circuitos Mundiais: Antigos e novos Consumos* (pp. 305–319). Porto: Instituto de História Moderna – Universidade do Porto.

Neves, R. (2004a). Figueira saltworks: Geography and salt history. In R. Neves, T. Petanidou, R. Rufino, & P. Pinto (Eds.), ALAS – All About Salt: Salt and salinas in the Mediterranean (pp. 19–21). Figueira da Foz: Intermezzo.

Neves, R. (2004b). Figueira da Foz – Organization and evolution of salinas on the Mondego estuary. In R. Neves, T. Petanidou, R. Rufino & P. Pinto (Eds.), ALAS – All About Salt: Salt and salinas in the Mediterranean (pp. 45–47). Figueira da Foz: Intermezzo.

Neves, R. (2004c). Local actions – Figueira da Foz. In R. Neves, T. Petanidou, R. Rufino & P. Pinto (Eds.), ALAS – All About Salt: Salt and salinas in the Mediterranean (pp. 94–96). Figueira da Foz: Intermezzo.

Neves, R. (2005). *Os salgados portugueses no séc. XX – que perspectivas para as salinas portuguesas no séc. XXI? In I Seminário Internacional Sobre o Sal Português* (pp. 129–133). Porto: Instituto de História Moderna, Universidade do Porto.

O'Connell, M. J. (2003). Detecting, measuring and reversing changes to wetlands. *Wetlands Ecology and Management, 11*(6), 397–401. doi:10.1023/B:WETL.0000007191.77103.53

O'Dell, T. (2005). Experiencescapes. In T. O'Dell & P. Billing (Eds.), *Experiencescapes: Tourism, culture and economy* (pp. 1–31). Copenhagen: Copenhagen Business School Press.

Pacitto, J. L., & Jacquemin, O. (2017). Salt Solar Wastelands: To new "saltscapes" resilient in the Mediterranean. In A. Kallel, M. Ksibi, & H. Dhia (Eds.), *Euro-Mediterranean Conference for Environmental Integration* (pp. 1005–1008). Cham: Springer.

Paredes, L., Rochette, A., & Marques, D. (2013). Environmental area applied to strategic projects: From education and training towards sustainable development based on territorial competitiveness. In *Proceedings 19th Congress of APDR – Resilient Territories: Innovation and creativity for new modes of regional development* (pp.1116–1126). Faro: APDR.

Petanidou, T., & Vayanni, L. (2004). Salinas and Tourism. In R. Neves, T. Petanidou, R. Rufino & P. Pinto (Eds.), ALAS – All About Salt: Salt and salinas in the Mediterranean (pp. 107–109). Figueira da Foz: Intermezzo.

Pinto, R., Patrício, J., Neto, J., Salas, F., & Marques, J. (2010). Assessing estuarine quality under the ecosystem services scope: Ecological and socioeconomic aspects. *Ecological Complexity*, *7*(3), 389–402. doi:10.1016/j.ecocom.2010.05.001

Ribeiro, A., & Fidalgo, V. (2015). O Turismo da Discórdia – Boom turístico em Lisboa e no Porto está longe de agradar a gregos e a troianos. *CM Jornal*. Retrieved December 18, 2017 from <http://www.cmjornal.pt/exclusivos/imprimir/o_turismo_da_discordia>

Rodrigues, C., Bio, A., Amat, F., & Vieira, N. (2011). Artisal salt production in Aveiro/Portugal – an ecofriendly process. *Saline Systems*, *7*(1), 3. doi:10.1186/1746-1448-7-3 PMID:22053788

Rufino, R. (2004a). Ecological features of the Mondego estuary and its salinas. In R. Neves, T. Petanidou, R. Rufino, & P. Pinto (Eds.), ALAS – All About Salt: Salt and salinas in the Mediterranean (pp.70–71). Figueira da Foz: Intermezzo.

Rufino, R. (2004b). Salinas and nature conservation. In R. Neves, T. Petanidou, R. Rufino & P. Pinto (Eds.), ALAS – All About Salt: Salt and salinas in the Mediterranean (pp. 77–81). Figueira da Foz: Intermezzo.

Sainz-López, N. (2017). Comparative analysis of traditional solar saltworks and other economic activities in a Portuguese protected estuary. *Boletin de Investigaciones Marinas y Costeras*, *46*(1), 171–189.

Saurí-Pujol, D., & Llurdés-Coit, J. (1995). Embellishing nature: The case of the salt mountain project of Cardona, Catalonia, Spain. *Geoforum*, *26*(1), 35–48. doi:10.1016/0016-7185(95)00016-E

Schmidt, L., Nave, J., O'riordan, T., & Guerra, J. (2011). Trends and dilemmas facing environmental education in Portugal: From environmental problem assessment to citizenship involvement. *Journal of Environmental Policy and Planning*, *13*(2), 159–177. doi:10.1080/1523908X.2011.576167

Sciolino, E. (2009, January 27). From a Portuguese marsh, salt the traditional way. *New York Times*, p. A12.

Teixeira, Z., Marques, C., Mota, J., & Garcia, C. (2018). Identification of potential aquaculture sites in solar saltscapes via the Analytic Hierarchy process. *Ecological Indicators*, *93*, 231–242. doi:10.1016/j.ecolind.2018.05.003

Termorshuizen, J., & Opdam, P. (2009). Landscape services as a bridge between landscape ecology and sustainable development. *Landscape Ecology*, *24*(8), 1037–1052. doi:10.100710980-008-9314-8

Thompson, I. B. (1999). The role of artisanal technology and indigenous knowledge transfer in the survival of a classic cultural landscape: The marais salants of Guerande, Loire-Atlantique, France. *Journal of Historical Geography*, *25*(2), 216–234. doi:10.1006/jhge.1999.0115

Urry, J. (1990). *The Tourist Gaze: Leisure and travel in contemporary societies*. London: Sage.

Vieira, N., & Bio, A. (2004). Artisanal Salina – Unique wetland habitats worth preserving. *Marine Science Research & Development*, 4-125. doi: .doi:10.4172/2155-9910.1000e125

Walmsley, J. G. (1999). The ecological importance of Mediterranean salinas. In: N. A. Korovessis & T. D. Lekkas (Eds.), *Proceedings of the Post Conference Symposium Salworks: Preserving Saline Coastal Ecosystems* (pp.81–95). Academic Press.

Wu, T. C., Xie, P. F., & Tsai, M. C. (2015). Perceptions of attractiveness for salt heritage tourism: A tourist perspective. *Tourism Management*, *51*, 201–209. doi:10.1016/j.tourman.2015.05.026

Zhang, H., & Lei, S. (2012). A structural model of residents' intention to participate in ecotourism: The case of a wetland community. *Tourism Management*, *33*(4), 916–925. doi:10.1016/j.tourman.2011.09.012

Chapter 3
Guest Retention Through Automation:
An Analysis of Emerging Trends in Hotels in Indian Sub-Continent

Partho Pratim Seal
Manipal Academy of Higher Education, India

ABSTRACT

The technology development in hospitality is continuing at a relentless pace which is challenging for the hospitality professional for both present and the future generations. The hotel front office is moving towards automation with less human interface. Reservations are mostly being made with help of booking engines and guest interaction with hotels are by apps and chatbots. Artificial intelligence (AI) also occupies a major role to facilitate and enhance guest experience. The trends now include use of augmented reality, predictive analysis, beacons, robotics, block chain technology, and biophilic designs in the hotel. The research is to study about how various hotel chains are adopting new technology and incorporating it in their establishment. The research is based upon data collected from hotel websites and other secondary sources to determine the acceptance of new trends by the hotel chains. The result suggests that though some international hotel chains have started accepting the new trends, the major Indian chains specially are lacking behind.

DOI: 10.4018/978-1-5225-8494-0.ch003

INTRODUCTION

As the service sector is growing across the globe the customers are becoming more demanding, sophisticated and experienced. The hospitality stream provides service excellence by continuous innovation and quality at price with unique points of distinction. Hospitality is a place which allows people to be exceptional individuals and extend their own personality and style. (Hogan, 2008) Hospitality is a part of consortium of company known as tourism and travel which assist in providing goods and services to the traveller. Hospitality and tourism are among the biggest and fastest growing industries across the world (Walker, 2010). Hospitality industry comprises of lodging industry along with food and beverage departments which provide accommodation, food and beverages and other recreational activities to the customer. To succeed in hospitality operations, the focus of an organisation should be towards adopting change and innovation (Walker, 2010).

For sustainable growth of hospitality industry, the experts in the field have a view that there has to be continuous improvement of quality of hospitality services so as to adapt to the changing needs of the customer. The use of technology is also to attract the new generation which is tech friendly and is keen to travel than their previous generations.

Current Trends in Hospitality

The tourism industry trends influence the hotel industry also and globalization has made it as a force for international business. By the passing days, the competition amongst the hotels is becoming more aggressive and is also becoming difficult for the hotels to be sustainable. Considering it hotel, or the hotel chains which have the vision to understand the need of emerging trends and amend both their product and services accordingly will take the opportunity to be the market leader while those not adapting to change will only be as spectators.

The future of the hospitality industry lies on Internet of things (IoT) technology which will help the organisation to be competitive in the market. The IoT will assist individuals in interconnecting regular usage physical devices such as sensors and mobile devices which connect or communicate with each other either directly or indirectly through local communication network or through Internet. An application of IoT is been given in Figure 1.

It will enable service providers to increase the back of the house efficiency with all the departments like connecting it with housekeeping. It will also enable various cost saving policies and smart energy management techniques. Some of the hospitality service new trends being provided by chain properties are been mentioned and denoted in Figure 2.

Figure 1. An example of IoT

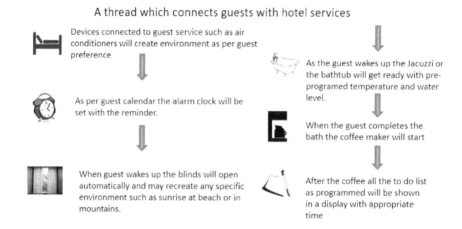

Predictive Analysis

It is a process which incorporates an array of statistical techniques which includes modelling, data mining, and machine learning to analyse both historical and current data so as to make future predictions for an event or of an individual (Suresh, 2016). It helps to create tailor made promotion offers for a guest considering the preference of the guests as they are more keen about their preference rather than the bouquet of options available. This will help in obtaining repeat guest to the establishment which will lead to increase in the hotel revenue. It enables the hoteliers to make more informed decisions considering their present problems to plan for the future (Hotelogix, 2018).

Virtual Reality

Virtual reality or VR is a favourable technology for hospitality industry as it makes an individual to believe about the virtual world with the aid of interactive 3D surrounding simulated with the help of computer. The simulations help the tourists to have a 3D view and makes the viewer feel present in the location which acts as an interface between the real world and virtual environment (Nayyar, Mahapatra, Le, & Suseendran, 2018). Use of VR has created a revolution in the advertising world how customers are being informed about various products and service on offer at the hotel. The technology assists the guests to make better decisions for opting for a hotel as compare to its competitors (Hotelogix, 2018).

Figure 2. Trends in hospitality industry

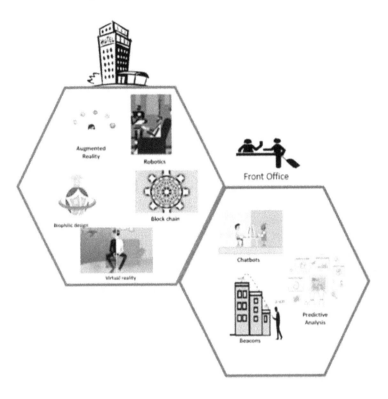

Augmented Reality

In a VR the user is transformed into an artificial environment with no connection with the real world whereas in Augmented Reality or AR the user can experience the real world along with the virtual entities (Azuma, 1997). It is an amalgamation of real world with the virtual world considering that it being an accumulation of information presented in virtual world. AR can revolutionize the tourist experience by planning, promoting and accessing the information about the destination in a better manner. It can provide guest with assistance during the whole trip and also individually planned tour. They can book hotel room, steer around the destination and select and choose local entertainment and dining options (Nayyar, Mahapatra, Le, & Suseendran, 2018). Some of the hotels have started using AR technology by designing their brochures which allows the guest to have a virtual realistic view of the property which enhances the booking of hotel rooms as the guest have an experiential view as if they are personally in the hotel. For tourism it can be used as an interactive museum in which various art forms, culture in the museum settings could be portrayed in a more interactive manner. AR could also be utilized in hotels and restaurants to know about guest preference and allergy if guest details are stored in the database. It also assists to know about guest purpose of visit which could be either official or recreational and would help the hotel to give more prioritize and better service.

Beacon

The beacon technology in hotel provides push announcements to the guests what the property is offering in the guest smart phone. The most preferred use of it is assisting guest by providing direction to the guest. Beacons with low- energy blue tooth connection assist in engaging guest to know about their buying behaviour and allows the hotel to prepare tailor made messages to market the products to preferred guest. They could also be used as devices for automatic check in and check out of the guest and could be used as a virtual key for unlocking doors with help of smart phone (Hotelogix, 2018).

Chatbots

A chatbot is a computer program which conducts dialogues with individual in their natural language similar to conversation made between two individuals through messaging apps or chat windows (Abu Sharwar & Atwell, 2007). A chatbot is equipped with artificial intelligence along with impression of a speaking human with advanced algorithm been used to analyse and reason text like a human (Gadiyar, 2017). The chatbots helps hotels to answer to the basic queries of the guest thereby enhancing communication provided to the guest. The chatbots been available 24×7 reduces the human interference as general queries could be addressed by them quickly and a customer service executive interacts when the query or the task is complex. A chatbot is more comprehensible as compared to humans and can be used for more of value creation process (Mittal, Agarwal, Chuksey, Shriwas, & Agarwal, 2016).

Robotics

Robots are described as "intelligent physical devices" (Chen & Hu, 2013) which have a partial degree of autonomy some sensory capabilities, mobility to perform tasks (Tan, Mohan, & Watanbe, 2016; Murphy, Hofacker, & Gretzel, 2017). Robotic application is considerable been used in manufacturing both inside and outside the establishment, in military operations, pharmaceuticals and in entertainment industry and it now been used in hospitality industry (Thrun, 2004). For hospitality industry the future will be for robots as already hospitality sector introduced in customer service. Some of the hotels have started up with self-service kiosks which allows guests to check in and check out without interacting with front office staff. Some hotels have allowed even check in through their mobile devices also. Robots are being used in hotels as front desk robot, concierge robot, vacuum robots, porter robots and room assistant robots. For restaurants robots' server, robot chef, robot bartender is being proposed (Ivanov, Webster, & Berezina, 2017). Robot butlers and robot bartenders would be staffing hotels by year 2020 as guest will be open for it as research suggests (Sophie, 2016). Restaurant in China and India have introduced robot waiters (Biswas, 2017). Japan is said to have robotic hotel (Martin, 2016). Aloft in the year 2014 had started with a robot which can navigate through the hotel, deliver some of the guest items to the room and even summon an elevator for the guest. Hilton hotels have also started using their robot "Connie" which uses artificial intelligence to communicate with the hotel guest (Hilton, 2016). Restaurants have started using robot chefs for preparing sushi (Sushirobo, 2016), sausage (Filloon, 2016), noodles (Elkins, 2015), burgers and in preparing mixed drinks (Sloan, 2017) and coffee (Fowler, 2017).

Block Chain

An online technology which chronologically records the transaction along with tracking the assets in a network (Peters & Panayi, 2016; Anderson, 2016) is block chain technology. Transaction could either be monetary or non-monetary. It also allows tracking of assets being leased to a third party by tracking ownership assets. In a block chain platform all records are duplicated and are been shared with all participants in the network, though they are protected by cryptographic keys.

A network of computers along with digital database is required for block chain to function (Gupta, 2017; Wright & De Filippi, 2015). All the transaction in a block chain are coded into blocks which are connected with each other in chain formation for which it is named block chain. The records stored in the block are sequentially time stamped with their unique identification number along with the previous blocks (Gupta, 2017). As the blocks are prepared and they are linked or chained the transaction in the record along with the sequence of the blocks cannot be altered which helps to store data in a manner which is secured (Gupta, 2017). Block chain technology is not being much preferred yet in hospitality and tourism industry but it is expected that it will improve guest satisfaction, service quality and profitability. Block chain technology could be used for tracking guest from home to airport to hotel and can help in reducing waiting time in the hotels though some of the guest privacy could be compromised upon. In restaurants block chain could be used along with supply chain management to control quality and ensure food safety for the guests. Along with the food suppliers, it allows the guest to check where the raw materials are grown and the path taken to reach the guest plate using block chain technology. Loyalty programs on hotels and airlines could be made with block chain technology and as rewards loyalty tokens can be issued to the guest (Kowalewski, McLaughlin, & Hill, 2017). Guest while travelling have to carry various IDs to pass security check in airport, hotels etc. Considering it blockchain platform can store all the IDs and can allow to check and validate the IDs (Davidson, De Fillipi, & Potts, 2016).

Biophilic Design

Biophilia is a Greek word meaning "love of life". Human beings have a distinctive connection between natural world and humans along with the philosphy which has an impact on the interior design of the hotels. It is an emerging trend characterized by natural lighting, naturistic view, vertical gardens along with sustainability of the resources. The benefits of the design leads to reducing stress, enhance air quality, lowers the energy cost and increases the positive views of the hotel guests. The Biophilic designs in hotel lobby also creates health and wellness benefits and the overall guest experience. The biomorphic patterens used in guest rooms have shown to reduce stress by shifting the focus and concentration (Joye, 2007). Many a times biophilic design patterns could also solve the design of the rooms with sufficient daylight and limited budget. The biophilic design could be used in food & beverage establishment such as bars and restaurants which helps the guest to connect with nature by an enhanced experience which is multisensory regarding sound, taste, smell,and the feeling (Browning, 2017).

Methodology

The International and domestic hotel chains with largest number of rooms in India were taken for the study considering that they would be the first to opt for trends. The top 10 hotels obtained from HVS report from top 20 were considered as in Table 1. The various hospitality trends as observed by these hotels chains were recorded. The data was collected by visiting the website of the hotel chain and other online secondary resources. The hotels website and other secondary resources were checked between July to August 2018. The hotels which used the technology either in India or abroad has been considered for the study.The study will help the highly competetive hotel industry to add on the new trends to be be more customer oriented and futuristics.

Table 1. Ranking as per total number of rooms

Hotel Brands	Rank
Marriot International	1
Taj Hotels, Resorts, Palaces, Safaris	2
Carlson Rezidor Hotels	3
Accor Hotels	4
ITC Hotels	5
Hyatt Hotel Corporation	6
Intercontinental Hotels Group	7
Lemon Tree Hotels	8
Sarovar Hotels & Resorts	9
Oberoi Hotels & Resorts	10

Source: HVS Research

ANALYSIS AND DISCUSSION

The secondary data collected from the websites of the hotels and articles in various magazines and reports are been checked for each hotels acceptance towards new technology. The results of all the top ten Indian hotel chains considering the inventory of rooms and the eight new trends has been put in Table 2. The study will help the highly competetive hotel industry to add on the services they are been not keen upon specially considering the Indian scenario where there is a stiff competition between the Indian hotel chains and the International chains. The analysis suggests that International chain Marriott is more trending, as all the new trends are been utilized by the property across the world while Accor and Intercontinental are just behind. The Indian hotel chains though seem to be lacking in accepting the new trends. Though some of the older hotel chains such as ITC and Oberoi have accepted some of the new trends Taj has been quite behind. The newer Indian hotel chains are yet to accept the new trends as the study found so which is not quite encouraging.

CONCLUSION

Tourism and Hospitality industry is growing globally with an increase in tourist's arrival and tourism expenditure. The trends which are most affecting the industry includes enhanced guest services, guest security and safety, and services which leads to additional methods to increase the revenue. The other major future trends

Table 2. Usage of trends by hotel chains

Hotel Chains	Predictive Analysis	Virtual Reality	Augmented Reality	Beacon	Chatbots	Robotics	Blockchain	Biophilic Design
Marriot International	Y	Y	Y	Y	Y	Y	Y	Y
Taj Hotels, Resorts, Palaces, Safaris	N	Y	N	N	N	N	N	N
Carlson Rezidor Hotels	Y	Y	Y	Y	N	N	N	Y
Accor Hotels	Y	Y	Y	Y	Y	Y	N	Y
ITC Hotels	Y	N	Y	N	N	N	N	Y
Hyatt Hotel Corporation	Y	Y	N	Y	Y	N	N	H
Intercontinental Hotels Group	Y	Y	Y	Y	Y	Y	N	Y
Lemon Tree Hotels	N	N	N	N	N	N	N	N
Sarovar Hotels & Resorts	N	N	N	N	N	N	N	N
Oberoi Hotels & Resorts	Y	Y	N	N	N	Y	N	N

include more green and boutique hotels with advanced technology along with social and virtual networks. The leading hotels of the country should be the major force for driving change. The hotels have to be more visionary about the future, have to critically enhance and restructure to meet the need of the modern technological advances. Indian hotel chains have yet to meet the challenges set by their international counterparts on the trends in hospitality. By the year 2025, hospitality industry is said to be evolved with their services coordinated in a manner, which have been transferred from the list of offerings made to the loyal customers to more tailored needs of each individual guests which are based upon innumerable variables and data points (Gadiyar, 2017).

REFERENCES

Abu Sharwar, B., & Atwell, E. (2007). Chatbots: Are they really useful. *LDV-Forum Journal for Computational Linguistics and Language Technology, 22*(1), 29-49.

Anderson, N. (2016, March). *Blockchain Technology: A game changer in accounting?* Retrieved from Deloitte: https://www2.deloitte.com/content/dam/Deloitte/de/Documents/Innovation/Blockchain_A%20game-changer%20in%20accounting.pdf

Azuma, R. (1997). A survey of augmented reality. *In Presence. Presence (Cambridge, Mass.), 6*(4), 355–385. doi:10.1162/pres.1997.6.4.355

Biswas, J. (2017, December 13). Chennai Restaurant Becomes India's First To Hire Robots As Waiters. *Analytics India Magazine*. Retrieved from https://www.analyticsindiamag.com/robot-waiter-india-chennai/

Browning, B. (2017). *Human Space 2.0: Biophilic design in hospitality*. Retrieved from www.humanspaces.com

Chen, Y., & Hu, H. (2013). Internet of intelligent things and robot as a service. *Simulation Modelling Practice and Theory, 34*, 159–171. doi:10.1016/j.simpat.2012.03.006

Davidson, S., De Fillipi, P., & Potts, J. (2016). *Disrupting Governance: The New Institutional Economics of Distributed Ledger Technology*. Retrieved from http://ssrn.com/abstract=2811995

Elkins, K. (2015, December 30). *This restaurant has a new secret weapon: a robot that slices the perfect noodle faster than any human*. Retrieved from Businessinsider.com: http://www.businessinsider.com/noodle-slicing-robot-could-revolutionize-the-restaurant-industry-2015-5

Filloon, W. (2016, December 30). *Bratwurst-Cooking Robot is a feat of German Engineering*. Retrieved from eater.com: http://www.eater.com/2016/7/19/12227128/bratwurst-robot-sausage-cooking-germany

Fowler, G. (2017). Robot baristas serve up the future of coffee at Cafe X. *The Wall Street Journal*. Retrieved from https://www.wsj.com/articles/robot-baristas-serve-up-the-future-of-coffee-at-cafe-x-1485781201

Gadiyar, A. (2017). *The Chatbot Imperative: Intelligence, Personalization and Utilitarian Design*. Retrieved from https://www.cognizant.com/whitepapers/the-chatbot-imperative-intelligence-personalization-and-utilitarian-design-codex2469.pdf

Gupta, M. (2017). *Blockchain for dummies*. Hoboken, NJ: John Wiley & Sons.

Hilton. (2016, February 3). *Hilton and IBM pilot "Connie" the world;s first Watson-enabled hotel concierge*. Retrieved from http://news.hiltonworldwide.com/index.cfm/news/hilton-and-ibm-pilot-connie-theworlds-first-watsoneabled-hotel-concierge

Hogan, J. (2008, September 19). *Hotel Online*. Retrieved from My definition of hospitality. What's yours?: http://www.hotel-online.com/News/PR2008_3rd/Sept08_HospitalityDefined.html

Hotelogix. (2018, February 7). Retrieved from https://www.hotelogix.com/blog/2018/02/07/top-hospitality-industry-technology-trends-2018/

Ivanov, S., Webster, C., & Berezina, K. (2017). Adoption of robots and service automation by tourism and hospitality companies. *Revista Turismo & Desenvolvimento*, 1501-1517.

Joye, Y. (2007). Architectural Lessons From Environmental Psychology: The Case of Biophilic Architecture. *Review of General Psychology*, *11*(4), 305–328. doi:10.1037/1089-2680.11.4.305

Kowalewski, D., McLaughlin, J., & Hill, A. (2017). Blockchain will transform loyalty programs. *Harvard Business Review*. Retrieved from http://hbr.org/2017/03/blockchain-will-transform-customer-loyalty-programs

Martin, H. (2016, June 18). Robots Deliver Fun with Hotel Room Service Orders, and they don't expect a tip. *The Los Angeles Times*.

Mittal, A., Agarwal, A., Chuksey, A., Shriwas, R., & Agarwal, S. (2016). A comparative study of chatbots and humans. *International Journal of Advanced Research in Computer and Communication Engineering*, *5*(3).

Murphy, J., Hofacker, C., & Gretzel, U. (2017). Dawning of the Age of Robotics in Hospitality and Tourism: Challenges for Teaching and Research. *European Journal for Teaching and Research*, *15*, 104–111.

Nayyar, A., Mahapatra, B., Le, D., & Suseendran, G. (2018). Virtual Reality (VR) & Augmented Reality (AR) technologies for tourism and hospitality industry. *IACSIT International Journal of Engineering and Technology*, *7*(2.21), 156–160. doi:10.14419/ijet.v7i2.21.11858

Peters, G., & Panayi, E. (2016). Understanding modern banking ledgers through blockchain technologies: Future of transaction processing and smart contracts on the internet of money. *Banking Beyond Banks and Monet*, 239-278.

Sloan, G. (2017, February 4). Robot bartenders? This new cruise ship has them. *USA Today*. Retrieved from USA Today: http://www.usatoday.com/story/cruiselog/2014/11/01/quantum-robot-bar-cruise/18308319/

Sophie, W. (2016, March 9). *Rise of the machines: Robots could be staffing hotels by 2020*. Retrieved from Big Hospitality: https://www.bighospitality.co.uk/Article/2016/03/09/Rise-of-the-machines-Robots-could-be-staffing-hotels-by-2020

Suresh, S. (2016). Big data and predictive analytics. *Pediatrics Clinics*, *63*(2), 357–366. doi:10.1016/j.pcl.2015.12.007 PMID:27017041

Sushirobo. (2016, December 30). *Sushi machines*. Retrieved from Sushirobo: http://www.sushirobo.com/#machines

Tan, N., Mohan, R., & Watanbe, A. (2016). Toward a framework for robot-inclusive environments. *Automation in Construction*, *69*, 68–78. doi:10.1016/j.autcon.2016.06.001

Thrun, S. (2004). Toward a Framework for Human-Robot Interaction. *Human-Computer Interaction*, *19*(1), 9–24. doi:10.1207153270511hci1901&2_2

Walker, J. (2010). *Introduction to Hospitality Management*. London: Pearson Education.

Wright, A., & De Filippi, P. (2015). *Decentralized Blockchain Technology and the Rise of Lex Cryptographia*. SSRN. doi:10.2139srn.2580664

Chapter 4
Restaurant Management System (RMS) and Digital Conversion:
A Descriptive Study for the New Era

Emel Memis Kocaman

https://orcid.org/0000-0003-4577-3421
Tokat Gaziosmanpasa University, Turkey

Mehmet Kocaman
Tokat Gaziosmanpasa University, Turkey

ABSTRACT

Customers expect a high standard and fast service from enterprises. In addition, competition among enterprises necessitates that enterprises renew themselves, meet customer expectations at maximum level, and raise the standard of products and services. Traditional restaurant management is inadequate to provide all this. This situation led to search, and restaurant management systems (RMS) have been developed. RMS, which emerged in the 1970s, are now much more developed, facilitating both the operation and management process and offering a professional management opportunity. RMS has made it possible for the restaurants to institutionalize and establish chain enterprises. Moreover, income and expense control can be made more effective via RMS. This chapter explains RMS and the operation of RMS via a sample program.

DOI: 10.4018/978-1-5225-8494-0.ch004

INTRODUCTION

Nutrition, which is the basic need of human beings according to Maslow's hierarchy of needs, has led to the emergence of food and beverage businesses. Today, due to the increase in the rate of eating out because of changing lifestyles (Fitzsimmons, & Maurer, 1991; Kant and Graubard, 2004; Lachat et al., 2012; Edwards, 2013) food and beverage enterprises developed, diversified, institutionalized, and has become a big sector with national and international chain enterprises. The businesses that provide services to meet the nutritional needs of people outside the home are called food and beverage enterprises because they have a common mission. However, there are a wide range of organizations that are shaped very differently in terms of purpose, scope, target group, product variety, service format and quality, service time and duration. Considering the food and beverage services offered within the cafes, bars, bakeries, restaurants, nightclubs, transportation vehicles (train, ship, airplane, etc.), public and private institutions (hospitals, factories, government offices, schools, military, elderly nursing homes, child protection agencies, etc.), hotel etc. accommodation companies, the broad scope of the concept of food and beverage enterprises is better understood (Edwards, & Hartwell, 2009). For this reason, the subject is limited to restaurants entering into food and beverage companies and the use of restaurant management systems (RMS) is emphasized in this section.

The restaurants also vary within themselves and it is possible to classify restaurants as shown in Figure 1.

Due to the development of information and communication technologies and software sector in recent years, various products have been developed to suit different areas of business life. These contribute to the success of businesses

Figure 1. Classification of restaurants
(Davis, Lockwood, AlcottandPantelidis, 2018)

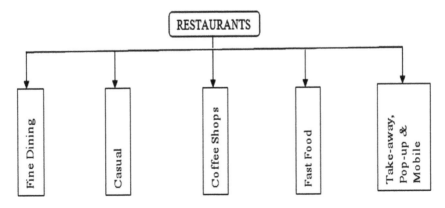

and to specialize in business planning (Acar, Ömürbek, & Ömürbek, 2003). The operation and management process is very complex because of the production of both products and services in restaurants. This situation increases the workload and stress of managers and restaurant employees as well as possible errors, disruptions and financial losses. Therefore, traditional methods in the management process are inadequate today (Memis Kocaman & Kocaman, 2014). Therefore, in order to minimize human factor based errors, RMS has been developed and these systems have provided significant advantages to business managers in the management process of restaurants. RMS has significant effects in terms of fast and accurate data flow, facilitating the effective execution of management process from planning to evaluation, enabling rapid production and service, increasing profitability, increasing customer satisfaction and competitiveness (Acar, Ömürbek, & Ömürbek, 2003; Memis Kocaman & Kocaman, 2014). In this section, it is aimed to introduce RMS, to give information about its usage in restaurants and to explain the contributions it will provide for both operation and managers.

BACKROUND

In traditional restaurant management, the waiter brings a printed menu booklet when the customer is seated. He leaves the table for the customer's review and decision. After a while, he comes to pick up the order. He writes customer orders to the tab. He goes to the kitchen and verbally passes the order to the kitchen staff. He follows the preparation of the meal by going between the kitchen and restaurant. When the meal is ready, he takes the meal to the customer's table. In this process, if the customer wants an additional food/beverage, the same procedure is repeated for the subsequent order. When the customer finishes his meal, the waiter is expected to come to the table. The waiter should follow up the meal, take the customer's collection to the cash point, collect the account in the vault, return to the table, take the customer's payment (cash, credit card, etc.) to the cash point and bring the cash/credit card back to the customer (Dorr, 1985). All this means a lot of waiting for the customer. It also increases the workload of waiters and slows down the speed of service. It also reduces the time spent by middle and top executives (chefs, managers) of the restaurant to take care of operations beyond the control. It is also difficult and time-consuming for the senior executives to check their accounting records, inventory and business sales manually. However, as a regular and rigorous control cannot be performed, a high degree of error control is performed.

All this has led to the search for making the restaurant management process easier, effective and efficient. Auger (1967) has developed a system to monitor the occupancy of tables in different rooms in the restaurant. Wolf (1967) developed an automation system where the customer order was entered a consoles by a waiter at a restaurant and the total invoice was calculated. This system also allows inventory control. Later, a system with multiple wireless hand-held terminals to which order entry can be made, has been developed (Sandstedt, 1983). The system, developed by Dorr (1985), aims to shorten the time spent in receiving and transferring orders for restaurant management and control. This RMS was working by the waiters to enter orders from portable equipment, to transfer the information to the central processor, and to send the central processor to the screen in the kitchen. At the same time, it also provided the accounting transactions and ordered products to be deducted from stock.

It has been also developed systems for fast food restaurants where customers can enter their own orders into a touchscreen monitor. These systems integrate with the cashier station, kitchen station and central processor. (Mueller, 1992; Mueller, Neimeister, Counter & Marcus, 1993). Tripp & Vaszary (2006) developed an RMS in the restaurant where the customer can enter the order on a monitor at his table. The RMS used today has been developed in addition to the performance of the enterprise, staff productivity, inventory control, accounting records, menu planning, pricing, supply/supplier follow-up, statistical reports and graphics for managers (Coleman, Davis, Morgan, 1997; Coleman, 1998; Leifer, 2003; Ge, Yang, & amp; Ge, 2003; Burns, Berenschot, Calabrese, Kasper, & Lovell, 2013).

THE SIGNIFICANCE OF RMS

Cash point management is also important in restaurants as in every business. More precisely, it is important that the payment instruments such as money etc. that occur every day in the enterprise are effectively managed, controlled and spent within the budget plan. Since the restaurant cash point is the payment place for the customers who receive food and beverage service, the account must be delivered via RMS in a way that does not give rise to any discussion. Because the fast and complete collection from the customer is the last stage of the service provided.

The orders that were taken by the waiters using the automation program are sent to the kitchen. In the event that the kitchen has approved the order, the order will be forwarded to the cash point as a table number or addition number. If the customer wants to come to the cash point and make payment, it will be enough to tell the table number or addition number. Therefore, it is possible to manage this situation smoothly, faultlessly and quickly by using RMS. The restaurants that use RMS have not kept their customers at checkout and most importantly collects the contents of their customers without sharing it with anyone. Because, in the classic restaurant management, when the customer goes to the cash point, the waiter comes to his side. He tells the attendant that the customer eats and drinks one by one. The cashier collects their prices, tells the customer the total amount and the customer pays. This process means that the customer waits and that the waiter and the cashier also lose time. (Dorr, 1985). Other customers wishing to make payment or hoping service will also be delayed. On the other hand, it is an application that is open to man-made errors due to the delivery of orders from the waiter to the cash point and/ or by the account at the cash point. With the RMS, both the process is accelerated and the risk of error is reduced.

By using RMS in restaurants, the time that managers spend on coordination and control also decreases. Waiter sales, business turnover, discounts, sales according to type of payment, detailed reports can be taken from the system. On the computer, it is possible for the managers to follow the whole process (especially for the chain businesses), to control them, to detect the possible errors/mistakes early and to intervene. Thus, administrators can allocate more time to other management functions.

FUNCTIONS OF RMS

By using RMS in a restaurant, it is possible to select menu items via digital display. Since all products presented in the restaurant are digitally defined, confusion in orders is prevented. Furthermore, if a digital hardware installed on the customer table or provided to the customer is used as a menu, it will be possible to offer a menu that can be updated more frequently than the printed menus. Thus, during ordering, the customer will be provided with accurate and complete information about the changes made in the menu. In addition, additional information such as the contents of the product, cooking method, calories, nutritional value can be given to the customer. This provides a wealth of use that will provide a positive impact for today's modern customer profile and also increase customer satisfaction (Tripp and Vaszary, 2006; Cheong, Chiew, & Yap, 2010 Rai, Shinde, Mhatre, Mahadik, 2014; Jayasekara, 2016).

Thanks to RMS, user-friendly operations are ensured with clear display images and guidance. This also means working efficiently. If the RMS software displays table status and status of the order with color codes, ease of use and increased service speed can be provided. In addition, the voice-visual stimulation of the waiter will speed up the process when the order is ready (Hodges, 2015). Again, it is possible for the waiter to add messages to the kitchen (such as "*rare*"). Since orders are saved in the system with date and time information, it provides managers with the opportunity to track and evaluate the time from receiving the order to the service.

If there is a takeaway service, it is easier to realize the service to be made out of the restaurant with the package/package tracking system in the RMS without any problem, faultless and fast.

With RMS it is possible to assign, add, delete, and merge people to the table. Thus, in the event that a new guest arrives at the table during the operation, that the customer wants to change places or that customers want to combine the table, the software gives them the opportunity and the table follow-up can be done without any confusion. In addition, it is possible to simplify the follow-up procedures by assigning tables only to the waiters. Seeing the status of the tables in the system also provides an opportunity to facilitate and accelerate the workflow. Because different payment points can be defined to the system, the customer can pay at the table without having to wait in the main cash point(Hodges, 2015).

The manager can monitor the instant status of the restaurant through the system. He/she can make changes in menu and recipes. He/she can make inventory tracking and stock management. He/she can view statistics and reports of different time periods of the restaurant (Hodges, 2015). Thus, managers can make faster, more accurate and effective decisions.

Administrators can see statistics for sales in RMS. Thus, by evaluating different menu items, it can provide sufficient supply for the products sold and can avoid unnecessary/over-supply for less-sold products. He/she can revise menu items according to sales rates.

RMS provides facility for senior managers to preserve the product and service standard, especially in chain businesses.

STRUCTURE AND USE OF RMS

Automation systems used in restaurants consist of hardware and software. Hardware consists of machines such as computer, monitor, printer, barcode reader, handheld terminal, kiosk, etc. Software consists of programs designed for work and operations in restaurants.

It is possible to manage kitchen and other departments effectively in restaurants using RMS. In order to do this, RMS software must have a good connection to the basic areas such as kitchen, order, safe and stock management.

Below is an attempt to explain the RMS program. Screenshots of some operations with RMS are shown with photographs.

Kitchen Module Operations and Applications Over RMS

In the context of the kitchen module operations, menu preparation, order taking and how to place the order on the program are explained below.

To Prepare the Digital Menu

It is possible to share all details visually such as displaying the menu items to the customers on a digital display, the ingredients of the food and beverages, cooking methods, garnishes, calorie information etc. Menu preparation operations in the program are carried out from the management panel of the program. This section is encrypted and unauthorized persons cannot make changes (adding and removing) in this field. Generally, the authorized persons of this field are business owners or managers. When they want to add a new menu, they firstly process that menu from stock entry to stock cards. During this process, the raw materials and/or semi-finished materials required in the production of the product are also processed or formed. Then the menu price and picture are added. Then, the process is the transfer process, which is the "send data to all cash points". At this stage, if the added menu is to be sold only in certain restaurants of the chain enterprises, it will be sent to that restaurant and not sent to others. In this way, the creation and addition of digital menu in the program is completed. (see Figure 2 and 3).

Taking an Order in RMS and Forwarding the Order to the Kitchen and Cash Point Management

When the program is entered with the selected products by the kiosk (see Figure 4), desk computer, mobile phone or hand terminal (see Figure 5), customers or order employees (waiters) in the automation program via the digital menu, this information will be first sent to the kitchen management. In the event that the kitchen management gives approval, the total account amount will be sent to the cash management.

If the customer service is to be done in the restaurant, the table number, the number of the waiter and the number of people receiving the service will be selected and registered to the order screen and the order taking process starts (see Figure 6). After that, the ordering process is completed by selecting the menu that is the customer request (see Figure 7).

If the restaurant has a business model that has fast food style and has sales and ordering status via telephone or website, the customer information screen is displayed on the program as shown in Figure 8 and customer's credentials, contact information and address information are recorded. When this customer orders again, if the name

Figure 2. Creating digital menu in RMS program

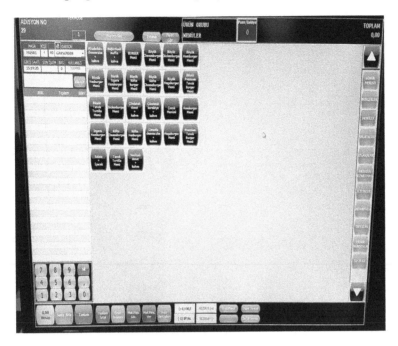

Figure 3. Creating digital menu in RMS program

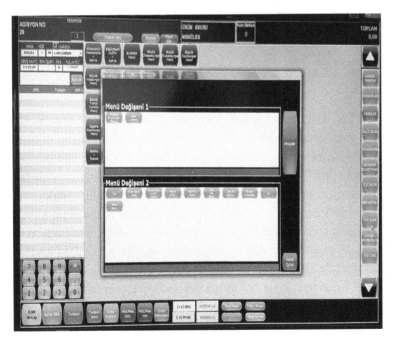

Figure 4. Restaurant kiosk

and surname are written, other information will be automatically displayed. This will provide great convenience to the person who is taking order in the takeaway restaurants. In addition, the customer will not have to give his contact information over and over again. Thus, the customer's satisfaction and loyalty of restaurant will increase. If the customer has already been registered with the program used in the restaurant, it will be sufficient to enter his/her name/last name or telephone number in the program The contact information of the person will be displayed on the screen.

Some special cases of the same menu can be sent to the kitchen via the program if the menu order has been received through the RMS program, whether he/she is a customer who has been registered to the defined customer card or is not registered. These messages are mostly messages that contain exceptions to the menu (*eg.*

Figure 5. Mobile application of the program

meatballs are rare). In Figure 9 and Figure 10, the message display for this status is shown on RMS.

When the order is taken in the restaurants using the RMS and the kitchen approves the order, the menu information will be transferred to the computer at the cash point where the payment is made. (see Figure 11). Here, when the person who will collect from the customer clicks on the account icon in the menu order screen, the display image in Figure 11 will appear . The first step here is to select the payment type by asking the customer. Because some customers pay by cash, some can pay by credit card or foreign currency. After this process is completed on the screen, payment type (cash, credit card, etc.) is processed in the program and '' finish sale '' then 'receipt or invoice' is selected, and then the payment process is completed. If the customer wants to have detailed information about the products he eats and drinks and to see their amounts, the bill is printed at the same time.

Figure 6. Opening order in restaurants

Figure 7. Display image of taking order and processing in restaurants

Figure 8. Customer card display image registered in the restaurant

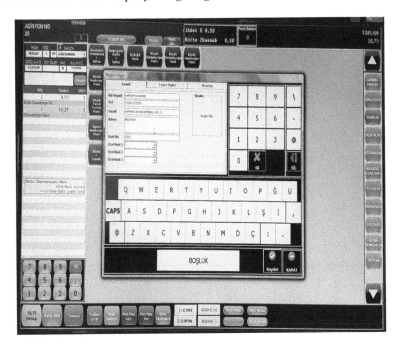

Figure 9. Kitchen message display image of the ordered menu in restaurant

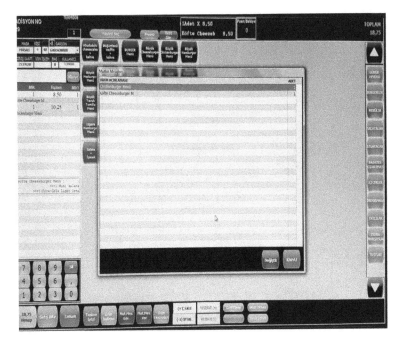

Figure 10. Kitchen message display image of the ordered menu in restaurant

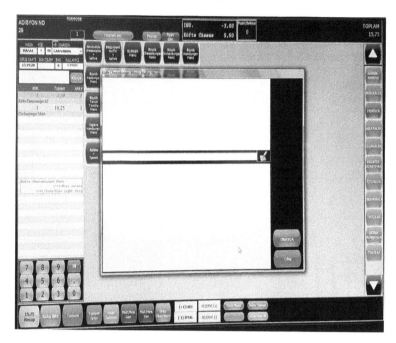

Figure 11. RMS payment screen display image

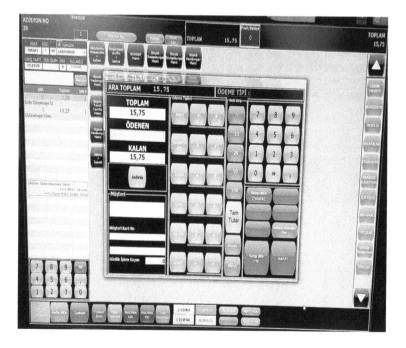

Cost Control Operations, Pricing and Prescribing Practices via RMS

Cost control, pricing and menu prescription applications are made through the management panel in the RMS program. Figure 12 is a screenshot of the management panel in RMS program. Here, restaurant managers can also monitor the cost control process.

The management section of the program includes purchasing management, sales management, retail sales management, warehouse management, restaurant management, customer relationship management, financial management, inventory management, general accounting, production management, e-invoice, definitions and reports.

Cost Control Operations in RMS Program

In this part of the program, studies that will affect the balance of income and expense of the restaurant are done. Correct recording of raw materials and stocks is the first of those. (see Figure 13.) All these operations are Cost Control operations. With the

Figure 12. RMS management panel display image

Figure 13. RMS program purchase management products section screenshot

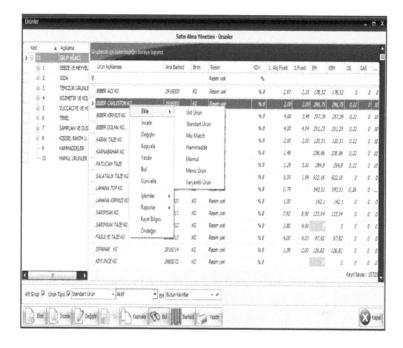

procedures performed in this section, it is possible to minimize the loss and leakage by personnel and to follow the raw material costs and to put the correct sales price. In addition, the purchase and sales invoices are followed, the receivables and debts of the enterprise are carried out in this field.

RMS Program Pricing

In the program, pricing is performed through the restaurant management module within the management panel. Figure 14 is a restaurant management module screenshot in RMS. Here, first the cost margins are taken into account when preparing cost records. If there are any changes in the prices of entered menus and drinks, the changes are made and recorded by entering the price change documents section . Then, the price changes made are sent to the cash registers in the retail sales via management section of the program. Figure 15 shows the RMS retail sales management information sending display panel. With these operations, the price change process is completed.

Figure 14. RMS restaurant management module display screen

Recipe Preparation Applications in the Program

The standard recipe application of food and beverages in the program is carried out from the product recipe panel in the production management section of the program. Figure 16 is a display image of this panel.

Standard recipes of food and beverages are prepared and recorded in the product recipe panel of the program. (see Figure 17.) The amount of raw material used by the personnel during food and beverage production will be indicated in this section. This is the standard recipe application. For example; how many cups from a bottle of drink will be determined by standard recipes. When it is sold through RMS, it will be provided to decrease the stocks according to these standard recipes. The standard recipe for meals prepared in restaurants is an important issue. In order to produce the same quality at every production time, not only in terms of accounting, but also production must be done by adhering to the standard prescription. As the RMS program is already entered as a stock in the recipe applications panel and the standard recipe menus are sold, the materials reduce from the inventories. Therefore, after a day or another time period, the remaining amount is displayed on the screen. For example, the standard ingredients of the food A to be produced are as follows;

Figure 15. Retail sales management information sending panel display image

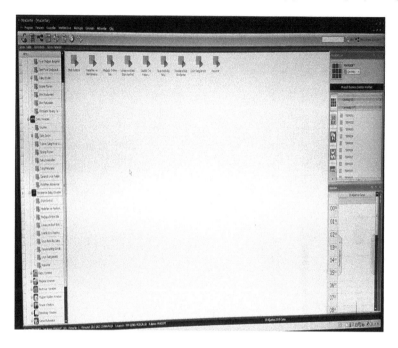

Figure 16. RMS program production management section, product recipes panel display image

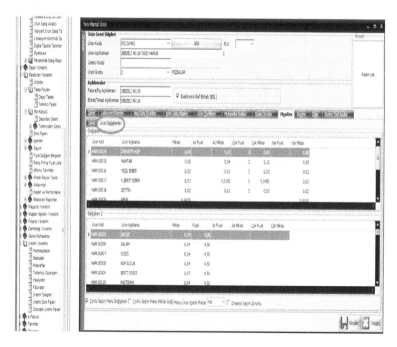

Figure 17. RMS program product recipes display image

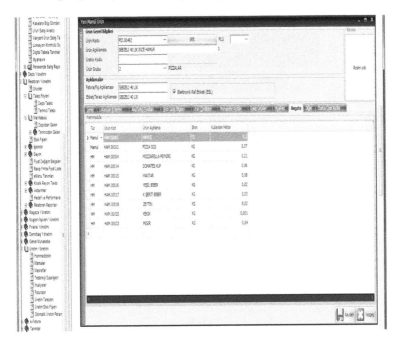

200 grams of beef, 100 grams of eggplant, 100 grams of beans, 50 grams of butter, 10 grams of black pepper, 10 grams of salt, 10 grams of cumin. Therefore, the materials used in this production of this A meal fall from stock and the remaining stock slips are seen in the RMS program. The manager of the restaurant, therefore, can receive the number of portions of the food received from the material and how much waste and loss during the production.

Stock Module Operation Applications via RMS

The stocks of the enterprise in the restaurants are monitored from the warehouse management stock slips panel of the program. At the same time the new stock is recorded from the same panel when it comes to the restaurant. Figure 18 is the display image of the stock slips panel. When stocks fall to the specified lower limit (when they reach the minimum stock level), the program gives an audible and visual warning message to the screen. In addition, inventory invoice entries are made in this module. As the added inventories are integrated with the sales management module, the inventories begin to decrease as sales are made over the system. For this reason, requirement list can be determined by the amount of stock to be removed

Figure 18. RMS program warehouse management section stock slips panel display image

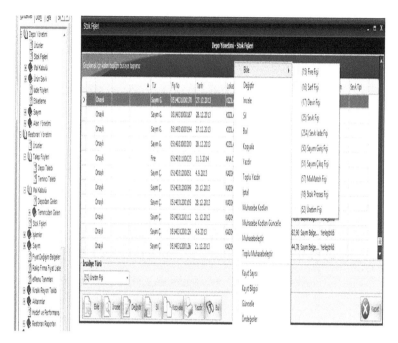

from the system in determined periods. Furthermore, by comparing the amount of stock in the system and the amount of stock in the actual situation (at the time of the counting in the enterprise), the leakage status can be easily determined.

RMS Purchasing Management Module Operations Applications

The purchasing management module ensures that all purchasing processes are carried out electronically and via RMS. This part of the program is carried out from the purchasing management module in the definitions section. The display image for this area is shown in Figures 19, 20 and 21. The suppliers are registered on the system. Company based and product based evaluation can be made. In addition, needs can be determined from the inventory module, and the demands and orders can be sent to the suppliers in electronic environment via e-mail or fax. The purchase process can be completed by giving the order confirmation according to the authorization status.

Businesses that make purchases in RMS save time significantly. The contract rules determined by the suppliers of the restaurant shall not be exceeded. Comparison of the price of the raw material product from the restaurant, taking into consideration

Figure19. Descriptions section of the RMS program, purchase management panel display image

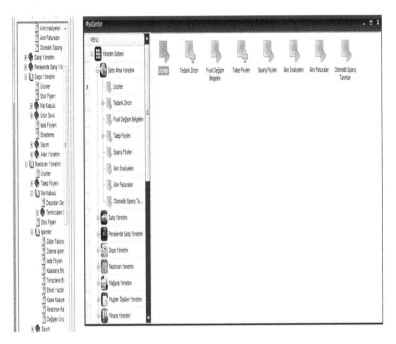

other criteria such as purchase period, usage amount etc. can be made. In addition, steps are taken to manage the restaurant according to the principles of efficiency and economy.

Cost and Sales Analysis Operations Applications via RMS

The program allows both restaurant manager and cashier to see sales reports and other reports according to hourly, daily, weekly or selected date range. The image shown in Figure 22 shows a report of all operations from the management panel. Figures 23, 24, 25, 26 and 27 are display images of cost and sales analysis that can be seen in case reports are entered without going into the sales module of the program. If this field is encrypted, only the administrator of the relevant restaurant can log in and view it. If the password application is not performed, the person/s responsible for the sale at the cash register can see the analysis and reports in this field.

The program allows the comparison between sales and purchases made at different times depending on the purchase and sales transactions in restaurants. It is also possible to analyze the following operations;

Figure 20. Descriptions section of the RMS program, purchase management panel products screen display image

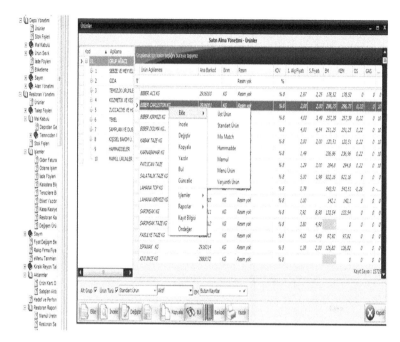

- During the day or in the selected time zone, you can see how much sales are made on the basis of prices and products.
- Comparisons and evaluations can be made by measuring the work efficiency of your employee personnel on a monthly weekly basis.
- When price changes are made, changes in sales can be seen and quick decisions can be made accordingly.
- Decreasing raw materials and other inventories can be followed immediately in the restaurant. In this way, production disruption is prevented by giving orders on time.
- Thanks to the customer registration system, it is possible to get information about the demographic characteristics of customers and their eating habits. Customer-based sales menu and other products can be analyzed and accordingly advertising and other campaigns can be planned according to the target audience.
- The sales performance of each branch in the chain enterprises can be compared daily or even by considering certain hours of the day. This information can be used in strategic decision-making.

Figure 21. Descriptions section of the RMS program, display image of the purchase management panel purchase contracts page

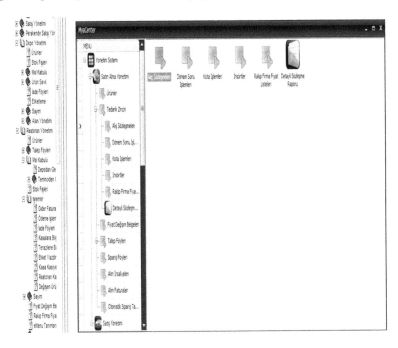

Figure 22. RMS program reports section display image

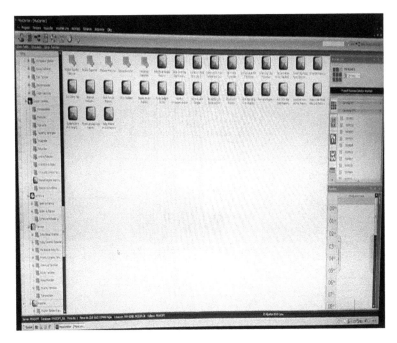

SOLUTIONS AND RECOMMENDATIONS

Besides all these, there are some difficult ways to use RMS. These are described below.

- Changes in the business such as menu, price, stock, table, task and authorization will require continuous updating in the system. Therefore, if there is a need for frequent changes to the system, the employment of an informed and experienced staff on computer programs, especially in a large-capacity/chain restaurant, may provide the opportunity to eliminate problems.

- With RMS, too much work can be carried out with less staff and employment is reduced. There will be a need for staff with knowledge and experience to use the program. Even without the need for waiter, the customer's order is entered into the system, the order is delivered to a customer an employee. Such RMSs are available (Mueller, 1992). Furthermore, the use of an automation system has started, where the order is delivered to the customer over a line instead of the waiter.

- Communication between departments may not be possible depending on the connection speed, internet and hardware infrastructure. For example, the waiter assumes that he handed the order from the handheld terminal to

Figure 23. RMS program login screen, reports section login screen image

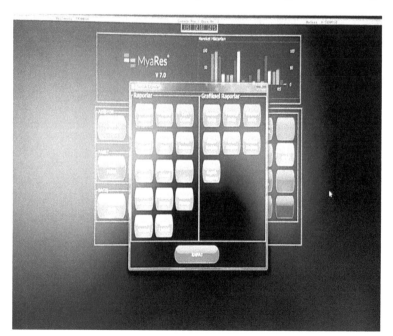

Figure 24. RMS program reports section product report display image

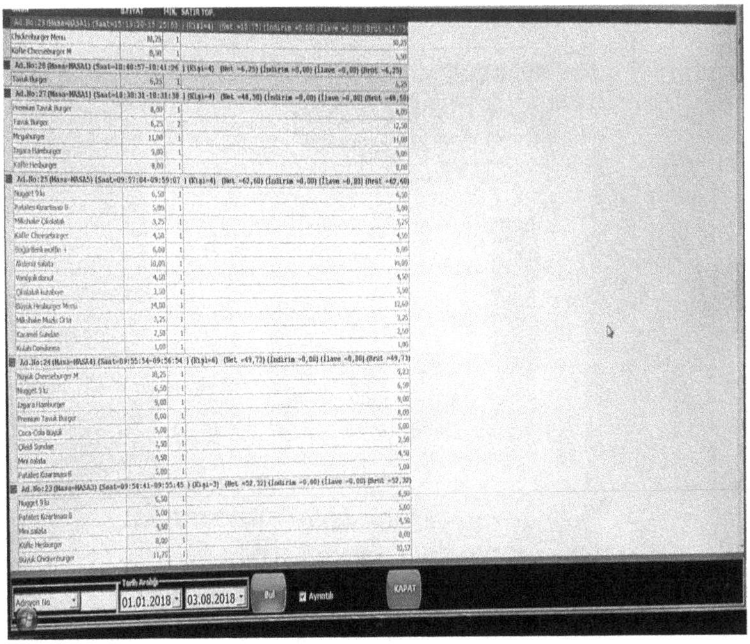

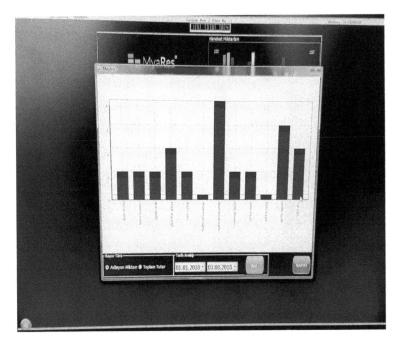

Figure 25. RMS program reports section bill list report image

Figure 26. RMS program reports section bill amount (by number of tables) report image

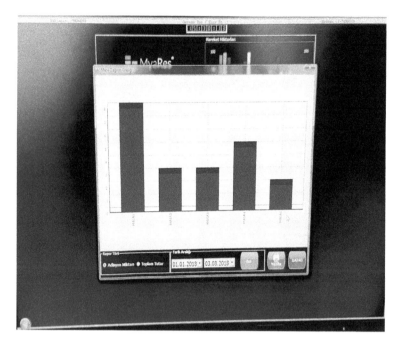

Figure 27. RMS program reports section product sales list report image

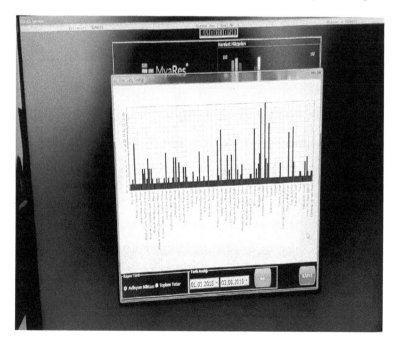

the kitchen, but the kitchen order might not have been received due to low connection speed or due to lack of connection/momentary interruption. This will cause the customer to wait for a long time for his order.

- As the automation systems used in restaurants and other businesses will appeal to different purposes, confusion increases if the RMS is not chosen well and integrated into the organization. For example, an automation system used in a market cannot be used in a restaurant. Similarly, the automation system in a fast-food business may be inadequate to the needs of the fine dining restaurant. Therefore, when choosing automation software, the structure, needs and capacity of the enterprise should be well defined and it would be appropriate to choose a fitted RMS. It will be easier to manage the tasks and processes on the system with easy and clear operation menus. Otherwise; personnel and managers working in the enterprise should be trained about the use of the system for a long time. This means an extra time cost for personnel who are already busy with workload. RMS, which has a complicated and hard-to-learn software, can cause delays, mistakes and disruptions to the service. In addition, starting with RMS, which has good hardware and software to prevent malfunctions such as failure of the program, connection problems, etc., will mean to eliminate many problems.

FUTURE RESEARCH DIRECTIONS

The effectiveness of the programs can be evaluated by performing field research for the benefits and challenges of RMS. Qualitative and quantitative research can be planned for that. Surveys in the sector to determine perceptions, attitudes and frequency of use for RMS can be planned.

CONCLUSION

RMS is the system that manages the process, management processes, stock follow-up and control operations, financial and statistical studies and also the advertising campaigns of the enterprises by taking into account the multiple business models in a standard way. Furthermore, in today's business, the way to use information and technology effectively is through programs. An effective and well-chosen RMS program will be sufficient to manage the complex relationships to be made with many people in a short and simple way.

Thanks to RMS, operations that will take a long time and require many people to work, can be done immediately and error-free. This allows businesses to grow thanks to effective management and human resource planning. Therefore, RMS adds value to enterprises as it institutionalizes restaurants, reduces managers' workloads and enables standard services and applications. For these reasons, enterprises must support the internal functioning systems, which are the invisible faces, with RMS.

ACKNOWLEDGMENT

Myares which was used in the writing of this section, was provided by RMS Adampos and technical support for the use of RMS was provided by the company when needed (http://www.adampos.com/English/restaurant-sector.aspx).

REFERENCES

Acar, D., Ömürbek, N., & Ömürbek, V. (2003). Bilgi Teknolojilerinin Gıda Sektöründe Kullanımının Analizi (Utilization of information technologies in food industry). *Süleyman Demirel Üniversitesi İktisadi ve İdari Bilimler Fakültesi Dergisi*, 8(2), 1–22.

Auger, U. G. (1967). *Method and Apparatus for Coordinating Restaurant Operation*. U.S. Patent No. 3,310,797. Washington, DC: U.S. Patent and Trademark Office.

Burns, J. W., Berenschot, C. E., Calabrese, G., Kasper, C. D., & Lovell, R. (2013). *Restaurant Management System and Method*. U.S. Patent No. 8,620,753. Washington, DC: U.S. Patent and Trademark Office.

Cheong, S. N., Chiew, W. W., & Yap, W. J. (2010, December). *Design and development of multi-touchable e-restaurant management system*. Paper presented at the meeting of the 2010 International Conference on Science and Social Research (CSSR 2010), Kuala Lumpur, Malaysia. 10.1109/CSSR.2010.5773867

Coleman, J. H. (1998). *Restaurant Management System*. U.S. Patent No. 5,839,115. Washington, DC: U.S. Patent and Trademark Office.

Coleman, J. H., Davis, J. C., & Morgan, R. L. (1997). *Restaurant Management System*. U.S. Patent No. 5,602,730. Washington, DC: U.S. Patent and Trademark Office.

Davis, B., Lockwood, A., Alcott, P., & Pantelidis, I. S. (2018). *Food and beverage management* (6th ed.). London: Routledge. doi:10.4324/9781315563374

Dorr, J. A. (1985). *Restaurant Management Information and Control Method andApparatus.* U.S. Patent No. 4,530,067. Washington, DC: U.S. Patent and Trademark Office.

Edwards, J. S. A. (2013). The food service industry: Eating out is more than just a meal. *Food Quality and Preference, 27*(2), 223–229. doi:10.1016/j.foodqual.2012.02.003

Edwards, J. S. A., & Hartwell, H. J. (2009). Institutional meals. In H. L. Meiselman (Ed.), *Meals in science and practice. Interdisciplinary research and business applications* (pp. 102–127). Oxford, UK: CRC Press, Woodhead Publishing.

Fitzsimmons, J. A., & Maurer, G. B. (1991). A walk-through audit to improve restaurant performance. *The Cornell Hotel and Restaurant Administration Quarterly, 31*(4), 95–100. doi:10.1177/001088049103100422

Ge, L., Yang, C., & Ge, R. (2003). Electronic Restaurant Service Management System. *U.S. Patent Application No. 10/104,187.*

Hodges, J. (2015). *Restaurant Management System.* 3rd Year Project Report. The University of Manchester School of Computer Science. Retrieved from http://studentnet.cs.manchester.ac.uk/resources/library/3rd-year-projects/2015/jonathan.hodges-2.pdf

Jayasekara, D. N. R. (2016). *Restaurant Management System* (Unpublished Doctoral dissertation).

Kant, A. K., & Graubard, B. I. (2004). Eatingout in America, 1987–2000: Trends and nutritional correlates. *Preventive Medicine, 38*(2), 243–249. doi:10.1016/j.ypmed.2003.10.004 PMID:14715218

Lachat, C., Nago, E., Verstraeten, R., Roberfroid, D., Van Camp, J., & Kolsteren, P. (2012). Eating out of home and its association with dietary intake: A systematic review of the evidence. *Obesity Reviews, 13*(4), 329–346. doi:10.1111/j.1467-789X.2011.00953.x PMID:22106948

Leifer, R. (2003). Restaurant Management System. *U.S. Patent Application No. 10/195,336.*

Memis Kocaman, E., & Kocaman, M. (2014). Yiyecek ve içecek işletmelerinde otomasyon sistemleri kullanımının yönetim sürecine etkileri [The effects of the use of automation systems in food and beverage business on the management process]. *Standard, 53*(625), 28–33.

Mueller, R. J. (1992). *Customer Operable Systemfor a Retail Store or Fast-Food Restaurant Having Plural Ordering Stations.* U.S. Patent No. 5,128,862. Washington, DC: U.S. Patent and Trademark Office.

Mueller, R. J., Neimeister, C. K., Counter, J. R., & Marcus, M. P. (1993). *Customer self-ordering system using information displayed on a screen.* U.S. Patent No. 5,235,509. Retrieved from http://patents.com/us-5235509.html

Rai, V., Shinde, S., Mhatre, B., & Mahadik, P. (2014). Restaurant management system. *International Journal of Research in Information Technology, 2*(3), 284–288.

Sandstedt, G. O. (1983). *Restaurant or retail vending facility.* U.S. Patent No. 4,415,065. Retrieved from http://patents.com/us-4415065.html

Tripp, T., & Vaszary, M. (2006). Restaurant Management Using Network With Customer-Operated Computing Devices. *U.S. Patent Application No. 11/024,105.*

Wolf, J. D. (1967). *Business Order Control System andApparatus.* U.S. Patent No. 3,304,416. Washington, DC: U.S. Patent and Trademark Office.

Chapter 5

Urban and Rural Ecotourism in and Around Bolpur:
A Study of Destination Marketing and Challenges – Ecotourism Practices in West Bengal, India

Debasish Batabyal
Amity University Kolkata, India

Dillip Kumar Das
University of Burdwan, India

ABSTRACT

Bolpur is a district town in Birbhum, West Bengal. This place is famous for Viswabharti in Shanti Niketan where a new school of thought was initiated by Rabindranath Tagore. Later on, the place became an epicenter for Bengali education and culture. Though the place has other noteworthy academic and cultural records, this place has immense scope for urban and rural ecotourism. With the blend of rural Bengal and its rich artistic and spiritual exuberance, Birbhum offers a lot. Now, as a mean of entrepreneurship and employment, ecotourism can provide the local people with new alternative scope and opportunities. This chapter is an attempt to revisit and reorganize destination Bolpur with a sustainable marketing orientation for ecotourism. Further attempt is also made to support industry leaders and tourism academicians interested to invest or study for business and commerce. Familiarization trip has been conducted along with a survey for the tourists to better understand their expectations and perceptions.

DOI: 10.4018/978-1-5225-8494-0.ch005

INTRODUCTION

Travel & tourism are among the world's fastest growing industries and are the major source of foreign exchange earnings for many developing countries. Tourism has emerged as an instrument for employment generation, poverty alleviation and sustainable human development. The increasing economic importance of tourism has captured the attention of most countries. Bolpur-Santiniketan is a municipality and headquarters of Bolpur subdivision in Birbhum District in the state of West Bengal, India. It is 145 km north of Kolkata and is best known for its proximity to Visva Bharati, the university set up by the Nobel laureate poet Rabindranath Tagore. Given its proximity to Santiniketan and Sriniketan, it is one of the seats of culture and education in West Bengal. About 150 years ago, Bolpur was a small village under supur porgana. Kalikapur a known place of Bolpur was the origin of the typical village in past. There were no rail lines, no developed roads. Paddy land were seen around the village. "Lalmati" (red soil) was found everywhere. Many villages named Sian, Dihipara, Khosakdampur, Paruldanga, Goalpara, Ballavpur, Bandhgara, Surul, Supur, Raipur were the boundary line around Bolpur.

East India company established the first railway line in 1859, when the Sahebganj loopline was extended beyond the river Ajay. Bolpur railway station was established in 1860. Along with this, court, police station, sub registry office, etc., were established in old Bolpur. Then people started residing here. Christian missionaries came; they founded a church that was known as Mission compound. Paddy storage house, stationary shops, grocery shops, garment shops etc. were on the east side near Bolpur railway station. About 19 husking machines were here at that time.

Maharshi Debendranath Tagore established a centre of religious mediation in Bolpur. Rabindranath Tagore established Visva Bharati Viswavidyalaya. These were the main reasons for the huge extension, development and popularity of Bolpur.

Provincial names proved the upcoming gradual development of Bolpur. Kachharipatti is just beside court house, Trishulapatti is the commercial paddy trading centre. Kalibaroarytala was the service place for Bolpur set up by some initiative people. Netaji made a conference. Here Harisava stood against "Bramhopasana". Every week these two conferences were held in Bolpur. Bijaykrishna Ghoswami, Shivnath Shastri, Shasibhusan Basu like many wisemen gave religious advice. Beside this, prayer committee was set up. There are direct trains from Bolpur to Howrah, Gaya, Jalpaiguri, Guwahati, New Delhi and Kolkata.

Bus and private cars are available from Durgapur City Centre Bus Stop and soon from Santragachi Railway Station in Kolkata.

The district lies between 280 32' 30" and 240 35' 00" North latitude and 880 01' 40" and 870 05' 25" East longitude. The district's immediate neighbours are Murshidabad in the east and northeast, Burdwan in the south and south-east and

Pakur, Dumka of Jharkhand in the west and north-west. The main floral species are Shorea robusta (sal), with associates like Pterocarpus marsupium (Piasal), Terminalia tomentosa (asan), Anogeissus latifolia(dhaw),Terminalia bellerica (bahera), T.chebula, Buchnania lanzan, Dalbergia sissoo etc. The degraded forest land is mostly planted with Akashmoni and Eucalyptus along with other misc. Species. An area of 2.021 sq km is declared as Ballavpur Wildlife Sanctuary u/s 18 (1) of Wild Life Protection Act, 1972 that also includes erstwhile declared Reserved forest, vides notification no. 4655 dated 11.07.1977 published in Calcutta Gazette on 18.08.1977 of Govt. of West Bengal, revenue & Forest department in Bolpur Range.

REVIEW OF LITERATURE

Ecotourism is often considered to be a potential strategy to support conservation of natural ecosystems while at the same time, promoting sustainable development (Ross & Wall; 1999). Ecotourism is usually considered to be more than just tourism to natural areas. The notion of ecotourism was initially developed in 1987 by Ceballos-Lascurain who defined ecotourism as an experience of *'travelling to relatively undisturbed areas with the specific objective of studying, admiring, and enjoying the scenery and its wild plants and animals as well as any existing cultural manifestation found in these areas'* (Boo, 1990). The definition by WTO also falls in this category. World Tourism Organisation (WTO, 1993) defined ecotourism as, *'tourism that involves travelling to relatively undisturbed areas with the specific objective of studying, admiring, and enjoying the scenery and its wild plants and animals as well as any existing cultural manifestation found in these areas'.*

The Ecotourism Society defines ecotourism as *'Purposeful travel to natural areas to understand the cultural and the natural history of the environment; taking care not to alter the integrity of the ecosystem; producing economic opportunities that make the conservation of the natural resources beneficial to the local people'* (Wood, Getz and Lindberg; 1995). Ecotourism is an amalgam of two separate concepts: *ecology* and *tourism*, but viewed jointly. The coinage assumes great significance both for ecological conservation and development of tourism. Tourism has been recognized of late as a revenue earner with the potential for generating employment for the local populace; on the other hand, an ecological perspective is considered significant for preserving the ecosystem of the earth, thus ecotourism has drawn the attention of the world community as a positive contributor towards the preservation of the natural and cultural resources and also towards the development of tourism.

In his article, "Marketing National Parks Using Ecotourism as a Catalyst", Wearing, S. (2008) addressed the confusion and controversies surrounding tourism practices in the places/ national parks where eco tourism played the role of a catalyst.

He emphasized more on marketing that brought an alternative paradigm and made it possible to increase the breadth and depth of understanding as to how these places/ parks were needed to shift their management approaches and to increase a 'new view'. Later he admitted that the low intensity, small scale ecotourism development may be feasible only in the early phases and will bring contention and contradiction with the passage of time as the intention of profit maximization increases. So, the generic term destination has several meanings ranging from the geographical perspective to a product to be consumed or an experience to be gained. It can be a place to be visited repeatedly to a place of life time experience. Having been extensively interrelated and interdependent with geography, sociology, environmental science, economics, anthropology, commerce and trade etc., modern tourism has always unified itself with a dominant role of marketing management. But the marketing orientation of tourist destination has been changing with the relevance and inclusion of many existing and new subjects as destination development literature needs a solid support from other subjects with respect to a specific market orientation i.e. the key factor of the demand-supply equilibrium in this open market economy of the world. Prioritizing destination marketing and its ever changing aspects will certainly contribute to the all stakeholders and as such will bring in an adoption of green marketing approaches. But destination marketing is different in that here the product formulation and the product itself are multiple and jointly contributing to the experience. Consumption of a place is also different from the residence of the customers and the derived demand should not exceed the actual demand though both of them need to be properly integrated.

In their article ' A framework for an industry supported destination marketing information system' Ritchie R.J.B. and Ritchie J.R. have introduced a new orientation of holistic destination marketing, which uses information to guide strategic marketing priorities and create cooperative marketing opportunities for industry. Here solutions were identified to deliver high quality information supported by research and intelligence at an affordable cost by preparing a useful framework for model building even for other jurisdictions seeking to develop a Destination Marketing Information System.

In his book " Tourism Product and Services: Development Strategy and Management Options" Sharma J.K. (2007) emphasized on product development and its improvement of quality related services. Contemporary tourism services, tourism product development, sustainable tourism product development, quality management in tourism, sustainable tourism certification and training, tourism product development strategy, management and research. Existing ecotourism enterprises often highlight some conservation activities like energy saving gadgets or restricted use of plastics, but tend to ignore the overall impact on the natural and cultural integrity of the destination. There are instances where this has either led to eventual degradation of the marketed tourism products themselves or to social unrest. Distinguishing the components of Ecotourism enterprises can clarify the ambiguity in the concept and practice of ecotourism in the country. In many countries, 'home grown' definitions are in vogue (Edward *et al*, 1998), groomed to meet specific needs of the context. Based on various definitions of ecotourism, one can distinguish ecotourism for our context by the following four essential characteristics.

- Nature based activities
- Eco-cultural Sustainability
- Conservation Education (for tour operator and the tourist) as a major component
- Significant involvement of and benefits to local people

PLACES OF INTERESTS

Considering the market trends through empirical evidences, ecotourism products in the study areas are broadly divided into two categories, viz. rural ecotourism products and urban ecotourism products.

Rural Ecotourism Products of Bolpur and Its Near Around Places: Artistic Leather Craft

Artistic leather craft is a contemporary craft believed to have been developed in this state by a group of artist craftsmen working at Bolpur and adjacent places in Burdwan district. The processes were developed and perfected and in course of time, W.B. came to occupy the foremost place as a seat of manufacture of fancy leather goods. Well-tanned sheepskin, the principal raw material however, is not much available locally and has to be imported to this state from outside, especially from Tamil Nadu. Besides, the few other articles that the artisans require include powder color, methylated spirit, gum acacia and different types of metallic fittings. The leather is marked carefully so as to minimize wastage and then cut to the required size. Designing is usually done by hand painting with brush and engraving is done by a modeler. Zinc and copper blocks are also used for deep lining. Batik work on leather is very much appreciated by the customers because of its intricate play of lines and colors. The technique is the same process of resist dying, very much similar to the process of batik printing on textile. The only difference being that a thick coating of gum acacia solution is applied a resist.

Artistic leather products have a special appeal for their beauty, plasticity and utility. The designs and motifs evolved and introduced by the artisans of Bhedia (near

Bolpur in Burdwan) have added to their charm. The products include a variety of utility articles like ladies' handbags, wallets, briefcases, travel bags moras etc. Very recently leather jackets are also in great demand particularly amongst foreign buyers.

Dokra

The name Dokra was used to indicate a group of nomadic craftsmen scattered over Bengal, Orissa and Madhya Pradesh who were identified by their beautifully shaped and decorated metal products. Many of these craftsmen have settled in Dariapur near Bolpur.

The Dokra system of metal casting is believed to be the oldest form of metal casting and is technically known as Cire Perdue or lost wax process. The technique is supposed to be of high antiquity in India. According to certain scholars, the small bronze statue of he dancing girl found in Mohanjodaro was probably done by Cire Perdue process. Ruth Reeves writes -The intricate pattern and design reproduced in casting the dancing girl would, however, indicate that most probably the lost wax process was employed, as direct casting from mould would not produce a bronze of such a fine finish."

The newcomers probably learnt it from them and added perfection to it. It has been one of the most accepted techniques of image casting including the famous South Indian Bronzes. However, what is peculiar to Dokra products is that the techniques, the form, the design and motif have been preserved in their primitive shape, unalloyed and unsullied by any outside interference. Like many other ancient crafts of India, the Dokra too was associated with the religious requirements of the people. The original ritual character of the Dokra products is now forgotten but these products are liked even today for their primitive simplicity.

In recent years, the products of Dokra artisans have been in great demand in India and abroad. Figures of birds and animals among which owl, peacock, horse and elephant are very popular, images of divinities, lamps, cascades, bowls, etc. constitute some of the distinctive and highly individualistic forms coming from the Dokra artisans.

Kantha Stitch

Every part of the world, embroidery work had been the special mean and way of the ladies of the household, wherein they could give expression to their creative abilities and artistic talents. The ladies of Birbhum and Burdwan have also been practicing this household craft since time immemorial and specimens of their work is best exemplified in the "kanthas" which have now become widely known and appreciated. Kanthas are discarded saries placed one upon another, sewn and quilted on which designs are embroidered with colored threads taken from borders of old saries. In some kanthas, the embroidery starts from the centre with a lotus motif and goes round and round to decorate the centre; in another, the tree of life starts from the four corners and reach towards the centre; and in yet another type, the available space is divided into panels, each filled in with rich embroidery. The designs are limitless, every women working on any innovation that takes her fancy. Traditional designs, ritual designs, are among the other vital categories.

Solapith

Sola (Aeschynomene Aspera) is a herbaceous plant growing wildly in the waterlogged marshy terrain of Bengal and Assam and in some parts of Orissa and the Deccan peninsula. The seeds germinate with showers in April and mature plants are collected in September/ October which are then dried in the sun and stored in shade for use throughout the year. The soft, white, light and lustrous inner portion of the plant is used by the artisans. Some areas in and around Bolpur has artisans making crafts made of this plants.

Wood Carving

The art of wood carving is also a very old craft. Man had traditionally looked to wood carving for decorating this home as well as for making dolls and toys for children to play with. The art of wood carving is a common heritage and exists in every human habitat. The Sutradgars, the traditional craftsmen of the past, were grouped into 4 categories- Kasthkar, Bhaskar, Mrittikar and Chitrakar in terms of profession and they used wood, stone, earth and color for painting respectively as raw materials for creation of their artifacts.

Cane and Bamboo

Cane and bamboo work, especially basketry, is one of the oldest crafts known to man and is universally practiced wherever necessary raw-materials are available. Birbhum has a rich store of raw-materials, and the artisans have a tradition of producing beautiful utility articles from bamboo and cane for household uses. Baskets of different kinds, from the day laborer's ordinary work basket to the very finely woven and decorated travel basket, has been a major item of production of bamboo artisans. Typical oval boxes and oblong boxes made of bamboo are going out of fashion and have largely been replaced by different metals. So the new avenues are required to popularize these products.

Centres of Handicrafts in Bolpur and Its Adjacent Places

- **Illambazar:** Lac artisans, locally called *nuris*, worked out a variety of lacquered items namely, cups, inkpots, bracelets and toys 'of excellent design and craftsmanship'. Some of the ornamental items were sent to the Great Paris Exhibition of 1855. Lot of rural artisans in and around Illambazar are found practicing kantha stitch today.
- **Dariapur:** The village is within Ausgram I – Village Panchayat. This village is famous for Dokra Craft. All the people of this village are involved with this craft.
- **Bannkapashi**: This village is within Mongalkot Anchal. Sola Pith craft is famous here. **Ausgram I**: The villages within this region are famous for sewing and needle craft.
- **Srikrishnapur**, one of these villages, is renowned for Kantha stitch sarees, dupattas. Kanthas for the kiddies have demand even in foreign countries.
- **Ausgram II**: Renowned for handicrafts made from canes and bamboos and needle works.

Ballavpur Danga is just two kilometers from Ballavpur sanctuary. This place is already famous tourist spot for rural tourism. The village of Ballavpur Danga is known for the handicrafts work made by the local artisans to earn their livlihood. The tribals of the village posses the rich art and craft culture. They are expert in mat weaving, broom binding, musical instruments, baskets, batik, leather work and making ornaments with date leaf, palm leaf, and bena grass. They pass this talent from generation to the other.

Fairs and Festivals

Karam is the most important festival celebrated among the tribes in the village. This festival falls in the month of September and October. On the auspicious day tribals thank their God and Goddess for every things they have and worship to have more. Another festival celebrated among the tribals in the village is called Chabbish Prahar. Villagers do not worship any idols. They follow the Sarna religion. The God and Goddess worshipped among the tribals in the village are Marangburu, Jaheraera, and Manjhi. They also pay respect to the ghosts and spirits like Kal, Sing, Lakchera,Beudarang etc.

Jaydev Kenduli mela, Sriniketan Krishi mela, Chandi Das and Pous mela are some of the major fairs that held every year in the village of Ballavpur Danga. Villagers of Ballavpur Danga love dance and music. They play great music using

Tirio (bamboo flute with the seven holes), Dhodro banam (which consists of belly called lac covered with an animal skin on which rests the bridge(sadam, lit, horse), an open chest(korom), a short neck (hotok)and a head(bohok), Phet banam (a fretless stringed instrument with three or four strings), Tumdak, Tamak, Junko and Singa.

Santhali Dance

At Ballavpur, one can enjoy the performance or you can be apart of the vibrant Santhal Dance performed by the Santhali women, dressed up in the red bordered white saris. The artists paint themselves with the different colors in order to depict the various mythological character and dance gracefully on the beats of the traditional music using the sticks.

Urban Ecotourism Products

Festivals and Fairs: These include Basanta Utsav, Barsha Mangal, Sharodutsav, Nandan Mela, Anandamela, Poush Mela, Magh Mela, Rabindra Jayanti to name a few. Of these, the Poush Mela is a major tourist attraction. It is a three-day fair (Bengali, mela means a fair), starting on the seventh day of the Bengali month Poush. Basanta Utsab is also celebrated each year on the occasion of Dol Yatra (Holi-the festival of colour) at the advent of the Vasanta (spring season in Bengal).

Deer Park in Shantiniketan

There is a Deer Park 3 km from Santiniketan. The entry ticket is 10 rupees. There are lots of deer but nothing else. Originally, the area was a fast eroding 'Khowai'. It is now a large wooded area with herds of deer and makes a natural bird sanctuary. 'Sonajhuri' is a tourist place, which is 3.1 km apart from santiniketan. Laal mati(red soil), sonajhuri (earleaf acacia), eucalyptus trees and erosion of land (khowai) give this place an extraordinary scenic beauty. The place is named after the tree sonajhuri. Here is a great abundance of these trees. This place sonajhuri is largely celebrated for 'Shonibarer Haat' (Saturday's market) which happens to situate here on every Saturday (nowadays also is in Sunday). This market is very remarkable for baul songs, handicrafts, handlooms, home decorating materials etc. People from the nearby villages and many artists from all over Bolpur earn their bread and butter from this market. This is the hub of bolpur crafts with all it's manifestation. This beautiful place bestows its people with the golden dusts of Sonajhuri trees that leaves people with a happy heart and complete bliss.

Ballavpur Wildlife Sanctuary

Ballavpur Wildlife Sanctuary started on 10th Feb 1967 as a Deer Park. Gradually it increased in size and species diversity with the passage of time. On 18.8.77 vide Notification No.4655-For dated 11.07.77, the Deer Park was notified as Ballavpur Wildlife Sanctuary, with an area of 200 ha. of this 35-40 hectare comprises of wetlands in three different patches. The Deer enclosure is of 40 hectare area and within it, Sal, Akashmoni, Minjiri, Mahul etc. are the principal species.

Amkhoi Fassil Park

The angiosperm wood fossils which are displayed here were collected during pond digging from Amkhoi village of Illambazar Forest, Birbhum District. These specimens are definite proof of the presence of a vast dry deciduous forest with a few evergreen elements in this area, which prevailed 15 to 20 million years before present (Late Miocene). Wood fossils can also be found in different places of Birbhum, Bardhaman, Bankura and Medinipur Districts of West Bengal as well as in Mayurbhanj District in Orissa. Few families and genera of the past forest of south West Bengal were identified by scientists. Dipterocarpacea, Anacardiacea, Combretacea and Leguminosae are some of these. At the present time these families occur in this area. However, some genera are extinct here, but occur in the present day forests of Western Ghats, Myanamar and Malaysia. This past forest thrived in the uplands of Rajmahal Hills and Chotanagpur Plateau at the North West of Birbhum. It is presumed that the trees were carried by occasional floods of the river system flowing from North West of the river basin towards South East in Birbhum, Bardhaman, Bankura and Medinipur Districts and deposited under find sand and clay gradually to transform into wood fossils. The petrified woods are found in two different laterite beds. This is a pioneering effort of West Bengal Forest Department in preserving the priceless fossils woods and to educate people about the natural heritage of West Bengal.

Proposed plan for the park is

1. Construction of Deer Park
2. Re-excavation of Ponds
3. Beautification of the Fossil Park
4. Construction of Children Park with children playing area in the Fossil Park
5. Landscaping
6. Development of Picnic Spot in the Fossil Park.

Banalakshmi

Banalakshmi or "Vanalakshmi Unmesh Samiti" is a Krishi Ashram and a small NGO in the Birbhum district of West Bengal. It is located near to the Santiniketan, the education centre set up by Rabindranath Tagore. It is connected by a highway to Ilambazar and Bolpur. The bus stop name is Banabhila . The Choupahari sal forests starts from here. Address is Vanalakshmi Unmesh Samiti, Banabhila, P.O. Dwaranda (via Sriniketan P.O.), Birbhum-731236. It is around 13/14 km towards Ilambazar from Shantiniketan. Contact Numbers are (03463) 271202 and 94344 46150. It is spread over an estimated area of 40 bigha (around 13 acres). It has vegetation grown on laterite soil which is the abundant red soil variety found in Birbhum. It has large forested tracts, orchards of various fruits—like mango and guava—and multiple crop cultivation the year round. The place is admirable for its scenic beauty. The road leading to Banalakshmi is also lined by dense to sporadic occurrence of tropical deciduous trees like sal and eucalyptus.

Objectives

The objectives of the study are based on ecotourism destination development and marketing for Bolpur and adjacent places with a sustainable practices. Objectives are set on the basis of familiarization trips and available literature based impact studies. This is for establishing the study area as ecotourism destination. So, the objectives are

1. To find out the avenues for rural ecotourism development and promotion in the study area with regard to sustainable principles .
2. To measure the expectation and experience of tourists before and after visiting the places for urban ecotourism in the study area.

RESEARCH METHODOLOGY

The research has carried both primary and secondary data collection. The primary data collection has been done during the peak months more specifically during Vasanta Utsav and Paus Mela. It has been done with the help of two schedules. Secondary data are collected mostly from the concerned officials and important websites. One schedule contains 18 questions. Out of these 18, 15 questions are asked with the help of five point likert scale with score 1 to 5, where 1 represents highly disagree and 5 represents highly agree. Out of these 15 questions the first six questions are with respect to the environmental conditions of the destination due to tourism and the remaining questions are regarding the initiatives to be carried towards the improvement of environment. The last three questions are about rate of water waste discharge and solid waste discharge; and loss of vegetation. An another schedule for pilgrims contains 7 statements about the conditions of environment and these statements are common to the statements of schedule for the officers. Here, the paired t- test has been applied to test the significance of difference of opinion among the tourists before the start of the visit and thereafter i.e. the difference between the expectations and the experiences of the tourists.

Data Analysis and Interpretation

The statistical treatment of the data from tourists and officers during Vasanta Utsab and Paus Mela reveal the statements over which tourists differ significantly with respect to their expectation and experience. It also reveals the statements over which tourists and officers agree and disagree with each other significantly as well as insignificantly.

The table 1 clearly shows that the mean values experience (3.9733) and expectation (3.793) are above the score 3. The positive mean difference confirms the expectation.

Table 1. Results of paired t- test between tourists' expectations and experience of the environmental aspects

S.No.	Statements	Experience mean	Expectation Mean	Mean difference	t-value
1	Vehicular traffic has affected the air quality during Mela and Utsav	3.9733	3.7933	.18	5.719
2	Mela and Utsav have increased the sewage problem	2.9867	2.9067	.08	3.6
3	Arrivals has increased the soil contamination	4.6000	4.3333	.2667	7.361
4	Increased number of tourists at the site has increased demand of water resources which has resulted in shortage of these resources	4.0	3.4667	.5333	8.082
5	Vegetation in and around Bolpur has been affected adversely due to the developmental projects at the destination	2.7333	2.9333	-0.2	8.761
6	Heavy rush of tourists during festivals cause congestion and suffocation.	4.7267	3.7267	1.0	3.737
7	There are frequent sights of garbage on the other side of the walking pathway	1.26667	1.6067	-0.34	22.538

Source: Field Survey, 2016-17

This shows that the vehicular traffic during Mela and Utsav have affected the air quality to some extent.

The mean value of 150 respondents for the statement *pilgrimage has increased the sewage problem that* is 2.9867 which is greater than experience mean value of 2.9067, having mean difference of .08. This shows that tourists are almost not sure about whether the sewage problems during the festivals have affected the place or not. This difference is quite significant as the p value being .000.

The statement *tourism has increased the soil contamination* has mean experience value 4.6000 and mean expectation 4.3333 with positive mean difference of .2667 along with significant difference of mean shows that tourists agree to the fact before and after the visit that the festivals have increased the contamination of soil.

The experience mean value 4.0000 and the expectation mean value 3.4667 for the statement *increased number of tourists at the site has increased demand of water resources which has resulted in shortage of these resources* reveal that tourists are having the disposition that the water resources have been affected due to heavy crowd and their experience too confirms their expectation. The significant difference with t value 8.082 emphasises that the matter needs a consideration.

Vegetation in and around Bolpur has been affected adversaly due to the development projects of the destination has mean value expectation 2.9333 and mean value experience 2.7333. The values reveal that the tourists are not so sure over the statement. The positive mean difference confirms their disposition that the vegetation has not been affected.

The experience mean value of 4.7267 and expectation mean value of 3.726 for the statement heavy *rush of tourists during festivals cause congestion and suffocation* show that the tourists agree to this fact that crowd at this area causes congestion and suffocation. The positive mean difference is also confirming the same. The mean value above 3 shows that they were almost agreeing to this fact before this visit. The positive mean difference confirms their earlier disposition

The statement *there are frequent sights of garbage on the other side of the walking path way* has mean value expectation 1.6067 and the mean value experience 1.2667 with negative mean difference (- .34). These values show that tourists disagree with any frequent sight of garbage.

Discussion of the Findings for Urban Ecotourism

Existence of significance difference in expectation and experience of pilgrims with respect to the environmental statements reveals that environmental features like air quality and water bodies have been affected adversely. In addition to it heavy rush at the destination causes congestion and suffocation. Tourists expressed their view that the over crowd deteriorates their satisfaction in paying obeisance to the goddess inside the cave (the final destination). So these issues need a special consideration from the authority. Vegetation and cleanliness are the two issues which are perceived at good side.

Discussion of the Findings for Rural Ecotourism

The *recent field visit and a survey* clearly show the three main loopholes for which alternative tourism is not developing in this area. These are pointed out here under.

1. Lack of initiative of the local entrepreneurs to nurture the business opportunities of tourism.
2. Lack of initiative of the government to properly assess the feasibilities of alternative tourism in suitable places.
3. Conventional avoidance of the domestic customer groups to emphasize on their near by places and/or attractions.
4. Lack of understanding the relationship between development and conservation.

The development of tourism in Birbhum and adjacent places in Burdwan is one of the emerging economic activities. Tourism at the domestic level needs to be developed following the pulse of the market and by considering the sustainable practices. Domestic population with high travel propensity, scarcity of holiday entitlement, increasing trend of excursion, many un-known information may be with historical and cultural evidences, overt and covert tribal and ethnic culture and above all the desire to know the places of ones own are some of the important factors of tourism motivation from within the region. Again the supply factors don't require massive investment often by multinational tourism developers that subsequently results in leakage of investment and major benefits are not accrued to the local people. So, considering the available attraction features, community needs, existing and possible supportive infrastructure and supply factors alternative tourism will be the best suitable tourism development option to extend tourism which is so far confined to an elitist tag.

Strategies for Zoning

After studying potential of ecotourism in Bolpur and its adjacent places, various strategies have been suggested. Activities like trekking along jungles, village visit and home stay, forest trails, nature walks, etc can be developed to attract ecotourists. All these activities have to be conducted in a manner that promotes awareness of environment and helps maintain the fragile ecological balance. These activities can be categorized under following zones:

- Leisure zone
- Cultural zone
- Educational zone

Leisure Zone

Bolpur and Shantiniketan have innumerable locations that can serve as quiet retreats for those seeking *Shanti* (peace) and leisure away from the stress of modern urban life and as Gurudev Tagore and family sought earlier. Leisure tourism would centre around places that offer possibilities of leisured relaxation through favorable environment, potential view points, picturesque village surroundings. However, this activity is still far from reaching its fullest due to present total inadequacy of the supporting infrastructure.

Cultural Zone

From the point of view of Bengali culture and post colonial heritage, Bolpur and Shantiniketan are el Dorado. These places are something like Mecca where every Bengali wants to experience in his or her life span. Again, these places are of national importance to all. From the University museum to near around places are seemed to have been an open air museum of cultural achievement and respect for all. Activities can be well integrated with the varied passive tourism facilities including yoga, meditation, religious and cultural discourses. Picnic and day spending with local people can also be arranged with the purpose of understanding the local culture & tradition.

Educational Zone

Shantinikatan is already an educational zone. This place is where one interlink book with nature and society and vice versa. Even today, this is equally relevant and dignified as suggested by Gurudev Tagore. Educational tours can be organized for the students and researchers. The traveler can explore the flora and fauna of the nearby region. Awareness programme for the local people, tourists and service providers for the protection of environment, plantation of trees and animal protection should be organized there. Video film, destination brochures and information brochures should also be provide to the tourists at the destination.

Some eco-initiatives that must be considered by the policy makers are:

- Tree plantation
- Using biodegradable products like jute bags
- Awareness of environment and culture among locals and visitors.
- Special attention on carrying capacity
- Code of conduct to check the behaviour of tourists

EMPLOYMENT OF LOCAL PEOPLE

Ecotourism aims to meet higher social and environmental goals. The site for ecotourism will not only be developed to entertain the people but also for the benefit of local people. The project will not be successful without the help of local people. It has been observed that communities located near the major attraction sites such as nature parks, reserves, historic sites, etc should have the opportunity to participate in tourism related activities. Local people can be employed in hotels, restaurants, shops, transportation, guide and escort service and other tourist facilities and services. Also, they can be employed in management and operation of the attraction feature. Concrete financial benefits are obviously an important part of such a partnership. Local people should be involved in the planning and decision making process and must have a final say about how much and what kind of tourism development they want in their area.

REFERENCES

Amatya, P. H. (1997). Nepal's Experience with Ecotourism in Annapurna Conservation Area Project. In World Ecotour' 97 Abstracts Volume. Rio de Janiero, Brazil: BIOSFERA.

Bagri, S. C. (2005). (Submitted to). Ecotourism in Kedarnath Musk Deer Sanctuary. *Major Research Project.*

Boo, E. (1990). *Ecotourism, the Potential and Pitfalls. World Wild life Fund* .

District Statistical Handbook. (2011). Govt. of West Bengal Economic Review of West Bengal.

Dowling, R. K. (1998) *The Growth of Australian Ecotourism.* Paper presented at the NZ Tourism and Hospitality Research Conference, Third Biennial Conference, Akaroa, Canterbury, NZ.

Edward, S. N., Mehaughliu, W. J., & Ham, S. H. (1998). *Comparative Study of Ecotourism Policy in the Americas.* University of Idaho, Organisation of American States.

Gandotroa, N. (2000). *Sustainable Tourism in Vaishno Devi Hills.* WWF Jammu.

Handicrafts of Burdwan District. (2008). Ministry of Textiles, Govt. of India.

Haque, S. M., & Dar, S. A. (2007). Sustainable Approach to Ecotourism. In S. P. Bansal & ... (Eds.), *Cutting Edge Research in Tourism - Emerging Issues and Challenges* (pp. 249–261). Chandigarh: Aman Publication.

Harrison, D. (1997). Ecotourism in the South Pacific: The case of Fiji. In World Ecotour' 97 Abstracts Volume. Rio de Janiero, Brazil: BIOSFERA.

Inskeep, E. (1999). *Tourism Planning: An Integrated and Sustainable Development Approach.* New York: Van Nostrand Reinhold.

Kamra, K. K. (n.d.). *Managing Tourist Destination: Development, Planning, Marketing, Policies.* Kanishka Publication.

Kelkar, O. P. (2002). Ecotourism and Green Productivity in India. In T. Hundloe (Ed.), *Linking Green Productivity to Ecotourism-Experiences in the Asia Pacific Region.* Printery, Australia: University of Queensland.

Lascurain, H. C. (1996). *Tourism, Ecotourism and Protected Area.* Gland, Switzerland: IUCN.

Mishra, J. M. (2005). *Ecotourism Planning in the Garhwal Himalaya - A case study of Chomoli district of Uttarakhand State* (Unpublished PhD Thesis). HNB Garhwal University, Srinagar Garhwal.

Mohanlal, K. G. (2002). Ecotourism in Kerala. In T. Hundloe (Ed.), *Linking Green Productivity to Ecotourism-Experiences in the Asia Pacific Region.* Printery, Australia: University of Queensland.

Negi, J. S. (2007). *Rural Tourism and Economic Growth.* New Delhi: Cyber Tech Publications.

Ross & Geoffery. (1999). Ecotourism Toward Congruence between Theory and Practice. *Tourism Management, 20,* 123 – 133.

Sharma, J. K. (Ed.). (2008). Tourism Planning and Development, A New Perspective. New Delhi: Kanishka Publishers.

Tourism Policy of West Bengal. (1996). The Government of West Bengal.

UNWTO. (2007). *World Tourism Barometer.* Madrid: World Tourism Organisation.

Wood, E., Gatz, M. F., & Lindberg, K. (1995). Ecotourism Society: An action Agenda. In J. Kusler (Ed.), *Ecotourism and Resource Conservation* (pp. 75–79). Madison, WI: Omnipress.

Chapter 6
Sustainable Development and Ecotourism Consciousness:
An Empirical Analysis for Kallakurichi, Tamil Nadu, India

Abhijit Pandit
ⓘD https://orcid.org/0000-0003-2122-3468
Amity University, India

ABSTRACT

This chapter focuses on how people of Kallakurichi, Tamil Nadu, India can become conscious of ecotourism, bio-cultural diversity, and sustainable development, vital for both present and future. It utilized a sustainable development framework for considering biological and cultural perspectives. The primary target audience of this research was 100 local people of this lesser known and sparsely populated area, and 31 questionnaires were found to be useful. Simple random sampling was used in this regard. The collected data were analyzed using mean, t-test, Pearson's product moment correlation, and regression analysis. The researcher concluded with findings that point to the need for shared community authority, management, and decision making; mutual benefits; recognition of the rights, values, norms, power structures, and dynamics of local populations; respect for belief systems as well as traditional and local ecological knowledge; and the importance of contextual adaptation.

DOI: 10.4018/978-1-5225-8494-0.ch006

PURPOSE

This paper focuses on how people of Kallakurichi, Tamil Nadu, India can become conscious of ecotourism, bio-cultural diversity and sustainable development, which is vital for both present and future. It utilized a sustainable development framework for considering biological and cultural perspectives including human rights and social justice, the contribution of traditional knowledge, community involvement, and the effects of human impact and globalization.

Methods

The primary audience of this research was 31 local people of Kallakurichi selected by simple random sampling method. The researcher highlighted issues related to minimizing environmental impact, respecting local cultures, building environmental awareness, community participation, environment and ecosystem improvement facility, and providing direct financial benefits for conservation. Primary data were collected using a standardized questionnaire and were analyzed using mean, t-test, Pearson's product moment correlation and regression analysis.

Findings

The researcher concluded with findings that point to the need for shared community authority, management, and decision making; mutual benefits; recognition of the rights, values, norms, power structures, and dynamics of local populations; respect for belief systems as well as traditional and local ecological knowledge; and the importance of contextual adaptation.

Implications

There is lot of opportunity for Government as well as local people of Kallakurichi in order to promote eco-tourism as well as facilitate sustainable development of community.

INTRODUCTION

The framework for sustainable development describes society's commitment to four interconnected objectives: economic development (including the end of extreme poverty), social inclusion, environmental sustainability, and good governance (including security). Each of these four dimensions of sustainable development contributes to the other three, and all four are therefore necessary for individual and societal wellbeing. Sustainable development is sometimes described by the first three dimensions: economic, social, and environmental. We add good governance and personal security as a fourth dimension to highlight several enabling conditions for sustainable development, including transparency, effective institutions, the rule of law, participation and personal security, accountability, and adequate financing for public goods. These standards of good governance apply to the public sector, the private sector, and civil society.

Sustainable development, as defined by The World Commission on Environment and Development's (the Brundtland Commission) report is "development which meets the needs of the present without compromising the ability of future generations to meet their own needs" (1987, p. 16). The United Nations Environment Programme (UNEP) together with the World Tourism Organization (WTO) (2005, p. 9) further divide sustainability into three subsections: social, economic, and environmental, which are defined as follows:

- Social sustainability means respecting human rights and equal opportunities for all in society. It requires an equitable distribution of benefits, with a focus on alleviating poverty. There is an emphasis on local communities, maintaining and strengthening their life support systems, recognizing and respecting different cultures, and avoiding any form of exploitation.
- Economic sustainability means generating prosperity at different levels of society and addressing the cost-effectiveness of all economic activity. Crucially, it is about the viability of enterprises and activities and their ability to be maintained in the long term.
- Environmental sustainability means conserving and managing resources, especially those that are not renewable or are precious in terms of life support. It requires action to minimize pollution of air, land and water, and to conserve biological diversity and natural heritage.

REVIEW OF RELEVANT LITERATURE

According to Maffi and Woodley's (2010) Biocultural diversity conservation: A global sourcebook, "comprises the diversity of life in all of its manifestations – biological, cultural, and linguistic – which are interrelated (and likely co-evolved) within a complex socio-ecological adaptive system."

Figure 1. Diagrammatic representation of sustainable development illustrating the environmental, social, and economic aspects and their overlaps

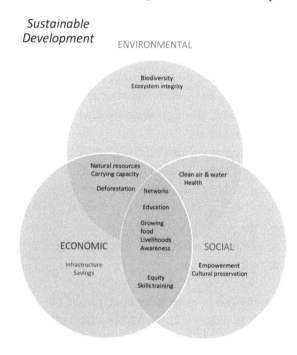

Figure 2. Diagrammatic representation of biocultural diversity illustrating how biological and cultural diversity influence conservation issues

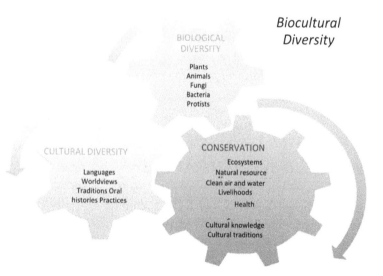

Figure 3. Responsible community-based ecotourism, involving both ecological and cultural responsibility

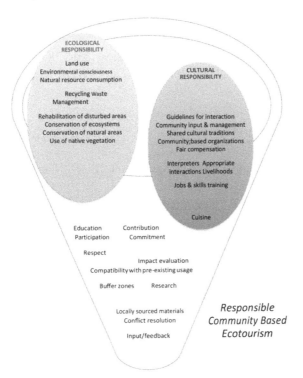

The concept of community-based ecotourism, which, in this context, is a combination of three definitions. The first one has been adopted by the IUCN (International Union for Conservation of Nature), which defines ecotourism as

"environmentally responsible travel and visitation to relatively undisturbed natural areas, in order to enjoy and appreciate nature (and any accompanying cultural features—both past and present) that promotes conservation, has low visitor impact, and provides for beneficially active socio-economic involvement of local populations" (Ceballos- Lascuráin, 1996).

The second definition by Martha Honey (2008) includes building environmental and cultural awareness, recognizing the rights and spiritual beliefs of the indigenous people in the community, and providing direct financial benefits for conservation.

The third definition by The International Ecotourism Society (2010) defines ecotourism as "responsible travel to natural areas that conserves the environment and improves the well- being of local people."

The conservation movement often includes a definition of natural areas that excludes human settlements and many forms of human activities, both past and present. All humans need clean air, clean water, food, shelter, and so on, but who is to decide where protected areas will be located, and who is to suffer the short-term consequences in exchange for long-term gains? Ecotourism can contribute by involving local stakeholders. This can reduce conflict and produce long-term sustainability within these protected areas (Elias, 2012; Klein, Réau, Kalland, & Edwards, 2007; Lepp & Holland, 2006; Snyman, 2012b, 2014a, 2014c).

OBJECTIVES

The objectives of present study are to determine:

1. The demographic profile of local people of Kallakurichi.
2. The level of attitude towards sustainable eco-tourism of local people of Kallakurichi.
3. Whether any significant association exists between demographic factors of local people of Kallakurichi and their attitude towards sustainable eco-tourism.

METHOD

The primary audience of this research was 31 local people of Kallakurichi selected by simple random sampling method. The researcher highlighted issues related to minimizing environmental impact, respecting local cultures, building environmental awareness, community participation, environment and ecosystem improvement facility, and providing direct financial benefits for conservation. Central research question is: *How can local people help to preserve the environment, be sensitive to local cultures, and contribute to a sustainable future?* Primary data were collected using a standardized questionnaire and were analyzed using mean, t-test, Pearson's product moment correlation and regression analysis.

PROCEDURE

The study is based on primary sources. Primary data were collected using simple random sampling from local people of Kallakurichi, Tamilnadu, India with the help of questionnaire consisting of two sections- the first section is related to demographic profile and second section is for capturing responses on attitude towards sustainable eco-tourism.

RESULTS

The means and standard deviations (SDs) of scores for main variables of study with 95% confidence intervals were calculated and presented in Table 1.

Correlation among various demographic parameters and various parameters of attitude towards community-based sustainable eco-tourism is shown in Tables 2 and 3.

Count of factors in-between various parameters is shown below in Table 4.

Following table shows Multiple Regression Analysis with Suggestions for Sustainable Eco-tourism as dependent variable and independent variables as Age,

Table 1. Descriptive statistics

		Value	95% Confidence Interval	
			Lower	Upper
Mean	Age	2.16	1.84	2.55
	Residence	2.68	2.32	3.03
	Marital_status	1.61	1.45	1.77
	Educational_qualification	2.42	2.03	2.84
	Occupation	2.45	1.97	2.93
	Monthly_income	2.81	2.26	3.45
	Socio_economic_impact	1.7323	1.5984	1.8609
	Improvement_facility	1.8848	1.6920	2.0822
	Ecotourism_impact_culture	1.7748	1.6371	1.9219
	Ecotourism_impact_ecosystem	1.7484	1.6065	1.9000
	Suggestions	2.0552	1.9113	2.2125
Std. Deviation	Age	1.003	.783	1.148
	Residence	.979	.755	1.141
	Marital_status	.495	.425	.508
	Educational_qualification	1.177	.877	1.407
	Occupation	1.410	1.180	1.567
	Monthly_income	1.740	1.311	2.022
	Socio_economic_impact	.37500	.30275	.43018
	Improvement_facility	.57411	.49285	.63386
	Ecotourism_impact_culture	.41749	.31833	.48090
	Ecotourism_impact_ecosystem	.40569	.31195	.47387
	Suggestions	.44036	.34697	.50068

Table 2. Correlations among demographic parameters

		Age	Residence	Marital_ status	Educational_ qualification	Occupation	Monthly_ income
Age	Pearson Correlation	1	.326	.600**	-.257	-.195	.114
	Sig. (2-tailed)		.073	.000	.163	.294	.542
Residence	Pearson Correlation	.326	1	.490**	-.284	-.229	.099
	Sig. (2-tailed)	.073		.005	.122	.216	.596
Marital_ status	Pearson Correlation	.600**	.490**	1	-.113	-.123	.220
	Sig. (2-tailed)	.000	.005		.547	.509	.235
Educational_ qualification	Pearson Correlation	-.257	-.284	-.113	1	.464**	.399*
	Sig. (2-tailed)	.163	.122	.547		.008	.026
Occupation	Pearson Correlation	-.195	-.229	-.123	.464**	1	.390*
	Sig. (2-tailed)	.294	.216	.509	.008		.030
Monthly_ income	Pearson Correlation	.114	.099	.220	.399*	.390*	1
	Sig. (2-tailed)	.542	.596	.235	.026	.030	
**Correlation is significant at the 0.01 level (2-tailed). *Correlation is significant at the 0.05 level (2-tailed).							

Residence, Marital status, Educational Qualification, Occupation and Monthly Income. Moreover results of paired t-tests between the dependent and all the independent variables taken one at a time are also shown.

DISCUSSION

Results indicated the following points:

1. There is significant association between the following pairs of demographic factors:
   a. Age and Marital Status,
   b. Residence and Marital Status,
   c. Educational Qualification and Occupation,
   d. Educational Qualification and Monthly Income,
   e. Monthly Income and Occupation.
2. There is significant association between the following pairs of factors measuring attitude towards community-based sustainable eco-tourism:
   a. Socio-economic Impact and Improvement Facility,
   b. Socio-economic Impact and Ecotourism Impact on Culture,

Table 3. Correlations among parameters to measure attitude towards sustainable ecotourism

		Socio_ economic_ impact	Improvement_ facility	Ecotourism_ impact_ culture	Ecotourism_ impact_ ecosystem	Suggestions
Socio_ economic_ impact	Pearson Correlation	1	.711**	.607**	-.249	.478**
	Sig. (2-tailed)		.000	.000	.176	.007
Improvement_ facility	Pearson Correlation	.711**	1	.710**	-.332	.727**
	Sig. (2-tailed)	.000		.000	.068	.000
Ecotourism_ impact_ culture	Pearson Correlation	.607**	.710**	1	-.111	.730**
	Sig. (2-tailed)	.000	.000		.553	.000
Ecotourism_ impact_ ecosystem	Pearson Correlation	-.249	-.332	-.111	1	.022
	Sig. (2-tailed)	.176	.068	.553		.908
Suggestions	Pearson Correlation	.478**	.727**	.730**	.022	1
	Sig. (2-tailed)	.007	.000	.000	.908	
**Correlation is significant at the 0.01 level (2-tailed).						
*Correlation is significant at the 0.05 level (2-tailed).						

c.   Socio-economic Impact and Suggestions,

d.   Eco-tourism Impact on Culture and Improvement Facility,

e.   Improvement Facility and Suggestions,

f.   Eco-tourism Impact on Culture and Suggestions.

3.   Positive association exists between suggestions for promoting sustainable ecotourism and independent variables: occupation, residence and age of local people of Kallakurichi.

4.   Local people of Kallakurichi have favourable attitude towards community-based sustainable eco-tourism.

Table 4. Between-subjects factors

		Value Label	**Count (N)**
Age	1	18-30 years	10
	2	31-40 years	9
	3	41-50years	9
	4	51 years / above	3
Residence	1	last 10 years	4
	2	11-20 years	9
	3	21-30 years	11
	4	31 years / above	7
Marital_status	1	single	12
	2	married	19
Educational_qualification	1	primary education	8
	2	secondary education	9
	3	graduation	9
	4	post graduation	3
	5	others	2
Occupation	1	agriculture	12
	2	small business	5
	3	job in hotel/restaurant/transport	4
	4	govt employee	8
	5	unemployed	2
Monthly_income	1	less than Rs 5000	9
	2	Rs 5001 to Rs 10000	7
	3	Rs 10001 to Rs 15000	7
	4	Rs 15001 to Rs 20000	1
	5	Rs 20000 to Rs 25000	3
	6	Rs 25000 or above	4

LIMITATIONS

The main limitation of the study is the sample selection. It is confined to 31 local people of Kallakurichi selected by simple random sampling method. The credibility of the results will be enhanced by increasing the sample size covering local people of different parts of the country having rich bio-cultural diversity. The second limitation

Table 5.

Parameters	Unstandardized Coefficients		Standardized Coefficients	t	Sig.
	B	Std. Error	Beta		
(Constant)	2.289	.398		5.745**	.000
Age	.041	.102	.092	.396	.696
Residence	.092	.098	.205	.942	.355
Marital_status	-.280	.221	-.314	-1.263	.219
Educational_qualification	-.121	.084	-.322	-1.433	.165
Occupation	.110	.067	.353	1.640	.114
Monthly_income	-.034	.055	-.134	-.616	.544
**. Correlation is significant at the 0.01 level (2-tailed).					
*. Correlation is significant at the 0.05 level (2-tailed).					

is that the findings are based on the responses to the questionnaire which may be different from actual behaviour. The third limitation is that the study only considers local people. Comparative study including local people, tourists and people from government and non-governmental sectors may be useful.

Another important influence is researcher bias: this paper was approached with a goal to preserve the environment. Did this bias the researcher away from cultural preservation? How it is possible to understand how people are living, who work and gather resources so they can put food on their table, take care of their families, and merely survive, while researcher is simply an observer. It comes around to starting at home: consuming less, reducing our natural resource usage, and so forth. In short, the Best Practices are not just for eco-tourist operators or government, they are for all of us to follow in our home environments as well. We must care for our environment, use natural resources sustainably, utilize local materials, promote local involvement, respect local cultures, increase public awareness, disperse benefits, address inequities, keep businesses and governments accountable, consider the rights of all species, and work together towards a solution.

Furthermore, it is not just about our own species, it is about all species, the interconnected nature of our planet is dependent upon the great diversity of ecosystems that work together to make it habitable for us all. Last but not the least, present study is a cross-sectional in nature. Longitudinal study may provide different insight.

IMPLICATIONS

Despite having limitations, the study has some significant implications:

- There is lot of opportunity for Government as well as local people of Kallakurichi in order to promote eco-tourism as well as facilitate sustainable development of community.
- The following list of questions that might help to further the research on the topic of environmentally and culturally responsible tourism, and ultimately, the goal of sustaining our planet:
  - ○ What would make the most impact to help support bio-cultural diversity?
  - ○ What could be derived from impact evaluations, and how could we use them?
  - ○ Where might our monetary support have the most influence?
  - ○ Are there general investments that are universally good for supporting cultural and biological diversity?

CONCLUSION

The researcher concludes by emphasizing the necessity for hands-on experience in this field of inquiry. Researcher's interest in bio-cultural diversity came from years of travel, looking for biodiversity around the world, while observing and appreciating the vast diversity of cultures that make it such an interesting place. There is necessity for intercultural communication through wanting to understand the influence international travel and conservation has on local communities. One must appreciate that conservation is not just about what is good for everyone (the "common good") but also about who can afford to care about their futures, not just day-to-day survival. We must open our eyes to the complexity of conservation practices, looking beyond sustainable development to the need for collaborative efforts in order to make this a reality and save our precious natural resources.

Having a local people who work in the field of conservation and ecotourism was crucial to completion of this research. It was important to this researcher that something that "made a difference" could be done. Seeking biologically diverse ecosystems requires travel to remote areas, and there must be a conscious decision made about resource use and cultural impacts. There is a start at certifying "green" tourist companies with programs such as The International Ecotourism Society (TIES) and Fair Trade Tourism, which have certification programs for the tourism industry that encourages responsible tourism (Harmony, 5/10/2008), but there are problems with certification, which is beyond the scope of this research work. Such issues as standardization, government support, criteria for certification, ongoing certification, and the question of how businesses in foreign countries become certified only begin to delve into the complexity of green ecotourism. This leads into the topic of impact assessments. It is nearly impossible to evaluate progress towards sustainable development without progress reports, and careful attention needs to be paid to make sure impact assessments are properly carried out and acted upon.

This paper is written from a sustainable development approach. One might find entirely different results if one were to look purely from a biological or anthropological perspective. It is not a socially just option to make decisions about which culture is more important to conserve than another, nor is it ethical to consider one species as more important than another. But it always comes around to who gets to make those decisions.

REFERENCES

Aas, C., Ladkin, A., & Fletcher, J. (2005). Stakeholder collaboration and heritage management. *Annals of Tourism Research*, *32*(1), 28–48. doi:10.1016/j.annals.2004.04.005

Apollo, M. (2018). Ethics in tourism as a key to development, prosperity and well-being of all stakeholders: 3rd International Congress on Ethics and Tourism, Krakow, 27–28 April 2017. *International Journal of Environmental Studies, 75*(2), 361–365. doi:10.1080/00207233.2017.1383076

Appiah-Opoku, S. (2007). Indigenous beliefs and environmental stewardship: A rural Ghana experience. *Journal of Cultural Geography*, *24*(2), 79–98. doi:10.1080/08873630709478212

Arunotai, N. (2006). Moken traditional knowledge: An unrecognised form of natural resources management and conservation. *International Social Science Journal*, *58*(187), 139–150. doi:10.1111/j.1468-2451.2006.00599.x

Baer, A. (1989). Maintaining biocultural diversity. *Conservation Biology*, *3*(1), 97–98. doi:10.1111/j.1523-1739.1989.tb00233.x

Balint, P., & Mashinya, J. (2008). CAMPFIRE during Zimbabwe's national crisis: Local impacts and broader implications for community-based wildlife management. *Society & Natural Resources*, *21*(9), 783–796. doi:10.1080/08941920701681961

Ballet, J., Sirven, N., & Requiers-Desjardins, M. (2007). Social capital and natural resource management. *Journal of Environment & Development*, *16*(4), 355–374. doi:10.1177/1070496507310740

Baskin, J. (1995). *Local economic development: Tourism - Good or Bad? In Tourism workshop proceedings: small, medium, micro enterprises*. Johannesburg: Land and Agriculture Policy Center.

Beck, J. A. (2012). A biocultural approach to development. *Terralingua, 3*. Retrieved from http://www.terralingua.org/bcdconservation/?p=1493

Becker, C. D., & Ghimire, K. (2003). Synergy between traditional ecological knowledge and conservation science supports forest preservation in Ecuador. *Ecology and Society*, *8*(1).

Berkes, F. (1999). *Sacred ecology: Traditional ecological knowledge and resource management*. New York, NY: Taylor & Francis.

Berkes, F., & Berkes, M. K. (2009). Ecological complexity, fuzzy logic, and holism in indigenous knowledge. *Futures*, *41*(1), 6–12. doi:10.1016/j.futures.2008.07.003

Berkes, F., Colding, J., & Folke, C. (2000). Rediscovery of traditional ecological knowledge as adaptive management. *Ecological Applications*, *10*(5), 1251–1262. doi:10.1890/1051-0761(2000)010[1251:ROTEKA]2.0.CO;2

Blaustein, R. J. (2007). Protected areas and equity concerns. *Bioscience*, *57*(3), 216–221.

Blount, B. G. (2001). Indigenous peoples and the uses and abuses of ecotourism. In L. Maffi (Ed.), *On biocultural diversity: Linking language, knowledge, and the environment* (pp. 503–516). Washington, DC: Smithsonian Institution Press.

BookDifferent. (2016). Retrieved from http://www.bookdifferent.com/en/

Borrini-Feyerabend, G., Dudley, N., Jaeger, T., Lassen, B., Broome, N. P., Phillips, A., & Sandwith, T. (2013). *Governance of protected areas: From understanding to action.* Retrieved from http://cmsdata.iucn.org/downloads/governance_of_protected_areas from_understanding_to_action.pdf

Bossel, H. (1999). *Indicators for sustainable development: Theory, method, applications.* Winnipeg, MB: International Institute for Sustainable Development.

Bourdieu, P. (1990). *The logic of practice.* Stanford, CA: Stanford University Press.

Breaky, N., Ruhanen, L., & Shakeela, A. (2004). The Role of Employment in the Sustainable Development Paradigm—The Local Tourism Labor Market in Small Island Developing States". *Journal of Human Resources in Hospitality & Tourism*, *10*(4). doi:10.1080/15332845.2011.588493

Bridgewater, P. (2002). Biosphere reserves: Special places for people and nature. *Environmental Science & Policy*, *5*(1), 9–12.

Brockington, D. (2007). Forests, community conservation, and local government performance: The Village Forest Reserves of Tanzania. *Society & Natural Resources*, *20*(9), 835–848. doi:10.1080/08941920701460366

Brohman, J. (1996). New Directions in Tourism for Third World Development. *Annals of Tourism Research*, 23.

Brohman, J. (n.d.). New Directions in Tourism for Third World Development. *Annals of Tourism Research, 23.*

Brohman, J. (1996). New directions in tourism for third world development. *Annals of Tourism Research, 23*, 48–70. Available at: http://www.ansvarligturisme.org/CapeTown.html

Brosius, J., & Hitchner, S. L. (2010). Cultural diversity and conservation. *International Social Science Journal, 61*(199), 141–168. doi:10.1111/j.1468-2451.2010.01753.x

Canavan, B. (2014). Sustainable tourism: Development, decline and de-growth. Management issues from the Isle of Man". *Journal of Sustainable Tourism, 22*(1), 127–147. doi:10.1080/09669582.2013.819876

Carlson, T. J., & Maffi, L. (2004). *Ethnobotany and conservation of biocultural diversity*. Bronx, NY: New York Botanical Garden Press.

Carroll, A. (1998). Corporate Social Responsibility. *Business & Society, 3*(38), 268–295. doi:10.1177/000765039903800303

Castellino, D. (2013). *Social inclusion & human rights: Implications for 2030 and beyond.* Retrieved from http://unsdsn.org/wp-content/uploads/2014/02/130114-Social-Exclusion-and-Human-Rights-Paper-for-HLP.pdf

Cohen, S., Higham, J., & Cavaliere, C. (2011). Binge flying: Behavioural addiction and climate change. *Annals of Tourism Research, 38*(3), 1070–1089. doi:10.1016/j.annals.2011.01.013

Cohen, S., Higham, J.E., Peeters, P., & Gossling, S. (2014). Why tourism mobility behaviours must change. In *Understanding and Governing Sustainable Tourism Mobility: Psychological and Behavioural Approaches*. Academic Press.

Croall, J. (1995). *Preserve or Destroy: Tourism and the Environment*. London: Calouste Gulbenkian Foundation.

Drake, S. (1991). *Local Participation in ecotourism project. In Nature Tourism* (p. 132). Washington, DC: Island Press.

Epler Wood, M. (1991). Global Solutions: on ecotourism society. In *Nature Tourism* (p. 204). Washington, DC: Island Press.

Friedman, M. (1962). *Capitalism and Freedom*. Chicago: University of Chicago Press.

Gössling, S., Ceron, J. P., Dubois, G., Hall, C. M., Gössling, I. S., Upham, P., & Earthscan, L. (2009). Hypermobile travellers Archived 2010-06-19 at the Wayback Machine. In Climate Change and Aviation: Issues, Challenges and Solutions. Academic Press.

Gossling, S., Hall, M., Peeters, P., & Scott, D. (2010). The future of tourism: Can tourism growth and climate policy be reconciled? A mitigation perspective. *Tourism Recreation Research*, *35*(2), 119–130. doi:10.1080/02508281.2010.11081628

Harrison, D. (1992). *International Tourism in the less developed countries*. Chichester, UK: Wiley.

Høyer, K. G. (2000). Sustainable tourism or sustainable mobility? The Norwegian case. *Journal of Sustainable Tourism*, *8*(2), 147–160. doi:10.1080/09669580008667354

Larsen, G. R., & Guiver, J. W. (2013). Understanding tourists' perceptions of distance: A key to reducing the environmental impacts of tourism mobility. *Journal of Sustainable Tourism*, *21*(7), 968–981. doi:10.1080/09669582.2013.819878

Lea, J. P. (1988). *Tourism and Development in the Third World*. London: Routledge.

Malhado A., de Araujo L., Rothfuss R. (2014). The attitude-behaviour gap and the role of information in influencing sustainable mobility in mega-events. In *Understanding and Governing Sustainable Tourism Mobility: Psychological and Behavioural Approaches*. Academic Press.

Moisey, R. N. (2008). Tourism, recreation, and sustainability: linking culture and the environment (2nd ed.). Wallingford, UK: CABI.

Monbiot, G. (1994). *No Man's Land*. London: Macmillan.

Mowforth, M., & Munt, I. (1998). *Tourism and Sustainability: New Tourism in the Third World*. London: Routledge. doi:10.4324/9780203437292

Mowforth, M., & Munt, I. (1998). *Tourism and Sustainability: New Tourism in the Third World*. London: Routledge. doi:10.4324/9780203437292

Mycoo, M. (2014). Sustainable tourism, climate change and sea level rise adaptation policies in Barbados". *Natural Resources Forum*, *38*.

Peeters, P., & Dubois, G. (2010). Tourism travel under climate change mitigation constraints. *Journal of Transport Geography*, *18*(3), 447–457. doi:10.1016/j.jtrangeo.2009.09.003

Peeters P., Gössling S., Ceron J.P., Dubois G., Patterson T., Richardson R.B., & Studies E. (2004). *The Eco-efficiency of Tourism*. Academic Press.

Pizam, A. (2009). Editorial: Green hotels: A fad, ploy or fact of life? *International Journal of Hospitality Management*, *1*(28). doi:10.1016/j.ijhm.2008.09.001

Queiroz, R., Guerreiro, J., & Ventura, M. A. (2014). Demand of the tourists visiting protected areas in small oceanic islands: The Azores case-study (Portugal). *Environment, Development and Sustainability, 16*(5), 1119–1135. doi:10.100710668-014-9516-y

Reay, D. S. (2004). New Directions: Flying in the face of the climate change convention. *Atmospheric Environment, 38*(5), 793–794. doi:10.1016/j.atmosenv.2003.10.026

Scheyvens, R. (1999). Ecotourism and the Empowerment of Local Communities. *Tourism Management, 20*(2), 245–249. doi:10.1016/S0261-5177(98)00069-7

Scheyvens, R. (2002). Backpacker tourism and third world development. *Annals of Tourism Research, 1*(29), 144–164. doi:10.1016/S0160-7383(01)00030-5

Thuot, L., Vaugeois, N., & Maher, P. (2010). Fostering innovation in sustainable tourism. *Journal of Rural and Community Development, 5*, 76–89. doi:10.25316/ir-138

Trejos, B., & Chiang, L. H. N. (2009). Local economic linkages to community-based tourism in rural Costa Rica". *Singapore Journal of Tropical Geography, 30*(3), 373–387. doi:10.1111/j.1467-9493.2009.00375.x

Twinning-Ward, L., & Butler, R. (2002). Implementing STD on a Small Island: Development and Use of Sustainable Tourism Development Indicators in Samoa". *Journal of Sustainable Tourism, 10*(5), 363–387. doi:10.1080/09669580208667174

WTTC, WTO & Earth Council. (1995). Agenda 21 for the travel and tourism industry: Towards Environmentally Sustainable Development. London: WTTC.

Chapter 7
Understanding the Importance of the Banking System in the Romanian Tourism and Hospitality Industry

Cristi Spulbar
University of Craiova, Romania

Birău Ramona
Constantin Brâncusi University of Targu Jiu, Romania

Jatin Trivedi
Amity University Mumbai, India

ABSTRACT

This chapter aims to provide an exhaustive overview of the importance of banking system in Romanian tourism and hospitality industry. Romania is a member of the European Union since 1 January 2007, but is not a member of the Schengen area and haven't adopted the euro currency yet. The banking system plays an essential role in financial intermediation being a major factor in raising productivity of Romanian tourism and hospitality industry. From a long-term perspective, a global perspective on the banking system can lead to the development of tourism and hospitality business. The interdependence between banking system and the tourism and hospitality industry in Romania is an increasing challenge for public and private investment. However, Romania's tourist attractions are still not capitalized due to the lack of financial investments. The Romanian tourism potential is significant, but the relatively low number of foreign tourists and even indigenous tourists reflects the lack of relevant financial investments and effective promotion.

DOI: 10.4018/978-1-5225-8494-0.ch007

INTRODUCTION

The main purpose of this book chapter is to provide a comprenhensive framework on understanding the essential role of banking system in Romanian tourism and hospitality industry. Tourism a multidimensional phenomenon with very complex implications. However, the banking system has a significant importance in terms of financial funding. Moreover, the acces to international bank funding provides a significant development opportunity for Romanian tourism and hospitality industry. Romania is a part in various international tourism agreements signed with countries all around the world. Naturally, every country in the world needs to exploit its tourism potential in order to attract foreign capital for sustaining tourism and hospitality industry. Romania is an European tourist destination with a a great growth potential. The natural landscape of Romania is centered on three main pillars, the Carpathian Mountains, the Danube River and the Black Sea.

Over the last few decades, Romania have signed bilateral tourism agreements with many countries all around the world. The development of tourism in Romania depends largely on the influx of foreign tourists and implicitly on attracting foreign investment capital. The international cooperation is an essential aspect for tourism development in Romania. At the local level, the development of Romanian tourism requires an accelerated improvement based on sustainable investment strategies. Governmental international agreement on cooperation in the tourism sector are very important for the development of this industry as well hospitality industry. The sustainability of Romanian tourism and hospitality industry is important in order to achieve economic growth. This book chapter also provides a complex analysis on the banking system in Romania highlighting theoretical aspects, official statistical data and comparative empirical investigations.

The legislative framework includes numerous international agreements on tourism cooperation between the government of Romania and the government of various countries, such as: Albania, Austria, Belarus the Federative Republic of Brazil, Bulgaria, China, Cyprus, Colombia, Croatia, Egypt, Philippines, Finland, Georgia, Greece, India, Iran, Israel, Italy, Yugoslavia, Macedonia, Morocco, Mexico, Libya, Peru, Poland, Portugal, Turkey, Hungary, Venezuela and many other countries (many of these agreements being signed before Romania's accession to the European Union on January 1, 2007). Romania shares borders with certain neighboring countries, ie Moldova and Ukraine lies to the east, Bulgaria lies to the south, Serbia and Hungary lies to the west, but also has a maritime delimitation, bordering the Black Sea. Romania has a strategic geographical position which can bring many benefits in the field of tourism.

Romania is a former communist Eastern European country. However, on January 1, 2007, Romania became a member of the European Union. Moreover, Romania became a member of the North Atlantic Treaty Organisation (NATO) on March 29, 2004. Romania joined this international alliance considering its significant implications for national security and stability. Romania and United States share an mature Strategic Partnership which generates strategic cooperation in various fields such as military, economical or political. However, this strategic partnership led to the installation of an important U.S. missile shield at Deveselu Air Base in Olt county, in southern Romania. This aspect provides increased security for Romanian citizens, including for foreign tourists in Romania in the context of rather frequent terrorist attacks across the globe.

Metaphorically, Romania is an island of pro-Western and pro-European democracy surrounded by various pro-Russian country positions. Romania has significant tourist potential, including castles, parks, historic buildings, natural landscapes, churches and monasteries as well as modern tourist attractions such as malls, luxury shops, workshops with traditional Romanian products. The uniqueness of certain transforms Romania into a very attractive tourist destination. Romania is famous for its mineral waters, thermal springs, balneotherapeutic resorts and natural spa resources. The beneficial effects of medical tourism in Romania are extremely varied considering the impressive natural potential. Nevertheless, rural communities is a major opportunity to exploit the tourism potential, especially with regard to special, particular natural areas. The Romanian tourism and hospitality industry is in a great measure affected by the lack of financial funds. Moreover, government authorities must implement sustainable development programs for tourism and hospitality industry.

LITERATURE REVIEW

In the literature there are numerous studies on tourism and its implications for the real economy of a country. Moreover hospitality industry is a complementary dimension but indispensable in managing efficient tourism policies. However, this professional symbiosis involves a complex activity that can lead to significant profits by implementing sustainable strategies. Busuioc, Simon, Niculescu and Trifanescu (2016) has analyzed the concept of ethnographic tourism and argued that it mainly consists of the link between two distinct cultures, that is, the culture of the tourist and the host, based on a multitude of events, festivals, celebrations and various other types of entertainment meant for enjoyment and spending spare time. Birau & Co (2015) investigated relevant issues on international tourism and hospitality by disseminating a variety of topics of great interest. Patrichi (2013) has provided an interesting study on dark tourism in Romania identifying certain places with great tourist potential, such as: Merry Cemetery in Sapanta, Bellu Cemetery in Bucharest or Sighetul Marmatiei Prison, one of the dark prisons of communism, especially used for the extermination of the Romanian elites.

Tutunea and Rus (2011) have conducted empirical research on Mobile-tourism in Romania in order to capture a detailed framework on mobile-services market in Romanian tourism thus identifying the existence of certain underdeveloped and unexploited market segments with significant marketing potential. In another train of thoughts, Khan, Khaled and Shambour (2018) investigated relevant aspects regarding mobile applications for Hajj and Umrah services in order to identify user behavior considering the annual magnitude of Islamic ritually pilgrimage. Furthermore, Tutunea (2016) has expanded empirical analysis by providing a study on Mobile applications for tourism based on a study regarding their use by Romanians and has concluded that the profile of tourist - user of mobile devices from Romania is based on three main pillars, ie: a socio-demographic profile, a mobility profile and a tourism-related mobile application user profile. Axinte and Spulbar (2009) have conducted a comprehensive analysis on tourism development in Romania and have highlighted the importance of tourism advertising and marketing as well as promoting tourism destination strongly based on competitive advantages.

Hall (1993) has conducted a research study on the ecotourism in the Danube Delta which is largely located on the territory of Romania and pointed out that it is probably "the most important wildlife area in Europe". In addition, Dragin, Jovičić and Lukić (2010) investigated the impact of the river Danube, ie the international cruises along the Pan-European Corridor VII also known as the Danube Waterway on the Serbia's tourism economy. Iorga (2015) conducted a research study on rural protected area from Romania by analyzing relevant aspects regarding economic and social development in the Danube Delta. On the other hand, Hein, Schwarz, Habersack, Nichersu, Preine, Willby and Weigelhofer (2016) have performed a more detailed analysis on restoration options for floodplains along the Danube River considering their status as essential ecosystems of riverine landscapes.

Another major tourist attraction in Romania is the castle of Count Dracula based on the Bram Stoker's classic novel of the vampire in Transylvania. Despite the fact that this type of tourism is especially preferred by a certain audience, the international recognition based on movies, commercials, music videos, books, documentaries is a major asset in attracting both foreign and Romanian tourists. Numerous research studies have been conducted on the impact of Dracula vampire bloody legend on Romanian tourism. In general, the profane Romanian customs, but historically unconfirmed analogy, associate the myth of Count Dracula with the Romanian voivode Vlad Tepes, known for his bloodless methods of punishing the enemies.

Razak and Ibrahim (2017) investigated the importance of myths and legends in tourism and suggested that these important elements can make a significant contribution to stimulating existing tourist attractions while being highlighted as tangible assets for tourists. Candrea, Ispas, Untaru and Nechita (2016) have conducted a research study on the potential of the Dracula's myth "as a unique competitive advantage" to revive Romanian tourism. Moreover, Light (2007) has highlighted relevant issues regarding Dracula tourism in Romania based on cultural identity and the state. Cosma, Pop and Negrusa (2007) also conducted a research study on the possibility that Count Dragula's myth might be a brand for Romanian tourism as tourist destination and concluded that, despite the negative impact of the character, it can be used as an intricate product for promoting Romanian tourism.

The hospitality literature is very vast and heterogeneous while reaching multiple interdisciplinary dimensions. Chan and Hsu (2016) provided a very comprehensive research study on environmental management (EM) research in hospitality industry based on the review of 149 hospitality -related studies published between 1993 and 2014 and have proposed new future research directions which to include green marketing, environmental technologies, environmental reporting, carbon footprint, employees' green behaviour, the effects of EM on hospitality firms' stakeholders and small - and medium - sized hospitality firms. Jogaratnam, McCleary, Mena and Yoo (2005) provides a complex overview based on research contributions on 11 leading hospitality and tourism journals from 1992 to 2001.

Kukoyi and Iwuagwu (2015) have analyzed relevant issues on the interconnection between service delivery and customer satisfaction in hospitality industry at the Divine Fountain Hotels Limited, Lagos, Nigeria and concluding that these two variables have a major implication in improving service quality and obtaining higher revenue. Moreover, Parsa, Harrington and Ottenbacher (2009) have provided a very interesting study based on a multitude of theoretical approaches from the literature. Li and Singal (2018) have conducted a research study on firm financial performance in the hospitality industry and have also highlighted the essential role of compensation practices in achieving the performance goals.

Obiora and Nwokorie (2018) discussed interesting issues regarding the performance of rural youth entrepreneurship in hospitality sector based on a case study of Ihitte Uboma, Imo State Nigeria by identifying relevant aspects that contribute to achieve this goal, such as urban drifts and development of local communities. In addition, Antara and Prameswari (2018) have provided a broad picture on the most significant push factors, ie status and personal development (F2), culture (F1) and interpersonal relationship (F4) and pull factors, ie people (F10), atmosphere and climate (F6), security and hygiene (F11), and opportunities for outdoor activities (F12) which are influencing the tourist option for the tourism destination of Bali, Indonesia. Kanaan (2018) investigated a number of practical aspects of high relevance on the concept of All-Inclusive (AI) hotel package but also taking into account highly challenging options such as Ultra inclusive, Super-inclusive, and Unlimited Luxury.

Bianchi and Chen (2015) have investigated the relationship between chief executive officer (CEO) compensation and the performance of firms in the hospitality industry and non-hospitality industries in the United States (US) over the period 1992–2010, and the author has identified on the basis of empirical evidence a higher salary level in non - hospitality compared to the hospitality industry. Gottschall, Gultek and Heroux (2018) have investigated relevant issues regarding hospitality industry focusing on identification both the similarities and differences in US and Canadian restaurant marketing approaches. and concluded that the differences were found in the case of casual dining restaurants while similarities have been identified in the case of fine dining restaurants.

ANALYZING ROMANIA AS A TOURIST DESTINATION

The Romanian Danube Delta Biosphere Reserve is included on the list of Unesco World Heritage since 1991. The Danube Delta is a tourist destination that attracts annually hundreds of thousands of tourists, both foreign and indigenous (Romanian tourists). However, many Romanian tourists visit this tourist destination several times a year. The Romanian government authorities implemented various modernization and maintenance measures in order to preserve the tourism potential of the Danube Delta. Moreover, private investments in the Danube Delta have led to the tourist development of the natural area. The biodiversity of Romanian Danube Delta is unique, extremely varied and impressive in its beauty. Numerous species of birds, animals and plants enrich the natural heritage of the Danube delta. A trip in this piece of heaven equates to an escape in the middle of wild nature. Tourists, both foreign and natives, are very attracted by the natural diversity of the Danube Delta. In the following subchapter we will also detail the attractive costs of a vacancy or trip in Danube Delta.

In another train of thoughts, the Romania Black Sea Coast is another major tourist attraction. However, in this case we were talking about seasonal tourism. The highest number of tourists coincides with the warm season. The Romanian Black Sea coast measures 245 km, ie a very large area, which has an impressive biodiversity. The Black Sea coastline is very interesting as biodiversity, but the sea water and its restless waves are not very crystalline, harmless and calm. Romanian seaside includes natural beaches where tourists are sun tanning, suntanning and swimming, otherwise just relaxing in lounge chairs or under special umbrellas arranged by the hoteliers.

The Carpathian Mountains, also known as or Carpathians, are distinguished by the special beauty of the mountain landscapes, numerous thermal springs and mineral waters, natural parks, virgin forests, a spectacular fauna and flora. In this sense, we can exemplify some representative mountains as well, such as: Fagaras, Piatra Craiului, Piatra Mare, Vrancei, Postavaru, Ceahlau, Stânişoara, Harghita and Calimani mountains. Moreover, Romania has several mountain resorts, such as: Poiana Brasov, Balea, Sinaia, Predeal, Paltinis, Stana de Vale and others. Another major Romania tourist attractions include archaeological sites and artifacts, ancient architectural buildings, traditional folkloric objects, museums and memorial houses, and historical monuments.

The Romanian Orthodox Church had a great influence over indigenous peoples over time, considering its very large properties, including numerous church buildings (church houses), heritage buildings and places of worship. Orthodox monasteries and churches are an essential dimension in Romanian tourism. The official statistics highlight the following structure of religious affiliation in Romania, ie: Orthodox - 16,307,004 persons, Roman Catholic -870,774 persons, Reformed - 600,932 persons, Pentecostal - 362,314 persons, Greek Catholic - 150,593 persons, Baptist - 112,850 persons, Seventh-day Adventist - 80,944 persons, Muslim - 64,337 persons, Unitarian - 57,686 persons, Christianity after the gospel - 42,495 persons, Jehovah's Witnesses - 49,820 persons, the Lutheran evangelical - 20,168 people, the Augustan-evangelical confession - 5,399 people, the Serbian Orthodox - 14,385 people, the evangelical Romanian - 15,514 people (the 2011 Population and Housing Census in Romania). Nevertheless, religious tourism is very attractive due to the numerous tourist destinations in Romania. The preference of certain tourists is obvious in this respect. In other words, official statistics on religious affiliation in Romania are more than edifying in order to understand the option for religious tourism.

In this book chapter we will provide a list of some of the most attractive religious tourist attractions in Romania. The Church Type "Rotonda" - Geoagiu Bai in Transilvania is a tourist attraction of great interest due to its special beauty. The Black Church in Brasov is beyond anything else an ancient and very impressive historical monument. Moreover, the Black Church in Brasovis is also considered one of the major tourist attractions in Romania because is being visited annually by tens of thousands of tourists. The Wooden churches of Maramureş in Transylvania also have significant tourist potential, being unique in their particularities. The Metropolitan Cathedral of Iasi is also an important tourist destination both as a religious motivation and as a preference for its spectacular architectural appearance. Furthermore, the "Three Holy Hierarchs" Church in Iaşi provides additional motivation for the city of Iaşi to become a major attraction for religious tourism. The Roman Catholic Church and Franciscan Monastery of Cluj-Napoca is also a Romanian religious tourism objective of high relevance and consideration. The following churches are very attractive in the context of religious tourism, ie: the Roman Catholic Church in Brasov, the Metropolitan Cathedral of Timisoara, the Viscri Fortified Church in Transylvania, the Roman Catholic Cathedral in Satu Mare, the Church on the Hill situated in Sighişoara in Mureş County, the Holy Trinity Church in Craiova, the Ursuline Church located in Marginimea Sibiului, the Wooden Church "The Holy Voivodes" located in Isverna (Mehedinţi County), the Stavropoleus Church in Bucharest and many others. Obviously, the list of Romanian churches that can be considered tourist destinations for religious pilgrims or visiting tourists is extremely wide.

The jewelery of religious tourism in Romania is represented by the Voroneţ Monastery in Bucovina, also known as the "Sistine Chapel of the East". The Voroneţ Monastery is a great tourist destination visited both by religious pilgrims and by simple recreational tourists. The shade of Voroneţ blue is an unique color in the world, so special that it could not be reproduced by other painters. In other words, the Voroneţ Monastery is proof that when originality blends harmoniously with artistic sensitivity results an architectural jewel. Moreover, the history of this holy place has magnified its value and tourist potential.

A complex series of Christian monasteries with great tourist potential for religious pilgrims or simple visitors include the following: the Putna Monastery in Bucovina, the Cozia Monastery in Olt, the Prislop Monastery in Transylvania, the Stanisoara Monastery in Olt Valley, the Curtea de Arges Monastery in Arges county, the Cârţişoara Monastery "The Holy Apostles Peter and Paul" in Marginimea Sibiului, the Râmeţ Monastery in Alba County, the Dragomirna Monastery in Suceava County, the Cheia Monastery in Prahova Valley, the Mraconia Monastery situated in Duhova commune in Mehedinti County, the Monastery of the Ialomita Cave situated in Bucegi Mountains, the Crasna Monastery in Teleajen Valley in Prahova County and the Barsana monastery in Maramureş County.

The Bran Castle, also known as the Castle of Dracula, has an impressive history of over 600 years. Dracula's castle annually attracts hundreds of thousands of tourists from all over the world. Foreign tourists are very interested in Dracula's castle due to its significant media coverage in horror films, videos, books, pictures, songs and publications with reference to bloody vampires and mysterious darkness. Practically, this tourist attraction is generated by an internationally recognized myth. However, the touristic potential of the Bran Castle is not being sufficiently exploited by the Romanian authorities.

The Romanian Hospitality Industry

Developing countries such as Romania assigns major importance to certain sectors with high potential for growth, as in case of tourism industry. The tourism and hospitality industry have an encouraging share in global economy of Romania. The official statistics provide an interesting overview of the tourism and hospitality industry evolution. Practically, the total number of establishments of tourists' reception with functions of tourists' accommodation and the tourists' accommodation capacity, by type of ownership and type of establishments, in 2017, is 7.905, and includes: hotels, motel, tourist inns, hostels, tourist villas, bungalows, tourist chalets, holiday villages, camping sites, school and pre-school camps, tourist halting places, tourist boarding houses, agro-tourist boarding houses, houselet-type units, ship accommodation places (Romanian Tourism Statistical Abstract 2018, National Institute of Statistics of Romania).

A very important aspect is highlighted by the structure of the most companies in the tourism and hospitality industry in Romania. Official statistics reveal that in the case of establishments of tourists' reception with functions of tourists' accommodation, by type of ownership, in 2017, there are a number of 240 as mainly state ownership and a number of 7.665 as mainly private ownership (Romanian Tourism Statistical Abstract 2018, National Institute of Statistics of Romania). A state-owned enterprise (SOE) involves significant state control that affects market economy and free competition. The predominant private ownership is preferable in order to attract financial investment fundings. However, inappropriately or insufficiently qualified staff is a major disadvantage for the hospitality industry. The human factor is essential in maintaining a successful business. Moreover, tourism and hospitality industry in Romania must be perceived as high priority industry due to its considerable impact on economic growth.

Romanian governmental authority is supporting the tourism and hospitality industry by implementing certain strategies at national level. The Government of Romania has established on the basis of the Governance Program 2017-2020, that all employees in the public system have to benefit of a holiday allowance or holiday bonus as the case may be, in the form of a holiday voucher equal to the gross minimum salary of that year (Government Emergency Ordinance 46/2017). Each public sector employees may receive one holiday allowance, at the value of currently Lei 1,450, during the July 2017 to November 2018 period. The Romanian Leu (the plural form is Lei) is the currency of Romania. The public sector employees can spend a holiday in Romania (exclusive) using holiday vouchers. In other words, holiday vouchers represent a dual opportunity considering that it stimulates the development of Romanian tourism and hospitality industry, but it also contributes to the relaxation/recreation of the public sector employees.

The governmental authorities in Romania also provide other opportunities for the development of local tourism. In quantitative terms, in Romania around 1.2 million employees work in the public sector. The International Workers' Day or Labor Day is celebrated annually worldwide on May 1. For public sector employees, the official working day of April 30, 2018 was set as free working day, but under the condition to prolong the subsequent work schedule corresponding to the working time until May 11, 2018 (Government Decision no. 207/2018). As a consequence, all employees in the Romanian budgetary sector had at their disposal a 4-day minivacation in order to enjoy the tourism offers and hospitality industry opportunities. Moreover, for public sector employees, the official working days of August 16 and 17, 2018 were set as free days, but the equivalent of these free days were equate to hours recovered in the subsequent period until September 7, 2018 (Government Decision no. 595/2018). One of Romania's bank holidays in 2018 was the Dormition of the Virgin Mary on August, 15 which is also a public national holiday for al Romanian citizens. Therefore all employees in the Romanian budgetary sector had at their disposal a 5-day minivacation for relaxing, visiting tourist destinations and benefiting from the services of the hospitality industry in Romania.

Official statistics have revealed a significant increase in earnings and profit during the period of these so-called minivacation for both Romanian tourism and hospitality industry. In addition, Romanian tourist agencies have provided special tourist packages in order to enjoy those minivacations. Concretely, each of these minivacation enjoyed several tens of thousands of Romanian tourists who have spent a total of several million euros each time. In other words, domestic tourist destinations represented the main attraction for Romanian tourists most of them being employees in the public sector. Thus the objective pursued by the governmental authorities was reached in optimal parameters. Moreover, taking into account the impressive results of the revival of national tourism, the Romanian government authorities decided to continue the programs on holiday vouchers for all employees in the public system.

Multidimensional Challenges of the Banking System

A comprenhensive approach on the multidimensional challenges of the banking system highlights certain characteristic features. The banking system plays an essential role in terms of Romanian tourism and hospitality industry. Financial funds, both domestic and international, form a central pillar of Romanian tourism and hospitality industry. The development of these industries depends on attracting financial investments. However, in the context of efficient bank management, challenges can be transformed into opportunities and benefits. Financial intermediation is one of the great challenges of modern finances. The major implications of the financial intermediation phenomenon are significant in the context of implementing sustainable development strategies for the tourism and hospitality industry in Romania. Moreover, the modernization and development process required by international standards involve significant financial investments. An adequate legislative framework would provide an improved perspective for the development of local entrepreneurs. The performance of the hospitality industry in Romania depends on customer satisfaction.

Various research studies have disseminated a related issues and have provided a significant number of very interesting conclusions. Spulbar and Niţoi (2012) have performed a complex comparative analysis of banking systems and suggested that the financial system is one of the most controlled sectors of the economy, and banks are among the most regulated financial institutions, considering the fact that banking regulation is a set of rules and practices imposed by public authorities aimed at establishing and maintaining financial stability. Spulbar and Nitoi (2015) investigated cost efficiency of certain commercial banks in Central and Eastern Europe and suggested that a high level of macroeconomic stability directly influences the efficiency of commercial banks. Moreover, Spulbar and Nitoi (2016) have conducted an empirical research study on the nexus between commercial banks' cost efficiency, risks and performance and productivity patterns in the Romanian banking system and concluded that there is a direct link between a reduced risk of failure, a higher level of liquidity, a higher rate of financial intermediation, a higher ROE on the one hand, and efficiency, on the other hand. Katircioglu, Katircioğlu and Altinay (2018) investigated relevant issues on the nexus between tourism growth and financial sector development based on a case study of Turkey and concluded that changes that occurred in the case of tourism volume precede changes that occurred in the case of financial volume given the existence of a long-term and reinforcing mutual influence.

The World Bank classify countries (economies) in four main groups according to the income criterion, ie low, lower-middle, upper-middle, and high based on gross national income (GNI) per capita, value calculated in the the currency of United States (dollars) by using the World Bank Atlas method. Synthesising this aspect we can emphasize the following classification of countries for the current 2019 fiscal year by using as a criterion the GNI per capita level for 2017 fiscal year: low-income economies ($995 or less), lower middle-income economies (greater than or equal to $996 but but less than or equal to $3,895), upper middle-income economies (greater than or equal to $3,896 but less than or equal to $12,055) and high-income economies ($12,056 or more). However, Romania is included in the category of upper-middle-income economies ($3,896 to $12,055).

Specific banking products and services can lead to development of Romanian tourism and hospitality industry. In other words, if commercial banks are launching innovative financial products or services addressed to local entrepreneurs or small and medium size businesses who want to invest in these particular areas, the prerequisites for quality improvement are favorable. In general, the main objective of any entrepreneur is earning high level of profit. In this context, the role of commercial banks is essential. Certain issues of major importance for the banking sector activity concern the level of performing financial deposits, the degree of nonperforming loans to total gross loans (%), the solvency regulations and optimal level of liquidity. The role of commercial banks is fundamental considering the importance of attracting additional sources of financial funding. Nevertheless it is very important for an entrepreneur to remain financially solvent. Moreover, Romania can access significant European structural funds for tourism development considering its European Union membership. This is an immense opportunity for potential investors in order to implement sustainable development strategies.

CONCLUSION

The importance of tourism and hospitality industry is generated by its various socio-economic implications. The progress of the tourism and hospitality industry in Romania depends directly on the access to financial funding sources. Nevertheless, implementing optimal strategy for the sustainable development of Romanian tourism is more convenient as a long-term approach. Government authorities in Romania must ensure legislative harmonization in relation to the European standards in the field of tourism. The international financial imbalances the global financial crisis generate severe turmoil in the banking system so the financing and lending mechanism is strongly affected. Moreover, such an extreme event determines negative repercussions in the case of attracting funding sources for supporting real investments in the tourism and hospitality industry in Romania. Global imbalances are perceived as a major risk factor for economic stability so it also affects the development level of the tourism and hospitality industry in Romania. A commercial bank must have the ability to provide integrated financial services in order to contribute to sustainable development of the tourism and hospitality industry in Romania. The customer portfolio is essential to optimize the banking system and the fierce competition will emphasize the vulnerabilities of small commercial banks. However, the knowledge of inflation dynamics is crucial in monetary analysis and this condition is very important for Romania in the view of recent fluctuations.

It is very important for Romania to attract European Union funds in order to implement sustainable development strategies for tourism and hospitality industry. Sustainable tourism is a concept with various implications for the economic growth in Romania. The foreign tourist influx to Romania is also considerably influenced by socio-economic issues such as: poorly developed infrastructures, increased inflation, financial instability, political disturbances, endemic corruption, inadequate and inaccurate legal regulations on certain sensitive issues. In this respect, the role of the banking system is essential. The major importance of financial innovation and financial deregulation influences considerably both the development and correction of financial imbalances and their implications on the real economy. The consequences of the accumulation of financial liabilities are devastating for an entrepreneur. A successful business depends on the credibility and solvency of the entrepreneur who has implemented a financial investment.

REFERENCES

Antara, M. & Prameswari, Y.A. (2018). Push and Pull Factors of Tourists Visit the Tourism Destination of Bali, Indonesia. *Journal of Tourism and Hospitality Management*, 6(1), 112-120. Doi:10.15640/jthm.v6n1a1

Axinte, G., & Spulbar, C. (2009). Critical Success Factors for Romanian Tourism. *Bulletin University of Agricultural Sciences and Veterinary Medicine (UASVM) - Horticulture*, 66(2), 22 – 28.

Bianchi, G. & Chen, Y. (2015). CEO compensation and the performance of firms in the hospitality industry: a cross-industry comparison. *International Journal of Tourism Sciences, 15*(3 – 4), 121-138. Doi:10.1080/15980634.2016.1181320

Birau, R. (2015). International Tourism and Hospitality in the Digital Age. In *The Global Implications of Ecotourism in Emerging Economies*. IGI Global. Doi:10.4018/978-1-4666-8268-9

Busuioc, M.F., Simon, T., Niculescu, A.C., & Trifanescu, R. (2016). New Opportunities For Niche Tourism In Romania: Ethnographic Tourism. *Romanian Economic Business Review*, 11(4.1), 35-43.

Candrea, A.N., Ispas, A., Untaru, E.N., & Nechita, F. (2016). Marketing the Count's way: how Dracula's myth can revive Romanian tourism. *Bulletin of the Transilvania University of Braşov*, 9(58), 83-90.

Chan, E. S. W., & Hsu, C. H. C. (2016). Environmental management research in hospitality, *International Journal of Contemporary Hospitality Management*, 28(5), 886–923. doi:10.1108/IJCHM-02-2015-0076

Cosma, S., Pop, C., & Negrusa, A. (2007). Should Dracula Myth be a Brand to Promote Romania as a Tourist Destination? Interdisciplinary Management Research, Josip Juraj Strossmayer University of Osijek, Faculty of Economics.

Dragin, A. S., Jovičić, D., & Lukić, T. (2010). Cruising along the river Danube: Contemporary tourism trend in Serbia. *Geographica Pannonica, 14*(3), 98–108. doi:10.5937/GeoPan1003098D

Gottschall, R., Gultek, M. & Heroux, L. (2018). Similarities and Differences in US and Canadian Restaurant Marketing Strategies: A Cross-Border Analysis of Menu Offerings. *Journal of Tourism and Hospitality Management*, 6(1), 1 – 8. Doi:10.15640/jthm.v6n1a1

Hall, D. R. (1993). ECotourism in the Danube Delta. *The Tourist Review*, *48*(3), 11-13. doi:10.1108/eb058125

Hein, T., Schwarz, U., Habersack, H., Nichersu, I., Preiner, S., Willby, N., & Weigelhofer, G. (2016). Current status and restoration options for floodplains along the Danube River. *Science of The Total Environment*, *543*(Part A), 778-790.

Iorga, A. (2015). Tourism and Protected Areas: Political Ecology of The Rural Tourism in Romanian Danube Delta. *Journal of Tourism – Studies and Research in Tourism*, *20*, 34-41.

Jogaratnam, G., McCleary, K. W., Mena, M. M., & Yoo, J. J. E. (2005). An Analysis of Hospitality and Tourism Research: Institutional Contributions. *Journal of Hospitality & Tourism Research (Washington, D.C.)*, *29*(3), 356–371. doi:10.1177/1096348005276929

Kanaan, K. (2018). Balanced Performance Evaluation in the Light of the Digital Hotels Era. *Journal of Tourism and Hospitality Management*, *6*(1), 100-111. Doi:10.15640/jthm.v6n1a10

Katircioglu, S., Katircioğlu, S., & Altinay, M. (2018). Interactions between tourism and financial sector development: Evidence from Turkey. *Service Industries Journal*, *38*(9-10), 9–10, 519–542. doi:10.1080/02642069.2017.1406479

Khan, E. A., Khaled, M., & Shambour, Y. (2018). An analytical study of mobile applications for Hajj and Umrah services. *Applied Computing and Informatics*, *14*(1), 37–47. doi:10.1016/j.aci.2017.05.004

Kukoyi, I. A., & Iwuagwu, C. (2015). Service delivery and customer satisfaction in hospitality industry: A study of the Divine Fountain Hotels Limited, Lagos, Nigeria, *Journal of Hospitality Management and Tourism*. *Academic Journals*, *6*(1), 1–7. doi:10.5897/JHMT2015.0139

Li, Y., & Singal, M. (2018). Firm Performance in the Hospitality Industry: Do CEO Attributes and Compensation Matter? *Journal of Hospitality & Tourism Research*. doi:10.1177/1096348018776453

Light, D. (2007). Dracula Tourism in Romania. Cultural Identity and the State. *Annals of Tourism Research, Elsevier Ltd.*, *34*(3), 746–765. doi:10.1016/j.annals.2007.03.004

Obiora, J.N.P., & Nwokorie, E.C. (2018). Impediments to Rural Youth Entrepreneurship towards the Hospitality Sector in Nigeria: The Case of Ihitte-Uboma, Imo State. *Journal of Tourism and Hospitality Management, 6*(1), 81-91. Doi:10.15640/jthm.v6n1a8

Parsa, H. G., Harrington, R., & Ottenbacher, M. (2009). Defining the Hospitality Discipline: a Discussion of Pedagogical and Research Implications. *Journal of Hospitality & Tourism Research, 33*(3), 263-283. doi:10.1177/1096348009338675

Patrichi, I.C. (2013). Dark Tourism – A Niche Segment For The Romanian Tourism. *Romanian Economic Business Review, 8*(4.1), 351-358.

Razak, N. A., & Ibrahim, J. A. (2017). From names of places to Mahsuri's curse: exploring the roles of myths and legends in tourism. *International Journal of Business, Economics and Law, 14*(2), 10 - 17.

Spulbar, C., & Niţoi, M. (2012). *Comparative analysis of banking systems*. SITECH Publishing House Craiova.

Spulbar, C., & Nitoi, M. (2015). An Examination of Banks' Cost Efficiency in Central and Eastern Europe. *Procedia Economics and Finance, 22*, 544–551. doi:10.1016/S2212-5671(15)00256-7

Spulbar, C., & Nitoi, M. (2016). The relationship between bank efficiency and risk and productivity patterns in Romanian banking system. *Romanian Journal of Economic Forecasting, 19*(1), 39–53.

Tutunea, M., & Rus, R.V. (2011). Mobile-Tourism in Romania. *Journal Studia Universitatis Babeş-Bolyai Negotia, 56*(1), 76-88.

Tutunea, M.F. (2016). Mobile applications for tourism. Study regarding their use by Romanians. *Annals of "Constantin Brancusi" University of Targu-Jiu, 4*, 78-84.

Chapter 8

Indian Tourism Industry:
Current Trends and Future Outlook

Natisha Saqib
University of Kashmir, India

ABSTRACT

The tourism industry certainly has been a formidable pillar as an unfailing and reliable source of revenue and capital for many nations. Many countries have been elevated from poor to appreciable economic statuses as a result of the invaluable contributions their tourism sectors have succeeded in adding to their overall economic growth. Tourism is a major engine of economic growth and an important source of foreign exchange earnings in India. Over the last decade, India has been the fastest growing tourism region in the world. This chapter primarily aims and seeks to identify and examine the paradigm shifts in the tourism industry over the seeming years and how the trends have behaved in India. It seeks to study the current trends in the tourism industry and evaluates the role of tourism in economic development. The future outlook is bright for the tourism sector, and the region is expected to maintain a high rate of growth well into the next century. The chapter contributes to an improved understanding of economic growth of a country because of tourism development.

DOI: 10.4018/978-1-5225-8494-0.ch008

INTRODUCTION

Tourism is a phenomenon of great social importance in modern society, a fact that is directly linked to historical aspects such as increased free time, improved communications, modern transport, and urbanization. Tourism is also an important economic activity in almost every country of the world and has experienced continued expansion and diversification, to become one of the largest and fastest growing economic sectors in the world. This sector has a direct impact on an economy of a country, the sector has reflected significant indirect and induced impacts over the past six decades;. As an engine for economic growth, tourism has been found to be resilient and offers scope for foreign exchange earnings, generating employment, revenue and stimulating domestic consumptions well (Gokovali & Bahar, 2006 ; Modeste, 1995; Steiner, 2006).Studies have demonstrated that tourism plays a significant role towards balanced sustainable development of an economy and that it can be effectively harnessed to generate net benefits for the poor (UNWTO, 2002). The potential of tourism as a tool for an economic growth and poverty reduction is derived from several unique characteristics of the tourism system (UNWTO, 2002).Tourism can play an important and effective role in achieving the growth with equity. Tourism has the potential to grow at a high rate and simultaneously ensure consequential development of the infrastructure of the destinations. It can help a nation to leverage upon its natural scenic resources and capitalize on the country's success in the services sector as well as provide sustainable models of growth. Tourism sector stimulates forward linkages and cross-sectorial synergies. Expenditure on tourism induces a chain of transactions requiring supply of goods and services from the related sectors. The consumption demand, emanating from tourist expenditure also prompts more employment and generates a multiplier effect on the economy as well as on the other allied economic sectors like agriculture, horticulture, poultry, handicrafts, transport, construction, etc. through its backward and forward linkages

According to the United Nations World Travel & Tourism Council (WTTC) 2015, the Travel & Tourism sector reported 2.8 per cent growth in 2015and outpaced that of the global economy i.e. 2.3 per cent along with the number of other major economic sectors such as manufacturing and retail. In total, Travel & Tourism generated US $7.2 trillion (9.8 per cent of global GDP) and generated 284 million jobs, equivalent to 1 in 11 jobs in the global economy. While traditionally Europe and America have remained high among the tourism markets, new emerging markets are expected to witness high growth in international tourist visits over the next decade. The WTO forecast indicates an increasing tourism preference towards East Asia, the Pacific,

West Asia and South Asia. With 279 million tourist arrivals, nearly one fourth of the world's total international tourists in 2016, Asia and the pacific is the second most visited region in the world with a 6 per cent growth rate. It is above the 4 per cent global average. Asia and the pacific continues to consolidate its position as one of the fastest growing regions in the world that is expected to increase its share of global tourism to 30 per cent in 2030 accounting for an estimated 535 million international arrivals. In Asia, China and India has emerged as a leading tourist destination and is poised to become the world's top tourist destination by 2020.

India has the potential to achieve considerable share of the world tourism market. India is a country of all reasons and all seasons, full of different natural resources and varieties of tourist destinations. India is having a rich traditional heritage, which has created magnificent architectural flairs, temple cities and towns with fascinating glorious monuments. Besides this, India is having a long and attractive coastline, history, cultural diversity, natural variations e.g., hilly areas, sea beaches, deserts, mangrove forest, and many historical and archaeological sites with a huge potential in the scenario of world tourism. More specifically, India offers 30 World Heritage Sites and 25 biogeographic zones. India has a suitable climate, improving tourism infrastructure and a tradition of hospitality. India has a diverse portfolio of niche tourism products – cruises, adventure, medical, wellness, sports, MICE, ecotourism, film, rural and religious tourism. In a true sense, India possesses the essential qualities of 'Incredible India' as it is a heaven for all types of tourists.

OBJECTIVES

The present study aims to achieve the following objectives:

1. To identify and examine the paradigm shifts in the tourism industry over the seeming years and how the trends have behaved in India and
2. To evaluate the role of tourism in economic development of India .

Methodology

The design used for this study was that of a descriptive research design which sought to examine, evaluate and assess the current trends in the tourism industry and also the role of tourism in economic development of India Data was collected for this research using secondary sources. To accomplish the objective proposed in this work the author compiled tourism statistics from 1991 to 2016 with a goal of finding no of domestic and foreign tourist visits to India for this period. The following databases were searched:

1. Ministry of Tourism, Government of India and
2. Indian statistics.

Economic Importance of Tourism in India

The WTTC has identified India as one of the world's foremost tourist growth centres in the coming decade. The sector is predicted to grow at an average annual rate of 7.5 per cent by 2025 (7.2 per cent of GDP) and is expected to achieve the fastest growth of economic activities via tourism sector. India attracted 14.57 million international tourist arrivals in 2016, compared to 13.28 million in 2015. According to the Ministry of Tourism, Govt. of India Report, 2017, India ranks 8th in the Asia Pacific region compare to 11th in 2013 and 24 globally compared to 41st in 2013. .India earned US$21.07 billion in foreign exchange earnings from tourism receipts in 2015 (Table 1).

The direct contribution of Travel & Tourism sector to GDP was INR2,668.3 billion (2.0 per cent of total GDP) in 2015, This primarily reflects the economic activity generated by industries such as hotels, travel agents, airlines and other passenger transportation services (excluding commuter services). It also includes, for example, the activities of the restaurant and leisure industries directly supported .The direct contribution of Travel & Tourism sector to GDP is expected to grow by 7.9 per cent per annum to INR6,115.5 billion (2.4 per cent of GDP) by 2026. The total contribution of Travel & Tourism sector to GDP (including wider effects from investment, the supply chain and induced income impacts) was INR8,309.4 billion

Table 1. Share of India in international tourist arrivals (ITA's) in world and Asia and the Pacific region (2013-2016)

Year	ITA's (in millions)			Percentage (%) share and rank of India in world.		Percentage (%) share and rank of India in Asia and the Pacific.	
	World	Asia and the Pacific	India	% share	Rank	% share	Rank
2013	1087.0	249.7	6.97	0.64	41st	2.79	11th
2014	1134.0	264.3	13.11	1.15	24th	4.86	8th
2015	1184.0	278.6	13.28	1.12	24th	4.72	7th
2016	1235.0	308.7	14.57	1.18	24th	4.72	8 th

Source: Author's Compilation based on secondary data from Ministry of Tourism, Govt. of India, 2017

Table 2. Contribution of travel and tourism to GDP and employment

Contribution	World	Asia pacific	India %
Direct contribution to GDP	3.0	2.7	2.0
Total Contribution To GDP	9.8	8.5	6.3
Direct contribution to employment*	3.6	3.7	5.5
Total contribution to employment *	9.5	8.6	8.7
Visitors exports	6.1	5.5	4.5
Domestic spending	4.7	4.4	4.4
Leisure spending	2.3	2.0	1.7
Business spending	0.7	0.6	0.3
Capital investment	4.3	3.7	6.0

Source: Author's Compilation based on secondary data from World Travel & Tourism Council (WTTC), 2015

*000 jobs

(6.3 per cent of GDP) in 2015, and is forecast to rise by 7.5 per cent per annum to INR18,362.2 billion (7.2 per cent of GDP) in 2026. Further Leisure travel spending (inbound and domestic) generated 83.2per cent of direct Travel & Tourism GDP in 2015 (INR 5,945.5 billion) compared with 16.8 per cent for business travel spending (INR1,198.9billion). Domestic travel spending generated 82.5 per cent of direct Travel & Tourism GDP in 2015 compared with 17.5 per cent for visitor exports (i.e. foreign visitor spending or international tourism receipts). Domestic travel spending is expected to rise by 7.8 per cent per annum to INR13, 305.5 billion in 2026. Visitor exports are expected to rise by 7.2 per cent per annum to INR2; 625.6billion in 2026. In 2015, Travel & Tourism directly supported 23,454,500 jobs (5.5per cent of total employment). This includes employment by hotels, travel agents, airlines and other passenger transportation services (excluding commuter services). It also includes, for example, the activities of the restaurant and leisure industries directly supported by tourists and is expected to rise by 2.0% pa to 29,629,000 jobs (5.8% of total employment) in 2026.In 2015, the total contribution of Travel & Tourism to employment, including jobs indirectly supported by the industry, was 8.7per cent of total employment (37,315,000 jobs). This is expected to rise by 3.0per cent in 2016 to 38,441,000 jobs and rise by 1.9per cent per annum to 46,422,000 jobs in 2026 (9.0per cent of total).Money spent by foreign visitors to a country (or visitor exports) is a key component of the direct contribution of Travel & Tourism. In 2015, India generated INR1, 249.3 billion via visitor exports. This is forecasted to grow by 7.2per cent per annum, from 2016-2026, to INR2, 625.6billion in 2026 (3.8 per cent of total). Travel & Tourism is expected to have attracted capital investment of INR2, 264.1billion in 2015. This is expected to rise by 4.8 per cent in 2016, and rise by 6.3 per cent per annum over the next ten years to INR4l, 356.7bn in 2026. Travel & Tourism's share of total national investment will rise from 5.9 per cent in 2016 to 6.0 per cent in 2026 (*Table -2*).

Trends in Tourist Arrivals in India

- **Foreign tourist arrivals (FTA):** Foreign tourist arrivals (FTA) during last 25 years in India are given in Table 3 and Figure 1 below. An Increasing trend can be seen from 2002 to 2015 except in 2009 when the country witnessed a negative growth of 2.2 per cent in FTAs due to economic recession. Foreign tourist arrivals increased from 7.68 million in 2014 to 8.0.3 million in 2015 registering an annual growth of 8.1 per cent over the previous year. By 2025, Foreign Tourist Arrivals in India is expected to reach 15.3 million, according to the World Tourism Organisation.

- **Foreign Exchange Earnings:** FEE from tourism has also increased significantly from 1991 to 2015. (Table 3 and Figure-2) However FEE's felt the repercussions of the economic recession in 2009 however a sudden increase of 18.1per cent in 2010 reflects the resilience that tourism has and the revival that it has brought in the economy. The Foreign Exchange Earnings (FEEs) from tourism during 2015 were US $21071 million with a growth of 9.6 per cent.

. FTAs and FEEs in India have seen somewhat of a dramatic turnaround since 2002 with a temporary declining trend has been reversed aggressively. This turnaround has been the result of several policies schemes and initiatives by Government of India such as "Incredible India" campaign, the tourism industry's constant search for new destinations, and to some extent improvement in infrastructure in specific areas such as better air connectivity of smaller and remote destinations.

There has been substantial growth in domestic and foreign tourists in India over the last two decades

- **Domestic Tourist Visits:** Domestic tourism plays an important role in overall tourism development in the country. Table 4 and Figure 3, shows an uninterrupted increase in tourist flows from 1994 to 2016. There have been some fluctuations in the tourist arrival from one period to another period but there is no negative percentage growth from 1994 to 2016 which is a positive

*Table 3. No of foreign tourist arrivals (FTA's) to all states/UT's in India, 1991-2015 &
foreign exchange earnings (FEEs) from tourism in India in (Us $millions) 1991-2015*

Year	No Of Foreign Tourist Arrivals (In Millions) To India	Foreign Exchange Earnings FEE From Tourism (In Millions) To India
1991	1.68	1861
1992	1.87	2126
1993	1.76	2124
1994	1.89	2272
1995	2.12	2583
1996	2.29	2832
1997	2.37	2889
1998	2.36	2948
1999	2.48	3009
2000	2.65	3460
2001	2.54	3198
2002	2.38	3103
2003	2.73	4463
2004	3.46	6170
2005	3.92	7493
2006	4.45	8634
2007	5.08	10729
2008	5.28	11832
2009	5.17	11136
2010	5.78	14193
2011	6.31	16564
2012	6.58	17737
2013	6.97	18445
2014	7.68	20236
2015	8.03	21071

Source: Author's Compilation based on secondary data from Ministry of Tourism, Govt. of India and Indian statistics website

Figure 1. No of foreign tourist arrivals (FTA's) to all states/UT's in India
Source: Author's Compilation based on secondary data from Ministry of Tourism, Govt. of India. and Indian statistics website

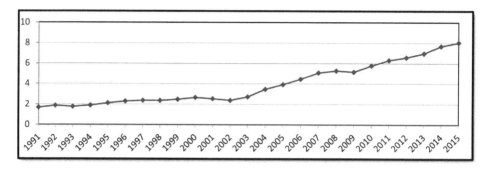

Figure 2. Foreign exchange earnings (FEEs) from tourism in India in (Us $Millions)
Source: Author's Compilation based on secondary data from Ministry of Tourism, Govt. of India and Indian statistics website.

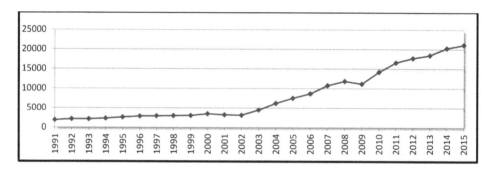

indication of bright future of tourism industry. The rise in domestic tourism is a symbol of increasing mobility of Indian travellers, enhanced spending power, better connectivity, affordability and a gradually evolving mind-set of Indian consumers, which motivates them to venture beyond their home towns. In 2009, when the country witnessed a negative growth of 2.2 per cent in FTAs, domestic tourist visits (DTV's) registered a growth of 18.8 per cent. This growth of DTVs sustained various tourism infrastructures during bad period for the tourism sector.1613.55 million domestic tourist visits were recorded in India during 2016 as compared to 1431.97 million in 2015, with a 12.7 per cent change over the previous year. Domestic travel revenues are anticipated to increase around USD 203.3 billion by 2026.

Table 4. No of foreign tourist visits (FTV's) and domestic tourist visits DTV's) to all states/UT's in India, 1991-2015

Year	No Of Foreign Tourist Visits (In Million) To India	No Of Domestic Tourist Visits (In Million) To India	No Of total Tourist Visits (In Million) To India
1991	3.15	66.67	69.82
1992	3.09	81.45	84.54
1993	3.54	105.81	109.35
1994	4.03	127.12	131.15
1995	4.64	136.64	145.14
1996	5.03	140.11	145.14
1997	5.50	159.88	165.38
1998	5.54	168.20	173.74
1999	5.83	190.67	196.50
2000	5.89	220.11	226.00
2001	5.44	236.47	241.91
2002	5.16	269.60	274.76
2003	6.71	309.04	315.75
2004	8.36	366.27	374.63
2005	9.95	392.01	401.96
2006	11.75	462.32	474.07
2007	13.26	526.56	539.82
2008	14.38	563.03	577.41
2009	14.37	668.80	683.18
2010	17.91	747.70	765.61
2011	19.50	864.53	884.03
2012	18.26	1045.05	1063.31
2013	19.95	1145.28	1165.23
2014	22.57	1281.95	1304.52
2015	22.33	1431.97	1454.3
2016	24.71	1613.55	1638.26

Source: Author's Compilation based on secondary data from Ministry of Tourism, Govt. of India and Indian statistics website

Figure 3. No of domestic tourist visits (in million) to India

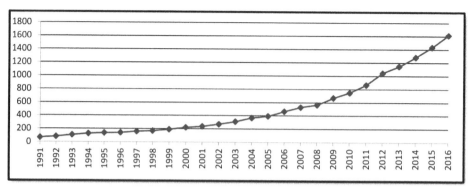

Figure 4. Number of foreign tourist visits (in million) to India
Source: Author's Compilation based on secondary data from Ministry of Tourism, Govt. of India and Indian statistics website

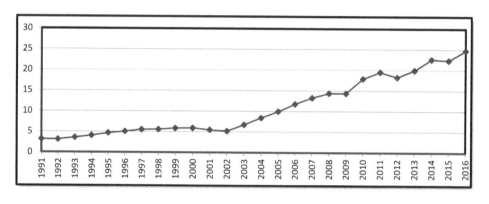

Figure 5. Number of total tourist visits (In Million) to India
Source: Author's Compilation based on secondary data from Ministry of Tourism, Govt. of India and Indian statistics website

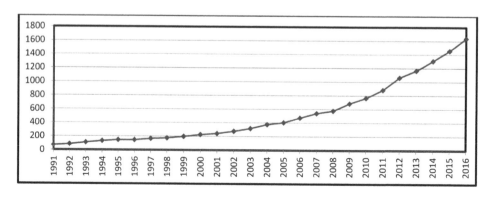

- **Foreign Tourist Visits:** Most promising sign of growing contribution of tourism has been the much awaited increase in the number of foreign tourist visits (FTVs) in India after 2002. The number of foreign tourist visits (FTV's) increased from 3.15 million in 1991 to 24.71 million in 2015, with a 5.92 per cent change over the previous year (Figure 4). Revenues earned from foreign visitors are projected to increase to US$40.11 billion by 2026.

To sum up, the tourism industry in India has come a long way from just 15,000 tourists in 1950 to 1638.26 million in 2016 (Figure 6). Total tourist visits in various states of India over a five year period reveal that States such as Tamil Naidu, Uttar Pradesh, Andhra Pradesh Karnataka and Maharashtra will continue to be the principal visitor generating market, while Tripura, Madhya Pradesh, West Bengal, Gujarat, Rajasthan, Uttarakhand, Bihar Punjab Delhi, Chhattisgarh Himachal Pradesh and Jammu and Kashmir has the potential to be the next major visitor generating market (Indian statistics report, 2017).

CONCLUSION

The tourism industry has emerged as one of the fastest growing sectors contributing significantly to global economic growth and development. It has been making a revolutionary and significant impact on the India Economic scenario over the last two decades. Tourism is one economic sector in India that has the potential to grow at a high rate and has the capacity to capitalize on the country's success in the services sector and provide sustainable models of growth. It is believed that India's competitive advantage lies in its mystical attractions with its ancient civilization and culture. The country has much to offer with attractions ranging from the world's highest mountains, vast coastline with excellent beaches, rich tropical forests, captivating wild life, desert safari, lagoon backwaters, ancient and majestic monuments, forts and palaces, diverse culture, colourful fairs, folk arts, unique hospitality etc. Indian tourism has vast potential for generating employment and earning large sums of foreign exchange besides giving a fillip to the country's overall economic and social development. Over the two decades, statistical data on domestic and foreign tourist visits to India has shown a rapid increase. FTAs and FEEs in India have also seen somewhat of a dramatic turnaround since 2002 with a temporary declining trend has been reversed aggressively. The future outlook is bright for the tourism sector, and the region is expected to maintain a high rate of growth well into the next century. The paper contributes to an improved understanding of economic growth of a country because of tourism.

REFERENCES

Annual Report 2016-17 Ministry of Tourism Government of India. (n.d.). Retrieved from: http://tourism.gov.in/sites/default/files/annualreports/MoT%20Annual%20 Report%20201617_English.pdf

Gokovali, U., & Bahar, O. (2006). Contribution of Tourism to Economic Growth: A Panel Data Approach. *Anatolia: An International Journal of Tourism and Hospitality Research*, *17*(2), 1–13. doi:10.1080/13032917.2006.9687184

IndiaTourismStatistics. (2003). Retrieved from: http://tourism. gov.in/sites/default/ files/Other/ INDIA%20TOURISM%20STATISTICS%202003.pdf

IndiaTourismStatistics. (2007). Retrieved from: http://tourism. gov.in/sites/default/ files/Other/ INDIA%20TOURISM%20STATISTICS%202007.pdf

IndiaTourismStatistics. (2014) Retrieved from: http://tourism.gov. in/sites/default/ files/ Other/INDIA%20TOURISM%20STATISTICS%202014.pdf

IndiaTourismStatistics. (2017) Retrieved from: http://tourism. gov.in/sites/default/ files/ Other/INDIA%20TOURISM%20STATISTICS%202017.pdf

Modeste, N. C. (1995). The Impact of Growth in the Tourism Sector On Economic Development: The Experience Of Selected Caribbean Countries. *Economic International*, *48*, 375–385.

Number of Domestic Tourist Visits in India. (1991 to 2015). Retrieved from: http:// www. indiastat. com/ tourism/29/stats.aspx

Steiner, C. (2006). Tourism, Poverty Reduction and the Political Economy: Egyptian Perspectives on Tourism's Economic Benefits in a Semi-Rentier State. *Tourism Hospitality Planning and Development*, *3*(3), 161–177. doi:10.1080/14790530601132286

UNWTO. (2002). *Tourism and Poverty Alleviation*. Madrid: United Nations World Tourism Organization.

Vaugeois, N. (2000). Tourism in Developing Countries: Refining a Useful Tool for Economic Development. *Proceedings of 6th World Leisure Congress*.

World Travel & Tourism Council (WTTC). (2015). *Travel & Tourism Economic Impact 2016*. Retrieved from: Https://Www. Wttc.Org//Media/Files/ Reports/ Economic%20impac t%20research/Regions%202016/World2016.Pdf

Chapter 9

Pricing for Hill Tourism Destination:
An Empirical Analysis of Sikkim Himalaya, India – Linear Price Model for Himalayan Hill Station

Debasish Batabyal
Amity University Kolkata, India

ABSTRACT

Pricing an alpine tourism is unlike pricing a tangible product. As a part of overall marketing strategy pricing a destination has lot of intricate issues that starts from the basic characteristics of the destination elements to the changing demand aspects. At the time of packaging, an alpine destination by a tour operator or destination promotion organization (DPO), a simplified model, is used that is not essentially limited to an absurd analysis of attraction features through FAM trips a priori. In almost all Indian leisure destinations, tourists are found to be price sensitive and per capita spending is not so high. So, an Indian alpine destination-specific model, based on simple linear regression equation, largely explaining the spending of tourists and thereby implying a modified landscape value has been explained here.

DOI: 10.4018/978-1-5225-8494-0.ch009

INTRODUCTION

All Indian alpine tourist destinations can be broadly categorized into two categories viz. Himalayan and Non-Himalayan. The important characteristic feature of all the destinations is having two different types of weather conditions and accordingly the attraction features. While the Himalayan alpine destinations enjoy a distinctive of two weather conditions and two different types of tourists, Non-Himalayan destinations are having the same salubrious environment. Sikkim is a small hilly state, bounded by vast stretches of Tibetan plateau in the North, the Chumbi Valley, and the kingdom Bhutan in the East, the kingdom of Nepal in the west and Darjeeling (West Bengal) in the south. The state lies between 27°04' 46 " N and 28° 07' 48" N and 88° 00' 58" E and 88° 55' 25"E covering an area of 7096 sq. Km. Sikkim is famous for scenic valleys forest, snow clad mountains, magnificent Buddhist culture and heritage and peace-loving people. Though small, the environmental, social and cultural diversities are not so. Some scholars believe that the word Sikkim involves Nepalese dialect and it refers to a *'new place'* or the term has been derived from a Sanskrit word which means a *'mountain crest'*.

The people of Sikkim have ethnic diversity. The Bhutias came from Tibet, the Lepchas were the aboriginal community, and the Nepalese came from Nepal. When Sikkim was an independent state and faced many invasions by its neighboring

Figure 1. Indian state Sikkim

countries and the king took the help of the British India and, later, gifted some of its region including Darjeeling to the British Government. Now this 22nd Indian State (joined Indian Union in 1975) has Over 81% of the total geographical area under the administrative managerial control of the Ministry of Environment and Forest, Government of India. Over 45% of the total geographical area of the state is under tree cover and nearly 34% of the geographical area is set aside as protected area network in the form of national park and wildlife sanctuary. The maximum summer temperature 28^0C and minimum winter temperature is 0^0C. Sikkim has a variety of mineral resources including coal, limestone, iron ore, graphite, pyrite etc. The temperature in the bottom of the valleys (up to 600 meters) situated at lower elevations, particularly during summers, are similar to the monsoon type of climate. The temperature starts falling between 600 meters and 2000metres above sea level and the place enjoys cool temperature climatic conditions and further up (2000 meters to 3000 metres) it is cold temperate climate. Arctic type of climate is found above 5000 meters. Sikkim is ecologically a fragile region. The state has the responsibility to conserve its rich biological diversity that includes coexistence and protection of over 5000 species of angiosperm (one third of the total national angiosperms). After becoming 25th state of the Union Government of India in the year 1975 the rapid development activities ushered in a new era of tourism in Sikkim. Increased accessibility by roadways and air transport, rapid socio-economic development, competitive advantage both from the side of the destination and geographical proximity to tourist generating states contributed to the development of tourism in Sikkim.

Sikkim accounts for the largest share of cardamom production in India, and is the world's second largest producer of the spice after Guatemala. Sikkim has the highest share of agricultural land dedicated to organic farming in India. It is also among India's most environmentally conscious states, having banned plastic water bottles and styrofoam products. Tourism is estimated to contribute to around 8 per cent of the state GDP in Sikkim.

Sikkim is increasingly emphasizing on industrial growth for higher rate of return and employment though the decreasing trend of service sectors is also evident there. It is also empirically true that more the conventional industrial growth is registered less sustainable practices are taken care of. Following is the trend given below from 2004 to 2012.

Again, it is empirically found that Sikkim depends heavily on service sectors for employment, mostly with lower rate of return. Amongst the existing service sectors transport, accommodation, travel agency and tour operations are predominating. The Chief Minister's self employment scheme for the recent year 2013 is clearly showing this trend below.

Table 1. Comparative position of Sikkim among top ten states/UTs w.r.t. per capita GSDP

State / *Union territory*	Rank	GSDP per capita
India (Country)	----------------------------	₹88,533 (US$1,300)
Goa	1	₹304,666 (US$4,500)
Delhi	2	₹275,174 (US$4,100)
Chandigarh	3	₹250,398 (US$3,700)
Sikkim	4	₹240,274 (US$3,600)
Puducherry	5	₹175,701 (US$2,600)
Haryana	6	₹165,728 (US$2,500)
Kerala	7	₹155,005 (US$2,300)
Uttarakhand	8	₹153,076 (US$2,300)
Maharashtra	9	₹152,853 (US$2,300)
Himachal Pradesh	10	₹147,330 (US$2,200)

Table 2. Contribution of different sectors to Sikkim's GDP, 2004-12

%	2004-05	2005-06	2006-07	2007-08	2008-09	2009-10	2010-11	2011-12
Agriculture	19	18	17	16	14	09	08	08
Industry	29	29	30	30	35	55	55	59
Services	52	53	53	54	51	36	37	33
	100	100	100	100	100	100	100	100

Source: SIDICO, as on 31 March 2013

Sikkim is one of the pioneering states developing infrastructure and public amenities. Though some transport development infrastructural projects failed, yet the State has a good record in growth and expansion of infrastructure and amenities to better off quality of human lives. NH-31 is the life line of Sikkim connecting the state with Siliguri of West Bengal and Assam indirectly. The state is connected by rail and helicopter services with the nearest rail head in New Jalpaiguri (about three hours by road) Bagdogra airport in West Bengal. Sikkim is ecologically a fragile region. The state has the responsibility to conserve its rich biological diversity that includes coexistence and protection of over 5000 species of angiosperm (one third of the total national angiosperms). Again this place has multi-ethnic communities. So the need for ecological, cultural, and social diversities is not only essential but

Table 3. Chief minister's self employment scheme, Sikkim

Sectors	Number of Beneficiaries	Comparative Rank
Industry	128	7
Agriculture	358	5
Animal Husbandry	1542	2
Service	304	6
Business	2856	1
Tourism	**941**	**3**
Vehicle/ Transport	94	8
Others	594	4
Total	6817	

Source: SIDICO, as on 31 March 2013

imperative as well. All these natural, cultural and social resources are directly contributing to the unique selling proposition (USP) of tourism development and marketing.

LITERATURE REVIEW

In their article, "Destination Price-Value Perceptions: An Examination of Origin and Seasonal Influences", Murphy, P. and Prichard, M. (1997) have put forward a consumer behavior model of price-value perceptions that is modified and examined in relation to a destination visit. The modification involves the addition of visitor

Table 4. Biodiversity of Sikkim

Taxa	Numbers	Taxa	Numbers	Taxa	Numbers	Taxa	Numbers
Flowering plants	4,458	Oaks 11	11	Bamboos 11	11	Reptiles 88	88
Orchids	527	Medicinal plants 700	700	Ferns and fern allies 480	480	Amphibians 50	50
Rhododendrons 38	38	Mammals 125	125	Tree ferns 9	9	Butterflies 689	689
Conifers 16	16	Birds 574	574	Primulas 58	58	Fishes 48	48

Source: http://sikkimforest.gov.in/Biodiversity-of-Sikkim.htm; Arrawatia and Tambe (2011).

origin and season of visit to take into account influential trip characteristics. The adapted model is investigated with a substantial database of visitor perceptions of Victoria, British Columbia. Statistical analyses reveal that origin and season both interact and separately influence the price-value perceptions of tourists. The evidence suggests that pricing strategies should consider the external influence of such trip variables on traveler value perceptions.

According to consumer behaviour research by Catterall et.al. (1992: 44) "consumers perception carry the greatest weight in the various decisions made by tourists - the choice of a destination, the consumption of commodities while on vacation, and the decision to return. Perception are the consumer's subjective reality. Perception is important because contemporary consumers are becoming more and more discriminating". They are more experienced travellers, older and more value conscious. It is important in influencing travel behaviour. To stay competitive in such a climate, the tourism product must be perceived as of a quality similar or better to that of other competitors, and its price must be perceived as attractive. Thus the information on tourists' perceptions of prices and quality and on the role price plays in tourist behavior is of the utmost importance. Meidan (1994: 357) reckons that when setting prices, the psychology of prices is very important in determining a person's price-value relationship. Attitudes to price are very closely related to the amount of risk the buyer feels is involved in the purchasing decision. Therefore cost-based methods of setting tourism prices could be dangerous - their real value is in determining the lower limits of price. According to Nellis and Parker (1992: 116-117) the essence of pricing strategies is choosing the appropriate price to charge for a good or service is one of the most important challenges facing management. ... therefore, economists call the price which exactly matches the supply and demand for a particular good or service, the equilibrium price". The 'best' or 'correct' price to charge must remain uncertain ahead of actual production and sale. Because market conditions are in a constant state of flux, pricing decisions contain risks. To achieve the optimal pricing strategy, there must be perfect information available to managers about consumer demand, competitors' reactions and supply costs, etc. They reckon managers might adopt various approaches to pricing.

According to Mill and Morrison (1992: 440-441), the factors that influence destination pricing policy are (i) supply and demand relationship of a destination, (ii) the expected length of the product life cycle and the destination or organization's position on it (iii) the extent to which the destination area or other tourism service is uniquely determines it and the (iv) needs of the selected target market(s). Middleton (1988: 59-60) is of the opinion that all marketing decisions involve costs for an organisation and implications for sales volumes. Three of the 4P's involve significant expenditure, which must be made in advance of the revenue it is expected to generate. Product changes, advertising, sales promotion, brochure production, and the organisation and servicing of distribution channels, are all financial commitments in the expectation of sales results. While pricing decisions do not involve costs in advance of sales, they surely determine the level of revenue achievable, and in the case of price discounting to unsold capacity, they represent revenue foregone. Vaccaro (1993: 84-85) reckons that price is traditional a basis for market segmentation. Price is perceived as a guarantee of confidence for the customer who does not have the experience and knowledge to assess product quality. Therefore, price should be viewed in many occasions as a psychological instrument for communicating the value of the brand.

As economic impacts are expenditure driven, theoretically, it would be useful if tourism expenditures were used more frequently in tourism demand studies. As Cai (1999, p. 16) remarked, "market demand, when expressed in dollar amount, should be a preferred measurement of its substantiality". Wang, Rompf, Severt, and Peerapatdit (2006, p. 333) also pointed out that tourism expenditure is "typically scrutinised by policy makers, planning officials, marketers and researchers for monitoring and assessing the impact of tourism on the local economy". Modelling tourist expenditure should consider not only tangible and functional factors, but also intangible and emotional factors. In this review, the two types of factors are classified as destination-related and psychological variables. 18 Psychological variables include traveller evaluation of trip/holiday/vendor, psychological characteristics, trip motives, and taste. Wang et al. (2006) examined the effect of traveller psychological characteristics on their total and disaggregated expenditure. Five psychographic variables presenting what travellers value most were incorporated in their study. Variables included were stability/excitement, self/family, being passive/being active, learning/dropping out and follow tradition/try new things. People seeking excitement had a higher expenditure than those seeking stability and self-oriented people spent more on accommodation than those who were familyoriented. Other studies found that people who travelled for ego / status enhancement tend to spend more than people travelling with other motives (Mehmetoglu, 2007) and the stronger the motive, the higher the expenditure would be (Thrane, 2002).

Much of the economic literature on landscape preferences until recently has been summary in style, as it addresses a 'price' to be placed on landscape, rather than the aspects of the landscape which are valued. The economic methodologies may be categorized into those which require some form of customer survey to elicit expressed values as stated preferences (for example, contingent valuation), those which use survey data other than stated preferences (for example, recent developments using the travel-cost method) and those which measure observed behavior as a proxy for values as revealed preferences (for example, hedonic pricing). Contingent valuation directly asks the respondent for their willingness to pay towards the preservation of an asset (Bateman et al. 1994; Grosclaude and Soguel 1994; Willis 1994; Tunstall and Coker 1995). Contingent valuation assumes hypothetical but structured markets to which respondents can give true valuations. It may be applied both to use-values (for example, of visiting a landscape) and to non-use values (for example, from knowing that a landscape exists although the beneficiary never actually visits it). However, the hypothetical nature of contingent valuation means that it has been found easiest to apply to things related directly to respondents' experiences; for example, a forest drive rather than the whole forest (Hanley 1989). Contingent valuation requires that individuals express their preferences for some environmental resources, or changes in the status of resources, by answering questions about hypothetical choices. This is approached in two ways: first, by questioning about how much the respondent is willing to pay for a welfare gain, so to ensure that this occurs, or pay to prevent a loss; second, by questioning about how much the respondent is willing to accept in order to tolerate a loss, as compensation for a welfare loss, or to accept in order to forgo a gain (Bateman and Turner 1993). It needs to be recognized that if uncritically used, contingent valuation is inherently susceptible to bias. An individual may deliberately underestimate or overestimate his or her willingness to pay. However, applications to cultural and landscape zv2 26 tourism have included Bateman et al. (1994), Garrod et al. (1994), Grosclaude and Soguel (1994) and Willis (1994), with the methodology increasing in popularity. The travel cost method assumes that landscape value is related to the travel cost incurred in reaching that landscape (Willis and Garrod 1991; Randall 1994). Whereas such a method may be valid for long journeys, the logic of interpreting travel costs as a valuation of the destination is less clear for more local travel which may be multifaceted. The method also only considers users, persons who have made the journey to the destination, thereby ignoring other types of consumption. The tourism settings provided by culture and landscape are a hallmark of post-modernity, since for many such transposition is no longer an extravagance but is perceived instead as a 'right' of modern affluence. Residential relocation to areas selected for their cultural or landscape value is the final manifestation of this 'right' and achievement of illusion; relocations are frequently the consequence of earlier tourist experiences. In view of this hallmark of contemporary western living, the present focus is on the consumers of cultural and landscape 'products' as tourists. The discussion originates from the belief that a sustainable product needs to be sustainable simultaneously in two ways and to two groups; namely in production and in consumption, and to destination communities and to tourists. This is a broader definition of sustainability than often used, definitions more usually focusing at least implicitly on host communities, that of tourism in harmony with its physical, social and cultural environment (Medlik ; 1993).

Cultural and landscape tourism is a much broader concept than a focus on palaces, cathedrals, temples and national galleries might imply. Its resources include those of historical geography, archaeology, literature and environmental management, to name but a few (Prentice; 1993). In essence, cultural and landscape tourism is about what a geographer would term *place,* the understanding of 'places as they really are' (Robinson and McCarroll ; 1990), and about *heritage,* things used as *tourism place-products,* 'which are literally or metaphorically passed on from one generation to the other' (Prentice 1993b: 5). At the same time cultural and landscape tourism is a form of self-initiated expressive behavior, but one which has for long been seen as potentially disruptive, if not destructive, of the places visited (Mathieson and Wall; 1982) and which is increasingly being seen as sub-optimal through tourist volumes and organization (Glasson *et al.* 1995).

OBJECTIVES OF THE STUDY

Destination product/ package pricing strategy needs to be formulated by the Destination Management Organization or the tourism department as the apex decision making authority. Regional disparity among tourists, seasonal fluctuations, difference among demographic and psychographic profiles of tourists, control and co-ordination between private and public sectors, extent of adoption of sustainable development principles are found to be the important parameters influencing destination product/ package relationship in Sikkim. A destination specific model, based on simple linear regression equation, was largely explaining the spending of tourists and thereby implying a modified landscape value. Actual landscape value was based on a travel cost that assumed 'landscape value is related to the travel cost incurred in reaching that landscape (Willis and Garrod 1991; Randall 1994). Based on the model, the objective of the study is –

1.   To identify the landscape value based travel costs and its implications in Sikkim.

   Therefore the hypothesis for the study is given below.

H0: There is no relationship among income of tourists, spending, duration of stay, earlier visit and number of times visited to Sikkim

Methodology

This study was conducted using self-administered questionnaires with the consent from the Hotel managers beforehand. Pilot testing was conducted using a small convenience sample of 35 respondents from various hotels in Sikkim. The respondents were informed that their participation was on a voluntary basis and all information provided would be kept private and confidential. Questionnaires were distributed only to those who agreed to participate in the study. The researcher then briefly explained the nature and requirement of the survey before the respondent filled up the questionnaire. For collecting the data from the primary sources, a structured questionnaire was prepared for tourists visiting Gangtok, Namchi, Mangan, Pelling. A total of 400 customers were contacted, and the overall response rate was 42.25 per cent (169 completed, usable questionnaires). The Ordered Probit Model is a generalization of the popular probit analysis to the case of more than two outcomes of an ordinal dependent variable. It describes the relationship among spending of tourists visiting Sikkim, average monthly income of tourists visiting Sikkim, length of stay of the tourists, past visit and its number(s) to measure tourist retention.

DATA ANALYSIS AND DISCUSSION

As this method was found to be relevant for long journeys, the logic of interpreting travel costs as a valuation of the destination was less clear for more local travel which may be multifaceted. So, modified landscape value for Sikkim was assumed to be the spending of tourists as majority of tourists are domestic and spend less to reach their destination. Here the model was given here under.

$$S=I+D+V+T+u$$

Here, S = spending of tourists, I = Average monthly income of tourists, D = Duration of trip in Sikkim, V = Visited Sikkim earlier or not and T = Number of times visited to Sikkim including the present visit. Ordered probit, a generalization of the popular probit analysis to the case of more than two outcomes of an ordinal dependent variable, was used to explain the relationship among spending of tourists visiting Sikkim, average monthly income of tourists visiting Sikkim, length of stay of the tourists, past visit and its number(s). Considering the relationship among these variables a, model was built with the help of calculated regression coefficients. Following result was computed for the model.

Table 5. The relationship among income of tourists, spending, duration of stay, earlier visit and times visited to Sikkim

Variables	Coefficient	Std. Error	z-Statistic	Prob.
INCOME (I)	0.362328	0.064406	5.625671	0.0000
DOTS (D)	0.135229	0.078971	1.712398	0.0868
VSE (V)	-0.660378	0.173713	-3.801543	0.0001
TVS (T)	0.179448	0.082577	2.173099	0.0298
Dependent Variable: Spending (S)	Method: ML - Ordered Probit		Sample: 169	

Source: Field Survey 2016-17
Note: Statistical analysis has been made using E-Views statistical Package

An interesting relationship was found among variables with calculated regression coefficients. The binary data "whether visited Sikkim earlier or not" was found to be negatively associated with the spending of tourists and the regression coefficient -0.660 was significant at 1% level. The same level of significance was also evident for the monthly average income of tourists which was 0.362.

The regression coefficient for the number of times tourists visiting Sikkim was 0.175 at 5% level of significance and a positive association was found whereas the same coefficient was 0.135 for duration of trip in Sikkim at 10% level of significance.

REFERENCES

Bateman, I., & Turner, R. K. (1993). Valuation of the Environment, Methods and Techniques: The Contingent Valuation Method. In R. K. Turner (Ed.), *Sustainable Environmental Economics and Management* (pp. 120–191). London: Belhaven.

Bateman, I., Willis, K., & Garrod, G. (1994). Consistency between Contingent Valuation Estimates. *Regional Studies*, *28*(5), 457–474. doi:10.1080/0034340941 2331348396

Cai, L. A. (1999). Relationship of household characteristics and lodging expenditure on leisure trips. *Journal of Hospitality & Leisure Marketing*, *6*(2), 5–18. doi:10.1300/J150v06n02_02

Cater, E., & Lowman, G. (Eds.). (1994). *Ecotourism*. Chichester, UK: Wiley.

Catterall, M., Maclaran, P., & Stevens, L. (2010). Postmodern Paralysis: The Critical Impasse in Feminist Perspectives on Consumers. *Journal of Marketing Management*, 489–504.

Garrod, G. D., Willis, K. G., & Saunders, C. M. (1994). The Benefits and Costs of the Somerset Levels and Moors ESA. *Journal of Rural Studies*, *10*(2), 131–145. doi:10.1016/0743-0167(94)90025-6

Glasson, J., Godfrey, K., Goodey, B., Absalom, H., & Van Der Borg, J. (1995). *Towards Visitor Impact Management*. Aldershot, UK: Avebury.

Grosclaude, P., & Soguel, N. C. (1994). Valuing Damage to Historic Buildings Using a Contingent Market. *Journal of Environmental Planning and Management*, *37*(3), 279–288. doi:10.1080/09640569408711976

Hanley, N. D. (1989). Valuing Rural Recreation Benefits: An Empirical Comparison of Two Approaches. *Journal of Agricultural Economics*, *40*(3), 361–374. doi:10.1111/j.1477-9552.1989.tb01117.x

Mathieson, A., & Wall, G. (1982). *Tourism: Economic, Physical and Social Impacts*. Harlow: Longman.

Medlik, S. (1993). *Dictionary of Travel, Tourism and Hospitality*. Oxford, UK: Butterworth Heinemann.

Mehmetoglu, M. (2007). Nature-based tourists: The relationship between their trip expenditures and activities. *Journal of Sustainable Tourism*, *15*(2), 200–215. doi:10.2167/jost642.0

Middleton, V. T. C. (1991). *Whither the package tour? Tourism Management*. Butterworth Heinemann.

Middleton, V. T. C., & Clarke, J. (2000). *Marketing in Travel and Tourism*. New Delhi: Butterworth Heinemann.

Middleton, V. T. C., & Hawkins, R. (1988). *Sustainable Tourism: A Marketing Perspective*. Butterworth Heinemann.

Mill, R. C., & Morrison, A. M. (1992). *The Tourism System: An Introductory Text*. Englewood Cliffs, NJ: Prentice Hall Publication.

Murphy, P., & Prichard, M. (1997). Destination Price-Value Perceptions: An Examination of Origin and Seasonal Influences. *Journal of Travel Research, 35*(3), 16–22. doi:10.1177/004728759703500303

Randall, A. (1994). A Difficulty with the Travel Cost Method. *Land Economics, 70*(1), 88–96. doi:10.2307/3146443

Richard, P. (2005). Cultural Landscape Tourism: Facilitating Meaning. In S. Wahab & J. J. Pigram (Eds.), *Tourism Development and Growth: The Challenges of Sustainability* (pp. 190–216). London: Routledge.

Robinson, V., & McCarroll, D. (Eds.). (1990). *The Isle of Man: Celebrating a Sense of Place*. Liverpool, UK: Liverpool University Press.

Thrane, C. (2002). Jazz Festival Visitors and Their Expenditures: Linking Spending Patterns to Musical Interest. *Journal of Travel Research, 40*(3), 281–286. doi:10.1177/0047287502040003006

Tunstall, S. M., & Coker, A. (1995). Survey-based Valuation Methods. In A. Coker & C. Richards (Eds.), *Valuing the Environment: Economic Approaches to Environmental Evaluation* (pp. 104–126). Chichester, UK: Wiley.

Wang, Y., Rompf, P., Severt, D., & Peerapatdit, N. (2006). Examining and Identifying the Determinants of Travel Expenditure Patterns. *International Journal of Tourism Research, 8*(5), 333–346. doi:10.1002/jtr.583

Willis, K. G. (1994). Taying for Heritage: What Price for Durham Cathedral? *Journal of Environmental Planning and Management, 37*(3), 267–278. doi:10.1080/09640569408711975

Chapter 10

FIBRAs as a Tool for Investment Diversification in the Mexican Hotel Sector:
The Case of FIBRA Inn

José G. Vargas-Hernández
University of Guadalajara, Mexico

Hugo Daniel González-Altamirano
University of Guadalajara, Mexico

ABSTRACT

This chapter seeks to make an approach to the financial instrument called REIT, Real Estate Investment Trust, specifically in the hotel industry in Mexico. This tool has allowed many investors to make business in the real estate sector, and it has provided a wider range of hosting services. This research takes us into the strategies the REIT leader in the hotel industry has implemented to position themselves as such. In large part this is explained by network theory and agent – principal theory. The study method is based on a literature review of several theories, as well as the study of a successful case. The analysis of results presents and describes the features that have contributed to business success.

DOI: 10.4018/978-1-5225-8494-0.ch010

INTRODUCTION

This work focuses on a problem facing investors in the Mexican country. Investments in real estate were unique to the few families with economic capacity to allow them to such investment, or for large foreign companies entering the country. The FIBRAs were born in the Mexican country only in 2004, but in the United States emerged in the early 60`s. Many countries have changed their laws to allow the FIBRAs figure, or its equivalent in the host country (Schachat, Fisher, Lowy, 2010)

These Trusts can be worked in three areas: The industrial area, the trade-services and the hotel industry. While the three sectors are attractive for investment, the industrial sector is the one that has had interest from investors. This sector includes rent mainly warehouses and offices (Howton, Howton, Lee, Mi. 2012). The hospitality sector has been, meanwhile, the least favored investment; perhaps because the hotels have a peculiarity, despite being part of the FIBRA to real estate aspects, the hotel management is in the hands of the franchise or original owner (Anderson, Benefield, Hurst, 2015).

The tourism sector in Mexico is one of the fastest growing clear that symbolizes a niche for all the potential opportunities it presents. While the increase in the number of rooms is remarkable, it is still insufficient for growth and economic development that presents Mexico. In part this lag is covered with franchises that through FIBRAs see the opportunity to enter the market, which also offers the attraction of goodwill and plus value or surplus. Thus, network management becomes essential for managers and investors because these networks that weave make the consortium stronger, besides reduce transaction costs and make the market more attractive. In this case, the multiple and various investments are a factor to minimize risk and offer more guarantees and certainty to investors. This paper discusses these strategies and recommendations that can follow this consortium organized to maintain business growth.

BACKGROUND OF THE PROBLEM

The markets have a wide variety of options to invest, in the case of Mexico, of all the assets of the most popular equity and known are the shares, which represent a fraction of the share capital of a company, issued by the same as a financing option and whose market value is affected by supply and demand. The shares have been part of the investment portfolios of Mexican investors for decades, so it is an investment option well known in our market (Cavazos González, Rodríguez García, Garza Sánchez, 2015)

In this same market, another active equity is FIBRAs (Trust Infrastructure and Real Estate). The FIBRAs are an investment instrument whose purpose is to finance the acquisition and / or construction of real estate for leaseback or acquire the right to receive income from the lease of such property. These trusts are responsible for renting and managing a portfolio of real estate such as office buildings, shopping centers, hotels, residential, etc.

While these assets are in the US market since the early 60s, known as Real Estate Investment Trust, REIT, it was in 2004 that these were introduced to the Mexican market with some adaptations, and since its introduction to the domestic market this option investment has gained popularity as a viable and confidence to bet their capital on other assets (Cavazos Gonzalez, et al. 2015) option.

The apparent stability of the Mexican economy to the global crisis during the years 2011 and 2012 contributed to the development of rental properties in the country, mainly in large and medium cities. The FIBRAs promoted the development of real estate in Mexico to be integrated as an instrument through which investors both its institutional and individual serve as a source of liquidity for developers and investors, and contribute to the diversification of risk for investor in real estate (De Leon, 2015).

An additional advantage is that they are very attractive instruments in times of uncertainty, aspects such as low oil prices and the depreciation of the Mexican peso against foreign currencies like the dollar. It should be remembered that the leases long term are linked to dollar and therefore have dollarized their income, with costs in Mexican pesos.

DELIMITATION OF THE PROBLEM

Before the implementation of the FIBRAs, the opportunity to participate in the development and leasing of commercial spaces in Mexico was restricted to a small group of families and wealthy businessmen, large foreign institutional investors and financial institutions. The commercial real estate in Mexico is characterized by a limited number of large-scale developers, who have financial strength and technical capacity to develop and complete large projects (Carranza Cedillo and Garcia Camargo, 2014)

As the FIBRAs are an opportunity for investment in real estate, are considered four main areas: industrial, commercial-retail, office and hotel sector. The main sector in which this type of trust is present today is the industrial wineries focused on logistics services, for example, and offices. Thus, the country offers opportunities and features that make it attractive (Makino, 2004) Although the FIBRAs share similar income indicators as the rate of occupation or income level, between sectors development has been uneven (Carranza Cedillo and Garcia Camargo, 2014). The FIBRAs have high performance in the industrial sector, commercial-retail and hotel sectors have maintained a lower profile, but with a perspective of strong growth (De Leon, 2015).

The operation of FIBRE is briefly described. Once legally constituted, properties are achieved for the real estate portfolio and certificates of participation therein are placed in the stock market. The trust is responsible for the administration of the property, ranging from maintenance to marketing (Cavazos Gonzalez, et al. 2015). It must be distributed annually, according to the Income Tax Law, in Articles 223 and 224, 95% of income derived property between certificate holders. The FIBRAs are a mixture of investment in fixed income and equity as it offers payments to investors in continued periods for income property, while allowing obtaining capital gains on the purchase and sale of certificates in the stock market, which change the price according to the surplus property portfolio.

In its publication, Cavazos González (2015) mentions some of the benefits of FIBRAs, which are listed below:

1. **Cost Control:** Because in this sector investors tend to manage their own hotels, FIBRA benefits from cost control, allowing achieves better operating margins.
2. **Accessibility:** FIBRAs offer an alternative investment through the Mexican Stock Exchange in real estate from accessible amounts to both individuals and corporations.
3. **Diversification:** The nature of the FIBRAs allows investing in a diversified way in the real estate sector including industrial buildings, shopping centers, offices and hotels, among others.
4. **Sources of Performance:** Through FIBRAs, investors earn two types of income: income flows in and gain surplus from the revaluation of real estate.
5. **Corporate Governance:** Investors can enjoy the benefits of the institutional legal framework of the FIBRAs, as well as its governance and operational transparency. The administration of the company is carried out with professionalism and experience that have the staff within the trust. The implementation of corporate governance practices avoids conflicts of interest between sponsors and related parties.
6. **Transparency:** The trust scheme provides simple and appropriate commissions, discloses information in detail and openly communicated to market participants.

The business model that includes FIBRA Inn is focused on specialization in business hotels, the operation with leading global brands, and preference in the acquisition of hotels before development and smart growth portfolio. This model has been useful for this trust, since the growth and expansion of the company has been remarkable in the last two years. Seeing this expansion and development, it comes to the question that this research seeks to answer.

What have been the strategies implemented FIBRA Inn to position itself as the largest hotel consortium in Mexico?

RATIONALE

This project was created to have an approach to the strategies that have generated success and diversification of a FIBRA in the competitive hotel industry in Mexico. In particular, strategies are analyzed from a theoretical point of view prior analysis of the literature, seeking explanations and suggestions for opportunities in a rapidly growing sector and the possibility of investing in real estate, a very attractive market.

This paper seeks to understand the management of networks as competitive sales of the consortium, to be more attractive to industry and investment. Besides, transaction costs tend to reduce, thanks to the strength of the institutions. In this case, the multiple and various investments are a factor to minimize risk and offer more guarantees and certainty to investors. This paper discusses these strategies and recommendations can follow this consortium organized to keep the company growing.

REVIEW OF THE THEORETICAL AND EMPIRICAL LITERATURE

First of all, speaking of FIBRAs, the talk is about tools for investment portfolios and so becomes inevitable resort to Modern Portfolio Theory, a classic financial theory developed by Markowitz in 1952. The fundamental concept of the Theory of Modern Portfolio states that individual investments in a portfolio should not be selected randomly, but must be the result of the optimum combination of actions, from a desired combination of investments with the combination of risks and returns (Markowitz, 1952, cited by Weyer, 2011).

One of the key points of the Modern Portfolio Theory as quoted by Markowitz (Weyel, 2011) is that a particular action is not only selected for its unique risk-return characteristics. On the contrary, the investor must consider as a group of actions covariate with the rest of the shares of a particular index. Also considering these covariates can build portfolios with the same expected return and lower risk, defining a region called Efficient Frontier (Markowitz, 1952, cited by Weyel, 2011).

Speaking of portfolio theory, it cannot be denied that while there is a Governing Board pointing the structure and delegating authority, the CEO becomes an agent that manages the capital of the principal, in this case, holders. Thus, the theory states that the principal agent hires someone to do his work, although this will always lead to conflict as they are not the same goals as the agent of the principal.

In this particular case, it can be seen more clearly the agent theory if it is identified the FIBRAs are financial instruments to open the possibility of investing in real estate. So FIBRA Inn what it does is to manage real estate investors have been on their hands, and while they may have functions to the direction and strategies to follow, are not owners but rather administrators (Collins, 1994). Various hotels in this consortium from different consortia are handled, but also hotels that retain their own administration.

While the theory states that agents are responsible for the goods of the principal, also it mentions the possible problems to which they would face: First that the information between the agent and the principal is asymmetric. Second, the agent's effort cannot be observed directly by the principal, so this imposes control systems to monitor the agent, which generates costs. Thirdly, it is mentioned that the actions and results of the agent depend not only on him but the number of externalities that are involved in his actions and decisions (Gorbaneff, 2003).

Given these externalities, it can be considered the core competencies, which are those that arise from the collective learning of the organization, especially those concerning how to coordinate the different production techniques. This type of skills is the real source of competitive advantage based on the ability to address the entire company that generates, besides professional skills (Markides and Williamson, 2007).

To summarize, it should be noted that a core competency is the logical result obtained by the combined valuation of three kinds of basic interrelated competencies that are technological, personal and organizational (Mahoney, 2012). The result of using these strategies must be reflected in a greater than the performance of competitors. As established in the so-called virtuous circle of Penrose, business expansion depends not only of demand but also the existence and adequacy of a company's own management services (Peng, 2012).

While it is important that the company generates this set of capabilities in management, the essence of the FIBRAs is working through networks. The network concept is currently a tool to explain the workings of society, and is of increasing relevance between various disciplines (Cabus and Vanhaverbeke, 2006 cited by Becerra, 2008); hence the importance that is given to understand social and economic situations where different agents are interconnected, and to explain individual behavior of these (Becerra, 2008).

The network is a mechanism or strategy of integration and coordination of different agents that have a goal that encourages them to ally themselves under this type of structure (Dabas, 2004 cited by Becerra, 2008). In areas marked by diversity, the network as a model of organization, does not seek to homogenize but organize heterogeneity, allowing the relative autonomy among its members. The network as such is an open system in which the exchange between its members and agents of other social groups allowing the potentiation of resources (Becerra, 2008) of the members individually and the network as a whole.

Systemic network structure comprises three basic elements: Nodes, which are the components, as individuals or organizations, between which links are given in the interest of the members (Becerra, 2008). Relationships or exchanges on information, knowledge, technology, goods and services define and govern, in essence, the network behavior. The third element is communication, which can be determined by social roles both formal and informal played by nodes within the network.

Formal social roles are often determined by groups, organizations or cultures, and reflect the formal designation of formal positions (Vargas, et al. 2014). While the formal aspect of networks plays an important role, sometimes casual aspect plays a more important role even so it is important that directors and managers know well the organizational culture of the company. In the specific case of FIBRA Inn networks play a substantial role, since it is precisely those relationships and contracts with franchises and leading companies that allow it to develop and maintain competitive advantage in this fast-growing industry

According to Cabus and Vanhaverbeke (2006) the main objectives of an enterprise network are: Increasing competitiveness and profitability of companies in the network induce specialization of businesses in some of the different stages of the production process, consolidate market presence of the companies that make up the network and facilitate business access to services which are inaccessible to them individually. As it can be seen, FIBRA Inn is a network that maximizes their opportunities and resources for the network that has to function properly.

Institutions are what give structure, regulations and seriousness to a society (DiMaggio, 1991), as it allows giving a more formal approach and reduce the uncertainty of entrepreneurs. In this case, the institutions are present from the same term FIBRA as it is a figure that Mexican legislation that responds to a problem. Before FIBRAs, the housing market was in the hands of a few families, and foreign companies. The FIBRAs have allowed investment in the purchase and development of Real Estate is a real option for many investors.

THEORETICAL ASSUMPTION

The rational use of relationships, the use of networks and portfolio diversification has allowed FIBRA Inn to become in just a couple of years in the consortium leader within FIBRAs exclusively focused on hosting and accommodation.

CONTEXTUAL FRAMEWORK

FIBRA Inn is a Mexican trust formed primarily to acquire, develop and rent a wide range of hotel properties in Mexico. FIBRA Inn owns a portfolio of high quality properties designed to serve the business traveler and is geographically diversified in 12 states, with more than 7,000 rooms.

Below there is a map showing the presence of FIBRA Inn in Mexico (FINN 2016). There are only two hotels on the coast, and of those, only Playa del Carmen is a tourist destination with high potential.

According to the official report, during the first quarter of 2016, FIBRA Inn grew by 80.5% in income before interest, taxes, depreciation and amortization. With previously mentioned, it can be observed that strive to fulfill its vision: To be the leading owner of hotels for business traveler in Mexico, while offering a memorable

Figure 1. Presence of FIBRA Inn in Mexico
Source: FIBRA Inn

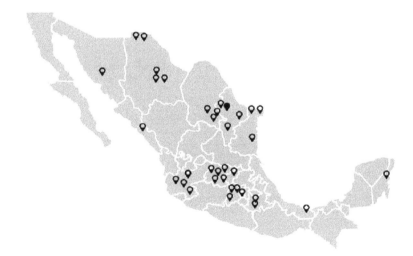

experience to guests, healthier and conducive environment for development of employees, exceeding expectations of investors. The knowledge strategy is composed as follows (FINN, 2016) on figure 2 below.

FIBRA Inn has entered into franchise agreements with IHG to operate its global brands including Holiday Inn, Holiday Inn Express and Holiday Inn Express & Suites. It also has licensing agreements and brand use with Hilton to operate Hampton Inn by Hilton; and Starwood Hotels and Resorts Worldwide to operate its Aloft brand. It has properties that operate with national brands such as Camino Real, City Express, City Express Junior, Casa Grande and Arriva Express, additionally has agreements with Marriott International and Wyndham Hotel Group to establish development agreements.

Figure 2. The Strategy followed by FIBRA
Source: FINN (2016)

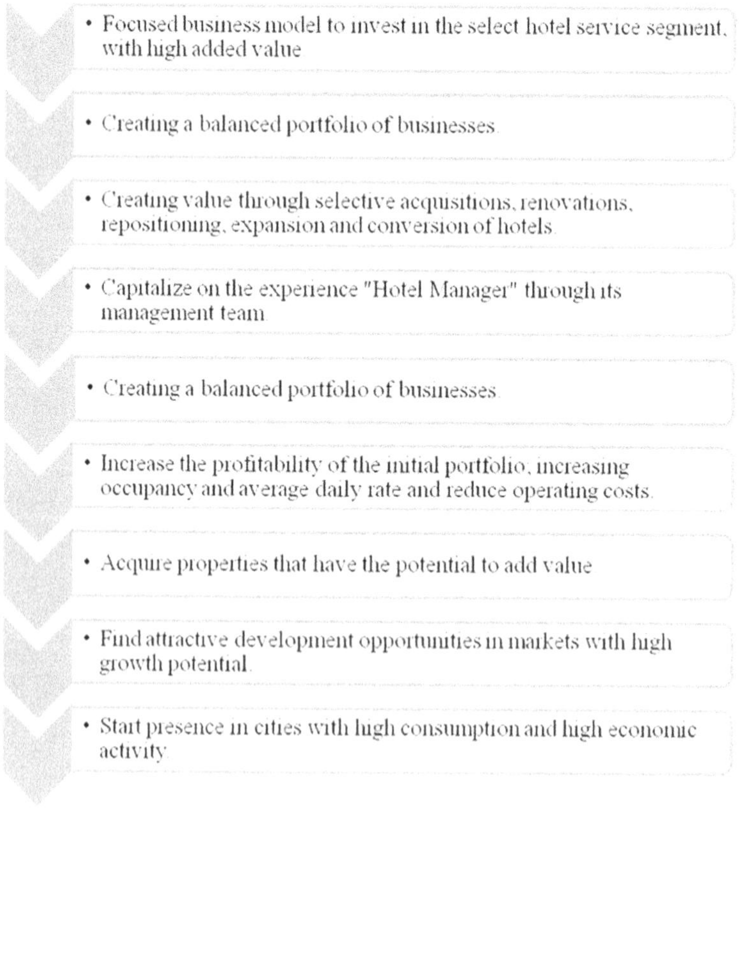

- Focused business model to invest in the select hotel service segment, with high added value
- Creating a balanced portfolio of businesses
- Creating value through selective acquisitions, renovations, repositioning, expansion and conversion of hotels
- Capitalize on the experience "Hotel Manager" through its management team
- Creating a balanced portfolio of businesses
- Increase the profitability of the initial portfolio, increasing occupancy and average daily rate and reduce operating costs
- Acquire properties that have the potential to add value
- Find attractive development opportunities in markets with high growth potential
- Start presence in cities with high consumption and high economic activity

Business strategy following this trust is clear: Meet the goal of increasing cash flow from operations portfolio, future potential acquisitions, and development opportunities so that sustainable growth is achieved long term to generate attractive returns to holders of stock certificates.

The ownership structure of the Trust is simple: 82.9% is owned by the investing public, while the remaining 17.1% is the trust of control. In turn, at least 51% of this trust is owned by the founders, and the remaining 49% are adherents invited to the trust control, which may include hotel managers, hotel operators, comprehensive services, to name a few. For its part, the organizational structure of the trust is made up as follows: holders are at the head of this structure, because debt holders have a priority claim on cash flows relating to shareholders who only they are entitled to the residual flow once paid to holders (Ehrhard, 2007).

Within this structure there is also a Technical Committee that the strategic decisions that the trust must follow, as the expansion to other cities or addition of other hotels to undergo FIBRA. Recall that one of the listed advantages over FIBRA is its corporate governance, because governance is crucial for the proper management of business element. In this case, the organizational structure has been added for better governance committees: Audit, practices and investments, nominations, and monitoring credit.

Figure 3. Organiational structure of FIBRA Inn
Source: FIBRA Inn

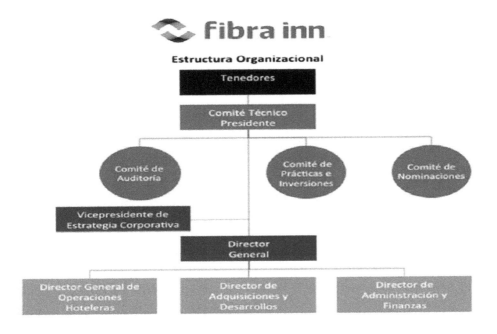

In all of the aforementioned committees, there are both independent members as equity members. Most members are specialists in their area and recognized members of society, so as to generate greater certainty to investors, while minimizing risk by taking decisions by the director of the trust.

Although the figure of the FIBRA has few years in Mexican country, the origin of FIBRA Inn dates back to the early 80's, as a family business, owned a unit Double Tree Hotels. It was in 1993 when got local partners with hotels of the size like Hampton Inn, later Quinta Real Hotel and in 2003 join the City Express hotels. From the year 2007 opens to private equity investments, and is finally in 2013 that FIBRA Inn is created, joining the capital market in Mexico (FINN, 2016).

By 2013, Dr. Peter Linneman macroeconomic analyst, consultant in real estate and professor at the University of Pennsylvania, in the United States wrote about FIBRAS in Mexico. He stated that the financial instrument in Mexico had gained the interest of investors in the previous two years, during the last two years and offered great potential at long-term real estate markets in Mexico. However, he considered substantially overvalued and with serious structural problems (Linneman, 2013). His analysis indicated that the furor even by Mexican FIBRAS end badly, especially because of the absence of leadership leaving behind a trail of disappointed investors (Linneman, 2013, page 1).

While during 2015, FIBRAS showed a negative performance in the stock market on the Mexican Stock Exchange. There are many diverse and solid reasons for this negative behavior throughout the year. However, it is important to remember a feature that makes the difference unlike other financial instruments: FIBRAS assets consist of real estate. The value of real estate tends to increase as time due to surplus and goodwill, and due among other things to the land meets the characteristics of the frame VRIO, is a valuable resource, rare, inimitable and is used in organization (Barney, 1996 cited by Arend and Lévesque, 2010).

Contrary to what happens with machinery and equipment, real estate is not depreciated with time. In this sense, an additional advantage is that the generation of surplus value does not depend on the ability of companies to market their products or services, but external factors such as location and some internal such as quality of construction. In addition to all this, the real estate generates steady income, because the tenants who rent pay regular rentals to the owners thereof (Gorbaneff, 2003).

Given these factors, it can be understood that a key factor in the poor performance shown by FIBRAS in 2015 is directly related to the loss of value of the Mexican peso against other currencies, particularly against the US dollar. Because foreign investors to participate in the local market, they must buy or sell pesos to perform operations. The impact is more relevant in this case because the FIBRAS distribute dividends quarterly, which are normally made in pesos due to a devaluation of the currency, the returns earned by investors is diminished by currency effects (De Leon, 2015).

With this diagnosis and prospects, it might consider a panorama with little favor for FIBRAs. However this is not the case. For testing, FIBRA Inn concluded the first quarter of 2016 with 40 hotels in operation and 2 in the purchase agreement, with that according to its quarterly results, accumulates 7, 027 rooms. On the revenue side is concerned, the amount totaled 412.8 million pesos, of which 391.8 million pesos are for lodging concept and 21.1 million are for lease, totaling an increase of 40.3% compared with the same period during 2015.

Net income exceeded 49 million pesos, the average occupancy rate rose to 59.9%, representing an increase of 3.7% over the first quarter of 2015. Meanwhile, the average daily rate also increased more than 11%, reaching a record high of $ 1,172.5 plus tax. And finally, another record figure for the company, room revenue to $ 702.7 spent an increase of 18.6% compared with $ 592.6 in the first quarter of 2015 (FINN, 2016).

This means that the outlook for FIBRAs in Mexico is encouraging, more in a sector unexploited as is the hotel industry, since according to data from INEGI 2016, is one of the industries that has shown higher growth, and overall, sustained growth, providing certainty to investors, while it can manifest itself in regional development if it can reach areas where the potential is high, and ease of investment that allows the instrument closer to a latent reality in the next years.

ANALYSIS OF RESULTS

Based on the analysis of literature, it can be said that the hotel industry is highly seasonal and particularly vulnerable to economic cycles and social changes. The main destinations in the country are: Mexico City, the Riviera Maya, Los Cabos and Acapulco (Secretaría de Turismo, 2016). According to the barometer of Tourism of the World Tourism Organization, Mexico is among the 10 most visited countries in the world by number of visitors, but falls 22nd place in terms of economic impact is concerned. It is noteworthy that in Mexico 70% of hotels are not affiliated with any franchise. The remaining 30% that is affiliated is located in large tourist centers and major cities.

Some of the main market opportunities FIBRA Inn has are those listed below:

1. Market. According to the Barometer of Tourism, prepared by the World Tourism Organization, Mexico is among the top destinations for global tourism receiving at around 30 million international tourists per year (Secretaría de

Turismo, 2016) measured by visitors at least one night staying. The entry of foreign currency from visitors represents the third largest source of income for Mexico, only after oil and remittances.

2.   Territory. Despite having more than 9,330 km of coastline in both the Pacific Ocean and the Gulf of Mexico, and there is more than 20 tourist destinations of relevance, including the Riviera Maya, Cancun, Acapulco, Los Cabos, Puerto Vallarta, Cozumel and Huatulco, the FIBRAs have not dabbled in beach tourism. Its focus is now more towards cities in central, northern and shallows, i.e. cities where most business is conducted.

3.   Independent hotels. Part of the strategy f FIBRA Inn is to acquire hotels operated independently. In Mexico there are 1,097 hotels aimed at business travelers, of which 405 (37%) are branded urban hotels, while 692 (63%) are independent urban hotels. This opportunity could be maximized to strengthen networks and linkages between small hotels and FIBRA Inn.

4.   Potential. Currently Mexico's economy is developing, since according to the data disclosed by both the World Bank and the UN (Naciones Unidas, 2011); economies in developing countries are those that allow the recovery of the world economy. The demand for accommodation in Mexico grows to be a country of opportunity; however, the lodging capacity is not sufficient in several medium-sized cities, allowing high development potential.

Among these opportunities, it can be found that competitive advantages of the company are closely linked to each other: The hotels of the company are located in high-growth cities. The properties are practically newly constructed; since 75% have less than 4 years, besides that meet high quality standards and maintenance. FIBRA Inn has strong business relationships with international brands that it handles. It offers attractive options for business travelers. In addition, the technology platform backed by a system of world-class reservations and customer service.

CONCLUSION AND RECOMMENDATION

Within the commercial, office and hotel sectors there is still a vast potential for growth given the greater degree of institutionalization that has barely begun to bear in recent years in the Mexican country, coupled with the growth in demand for this type of real estate spaces and the great backlog that exists in income levels in Mexico compared to other countries in Latin America.

The FIBRAs that have the best relations with strategic partners, developers and key customers within these sectors will be those that can sustain higher growth in the long term. Thanks to the benefits offered by the basic local real estate sector, all FIBRAs of commercial, office and hotel sectors are well positioned to capture this growth. The FIBRAs have met to give possibility to investors to get involved in the real estate market with an investment that is not as great as it would directly buy the property.

Undoubtedly, the advantages FIBRA Inn to investors are varied: From the platform investment in high-quality hotels, in a segment with relatively low volatility and attractive growth. Recognition of partner brands is a competitive advantage. The operational flexibility of FIBRA Inn is focused on creating an efficient and scalable platform resulting in a high guest satisfaction. The ability to generate attractive margins above market levels, the attractive capital structure with a conservative financial policy, obtaining attractive financing, the sound macroeconomic environment in Mexico are among other competitive advantages.

Another consideration to stress on FIBRA exposed to the hospitality industry is that its business model differs from the rest, as it tends to manage its own hotels when the rest delegated this operation to third parties.

Some of the proposals that FIBRA Inn can follow to continue:

1. Increase the number of hotels in coastal areas, mainly in the better-paid areas, such as Los Cabos, Cancun or the Riviera Nayarit. Currently there are only a couple of hotels on the coast: One in Playa del Carmen and the other in Coatzacoalcos.
2. In the Mexican country, there are still many independent hotels, so incorporating them into the corporate real estate, but not necessarily to the hotel management. It will give in addition to greater presence; it would increase in the number of rooms available.
3. Diversify and exploit opportunity areas for real estate development, especially in the three largest cities, because the location is important to achieve greater presence among consumers factor.
4. Increase presence in medium-sized cities, but commercial and industrially attractive, Aguascalientes, San Luis Potosí, Tijuana or Torreon.
5. Focus on mixed-use projects in the real state sector, including services such as offices, hospitals, shopping malls, hotels especially in dynamic cities such as Mexico City, Guadalajara and Monterrey.

REFERENCES

Anderson, R., Benefield, J., & Hurst, M. (2015). Property-type diversification and REIT performance: an analysis of operating performance and abnormal returns. Journal of Economics & Finance, 39(1), 48-74.

Arend, R., Lévesque, M. (2010). *Is the Resource-Based View a Practical Organizational Theory?* Doi:10.1287/orsc.1090.0484

Becerra, F. (2008). Las redes empresariales y la dinámica de la empresa: aproximación teórica. Revista Innovar: estrategia e innovaciones, 18(32).

Carranza, M., & García, P. (2014). *Fideicomisos de infraestructura y bienes raíces (FIBRAS) para incrementar el rendimiento de la cartera de inversión de una sociedad de inversión especializada en fondos para el retiro (siefore).* Monterrey: Universidad Panamericana.

Cavazos, M., Rodríguez, M., & Garza, H. (2015). *Análisis del desempeño financiero de portafolios de inversión en FIBRAs y acciones.* Monterrey: Universidad Autónoma de Nuevo León.

Collis, D. (1994). How valuable are organizational capabilities? *Strategic Management Journal, 15*(S1), 143–152. doi:10.1002mj.4250150910

De León, P. (2015). *Más allá de las tasas, los factores detrás del bajo rendimiento de FIBRAS en 2015.* DF, México: Reporte Actinver.

Di Maggio, P., & Powell, W. (1991) *El nuevo institucionalismo en el análisis organizacional.* Laboratorio de Análisis Institucional del Sistema Universitario Mexicano. Recuperado de http://laisumedu.org

Ehrhard, M., & Brigham, E. (2007). *Finanzas corporativas.* DF, México: Cengage Learning.

FINN. (2016). *Reporte trimestral Enero-Marzo 2016 FIBRA Inn.* Recuperado de http://www.FIBRAinn.mx

Gorbaneff, Y. (2003). *Teoría del agente principal y el mercadeo.* Revista Universitaria EAFIT.

Howton, S., Howton, S., Lee, J., & Mi, L. (2012). REIT Ownership and Property Performance: Evidence from the Lodging Industry. Journal of Real Estate Portfolio Management, 18(2), 169-185.

Linneman, P. (2013). Outlook for Mexican FIBRAs: A call for educating investors and raising standards. Retail Property Insights, 20(3).

Mahoney, J. (2012). *Economic Foundations of Strategy*. Thousand Oaks, CA: Sage Publishing.

Makino, S., Isobe, T., & Chan, C. (2004). Does country matter? *Strategic Management Journal*, 25(10), 1027–1043. doi:10.1002mj.412

Markides, C., & Williamson, P. (1994). Related Diversification, Core Competencies and Corporate Performance. *Strategic Management Journal*. doi:10.1002mj.4250151010

Organización de las Naciones Unidas. (2011). *Situación y perspectivas para la economía mundial 2011*. Recuperado de http://www.un.org

Peng, M. (2012). *Estrategia global*. México: D.F. Cengage Learning.

Schachat, R., Fisher, M., & Lowy, J. (2010). Real Estate Investment Trust Corner. Journal of Passthrough Entities, 31(6), 39–42. Retrieved from http://www.sectur.gob.mx

Vargas, J. G., Guerra, E., Bojórquez, A., & Bojórquez, F. (2014). *Gestión estratégica de organizaciones. Ciudad Autónoma de Buenos Aires*. Elaleph.

Weyel, P. (2011). *Portfolio Theory and the Financial Crisis*. Norderstedt. Grin Verlag.

Chapter 11
Christianity and Tourism Development in Nigeria:
A Socio-Economic Discourse

Floribert Patrick C. Endong
University of Calabar, Nigeria

ABSTRACT

Most of the spiritual programs organized by mega Pentecostal and charismatic churches in Nigeria constitute serious touristic attractions, which over the years, have immensely been contributing to socio-economic development in the country. These programs pull a multitude of national and international expectant tourists, who in the course of satisfying their various spiritual pursuits, often get involved in many other cultural and recreational activities. Hinging on empirical understandings, this chapter examines the extent to which these religious programs contribute—or may contribute—to tourism and socio-cultural development in Nigeria, particularly in host communities. The chapter equally explores some of the challenges of religious tourism in Nigeria. It is specifically anchored on the three following questions: (1) Which are the major religious activities attracting tourists in Nigeria? (2) To what extent foreign tourists' attendance at these programs does not only benefit the churches? and (3) How could these programs further contribute to tourism development in Nigeria?

DOI: 10.4018/978-1-5225-8494-0.ch011

INTRODUCTION

According to many exocentric observers, Nigeria is not only a very religious nation, but the cradle and centre of many transnational African Christianities. This myth is not unconnected to the fact that many Pentecostal and charismatic spiritualities – which have successfully proliferated across the Black Continent and other parts of the world – are founded or headed by Nigerians. In other words, they have Nigerians as their originators and overseers. Egregious examples of such Nigerian-born transnational Churches include A. Adeboye Eunoch's Redeemed Christian Church of God (RCCG), Odeyepo's Living Fountain Church, Chris Oyakhilome's Christ Embassy, Kumuyi's Deeper Christian Life Ministry and Timotope B. Joshua's Synagogue Church of All Nations (SCOAN) among others. These mega churches have spread their tentacles to most parts of Black Africa and in some climes in the west, engulfing an international pool of both nominal and fervent followers.

The above mentioned Nigerian born churches have, these last years, embarked on the tradition of organizing giant annual or seasonal programs as well as transnational religious services which attract myriads of foreign and national publics to various locales in Nigeria. Though it may be herculean to find credible statistics to describe or measure the social and economic implications of these spiritual activities, one easily observes that events such as Redeemed Christian Church of God's Holy Ghost Congress have been attracting thousands, if not millions of religious tourists to Nigeria. So too have the end of year conventions organized by churches such as Kumuyi's Deeper Christian Life Ministry and Chris Oyakhilome's Christ Embassy, pulled considerable amounts of foreign publics to Nigerian cities. Besides these examples, one notices that the spiritual temples of some of these Nigerian based churches have quickly become kinds of sanctuaries and solution centres to many local and foreign tourists. Indeed, thousands of tourists daily converge to many of these spiritual temples in search for healings, prophecies, miracles, spiritual guidance, spiritual relics/talismans and multiform esoteric fortifications among others. It is for instance believed that SCOAN's Ikotun spiritual temple[1] in Lagos State has these last years, become a prime destination and a last resort to both nationals and foreign publics in ardent search for the elixirs of their spiritual dilemmas. At present, the temple is the major touristic attraction in the country and the most visited in the whole of West Africa.

Religious tourists irrespective or race, nationality, social classes and age have, these last years, become visitors to the temple for reasons which even go beyond the spiritual to include the political. According to an article published in the British tabloid *The Guardian*, SCOAN's spiritual temple attracts more weekly attendees than the combined number of visitors to the Buckingham Palace and the Tower of

London (Mark 2013). The Sunday service held at its Ikotun temple in Lagos State (of Nigeria) is said to attract a minimum of 150 000 attendees every week. Among these attendees, thousands are foreign tourists including high profile entities (SCOAN, 2016; Opara & Onoriode, 2017).

It therefore goes without saying that the spiritual programs organized by many Pentecostal and charismatic churches in Nigeria constitute a serious touristic attraction. They pull multitude of both national and international expectant tourists who, in the course of satisfying their various spiritual pursuits, often get involved in many other cultural and recreational activities. This chapter critically examines the extent to which these religious programs contribute – or may contribute – to tourism development in Nigeria. It is specifically anchored on the three following questions: (i) which are the major religious activities attracting tourists in Nigeria? (ii) To what extent foreign tourists' attendance at these programs does not only benefit the churches; and (iii) how could these programs further contribute to tourism development in Nigeria? Following these interrogations, this chapter is divided into five main sections. The first section provides a conceptual framework composed of tourism development, religious tourism and Pentecostal and revival churches. The second section explores the relationship between religion and tourism. The third section deals with the issue of religious tourism in Nigeria. The fourth section explores the touristic potential of Christian temples and religious programs organized by mega churches in Nigeria while the last section delves into the challenges of religious tourism in Nigeria.

CONCEPTUAL FRAMEWORK

To ensure clarity of analysis, it will be expedient from the onset, to provide the definition of two key concepts used in this discourse namely tourism development and religious tourism.

Religious Tourism

As its name indicates, religious tourism is a typology of tourism which is principally or solely motivated by faith or spiritual factors. Such factors may include the desire (by the tourist) to confirm, deepen or reflect upon his/her faith. In line with this, Jongmeewasin (cited in Ele and Aniche, 2017) defines religious tourism as a form of tourism whereby people of faith travel individually or in groups for motives which are related to religion or spirituality in their quest for meaning. Most religious tourists thus embark on faith-based travels to (i) have greater understanding and a better appreciation of their faith, (ii) connect personally with holy places or temples, (iii) escape worries connected with spiritual problems and (iv) find peace and meaning in life (Stausberg, 2011). Examples of religious tourism activities include spiritual retreats, pilgrimages, visits to religious touristic attractions, missionary journeys, faith-based camps and cruises among others.

Though religious tourism is, in principle, associated with faith-based travels, some authors are of the persuasion that the religious or spiritual reasons driving such a travel may, in some cases, only be secondary. No doubt the online magazine *Tourism and More* (2014) observes that religious tourism is far from being a visitation to a holy place which is strictly driven by spiritual motives; it may take place during a travel which is primarily motivated by humanitarian factors among other reasons. Spiritual gratifications may be the primordial motives for a trip but they can as well be part of a trip and provide a destination with additional attractions. Another important issue in the definition of religious tourism is that, the religious travellers must not be of a particular religion – when embarking on the visit – for his or her act to qualify as religious tourism. This can be illustrated by the fact that not all those who visit Christian holy sites (such as Rome's Basilica or Notre Dame's Cathedral of Paris) are Catholics or Christians. Adherents of other religions do visit such holy sites, both for their spiritual value and architectural beauty.

Tourism Development

Tourism development on the other hand has to do with the intelligent act of designing strategies and plans to increase, develop and encourage tourism in a well defined country or region. It generally aims at providing services for tourists. No doubt, Ekundayo and Abatu (2015) construe it as "a positive change resulting in the improvement of tourism product for the enjoyment of tourists, good return of investment to the developer and socio-economic benefit to the host Community". Apart from providing services to tourists, the paradigm aims at diversifying the economy and ameliorating the country's GDP (Alberta Tourism 2016; Awang, Wan & Zahari 2009). Tourism development is therefore a way of generating income through employment. It may include heavy investments in sectors such as transport infrastructures and hospitality businesses (hotels, restaurants and careering among others). It may also entail measures taken by government and other stakeholders to improve the financial system of the country, security, as well as investment in programs geared towards ecological sustainability.

RELIGION AND TOURISM

There is a visible symbiosis between religion and tourism. This is so as the two sectors have, over the years, affected one another. Indeed, the sector of religion has in various ways kept the tourism sector active. One key dimension of the impact of religion on tourism lies in the fact that many – if not all – major religious sites in the world double as touristic attractions, pulling cohorts of local and international publics yearly. Two Egregious examples are the Meiji Shrine and the Sensoji Temple (in Tokyo - Japan) which each attract at least 30 million (national and international) visitors each year. Other examples include Al Haram mosque (in Mecca), Kashi Vishwanath Temple (in India) as well as Italy's Pad ova, Torino and Pompeii among others, which similarly attracts millions of tourists throughout the years. Also important to mention here is the fact that towns such as Jerusalem (in Israel), Medjugorje (in Herzegovinia), Fatima (in Portugal), Louvre (in France) and Mecca (in Saudi Arabia) –just to name a few – are prime touristic attractions in the world, mainly because of the fame of most of their religious sites and temples. It is for instance documented that the Basilica of Our Lady of Guadalupe and Notre Dame Cathedral respectively attract over 20 million religious visitors to Mexico city (in Mexico) and 13.65 million visitors to Paris (The European Network for Historic Places of Worship, 2013). According to the World Tourism Organization (cited in Ashiegbu & Achunike 2014), an estimate of 300 to 330 million tourists undertake religious pilgrimages yearly to religious places.

Faith-based activities and festivities represent another way in which religion keeps the tourism sector active. In effect, religious and cultural festivals and programs have become veritable natural resources and magnets with potential to attract waves of tourists. Spiritual gathering such as Muslims' yearly come-together in Mecca to stone Satan have serious implications for tourism development in Saudi Arabia. The Mecca spiritual gathering in particular pulls Muslims from all over the world, thereby boosting not only the city's tourism but other industries within the countries. Other activities such the Kumbh Mela festival often draw about 60 million Hindus when organized after 12 years. In a similar way, the visits of prominent religious figures in specific places are big avenues for tourism. In tandem with this, towns which receive papal visits most often turn out to witness massive immigration of tourists coming from various climes of the world. Such tourists come to see and listen to the pope. Given the enormous potentials of religious activities, most politicians and administrations have these last years been bent on transforming religious events to touristic ones. Saudi Arabia for instance has for some years now capitalized on the *hadj* pilgrimage to diversify her pilgrim market and limit her reliance on the oil industry. Similarly, countries like Israel have been seeking the collaboration of iconic religious figures, in view of creating new and more attractive religious sites in their territory. Recently for instance, the mayors of Jerusalem, Tiberia and the Jordan Valley offered to provide land and some facilities to crowd-pulling Nigerian religious figure (T.B.Josua) to spur him into relocating his head quarter to Israel (Henama 2017). The action was visibly aimed at ensuring a diversification of Israel's religious pilgrim market.

In view of all the issues discussed above, it may be argued that religion has a direct impact on tourism. In effect, tourism development is partly determined by religion. All these factors have made religious tourism one of the most important forms of tourism in recent times. As observed by Johansen (cited in The European Network for Historic Places and Worship 2014), the sub-sector is big and getting bigger. It is equally identified as an industry which is more resilient to recessions than secular leisure travel. The global faith-based travel sector is worth $18 billion and includes 300 million travellers a year, the majority well educated and with comfortable incomes. Studies equally show that over 35 per cent of travellers want to take a faith-inspired vacation, so the market potential remains enormous.

RELIGIOUS TOURISM IN NIGERIA

Religious tourism is classified among the earliest forms of tourism in the world. This is evidently connected to the popular belief that, the culture of undertaking religious pilgrimage began with the dawn of humanity. Therefore, from time immemorial, men had the culture of travelling to holy sites for worship, retreat and other spiritual assignments/purposes. In Nigeria precisely, religious tourism could be said to have started before the advent of imported religions (namely Islam and Christianity) as well as before the coming of the European colonizers in the country. The African traditional Religion (ATR) which prevailed during this pre-colonial period integrated a range of rituals, traditional festivals and other cultural activities which encouraged various forms of religious tourism in what territorially constituted Nigeria during that time. In such zones as Igboland and most of today's eastern Nigeria, socio-religious activities such as "New Yam festivals" and masquerades (notably the *Mmanwu*, *Odo* and *Omabe* masquerades in Enugu) often constituted strong motives for and enablers of religious tourism. This was so as festivals and masquerades have been media par excellence to venerate particular deities in view of receiving various forms of blessings and gratifications. Adherents of ATR and fans of these religious activities often travelled from near and far to attend these ceremonies and fulfil some of their religious obligations.

These activities (traditional festivals and masquerades) have survived the test and taste of time; and are today viewed as immense natural resources to be exploited by the tourism industry in Nigeria. Indeed, they continue to be major touristic attractions in the country not only for followers of the African Traditional Religion but equally for non-religious and non-animist publics. In tandem with this, one may observe that traditional festivals such as the Argungu Fishing Festival (in Kebbi State of Nigeria), the Osun-Oshogbo Festival (in Osun State of Nigeria) and the Olokun festival (in Yoruba land) among others continue to be major attractions for both religious and non-religious tourists, some of which originate from foreign countries. The Osu-Oshogbo Festival in particular is known to attract international tourists from China, Brazil, America, Cuba, U.K. and other European countries as well as a huge African Diaspora who use it (the festival) as an opportunity to reconnect to their roots. "Their moods, dances, worships and cheers earnestly yearn for this needed connection as they join the Oshogbo people in the communal identity that reflects in the strong bond that exists among the founding fathers of the town and its celebrated cultural heritage" (Emelike 2011).

The traditional African religion has thus been one of the important pillars of tourism and economic development in the country. As remarked by Iheanacho (2015), the cultural activities organized under the auspices of the TAR have seriously "added to make religious tourism a beautiful bride that may become a platform for explosion of the modern tourism industry in Nigeria" (p. 279). Besides the rituals and festivals organized by adherents of traditional African religion, numerous shrines have represented first class tourism products pulling pilgrims from near and far. Major among these shrines include the *Olokun* Shrine, the *Ogbuide* shrine in Oguta Lake, the *Arochukwu* shrine, the *Amadioha*, the Ozuzu shrine in Etche Rivers State and most especially the *Osun Oshogho* sacred grove and shrine which have been acclaimed by UNESCO and the World Tourism Organization as international cultural tourism sites of human heritage. It is partially thanks to these natural touristic resources that Nigeria has enjoyed a high religious tourism profile in Africa. As put by Iheanacho (2015), it is, in effect, on account of these religious heritage and cultural products that "Nigeria has maintained an impressively rising profile in UNESCO", and has occupied "sensitive positions in the organization's culture and heritage committees, and related agencies" (p. 280).

Other religious denominations particularly the Christian and Islamic faiths have equally constituted the pivot of religious tourism in the country. This could be evidenced by the fact numerous Christian and Islamic holy sites serve as major tourist sites in the country. Some of these sites include the National Mosque in Abuja, the National Ecumenical Christian Centre (Abuja), the Redemption Camp (Lagos), The Canaan Land Ota (in Ogun State of Nigeria), the Catholic Cathedral

Falomo (Lagos), Aokpe Pilgrimage Centre and the Awhum monastery (Enugu) among others. These holy sites have been major attractions to both international and local tourists. Nweze (2016) corroborates this observation with close respect to the Awhum monastery. He concedes that:

Awhum Monastery precincts [has been] a very busy tourism centre [...] The kind of tourism seen is almost exclusively religious or spiritual tourism; and lots of individuals and groups [that visit the site] come from far and near; some from far parts of Nigeria such as Lagos, Port-Harcourt Aba, Onitsha, and from outside Nigeria, for various kinds of prayer activity. It [is], more or less a pilgrimage destination of a special spiritual appeal – for Catholics mainly, and non-Catholics alike. (p.34)

Christian denominations' contribution to religious tourism could equally be illustrated by the fact that myriads of both local and international tourists (including dignitaries and heads of governments) have, in recent times, been visiting Nigeria to seek spiritual solutions from specific Nigerian pastors or spiritual initiatives. A case in point is the interminable waves of visits made by national and international tourists to renowned solution centres as the Synagogue Church of All Nations (SCOAN). As shall be discussed in greater details in the subsequent sections of this chapter, the overseer of this spiritual ministry (Prophet T.B. Joshua) has been the last resort of a multitude of both local and international tourists. High calibre politicians, dignitaries and celebrities have travelled long distances to meet him for reasons which range from spiritual restoration to physical deliverance. Similarly to the deliverance services offered by the SCOAN through its initiator, the religious activities of many Nigerian based churches have been valuable touristic resources, pulling waves of expectant publics from Africa, Asia and Europe throughout the years. This has made Nigeria to become one of the leading destinations in the African continent when it comes to religious tourism.

EXPLORING THE TOURISTIC POTENTIAL OF THE FAITH-BASED ACTIVITIES ORGANIZED BY MAJOR CHRISTIAN INSTITUTIONS IN NIGERIA

Christian denominations – particularly the Pentecostal and charismatic spiritualities – are the leading contributors to the vibrancy of religious tourism in Nigeria. This is thanks to the giant international activities they organized yearly and seasonally in view of pastoring their members and wining souls for their God. In effect, these activities – which include retreats, seminars, conventions, evangelization campaigns, come together services and prophetic nights – have constituted veritable magnets pulling millions of tourists yearly in the country. The Holy Ghost Congress organized yearly by the Redeemed Christian Church of God [RCCG] for instance is known to always pull multitudes which are roughly estimated in hundreds of thousands (Opara & Onoriode 2017). Some sources claim that at least five hundred thousand national and international tourists attend the event each year. Other crowd-pullers include Deeper Life Church's annual spiritual campaign brand named "Retreat". Held usually from the 23ʳᵈ to the 26ᵗʰ of December at the church's Conference Centre in Ibadan[2], this program is a beehive of activities and attracts thousands of religious tourists from other parts of Nigeria and the world. Foreigners throng the venue of the retreat for reasons which range between spiritual enlightenment to physical restoration and financial embellishment of their lives.

Similarly, House on the Rock Church annually organizes a mega concert christened "The Experience". This concert pulls an estimate of 750 000 worshippers during the Charismas and end of year period in Lagos. Many of the worshippers who attend the musical event are foreigners from Africa, Europe and Asia. A similar gospel music program titled "The Carol Night" is stage managed around the same period in Akwa Ibom State (of Nigeria), targeting religious tourists from within and outside Nigeria. According to Ibom Tourism (2016), the 2015 edition of the programs pulled over 30 000 attendants from various countries. Other major religious events which are veritable crowd-pullers during end of year periods in Nigeria include Living Faith Church's annual spiritual festival christened "Shiloh" held at Otta (where is located the church's hindquarter) and a wide range of spiritual programs organized by the Synagogue Church of All Nations (SCOAN). In fact, of all the Christian churches and spiritual initiatives contributing immensely to tourism development in Nigeria, the SCOAN is the most visible. According to the Nigerian Immigration Services (2012), most of the international tourists that visit Nigeria are not only motivated by religious factors but are particularly attracted by the SCOAN. The government agency observes that 6 out of each 10 tourists who visit Nigeria are motivated by the desire to consult Prophet T.B. Joshua (the pastoral head of the church) or attend the church's spiritual activities. In line with this, SCOAN's spiritual temple in Ikotun-Egbe (Lagos) has these last years been a crowd-pulling site, nay a Jerusalem of a sort to many international tourists. While T.B. Joshua's popularity (as a solution provider for all sorts of spiritual problems) has pull many expectant tourists from near and far, SCOAN's temple has become the most visited spiritual site in the whole of West Africa. According to Opara and Onoriode (2016), out of the over 2 millions religious tourists who visit Nigeria yearly, at least half are principally attracted by SCOAN's spiritual programs.

A good number of dignitaries, business gurus, celebrities and high profile politicians (from a multitude of African, European and American countries) have in one time or the other thronged the temple to find solutions to their problems. Among some of the high calibre figures to have visited the temple and consulted the Prophet, one may count former Ghanaian President Atta Mills, Zimbabwe's Prime Minister Morgan Tsvangirai, former Malawian President, Joyce Banda, former President Pascal Lissouba (of Congo Brazzaville), South Africa's Winnie Mandela, Julius Malema, the Zulu King, late President Omar Bongo (of Gabon) and late Zambian President Frederick Cheluba among others.

It goes without saying that religious tourism facilitated by the activities and programs of Nigerian Christian churches has a vast avalanche of socio-economic potential. In effect, this form of tourism has had a visible impact on Nigerian communities at the levels of employment, infrastructure development and living standard. The influx of religious tourists in deferent times of the year in Nigeria directly affects the Nigerian government revenue through visa issuance at various Nigerian embassies abroad. It is assumable that most of the international tourists (particularly those coming the West and Asia) pay for their stay in the country, thereby contributing to the Nigerian government's revenue. If one considers statistics provided by the Nigerian Immigration Services, much of the revenue derived by government from visa issuance would be from taxes paid by religious tourists. According to Nigerian Immigration Services' records, over 60% of international tourists visit Nigeria to attend SCOAN's spiritual programs or to consult its general overseer. This in itself is an indication that much of the revenue generated by government through issuance of visas to tourists come from religious tourists.

A very palpable impact of religious tourism in Nigeria is at the level of employment. It has been observed that religious tourism has been fuelling seasonal but thriving businesses in communities that host religious activities. Christian festivals organized in the countries have most often been beneficial to the hospitality industry, as well as to transporters who shuttle visitors to their hotels, hostels or church destination. In his review of the contribution of SCOAN's spiritual activities to tourism development and the local economy, Gboyega (2013) quotes a wide range of observers who claim that at least five big hotels have been founded by private investors in the Ikotun-Egbe area – where the highly visited Synagogue is based – following the great number of foreign tourists' visitations of the temple. In addition to this, various other lucrative initiatives have been developed by endogenous entities to provide accommodations and other facilities to the visiting members of the Synagogue. As noted by Gboyega,

Close observers of happenings in the church [SCOAN[and even residents of the [Ikotun-Egbe] area would swear that the level of growth in the last decade or so has been unprecedented, with its impact on its immediate environment very evident.

[...] The church's growth has led to an economic boom in the area. [...] every single business embarked on anywhere within the vicinity of the church is bound to be successful because of the mammoth crowd that now regularly visit the area. More especially, hospitality businesses, such as hotels and lodges, restaurants, cybercafés and other service delivery businesses have benefited the most. In the last year or two, [there are] five hotels that have sprung up in the area, mainly to service visitors and worshippers of the church. And that excludes the landlords and property owners in the area who have converted their houses and homes to informal lodging facilities to do business and make quick money. (p.23)

Another visible impact of Christian churches' spiritual activities on host communities is at the level of infrastructure development. This could vividly be illustrated by the fact that the need to accommodate or carter for the growing number of visitors and attendants at their programs has pushed most Christian churches to undertake immense development works in their respective spiritual camps. A case in point is the Redeemed Christian Church of God which, in the course of years, has developed its Redemption Camp into a vibrant town. The church has upgraded various facilities within the camp for the benefit of visitors and tourists who, during end of year periods, attend its Holy Ghost Congress in the camp. In praise of the Church's effort towards the development of the camp and the community (Kilometre 46, Lagos-Ibadan Expressway) where it is located, Eyokoba and Olayinka (2016) note that "the Redeemed Camp is a town that works. [...] The roads are free of potholes, and the general decay associated with urban living in Nigeria is almost non-existent [there]. Electricity supply is uninterrupted, clean water runs at the tap, environment is sanitised and decent transportation system is in place. Sanity and serenity of the City might not be as a result of prayers, praise and worship. Rather, authorities in the town have made deliberate efforts [...] to ensure that the place is not turned to another Nigerian nightmare" (p.45). It could therefore be enthused that churches' efforts towards catering for a growing number of visitors or tourists to their spiritual camps are directly or indirectly leading to infrastructural development in some Nigerian localities.

CHALLENGES OF RELIGIOUS TOURISM IN NIGERIA

Though religious tourism could arguably be described as the fastest growing type of tourism in the country, a multitude of factors hampers its optimum development. Three of these factors include underdeveloped tourism infrastructures, limited efforts by government to harness religious tourism resources and insecurity among others.

Underdeveloped Tourism Infrastructure

This challenge can be illustrated by the fact that key sectors such as hospitality, transport and electricity supply are still seriously underdeveloped in Nigeria. In line with this, many religious touristic attractions (holy sites) are hardly accessible by road because of the poor nature of the traffic management in many localities within the country. A good example is the pot-hole ridden roads that lead to Ikotun-Egbe area where the most visited religious site of the country (SCOAN's temple) is found. According to some observers, the terrible state of the roads leading to this area causes a daily aggravated vehicular traffic which, arguably, ranks among the worst in Lagos. This unfavourable traffic seriously complicates the movement of tourists from the Lagos airport to the Synagogue. The deplorable state of these roads is a serious threat not only to religious tourism but equally to the image of Nigeria. This is so as they (the deteriorated roads) do not encourage visitors to repeat their religious tourism experience (their visitation of the Synagogue); worse, many international tourists tend to view these roads as a trustworthy indicator of poor traffic management and infrastructure development in the whole of Nigeria.

Limited Attention Given by Government to Religious Tourism Development

From many indications, the Nigerian government has been according just little attention to the tourism sector in general and the religious tourism sub-sector in particular. Although government has recognized a number of religious sites in the country notably the Christian Ecumenical Centre (in Abuja) and the Aokpe Pilgrimage Centre (in Benue State) among other Christian holy sites as valuable touristic resources, religious tourism has for decades remained a mainly untapped market. Like in many other Black African countries, the tourism sector is among the economic sectors that received the least treasury support. In other words, the budget allocated to tourism in general and religious tourism is very meagre. In 2016, Nigerian Minister of Culture and Tourism (Mohammed Lai) described the budget allocated to the tourism sector as "mere tokenism". He noted that some administrations – notably that of President Goodluck Jonathan in 2015 – had no allocation for the completion of very vital projects in the sector. In view of these indexes it may be plausible to believe that religious tourism development is mainly left in the hands of the individual churches or spirited faith oriented initiatives which assumedly may not have the kind of means the government possesses.

Another index of government's lukewarm attitude towards religious tourism development is seen in its (government's) failure or reluctance to adopt well thought policies that will specifically encourage distinguished/mega churches and religious figures who are veritable pillars of the sector (religious tourism) in the country. Government has for instance often failed – or rather been slow – to provide a serious support to such religious initiatives as the SCOAN which have immensely contributed to tourism and economic development in Nigeria. The visible lack of such support has caused some of these religious initiatives to envisage relocating their churches to foreign countries which have the potential to provide them a better operative environment. A case in point is T.B. Joshua who envisaged relocating his ministry to Israel where over three mayors (Jerusalem, Jordan Valley and Tiberia) were seriously "wooing" him with offers of land and other vital facilities. While lamenting government's limited attention given to religious tourism development, Ojewusi (2015) enthuses that:

[I] always wondered what my compatriots at the Federal and State tourism organizations are doing to recognize this 'hidden' tourism treasure [SCOAN] and explore its fantastic opportunities to further boost the image of Nigeria. So much has been done in the tourism ministries to promote the image of Nigeria at home and abroad without any seriously positive and discernible outcome. We spend millions on tourism fairs, gatherings and events worldwide yearly with trickles coming as dividends. Have we really considered the tourism potentials of places like the Synagogue in bringing positive light upon our nation around the world; in attracting thousands of foreign visitors to Lagos – visitors who come here to see the good side of our land and relatively boost our economy while also boosting their personal spiritual well-being? The Synagogue has helped to advance our tourism industry. The earlier the tourism authorities [find] a way of reaching out to institutions like this for collaboration and idea exchange, the better for us. (p.5)

As contended by Ojewusi above, the Nigerian government tends not to fully view the touristic and economic values of some major religious activities and spiritual sites existing in the country. In different platforms, many government officials have expressed Nigerian government's desire to support religious tourism in Nigeria (Makinde 2011. Mbanefo 2016. Oredola 2016). However, from the palpable indexes discussed above, one may say that much is still expected from government as a form of support to religious tourism development in the country.

Insecurity in Some Religious Touristic Sites

The recrudescence of ethno-religious wars and terrorists attacks in various parts of Nigeria has caused the Nigerian destination to mostly been seen by the outside world as an unsafe one. This perception has been justified by the fact that, in recent times, there have been incidents of terrorist attacks or mortal accidents in some religious touristic sites, causing the death of many pilgrims or tourists and discouraging some potential visitors to throng such sites. A case in point is the September 2014 collapse of a five storey building in the premise of the SCOAN in Ikotun-Egbe. The incident - which led to the death of about 100 pilgrims and the injury of many others –was variously interpreted as a terrorist attack, the result of criminal negligence by the church or an unpredictable accident. It seriously affected the image of the SCOAN and that of its overseer as well as international perceptions of religious sites in Nigeria, having a negative effect on religious tourism in Nigeria.

Directly after the incident, the SCOAN became a less attractive destination for many international tourists. In a broader sense, it (the incident) negatively affected the number of religious tourists coming into Nigeria. This was promptly felt by car hire operators at the Murtala Muhammed International Airport (Ikeja, Lagos) Akinto (2017). A statement issued by the Airport Car Hire Association (ACHAN) International terminus Zone of the Murtala Muhammed International Airport clearly made allusion to the negative effects of the incidence on foreigners' patronage of car hire operators in particular and on religious tourism in Nigeria in general. This statement underscores that the incident did not only affect The SCOAN but the Nigeria's economy as a whole. "What happened is a big blow to the economy of the nation, most especially, the airport, as a whole, as most of the tourists to Nigeria are coming to visit The SCOAN; I mean, six out of every 10 tourists come to Nigeria visit The SCOAN. Since this happened, there is no more business and we cannot go on the street anymore" (cited in *The Maravi Post*, 2014).

From many indications, the SCOAN has progressively recovered from the image crisis and the legal actions that were triggered by the incident. However, the incident remains a stigma the SCOAN and its founder will have to bear for the rest of their existence.

CONCLUSION

Religious tourism is one of the most thriving forms of tourism in Nigeria. This has partially been thanks to the crowd-pulling nature of church activities, popular ecclesiastical figures and mythologized spiritual temples owned by some Christian bodies based in the country. Popular church programs organized by mega Nigerian churches such as RCCG's "Holy Ghost Congress", Deeper Life Bible Church's "Retreat", Living Fountain Church "Shiloh" and House on the Rock's "The Experience" have been major touristic attractions for tens of thousands of local and foreign tourists in specific periods of the year. Similarly, various Christian holy sites such as the National Ecumenical Christian Centre (Abuja), the Redemption Camp (Lagos), The Canaan Land Ota (in Ogun State of Nigeria), the Catholic Cathedral

Falomo (Lagos), Aokpe Pilgrimage Centre and the Awhum monastery (Enugu) among others have constituted a big magnet, pulling multitudes of pilgrims and expectant worshipers from diverse climes of the planet. As the most visited holy site in the country, SCOAN's temple alone has attracted over 60% of the foreign tourists who visit Nigeria at specific periods of the year.

As argued in this chapter, the economic and social impact of these religious activities and sites have been enormous as they have contributed to the local economy by creating (seasonal) employment opportunities and new avenues for government to generate revenue (through issuance of visas); as well as by seriously boosting businesses in the communities that host them (the programs and sites). It could therefore be enthused that religious tourism is one of the rare sub sectors that provide employment opportunities to large pockets of people who ordinarily wouldn't have been employable due to lack of skills or lack/insufficient education. Other positive effects of religious tourism is infrastructure development in host communities in the form of building of hotels and restaurants as well as the creation of other necessary facilities to carter for the growing population of pilgrims and visitors to specific holy sites in the country.

Despite the enormous potential of Christian religious programs and holy sites, faith-based tourism faces a number of serious challenges in the country. Some of these challenges include the lack of infrastructure development, the limited attention given by government to religious tourism development in the country and insecurity in some holy sites among others. In view of these challenges and many other factors, the following strategic actions may be recommended:

1. The Nigerian government should accord a greater attention to the tourism sector in general and the religious tourism sub-sector in particular. Such an action entails seeing this subsector as an area which should be developed and made to be a greater source income for the state. Developing the tourism sector will enable a diversification of the economy. Countries such as Saudi Arabia have understood and embraced this maxim with impressive results. It is therefore high time the Nigerian government emulates such examples.
2. Nigerian government officials should work in collaboration with religious organizations in their conception and execution of tourism development policies. Specific Nigerian churches and ecclesiastical figures should be provided full governmental support in the organization of their programs.
3. Nigerian government services such as the Nigerian Immigration Services should have a special desk for mega churches at strategic airports within the country, to facilitate the issuance of visas to religious pilgrims or visitors on their arrival on Nigerian soil.

4. The government should use specific mega churches and crow-pulling ecclesiastical figures such T.B. Joshua, Chris Okilome and E.A. Adeboye as well as the various international media outlets operated by these religious entities to advertise the good things that could pull tourists to Nigeria. The government should equally encourage these ecclesiastical figures to use their media to promote Nigeria as an attractive touristic destination, a land of God-fearing and peaceful people. Such actions, combined with others may contribute to countering the negative image of Nigeria in the international scene, a factors which for years has militated against tourism in the country.

5. Nigeria-based Christian churches should increasingly invest in research to have better and clearer figures of (foreign) pilgrims that visit their spiritual sites. This may not only help in the planning and management of their spiritual programs but provide serious illumination that may inform governmental support of their programs.

6. A better security design/engineering should be applied at religious sites to ensure the protection of tourists. This may help tackle insecurity concerns which have contributed in discouraging many foreign tourists from visiting the country and religious sites within it.

7. Government should emulate the example of some foreign countries (notably Israel) which adopt enticing policies to spurred foreign spiritual leaders to come and settle in their countries.

REFERENCES

African Travel Times. (2016). Synagogue Church: The vanguard of Nigeria as religious destination. *African Travel Times*. Retrieved from http://africantraveltimes. com/news/synagogue-church-the-vanguard-of-nigeria-as-religious-destination/

Akinto, O. A. (2017). How Nigeria will lose billions where Israel and Saudi Arabia gain. *Nairaland Forum*. Retrieved September 2017, from http://www.how-nigeria-will-lose-billions-where-israel-and-saudi-arabia-gain/nairalandforum.com.

Alberta Tourism. (2016). *Tourism development guide. A guide to help navigate the tourism development process*. Edmonton: Alberta Tourism.

Ashiegbu, O. P., & Achunike, H. C. (2014). Religion and tourism in Nigeria. *Research on Humanities and Social Sciences*, *4*(15), 130–139.

Awang, K. W., Wan, M. W. H., & Zahari, M. S. M. (2009). Tourism development: A geographical perspective. *Asian Social Science*, *5*(5), 67–76. doi:10.5539/ass.v5n5p67

Dallen, J. T., & Olsen, H. D. (2006). *Tourism, religion and spiritual journeys*. London: Routledge.

Ele, C. O., & Anicher, A. (2017). Religious tourism in Nigeria: The economic perspective. *OJAMSS: Online Journal of Arts. Management and Social Sciences*, *2*(1), 220–232.

Emelike, O. (2011, September 12). Osun-Osogbo festival: Heritage beyond religion and race. Gateway Nigeria, 11-14.

Eyoboka, S., & Latona, O. (2016, December 8). Holy Ghost Congress: RCCG turns forest to city. *Vanguard*, 32-35.

Federal Republic of Nigeria. (2006). Nigeria tourism development master plan. Institutional capacity strengthening to the tourism sector in Nigeria. Abuja: Federal Republic of Nigeria & World Tourism Organization (WTO).

Gboyega, A. (2013). Religious tourists experience Nigeria in rundown Lagos suburbs. *The Nation*. Retrieved September 29, 2017 from http://thenationonlineng. net/religious-tourists-experience-nigeria-in-rundown-lagos-suburb/

Gedecho, E. K. (2014). Challenges of religious tourism development: The case the Gishen Mariam, Ethiopia. *American Journal of Tourism Research*, *3*(2), 42–57. doi:10.11634/216837861403567

Henama, U. (2017). T.B. Josua emigrating to Isreal: Lesson for South Africa on religious tourism. *The Cable*. Retrieved September 20, from https://www.thecable. ng/tb-joshua-emigrating-israel-lessons-south-africa-religious-tourism

Ibagere, E., & Adeseye, B. O. (2016). *Aesthetic of indigenous faith tourism in Nigeria*. Retrieved September 21, 2017, from http:www.ojs.mona.uwi.edu/index. php/cjp/article/view/4374/3336

Iheanacho, N. (2015). Nigerian praxis of religious tourism and pilgrimage motivations in a globalizing world. *Ciencias da Religiao: Historia e Sociadade, 13*(1), 259–284.

Makinde, D. O. (2011). Potentialities of the Egungun festival as a tool for tourism development in Ogbomoso, Nigeria. *WIT: Transaction on Ecology and the Environment, 148*, 583–593. doi:10.2495/RAV110531

Mark, M. (2013, September 1). Lagos business cash in on lure of super pastor TB Joshua. *The Guardian*, 37-40.

Mbanefo, S. U. (2016). *Accountability now*. Abuja: Nigerian Tourism Development Corporation.

Nweze, C. C. (2016). *Awhum monastery or tourism destination*. Enugu: Fountain of Reason. Retrieved September 25, 2017, from https://fountainheadrepository. com/2017/06/11/awhum-monastery-or-tourism-destination/

Obasola, K. E. (2014). Religious tourism and sustainable development: A study of Eyo festival in Lagos, Nigeria. *International Journal of Social Sciences and Education, 4*(2), 524–534.

Ojewusi, S. (2015, March 23). T.B. Joshua and Synagogue tragedy: Another perspective. *The Authority*, 17-21.

Okonkwo, E. E., & Nzeh, C. A. (2016). Faith-based activities and their tourism potentials in Nigeria. *International Journal of Research in Arts and Social Sciences, 1*(1), 286–298.

Oluwa, A. O. (2016). *How Nigeria will lose billions where Israel and Saudi*. Retrieved September 18, 2017 from http://www.nairaland.com/3800455/how-nigeria-lose-billions-where

Opara, C., & Onoriode, L. G. (2017). *Tourism: Impact of churches' December crusade rush in Nigeria. In African travel times* (pp. 1–16). Lagos: ATT.

Oredola, A. (2016). Aokpe Pilgrimage Centre thrives as a tourist product. *Business Hallmarknews*. Retrieved September 30, from http://hallmarknews.com/aokpe-pilgrimage-centre-thrives-as-a-tourist-product/

SCOAN. (2016). *Synagogue Church of All Nations*. Retrieved May 15, 2017, fromhttps://www.revolvy.com/main/index.php?s=Synagogue%20Church%20Of%20All%20Nations&item_type=topic

Stausberg, M. (2011). *Religion and tourism: crossroads, destinations and encounters*. London: Routledge.

The European Network for Historic Places of Worship. (2013). *World – Growth of religious tourism*. Retrieved September 20th, 2017 from http://www.frh-europe.org/world-growth-of-religious-tourism/

The Maravi Post. (2014, October 12). SCOAN update: Tourism hard-hit by Synagogue building collapse, say airport transport operators. *The Malavi Post*, 21-22.

Uchenna, H. O., & Okpoko, P. U. (2017). Impact of religious tourism in southeastern Nigeria. *Journal of Tourism and Heritage Studies*, 6(1), 99–112.

Vukonic, B. (1998). Religious tourism: Economic value or an empty box? *Zagreb International Review of Economic and Business*, 1(1), 83–94.

END NOTES

[1]   Ikotun is a locality situated in the Lagos State of Nigeria. It harbors SCOAN's Head Quarter and one of its principal temples.

[2]   Ibadan is a major town situated in the south-eastern part of Nigeria.

Chapter 12
Assessment of the Internal Control System in the Accommodation Firm and Its Relation to Performance

Murat Erdoğan
https://orcid.org/0000-0002-4506-0731
Akdeniz University, Turkey

ABSTRACT

An effective internal control system will help achieve performance and profitability targets within the core objectives of the business, help to prevent the need for loss of resources, and ensure that financial reporting is realistic and reliable. The purpose of this chapter is to identify the components of the internal control system in the enterprise and to show whether these factors affect the firm performance. When the results of the study are evaluated in general, it has been determined that the elements of the internal control system of the companies have an effect on the firm performance. According to this, the control environment 1, the control environment 2, the risk evaluation, the control activities, the information and the communication, the monitoring variables are effective on the positive side and the control variables on the firm performance have positive effect on the firm performance of the operation bed capacity, the operation period, and the existence of the internal control unit.

DOI: 10.4018/978-1-5225-8494-0.ch012

INTRODUCTION

The fraudulent financial reporting, accounting scandals and economic crises, which are effective on the global scale, have faced important negativities and the need for control and audit activities has gained increasing importance (Amudo & Inanga, 2009). These developments have led to the implementation of important internal control and internal control models in the UK, Canada and the European Union, mainly in the United States of America, on internal control. In addition, the growth and complexity of the organizational structures of enterprises today, developments in technology, the need for knowledge, increasing competition environment, institutional management requirements and so on have revealed the necessity of an internal control system within the framework of the control function, which is one of the basic functions of management.

Establishment of internal control system effectively and its practice will make important contribution to achievement of performance and profitability targets within the main objectives and goals of the firms, prevention of resource losses, establishment of reliable and realistic financial reporting structure, etc.

When it is evaluated from the perspective of accommodation operations, it is observed that such enterprises are located in a labor intensive sector, the number of personnel is high and the turnover rate is high, the intensity of monetary transaction, the existence of products with high unit price, it is extremely important to establish and operate an effective internal control system in such enterprises (Okutmuş &Uyar, 2014). This study has made the necessary evaluations about the internal control systems in the hospitality enterprises and revealed the relation between the elements included in the internal control system and the performance of the accommodation enterprises.

Control is any action specified by the management to increase the likelihood of achieving objectives or goals. In other words, controls are actions designed to keep institutions in compliance with standards or plans (Hermanson & Hermanson, 1994). The control function is one of the firm functions and it generally draws attention as a coordinated process as a whole to ensure the comparison of the activities that are performed and the activities that are planned to perform result (Olalı & Korzay, 1993). In other words, control can also be expressed as a set of movements that will ensure successful achievement of foreseen goals, plans, policies and standards in the firm.

The basic steps of an effective control process are shown in Figure 1. When assessed in general terms, the control stage begins with the determination of standards; it goes on with measurement of outcomes and comparison the reel outcomes with expected results and it finally ends up with the review of the process by making necessary corrections.

Figure 1. An effective control process

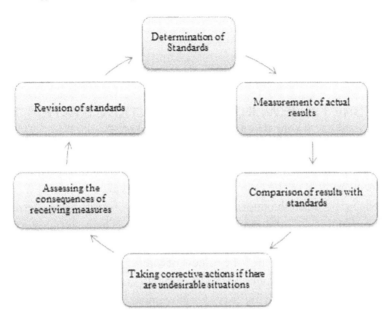

Establishment and operation of an effective internal control system will enable displaying behaviors of workers suitable with the aim of the firm and measurement of the effectiveness of these behaviors, the ability to clearly define the job descriptions of the people responsible for financial and non-financial transactions, the determination of the possible errors, frauds and risks in a comprehensive manner. It will also enable precautions taken in time and correctly in this way. In addition, it will contribute to the corporate governance of the business under the principles of transparency, equality, accountability and responsibility (Atmaca, 2012).

For example, abuse of assets is a common occurrence in every business wherever they operate. This is usually done by the staff of the firm. Abusive use of assets, defalcation, theft, use for personal purposes of assets, unauthorized access to information in the database, and the provision of personal benefits can be detected by means of effective internal control system and this system contributes to taking reasonable precautions in this way (Okutmuş & Uyar, 2014). On the other hand, control systems do not allow the avoidance of all adverse situations, and the responsibility of the management in this direction does not go away with the existence of the control system (Jagels & Ralston, 2007).

The design and implementation of an effective internal control system has a crucial significance of continuity and growth of the firm far beyond the level of minimizing the mistakes and abuses that occur within the firm. Firms need a healthy working internal control system whether they are open or closed to the public, or regardless of the distinction of family or single-person businesses. It is extremely clear that the existence and effectiveness of the internal control system has an indispensable significance such as continuity, performance and growth (Sebilcioğlu et al., 2013).

LITERATURE REVIEW: INTERNAL CONTROL SYSTEM AND ITS IMPACT ON FIRM PERFORMANCE

When sources related with internal control are examined, there are studies dealing with the measurement of the effectiveness of the internal control system, as well as the relationship between the internal control system and corporate governance, and whether the effectiveness of the internal control system influences firm performance. If so, in what ways does it affect? These studies are given below.

Elbannan (2009) investigated the effects of internal control quality on financial reporting, corporate governance and credit rating. In the survey, "Disclosing internal control weakness" of 171 firms between November 2003 and May 2005 is used in the US Securities and Exchange Commission (SEC) applications. The logistic regression was used to measure the relationship between internal control quality and credit rating. As a result of the study, some evident that support the idea firms with weak internal control controls are more likely to have a lower credit rating, lower profitability, lower cash flow for firm activities, net loss in current and previous fiscal years, more possibility on having high volatility in income than the firms with internal controls are found. There is also a strong positive relationship between corporate governance and credit rating and credit support, which supports the argument that strong corporate governance, reduces representation conflicts.

Food and beverage cost control methods are examined by Çiftçi & Köroğlu (2008) the in the study conducted in the accommodation firms operating in the province of Marmaris by using questionnaire method. According to the results of the analysis, it is determined that the number of departments depending on the star numbers of the firm, applied cost control method and existence of an independent unit related to cost control are different. In addition, it has been determined that cost analysis periods of hotels' star numbers are not determinative on stock valuation methods and computer systems used in cost analysis.

Dalgar (2012) used a one-to-one interview method in a large-scale production firm in order to establish an internal control system to prevent possible mistakes and missteps in the accounting departments where financial errors and tricks are frequently encountered in the firms and in order to determine it with the implementation model. It is emphasized that the internal control systems created in the firms as a result of the analysis made are required to be designed and maintained by the senior management in a structure that will be appropriate for the firms and to make the transactions fast and reliable. In addition, it has been stated that the internal control system that is created should be continuously monitored, the elements causing excessive bureaucracy and costs should be removed from sight and risks should be analyzed periodically.

In the study conducted by Can (2014), face-to-face and electronic questionnaires were used to evaluate the effectiveness of the internal control system in private hospitals operating in Istanbul. As a result of the study; these outcomes have been achieved; existence of the audit committees included in the organizational chart of the hospital firms affects control environment positively, emphasis should be given to the applications of the accreditation so that the internal control system can be operated effectively, the importance of periodical use of independent audit services during the execution of the internal control system.

Sharari (2006) conducted surveys on managers and employees at different levels of management in pension companies operating in Saudi Arabia to examine the relationship between internal control system and employee performance. As a result of the study, there is a strong positive relationship between internal control system elements and employees' performance and emphasized the necessity of effective implementation of internal control elements in order to improve employee performance.

The study by Judeh, Sheikh &Sbugh (2009) evaluated the control and accounting practices in four and five star hotels operating in Jordan. The study concludes that an integrated reporting system exists in the control and performance evaluation process, and that the incentive systems are operated effectively. In addition to the study, the necessity that the effective relationship and cooperation between the centers of responsibility established in the firms, especially the necessity of activating the planning and budgeting activities in the control area and the importance of forming the reporting systems in this context have been mentioned.

However, a study by Ama (2012) was conducted to evaluate the internal control systems of accommodation firms, and two accommodation firms operating in Ghana were handled and a case analysis was conducted through questionnaire application at the related firms. As a result of the analysis made, most of the participants stated that no pre-established accounting policies and procedures were systematically established. But they pointed out that there is an organizational scheme in which the duties and responsibilities of employees are clearly defined. When the internal control system is evaluated in terms of effectiveness, in the study, all other internal control system components are concluded to be created and implemented and control activities are handled in all organizational functions.

When measurements are made on the performance of the firm, both the subjective and the objective indicators are given as the indicators of the performance of the firm (Ejoh & Ejom, 2014). Performance indicators can include profitability, efficiency of firm operations, firm life time and the response of the firm to environmental opportunities and threats. How effectively firm resources are used to achieve firm objectives is one of the firm performance indicators (Mawanda, 2008). Also, the return on assets, sales, equity profit, return on investment, size of sales are also indicators of the performance of firms that is used as measurement (David, 2001).

When evaluating the studies on the relationship between internal control system and firm performance, Tang and Xu (2007) is the first writer to address the relationship between internal control weakness and firm performance. As a result of the analysis, there was a significant relationship between the performance of the company and the weakness of the internal control system. Similar to the work of Leenen (2008), Tang and Zou (2007), Tang and Xu evaluated the inadequacies in the internal control system. It is stated that the internal control system is influential on the operational performance and the weakness of the operational activities is the reason for the inadequacy of the internal control system (Soodanian, Navid & Kheirollahi, 2013).

In the study conducted by Chan Li, McVay &Skaife (2015), the effectiveness of inventory management and the operation of the internal control system was investigated. The relationship between the firm cycle rates used in assessing firm performance and the effectiveness of the internal control system in financial reporting has been assessed. According to the results obtained, it was seen that the internal control system was not effective in the companies with low inventory turnover rate. It has been determined that cash flow coming from transaction, gross profits and sales increase in the firms where the internal control system is improved.

The study by Ge & McVay (2005) shows that the internal control system is weak in the firms that are complex, small and less profitable. In the study conducted by Doyle (2007), which confirms the work of Ge and McVay, it is seen that the weaker firms of the internal control system are the ones that are young, showing fast-growing effort and insufficiently structured. Ejoh & Ejom (2014) conducted a survey and interview method in the Tertiary institutions operating in Nigeria to examine the relationship between internal control activities and firm performance. As a result of the study, there is no significant relationship between firm performance and internal control activities. The fact that all activities are reviewed by senior management and the financial statements are audited annually by external auditors and from the other side all financial information is easily accessible by only one staff in an unauthorized way to important financial information, the establishment of an effective internal control system and the prevention of unauthorized access and the creation of security nets should prevent fraud, theft and misuse of assets that may arise has been emphasized.

In the study by Mwakimasinde, Odhiambo & Byaruhanga (2014), the effect of the sugar cane companies operating in Kenya on the financial performance of internal control systems was investigated using primary and secondary data. Surveys were conducted as primary data, and annual reports, publications and documents of enterprises were used as secondary data. As a result of the study, it is seen that the internal control system has a positive relation with financial performance. Muraleetharan (2010) attempted to assess whether the internal control system would lead to increased operational performance in his study. While the internal control system is measured by the control environment, risk assessment and control activities, the firm performance is generally measured by profitability, productivity and liquidity values. By means of questionnaires and observations, 181 samples were analyzed and regression applied. As a result of the study, there appears to be a statistically significant relationship between internal control and financial performance. When positive findings were obtained between internal control and performance, no significant relationship was found between control environment and performance. The impact of an effective internal control system on performance is thought to be significant and effective in all firms. This is because of the idea internal control practices can detect and prevent fraud and errors in the organization.

In the study conducted by Mwakimasinde, Odhiambo & Byaruhanga (2014), the effect of the elements of internal control system on financial performance was tried to be investigated. In this context, while financial performance seen as dependent variables was determined as cost per unit in model 1, market value in model 2, profitability in model 3, dependent variables in all models include control environment, control activities, risk assessment, information and communication and monitoring elements of the internal control system. It has been determined that the internal control system elements have an explanatory effect on the financial performance expressed in cost per unit, market value and profitability.

Dineshkumar &Kogulacumar (2013) examined the impact of internal control elements on firm performance at the Sri Lanka Telecom Operation, stating that the elements of the internal control system will contribute in the performance of the firms. In the study with the primary and secondary data, the survey application was carried out predominantly. Interviews with 60 employees working in business were evaluated by correlation and SWOT analysis. The results show that there is a strong relationship between internal control system and firm performance. It is also concluded that the internal control system implemented in Sri Lanka Telecom firm will increase the expectation of the firm performance of the firm for the future.

When the litterateur is examined, it is seen that the studies related to internal control are generally aimed to measure internal control effectiveness and the effectiveness is related to performance. In this study, which is different from other studies, the effect of each of the internal control elements on the various elements of firm performance was evaluated and a comprehensive solution about the internal control elements was introduced by examining this relationship statistic through the models.

Data, Hypothesis Development and Methodology

Three models were established to determine the relationship between internal control elements and firm performance. The above mentioned models are as follows.

Model 1;

$$GPM_i = \beta_0 + \beta_1 CE1_1 + \beta_2 CE2_2 + \beta_3 RA_3 + \beta_4 CA_4 + \beta_5 IC_5 + \beta_6 MO_6 + \beta_7 FA_7 + \beta_8 IAU_8 + \beta_9 FBC_9 + e_0$$

Model 2;

$$ROA_i = \beta_0 + \beta_1 CE1 + \beta_2 CE2_2 + \beta_3 RA_3 + \beta_4 CA_4 + \beta_5 IC_5 + \beta_6 MO_6 + \beta_7 FA_7 + \beta_8 IAU_8 + \beta_9 FBC_9 + e_0$$

Model 3;

$$AT_i = \beta_0 + \beta_1 CE1_1 + \beta_2 CE2_2 + \beta_3 RA_3 + \beta_4 CA_4 + \beta_5 IC_5 + \beta_6 MO_6 + \beta_7 FA_7 + \beta_8 IAU_8 + \beta_9 FBC_9 + e_0$$

Hypotheses created for these models:

Ho = The elements of the internal control system have no effect on the firm performance.
H1 = The elements of the internal control system have effect on the firm performance.

The dependent variables were determined as shown below;
In Model 1 gross profit margin, In model 2 active asset profitability, In model 3 active asset turnover. The independent variables used in the models are the variables related to the internal control elements (control environment, risk assessment, control activities, information and communication, monitoring) shown in Table 1 and Figure 2, appearing in COSO Model and control variables are specified as the duration of firm activity, the existence of the internal audit unit and the firm bed capacity.

Table 1. Research variables

Dependent Variables	Descriptions
GPM	Gross Profit Margin
ROA	Return on Assets
AT	Asset Turnover
Independent Variables	**Descriptions**
CE1	Control Environment 1
CE2	Control Environment 2
RA	Risk Assessment
CA	Control Activities
IC	Information and Communication
MO	Monitoring
Control Variables	**Descriptions**
FA	Firm Activity
IAU	The Existence of the Internal Audit Unit
FBC	Firm Bed Capacity

Figure 2.

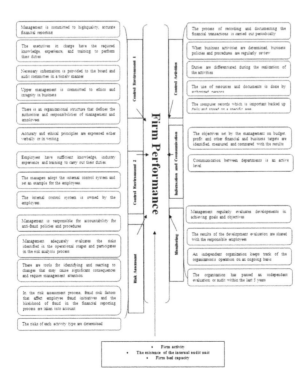

Method

For the purpose of the study, First of all, it is aimed to examine the relation between the control environment, risk assessment, control activities, information and communication and monitoring elements in the internal control system of accommodation firms and firm performance. Thus, firstly, demographic questions related to firms and questions that can represent elements of internal control system were prepared on the scale of Likert Type scale. Expressions in the questionnaire are prepared compiling from the article "How Effective are Organizations' Internal Control Inside Into Specific Internal Control Elements" published by Dana R. Hermanson, Jason L. Smith &Nathaniel M. Stephens in "Current Issues in Auditing" magazine in 2012 and the book entitled "Independent Audit" written by Usul in 2013 (Hermanson, Smith & Stephens, 2012; Usul, 2013). A questionnaire implementation was done using face to face interview technique using generated Likert Type scale with the people working in the position of department manager and worker in five stars accommodation firm running in the region of Turkey's one of the most important tourism cities Belek and Kundu in Antalya.

In order to determine the sub-dimensions of the internal control elements (control environment, risk evaluation, control activities, information and communication, monitoring) within the internal control system, reliability analysis of the factors after validity and explanatory factor analysis were performed first. A multiple regression model was developed and tested to evaluate the effect of each dimension of internal control elements on firm performance.

Analysis Results

To test the validity of the regression model, when we analyze R^2, which is a release power of dependent variable of independent variables, it is seen that at the 1% level of significance for Model 1, the internal control elements explain about 35% of the firm performance expressed by the gross profit margin.

When the results of the regression analysis are evaluated, it is seen that the risk evaluation variable from the internal control elements affects the firm performance indicated by the gross profit margin positively at the 1% significance level for the sample group examined. In addition, it has been determined that the firm activity duration (IFS) affects positively the firm performance at the 1% significance level.

To test the validity of the regression model, when we analyze R^2, which is a release power of dependent variable of independent variables, it is seen that at the 1% level of significance for Model 2, the internal control elements explain about 39% of the firm performance expressed by return on assets.

Table 2. Model 1 analysis research

	Gross profit margin		
	Beta	**T Statistics**	**P Value**
CE1	,089	,949	,344
CE2	,036	,432	,666
RA	,282	2,812	,005*
CA	,072	,841	,401
IC	,005	,062	,950
MO	-,144	-1,623	,106
FA	,263	3,339	,001*
IAU	-,039	-,409	,683
FBC	,025	,350	,726
(Constant)		11,909	,000
R2	0,352		
F	3,019		0,002

When the results of the regression analysis given in Table 3 are evaluated, it is seen for the sample group that the control environment expressed by the control environment 1 and control environment 2 variables of the internal control elements affects the firm performance indicated by the asset profitability in the positive direction at the level of 5% significance level. In addition, it has been determined that the firm activity duration (IFS) affects firm performance positively at the level of significance of 5%; the presence of the internal audit unit (IDB) and the operating bed capacity (ILC) affects firm performance positively at the level of significance of 1%.

To test the validity of the regression model, when we analyze R^2, which is a release power of dependent variable of independent variables, it is seen that at the 1% level of significance for Model 3, the internal control elements explain about 38% of the firm performance expressed by asset turnover.

When the results of the regression analysis given in Table 4 are evaluated, it is seen for the sample group that information and communication monitoring elements of the internal control elements affect the firm performance in the positive direction at the level of 1% significance level, control activities affect the firm performance indicated by the asset turnover in the positive direction at the level of 5% significance level. The presence of the internal audit unit (IAU) and the operating bed capacity (FBC) of the control variables are among the variables that affect the firm performance positively.

Table 3. Model 2 analysis research

	Return on assets		
	Beta	**T Statistics**	**P Value**
CE1	,187	2,224	,027**
CE2	,122	2,293	,021**
RA	,106	1,177	,241
CA	,066	,826	,410
IC	,018	,234	,815
MO	-,074	-1,062	,290
FA	,145	2,036	,043**
IAU	,176	2,084	,018**
FBC	,492	7,663	,000*
(Constant)		2,683	,008
R2	0,389		
F	8,652		0,000

Table 4. Model 3 analysis research

	Asset turnover		
	Beta	**T Statistics**	**P Value**
CE1	-,003	-,031	,975
CE2	,060	,790	,431
RA	-,105	-1,155	,250
CA	,149	1,919	, 050**
IC	,202	2,877	,004*
MO	,397	4,917	,000*
FA	,054	,751	,454
IAU	,351	4,017	,000*
FBC	,251	3,869	,000*
(Constant)		2,683	,008
R2	0,376		
F	8,114		0,000

EMPIRICAL RESULTS

The quality and functioning of the internal control system in the accommodation firm have qualification of guide for managers. Inadequate and ineffective functioning leads to management errors and thus negatively affects firm performance (Feng et al., 2009). The internal control system has a number of aims that will increase firm performance such as correcting low incomes arising from information deficiencies and abuses, firm debt follow, cash management, asset management (stocks, receivables etc.),efficiency of activities (Beeler et al., 1999). Jokipii (2010) emphasized that the key to firm success is the effectiveness of the implementation of the internal control system; while Schneider & Church (2008) pointed out that an effective internal control system plays a key role in effectively implementing cash management.

Assessment of Control Environment

It is based on the baseline control environment of an effective internal control system. The fact that the control environment is not strong will possibly eliminate the possibility of other elements' establishment and application while the strong control environment will directly contribute to the effective operation of the internal control system. Honesty and ethic values, professional competence, board of directors and audit committee, philosophy and style of management, organizational structure, authority and responsibility distribution and human resources policies and practices constitute elements of the control environment. The design and implementation of the said elements in line with the objectives and objectives of the firm will also contribute significantly to the effectiveness of the firm activities and the performance of the firm in this context (COSO, 1992). Analyzes made within the created model conclude control environment has a positive effect on the firm performance.

The subject-matter relationship that emerged when compared in terms of the litterateur has been examined by Mawanda (2008) in Uganda with a study of the relationship between Higher Education Institutions' internal control systems and firm performances, Kinyua et al. (2015) by a study of the relationship between internal control environment and firm performance on companies traded on the Nairobi Stock Exchange, show similarity to the Khamis's (2013) study of a bank operating in Zanzibar that examines the relationship between internal control system and firm performance. Although it is generally similar to the study of the relationship between the internal control systems of the public and private firms and the performance of the firm by Muraleetharan (2010), the study shows that there is no positive relationship between the control environment and the firm performance in the study.

Assessment Related With Risk Evaluation

Risk evaluation, which is among the elements of internal control, is one of the factors affecting the performance of the firm. The continuity of the firms, the ability to compete successfully in the sector in which they operate, the financial strength, the positive image and so on are extremely important and critical for firms. The effectiveness of the internal control system is directly related to the success of risk evaluation activities. The risk evaluation element will positively affect performance as a mechanism to remove the risks that may arise due to errors, fraud and abuse (Njeri, 2014). On the other hand, management should be prepared against the risks that may arise about the activities and also management should predetermine the necessary risk evaluations; that will contribute to firm performance. In the analysis made under the model created, it is concluded that risk evaluation factor affects the firm performance positively.

The subject-matter relationship that emerged when compared in terms of the litterateur has been examined by Mawanda (2008) in Uganda with a study of the relationship between Higher Education Institutions' internal control systems and firm performances, Kinyua et al (2015) by a study of the relationship between internal control environment and firm performance on companies traded on the Nairobi Stock Exchange, Khamis's (2013) study of a bank operating in Zanzibar that examines the relationship between internal control system and firm performance, the study of the relationship between internal control systems of public and private firms and firm performance by Muraleetharan (2010), Mwakimasinda, Odhiambo & Byaruhanga (2014) study on the effect of internal control systems on firm performance of sugar cane companies operating in Kenya, a study that seeks efficiency between internal control system and firm performance by ChanLi, Mc Vay & Skaife (2015) shows similarity.

Evaluations on Control Activities

Control activities, which are among the elements of internal control, are another factor that affects firm performance. Control activities are expressed as policies and procedures that are developed against the risks and threats encountered in the process of reaching the objectives of the operator and that provide data on this issue to the management (COSO, 1994). Control activity is an element that is effective in all levels and functions of an firm (Moeller, 2009). In this context, the creation and effective operation of control activities by the management will contribute positively to the performance of the firm.

The subject-matter relationship that emerged when compared in terms of the litterateur has been examined as explained in the followings; by Dineshkumar (2013) in Sri Lanka with a study of the relationship between internal control systems and firm performances in Telekom Firm, by Mawanda (2008) in Uganda with a study of the relationship between Higher Education Institutions' internal control systems and firm performances, Kinyua et al (2015) by a study of the relationship between internal control environment and firm performance on companies traded on the Nairobi Stock Exchange, Khamis's (2013) study of a bank operating in Zanzibar that examines the relationship between internal control system and firm performance, the study of the relationship between internal control systems of public and private firms and firm performance by Muraleetharan (2010), Mwakimasinda, Odhiambo & Byaruhanga (2014) study on the effect of internal control systems on firm performance of sugar cane companies operating in Kenya, a study that seeks efficiency between internal control system and firm performance by ChanLi, Mc Vay & Skaife (2015) shows similarity.

Evaluations on Information and Communication

Information and communication that are among the elements of internal control are another factor affecting firm performance. One of the most important resources of firms, information is widely used in all activity processes of the firms. In this context, firms producing and using information effectively improve their performance continuously by providing quality products and services (Demirel, 2007).

The information and communication element is of interest as an element that encompasses all of the other elements of the internal control system and is of critical importance in the realization of the overall objectives of the internal control system. There is a need for information throughout the organizational structure for the achievement of firm objectives. The ability of management to make effective decisions is directly proportional to the quality of the information. In this context, the information to be obtained must be provided in a timely, correctly, suitably for the need manner (Akyel, 2010). Analyzes made within the model were found to have a positive effect on the firm performance of information and communication element.

The subject-matter relationship that emerged when compared in terms of the litterateur has been examined as explained in the followings; Kinyua et al. (2015) by a study of the relationship between internal control environment and firm performance on companies traded on the Nairobi Stock Exchange, Khamis's (2013) study of a bank operating in Zanzibar that examines the relationship between internal control system and firm performance, the study of the relationship between internal control systems of public and private firms and firm performance by Mwakimasinda, Odhiambo & Byaruhanga (2014) study on the effect of internal control systems on firm performance of sugar cane companies operating in Kenya, another study that seeks efficiency between internal control system and firm performance by ChanLi, Mc Vay & Skaife (2015), A study by Darroch (2005) on the relationship between information and firm performance on firm operating in different sectors in New Zealand, Özaralli's study (2006) on the relationship between information and information sharing on different sectors and firm performance and Demirel (2007) shows that the information and communication on the banking sector is similar to those studies that examine the relation with the firm performance.

Assessment on Monitoring

Monitoring among internal control elements is another factor that affects firm performance. The purpose of monitoring the internal control system is to determine whether the system is functioning effectively, to identify possible changes in the condition and to provide the necessary compliance (Njeri, 2014). It is also an important factor in assessing whether or not the monitoring entity is able to perform its overall objectives in parallel with its mission and in the definition of internal control (INTOSAI, 2006; Understanding Internal Controls, 2015). Therefore, it is expected that the monitoring element will affect the firm performance. Firms that effectively carry out the necessary monitoring processes on business activities and internal control system will make a positive contribution to firm performance by increasing operational efficiency in the short term or in the long term in accordance with the objectives and targets set (Njeri, 2014).

The subject-matter relationship that emerged when compared in terms of the litterateur has been examined by Mawanda (2008) in Uganda with a study of the relationship between Higher Education Institutions' internal control systems and firm performances, Kinyua et al. (2015) by a study of the relationship between internal control environment and firm performance on companies traded on the Nairobi Stock Exchange, show similarity to the Khamis's (2013) study of a bank operating in Zanzibar that examines the relationship between internal control system and firm performance. The study of the relationship between internal control systems of public and private firms and firm performance by Muraleetharan (2010), the study of the relationship between internal control systems of public and private firms and firm performance by Mwakimasinda, Odhiambo and Byaruhanga (2014) study on the effect of internal control systems on firm performance of sugar cane companies operating in Kenya, another study that seeks efficiency between internal control system and firm performance by ChanLi, Mc Vay ve Skaife (2015) shows similarity.

CONCLUSION

The increasing need for institutionalization in firms, transparency and execution of activities in a more efficient level, and so on have brought along the need for control requirements. In this context, necessary internal control models have been developed and put into practice widely all over the world in order to be able to meet the need for such control systems. Among the different models created, the COSO Internal Control Model is the most widely used internal control model. The model published in 1992; it continues to be implemented in a dynamic structure by making necessary updates within the framework of changing needs, expectations and conditions.

The COSO Internal Control Model consists of five interrelated components. These components constitute a general framework for firms and guide the governance system for the establishment and effective operation process. The level of implementation of the components differs according to the type of management, the size of the firms, purpose of the establishment etc. In addition, these components are demonstrations that the internal control system in a firm exists in sufficient size. In the light of this information, the evaluation on the internal control system in accommodation firms and its relationship with the firm performance are based on the COSO Internal Control Model in this study.

It is recognized that the effectiveness of the internal control system, which constitutes the policies and procedures established to provide reasonable assurance of management in achieving the objectives of the enterprise, is considered to be effective in providing firm activities and revealing the achievement of specified business objectives. Absent or ineffective internal control system can lead to loss of assets, incomplete or incorrect decisions of the management, abuses and various different losses. Therefore, establishing the internal control system and effective operation of it in the firms has a critical importance for the firms.

The elements such as labor intensity in structure of the accommodation firms, high number of personnel employment and very high turnover rate of personnel, the density of monetary transactions, the existence of products with high unit price, the continuity of service, the multiplicity of income centers etc, have greatly increased the need for the internal control system in such firms. From this point of view, control environment which in included in internal control system in accommodation firms, risk assessment, control activities, evaluation of information and communication and monitoring elements and investigating their relation with the firm performance constitute the scope of the study.

This study examines the relationship between the evaluation of the internal control system and the firm performance. When the results obtained from the multiple regression analysis are evaluated, it is determined that there are meaningful positive correlations between the indicators of firm performance and internal control elements such as control environment, risk evaluation, control activities, information and communication and monitoring elements. Similar results are obtained when the litterateur is evaluated. The internal control system has a number of aims that will increase firm performance such as correcting low incomes arising from information deficiencies and abuses, firm debt follow, cash management, asset management (stocks, receivables etc.), efficiency of activities. It is expressed in studies that an effective internal control system plays an essential role in the effective realization of cash management. It is also expressed that the element which comes to the forefront for firm success is the effectiveness of the implementation of the internal control system.

In summary, control is an important management function, not a preferred management approach. Especially a number of elements such as the complex structure of accommodation firms, the multiplicity of revenue centers, the continuity of service, and so on, make it difficult for senior executives in the business to effectively perform their management duties. Through an effective internal control system, managers will be able to perform all necessary control processes at a more efficient level and comprehensively monitor all activities that carry strategic importance. In addition, the strong internal control system will provide significant advantages such as the prevention of major mistakes, fraud and corruption in the firms, acting of management more effectively in decision-making processes, minimizing resource losses, bringing competitive advantages to firms and transforming firms into a more institutional structure. In this context, it will positively contribute to the performance of the firms.

REFERENCES

Akyel, R. (2010). Türkiye'de İç Kontrol Kavramı, Unsurları ve Etkinliğinin Değerlendirilmesi. *Yönetim ve Ekonomi Dergisi, 17*(1).

Ama, A. J. N. (2012). An Assessment Of Internal Control System On The Image Of The Hospitality Industries. In *Royal Mac – Dic Hotel And Capital View Hotels*. Kwame Nkrumah University of Science and Technology.

Amudo, A., & Inanga, E. L. (2009). Evaluation of Internal Control Systems: A case study from Uganda. *International Research Journal of Finance and Economics, 27*.

Atmaca, M. (2012). Muhasebe Skandallarının Önlenmesinde İç Kontrol Sisteminin Etkinleştirilmesi. *Afyon Kocatepe Üniversitesi İİBF Dergisi, 14*(1).

Can, E. N. (2014). *Hastane İşletmeciliğinde İç Kontrol Sisteminin Etkinliği. Yayımlanmamış Doktora Tezi*. İstanbul: Marmara Üniversitesi Sosyal Bilimler Enstitüsü.

Chan Li, M. F., Mc Vay, S. E., & Skaife, H. (2015). Does Ineffective Internal Control over Financial Reportind affect Firm's Operations? Evidence from Firms' Inventory Management. *The Accounting Review, 90*(2).

Çiftçi, Y., & Köroğlu, Ç. (2008). Otel İşletmelerinde Yiyecek İçecek Kontrol Yöntemlerinin İncelenmesi (Marmaris İlçesi Örneği). *Manas Üniversitesi Sosyal Bilimler Dergisi, 19*.

COSO. (1992). *Internal Control Integrated Framework*. Retrieved from www.coso.org

Dalgar, H. (2012). İşletmelerin Muhasebe Departmanlarında Hata ve Hileleri Önlemeye Yönelik İç Kontrol Sisteminin Oluşturulması: Bir Vaka Çalışması. *Muhasebe Öğretim Üyeleri Bilim ve Dayanışma Vakfı Dergisi, 3*.

Demirel, Y. (2007). Bilgi ve Bilgi Paylaşımının İşletme Performansı Etkisi Üzerine Bir Araştırma. *Yönetim Bilimleri Dergisi, 5*(2).

Dineshkumar, S., & Kogalacumar, P. (2013). Internal Control System and its impact on the Performance of the Sri Lanka Telecom limited in Jaffna District. *International Journal of Advancements in Computing Technology, 2*(6).

Doyle, J. T., Ge, W., & McVay, S. (2007). Accruals Quality and Internal Control Over Financial Reporting. *The Accounting Review, 82*(5), 1141–1170. doi:10.2308/accr.2007.82.5.1141

Ejoh, N., & Ejom, P. (2014). The Impact Of Internal Control Activities on Financial Performance of Tertiary Institutions in Nigeria. *Journal Of Economics and Sustainable Development*, 5(16).

Elbannan, M. A. (2009). Quality of Internal Control Over Financial Reporting, Corporate Governance And Credit Ratings. *International Journal of Disclosure and Governance*, 6(2), 127–149. doi:10.1057/jdg.2008.32

Feng, Li., & McKay. (2009). Analysis of the Relationship Between Listed Companies' Earnings Quality and Internal Control Information Disclosure. *Modern Economy*, 2009, 2.

Ge, W., & Mc Vay, S. (2005). The Disclosure of Material Weaknesses in Internal Control after the Sarbanes-Oxley Act. *Accounting Horizons*, 19(3), 137–158. doi:10.2308/acch.2005.19.3.137

Hermanson, D. R., & Hermanson, H. M. (1994, Winter). The Internal Control Paradox: What Every Manager Should Know. *Review of Business*, 29–32.

Hermanson, D. R., Smith, J. L., & Nathaniel, M. S. (2012). How Effective are Organizastions' Internal Controls? Insights into Specific Internal Control Elements. *Current Issues in Auditing*, 6(1), 31–50. doi:10.2308/ciia-50146

INTOSAI. (2006). *International Organizastion of Supreme Audit Institutions*. Retrieved from www.intosai.org

Jagels, M. G., & Ralston, C. E. (2007). *Hospitality Management Accounting*. Wiley&Sons Inc.

Jokipii, A. (2010). Determinants And Consequences Of Internal Control In Firms: A Contingency Theory Based Analysis. *The Journal of Management and Governance*, 14.

Judeh, A,. Sheikh, I., & Sbugh, S. (2009). The Application Of Accounting Responsibility In The Jordanian Hotels: A Case Study. *Alzarqa Journal For Humanities Research*, 9(9).

Khamis, H. A. (2013). *Contribution of Internal Control System to the Financial Performance of Financial Institution. A Case of People's Bank of Zanzibar Ltd.* Mzumbe University Accounting and Finance Institute.

Kinyua, J. K, Gakure, R., Gekara, M., & Orwa, G. (2015). Effect of Internal Control Environment on the Financial Performance of Companies Quoted in the Nairobi Securities Exchange. *International Journal of Innovative Finance and Economics Research, 3.*

Mawanda, S. P. (2008). *Effects of Internal Control System on Financial Performance in Uganda's Institution of Higher Learning.* Dissertation for award of MBA in Uganda Martyrs University.

Moeller, R. R. (2009). *Brink's Modern Internal Auditing.* John Wiley&Sons.

Muraleetharan, P. (2010). *Internal Control and Impact of Financial Performance of The Organizations.* Academic Press.

Mwakimasinde, M., Odhiambo, A., & Byaruhanga, J. (2014). Effects of Internal Control Systems on Financial Performance of Sugarcane outgrowercompanies in Kenya. *Journal of Business and Management, 16*(12).

Njeri, K. C. (2014). *Effect of Internal Controls on The Financial Performance of Manufacturing Firms in Kenya.* University of Nairobi.

Okutmuş, E., & Uyar, S. (2014). *Yiyecek İçecek Departmanında Yapılan Bir Hilenin Tespiti: Vaka Analizi.* Mali Çözüm Dergisi, Ocak-Şubat.

Olalı, H., & Korzay, M. (1993). *Otel İşletmeciliği.* İstanbul: Beta Basım Yayım Dağıtım.

Schneider, A., & Church, B. K. (2008). The Effects of Auditors' Internal Control Opinions on Loan Decisions. *Journal of Accounting and Public Policy, 27*(1), 1–18. doi:10.1016/j.jaccpubpol.2007.11.004

Sebilcioğlu, F., Karaağaoğlu, S., & Karacacay, G. (2013). *Kurumsal Yönetim İlkeleri Işığında Aile Şirketleri Rehberi.* İstanbul: Türkiye Kurumsal Yönetim Derneği.

Sharari. (2006). *The Relationship Between Internal Control and Performance of Staff In The PPA in the Kingdom of Saudi Arabia: Attitude of the staff* (Unpublished Master's Thesis). University of Jordan, Amman, Jordan.

Soodanian, S., Navid, B. J., & Kheirollahi, F. (2013). The Relationship Between Firm Characteristics and Internal Control Weaknesses in the Financial Reporting Environment of Companies Listed on the Tehran Stock Exchange. *Journal of Applied Environmental and Biological Sciences, 3*(11), 68–74.

Tang, A., & Xu, L. (2007). *Institutional Ownership, Internal Control Material Weakness and Firm Performance.* Working paper, Morgan State University.

Understanding Internal Controls. A References Guide for Managing University Business Practices. (n.d.). Retrieved from http://www.ucop.edu/ctlacct/under-ic.pdf

Usul, H. (2013). *Bağımsız Denetim.* Ankara: Detay Yayıncılık.

KEY TERMS AND DEFINITIONS

COSO: The Committee of Sponsoring Organizations of the Treadway Commission, COSO, is dedicated to providing thought leadership through the development of comprehensive frameworks and guidance on internal control, enterprise risk management, and fraud deterrence designed to improve organizational performance and oversight and to reduce the extent of fraud in organizations.

Internal Control: Internal control is a process, effected by an entity's board of directors, management, and other personnel, designed to provide reasonable assurance regarding the achievement of objectives relating to operations, reporting, and compliance.

Internal Control System: System of internal control is expected to provide an organization with reasonable assurance that those objectives relating to external reporting and compliance with laws and regulations will be achieved. Achieving those objectives, which are based largely on laws, rules, regulations, or standards established by legislators, regulators, and standard setters, depends on how activities within the organization's control are performed. Generally, management and/or the board have greater discretion in setting internal reporting objectives that are not driven primarily by such external parties. However, the organization may choose to align its internal and external reporting objectives to allow internal reporting to better support the entity's external reporting.

INTOSAI: The 1992 INTOSAI guidelines for internal control standards were conceived as a living document reflecting the vision that standards should be promoted for the design, implementation, and evaluation of internal control. This vision involves a continuing effort to keep these guidelines up-to-date. The 17th INCOSAI recognized a strong need for updating the 1992 guidelines and agreed that the Committee on Sponsoring Organisations of the Treadway Commission's (COSO) integrated framework for internal control should be relied upon. Subsequent outreach efforts resulted in additional recommendations that the guidelines address ethical values and provide more information on the general principles of control activities related to information processing. The revised guidelines take these recommendations into account and should facilitate the understanding of new concepts with respect to internal control.

Chapter 13
Academic Tourism:
A Segment on the Rise

Jakson Renner Rodrigues Soares
UDC, Spain

ABSTRACT

This chapter aims to present the academic tourism segment as a rising trend that can improve indicators, both academic and marketing, of tourist destinations. On the one hand, economistic arguments were presented; on the other, the academic tourist can be highlighted as a source of reliable information about the destination. That is, returning to their place of origin, the individual will share their experience with other people, including students, commenting on their experiences at the university, and of course, on the receiving destination. At this time, both the power of attraction of their listeners to the place will increase and will act as a paradiplomacy. However, both financial aspects (impacts of academic tourism) and marketing (influence on the image of the destination) are strong arguments for betting on this segment, both from the academic literature, as well as destinations with good universities.

DOI: 10.4018/978-1-5225-8494-0.ch013

ACADEMIC TOURISM: A SEGMENT ON THE RISE

Academic tourism, although it is a segment that has grown a lot in recent years, is not new. Already the World Tourism Organization said that there has been a significant increase in diversification in tourism. This segment is closely related to university exchanges that have been part of the very essence of universities. Although it was little investigated from the academy, academic tourism was widely explored by companies in marketing campaigns for international studies. That is to say, it is a segment with little presence in the academic literature, but it is widely used as a marketing claim for journalistic information that deals with university exchanges.

This segment has a relevant role in the deseasonalization of tourism and can be a good option for places that are not yet developed touristically. This is because it has outstanding qualitative characteristics in the context of the traditional demand for tourism, given that the academic tourist stays longer in the destination, has greater spending capacity, given that his stay is longer over time. This market niche is appealing, given that the economic success that makes the academic tourist attractive: it has a higher average cost than other types; your average stay is longer; and travels and stays at the destination out of season.

The destinations must offer access to their university education system to foreign students to produce income from their academic attributes, specifically, universities. This generates an impact on the local economy thanks to the ability to generate foreign currency with the consumption of products and services during the tourist's long stay, or the great possibility of loyalty and recommendation. That's because the exchange can provoke the attraction of new tourists (family and friends) who come to visit academic tourists. That is why it is also a growing trend, due to its capacity to induce new displacements. In addition, in the future, many of these academic tourists may occupy influential roles in governments, business councils or organizations, which leads to believe that the relationships established during the tourist stay can be strategic for subsequent negotiations between countries.

The educational offer of a country can become an important tourist attraction that destinations have to know how to take advantage of. Traditionally, the United States, the United Kingdom and Australia were the main destinations for international students in the world. This is due both to the universality of English (characterizing tourism as language) and to the quality of its universities (characterizing tourism as academic). But more recently, Spain has realized that education can be a fundamental element to boost tourism in the country, diversifying its multi-destination matrix. With all that said, by betting on the segment in question, the destinations are investing in the improvement of the economic indicators of the satellite account of tourism, involving feasible solutions for the problem of the seasonality of the sector and, transversally, influencing the attraction of new visitors.

This chapter aims to preset the academic tourism segment as a rising trend that can improve indicators, both academic and marketing, of tourist destinations. On the one hand economistic arguments were presented, on the other the academic tourist can be highlighted as a source of reliable information about the destination. That is, returning to their place of origin, the individual will share their experience with other people, including students, commenting on their experiences at the university, and of course, on the receiving destination. At this time, both the power of attraction of their listeners to the place will increase, as will act as a paradiplomacy. However, both financial aspects (impacts of academic tourism) and marketing (influence on the image of the destination) are strong arguments for betting on this segment, both from the academic literature, as well as destinations with good universities.

ACADEMIC TOURISM AS A SEGMENT

This research has tried to revise some types of tourism with related motifs, comparing these different motivations that, after all, coincide in the definition that is closer to this type of tourism. According to the literature consulted, in general, when it comes to the trips made by students for study purposes, many are the terms that attempt to characterize them. Before dealing directly with this topic, it should be noted that according to Asquerino (2013), the educational offer of a country can become an important tourist attraction that destinations need to know how to take advantage. The paper refers to the term tourism studies as a market niche with tourist particularities that differentiate it from other passenger profiles.

In 2009, international students were vital to the British university system, contributing around 8% of the total income of their universities. Yet, already in 2013 that Spain was located realizing that education could be a key element to boost tourism in the country. In particular, destinations must create ways to attract this tourist, because according to Hosteltur (2013), tourists who travel for study purposes may end up acting as an ambassador of destiny, depending, of course, on the satisfaction with this.

In the studies of Limanond, Butsingkorn and Chermkhunthod (2011) on the behavior of trips on the campus, the authors refer to the activities in which the university students participate will eventually influence their behavior. Still following these authors, many of the students will happen to play roles of influence in the government, in the companies and in other organizations, for that reason it is possible to fit a positive relation with them. In the same way that Soares (2013) concludes that students who study outside their place of origin, upon returning to this, are an important source of information for others.

This monitoring moves millions of tourists a year and how these appeasible numbers are and knowing that the United States, the United Kingdom and Australia are the major destinations attracting international students, some countries, such as Spain, have fallen short of their interest in emerging markets (HOSTELTUR, 2013).

Within the varied tourist modes that young people practice, some subsectors can be highlighted: independent vacation trips, language tourism, jobs and studies where they combine vacations with a temporary job, volunteers and university students who carry out stays abroad. And, from the subsectors presented previously, this research will explore the tourism of university students, more specifically in aspects related to their experience abroad to be part of their academic training at a university other than their origin.

According to the review of the bibliography, there are three key factors that make up this segment of study in question: linguistic, tourist and more economic (BARALO, 2006; PAWLOWSKA; MARTÍNEZ, 2009; BERDUGO, 2012). In this case, when conducting a trip for study purposes, it is most likely that both aspects of the language and the tourism sector are present in the motivation of this. Many are the terms used to define this tourist phenomenon, but in the end, it can be said that it is a segment that has not been explored and lacks in-depth empirical research. The terms most commonly used to treat travel by studies are: educational tourism, exchange tourism, scientific tourism, student tourism, language tourism, linguistic tourism, language stays and more recently, academic tourism.

According to WYSE[1], when it comes to the young tourist, there are very important aspects that identify the issue in question: the desire to experience other cultures, build a life experience and / or benefit from formal or informal learning opportunities in an environment that is not usual. In this way, it is therefore possible to begin to explore the different contributions found in the literature review of travel for study purposes.

In the case of student tourism, the increase in commercial, political and academic interest in young tourists has stimulated a wide range of research (RICHARDS; WILSON, 2003). According to these authors, more and more young people travel abroad to study, and when you do this, you are learning about a different people, their culture and their customs (VICTER, 2009). According Limanond, Butsingkorn e Chermkhunthod (2011), college students are a social group that tends to have a complex and unique travel behavior. They have considerable freedom and are essentially autonomous in their decisions related to their daily activities. In addition, they live, study, and socialize with other students, which makes their decisions be influenced by these.

One can say that some remarkable features of this type of tourism are related both to economic aspects and to mercantile aspects. That is, research on the young tourist wakes up a lot of interest due mainly to the growing size of the market in question (study trips). In Table 1 next, we present both the mercantile and economic characteristics influenced by this segment, found in some of the investigations that dealt with this type of tourism.

Own elaboration based on the studies of Richards; Wilson (2003); Park; Latkova; Nicholls (2006); Embratur (2009); Pawlowska (2011).

It is understood that the motivations that lead a person to make a trip are many, and the displacement with the reason to reach new knowledge is one more. As you can see, according to Moiteiro (2010)

The displacement of people with the motivation to extend their horizons, to seek knowledge and emotions through discovery and contact with cultural, material or immaterial assets, has been representing an increasing importance in the last decades in the framework of the international tourism phenomenon (MOITEIRO, 2010, p. 141).

Both the Richards and Wilson studies (2003) and Park, Latkova and Nicholls (2006) emphasized that the research that analyzed this target audience was very scarce for years. This is because they are often young students, and because of the long-term prejudice that they had a low level of spending. But, what was previously

Table 1. Mercantile X economic characteristics

Mercantile	Economic
It creates bridges between people and cultures, approaching countries	It tends to concentrate more spending on the place where he studies
It works, or it can work, as a trend engine, presenting new destinations to the world	It stays longer in the destination, consequently it increases its cost in the place
Create or create new attractions, as well as help consolidate destinations	Even without much capital, it tends to carry a considerable amount of foreign exchange for the destination (it saves money before traveling)
You are generally more likely to travel than other segments	It is a type of tourism that can happen at any time of the year
You can end up as the ambassador of the destination according to your satisfaction	Have more free time to spend on destiny

despised, even excluded by many destinations, in recent years has become a highly desired market segment (RICHARDS; WILSON, 2003).

Within this diversification, an article published in The Economist on October 9, 2012, that is, for several years, it was widespread that countries should understand that offering access to education to tourists students[2] is an important way of producing wealth. This was due to basic aspects such as: first, the ability to generate wealth in the destination with the consumption of products and services during your stay (PAWLOWSKA, 2011); second, the great possibility of loyalty (FOREIGN..., 2012) or also to the recommendation that these do (RAMOS; SUÁREZ; URGORRI, 2014).

In this same article, there are three great reasons to attract tourists' students. In the first one, it cites that foreign students in the USA pay generous amounts of money for enrollment, textbooks and end-of-year parties. Secondly, by mixing with bright people from other places, the students of receiving destiny have a great opportunity to understand the globalized world, in which they will then look for work, and finally, foreign students forge connections that can last a lifetime. Enter here the concept of loyalty, an aspect that destinations must consider to stay competitive.

It is even noted that this stay is a great opportunity for the recipient destination to obtain the loyalty of the student tourist, given that in the future he will be more likely to do business with that country when they finally return home. This is what Hosteltur (2013) defines as ambassadors of destiny. In addition to the three characteristics cited above that emphasize the possibility of receiving foreign students, countries should also consider that during their stays, they may cause the attraction of new tourists: family and friends, who visit them, generating a significant impact in the economy of the place (PAWLOWSKA, 2011).

Chen, Chen e Okumos (2013) they relate the restrictions that tourists find when it comes to organizing the trip with the image of the destination. In these studies, it tries to identify the negative effects of the restrictions on accessing the destination by a segment of tourists with significant purchasing power and that they often travel more frequently than other segments, that is, graduate and postgraduate students. In this context, Embratur (2009) points out that one of the reasons why tourists decide on the destination they visit is the ease of obtaining permission to enter the country. More than a motivation, this should be faced as a restrictive aspect of access to the international market. In the same way, it indicates how influential aspects of choosing the quality of education; the recognition of the course; the facility of university admission; the financing options available; the cost of living; personal security; as well as linguistic aspects; cultural and social factors and the marketing of destiny.

Tourism due to study reasons is not sensitive to seasonality, which should be considered as a solution for periods of low tourist flow, since it can be carried out throughout the year, regardless of the season. In addition, this type of tourism can be used as attractive to places that do not yet have consolidated tourist routes, contributing to this activity adding more value to PIB than the countries that bet on it (VALDÉS, 2003). But it should be emphasized that positioning a target for a target audience requires an analysis of cognitive and affective images maintained by potential visitors (MARQUES, 2011). In addition, it must be considered that the image of a place also depends, to a large extent, on the operational and functional behaviors of the intervening actors and residents of the destination, as well as on the communication, advertising and promotion actions of this (AZEVEDO; MAGALHÃES; PEREIRA, 2010). As Hassan (2000) states that all actors directly involved with the tourism product must contribute to create added value capable of sustaining the resources of the destination to position itself in the market.

A great majority of the studies considered the profile of the tourist who travels by motivation of studies like a foreign tourist but it is not possible to be avoided that within a same country, the possibility exists that the university student realizes short stays in a university different from its original one, like This is the case for students SICUE/SÉNECA[3] in Spain. Therefore, this research understands that academic tourism is a modality practiced by students when they decide to spend an academic season in another university that is not their origin, allowing coexistence with other cultures and contact with educational and research institutions (even within their own borders). Not only that, since they can also be related to companies or organizations that will eventually influence their personal and professional training.

It is notorious that, even considering that there is a shortage of research on this segment, it becomes essential to explain before it important aspects that characterize it as a modality of tourism. This turns it into a more product to be marketed by tourist destinations, which need to have a competitive image to attract future student tourists. In order for there to be study motivation trips, there must be both attractive academic (universities, research centers...) or linguistic (that is, relating an activity related to the learning of a second language) as tourist attractions (cultural visits, public transport, security) (GARCÍA; COLLADO, 2007; PAWLOWSKA; MARTÍNEZ, 2009; BERDUGO, 2012).

In addition, according to García and Collado (2007), the study trip could be considered as a type of cultural tourism, but for that, the specific nature of supply and demand must also be considered. From this statement we can understand that the offer has to consider the key aspects to attract the student audience, based on the needs that these demand as tourists students. And not only that, when dealing with supply and demand, the authors denounce it is the need to know well what attributes of the destination (offer) can serve as a claim to attract the attention of the tourist. In addition, even according to them, together with the learning of a language, there are complementary elements that make up the tourist product. That is to say, there are not only aspects related to the trip -despray, accommodation and tourist visits-but also services of public libraries, sports centers, museums, where museums are or should be mirrors of society, its development and culture, of the past and of the present (GONÇALVES, 2010).

Studies dedicated to conceptualizing academic tourism also had approaches to the term linguistic tourism, as according to Baralo (2006), this tourism is related to trips to foreign countries in order to specify activities related to the learning of the language of this country. Even providing valid information (learning motivation) this definition is short to characterize academic tourism because it simply deals with the possibility of studying: one, languages, and two, abroad. Nevertheless, for the segment of the academic tourism it is proposed that the tourist student can travel to any destination that is not their home to study part of their academic career, without having the language as main motivation.

Continuing in the same line of investigation, there is another definition that was also used previously to help conceptualize academic tourism. In this case, we present the definition of language tourism that, in turn, is expanding, especially in traditional destinations, which innovate by offering this type of tourism segment (CANALIS, 2013). This term is totally related to this research, since it identifies both aspects related to studies (linguistic immersion for example) and aspects directly related to tourism (activities carried out during the trip, temporary displacement). What is most influencing the evolution of this work is that this research understands that the academic tourist can hold a language tourism stay at the same time that he is completing his academic stay, but learning another language is not the main reason for academic tourism.

Another term that can also be used to help to conceptualize this type of tourism is the tourist designation of studies and exchange, that is constituted of the tourist movement generated by activities and programs of learning and experiences for the purpose of qualification, extension of knowledge and development personal and professional (MTUR, 2008, p. 15). Relating this definition to the proposal for this modality, it is necessary to emphasize that there is no difference as far as the level of studies of the tourist of exchange, that is to say, it does not distinguish if this individual who makes the exchange is a student of primary, secondary or university, consequently It does not consider motivations, experiences, or its cultural level. At the same time, this definition ignores the possibility of carrying out learning programs within the same borders of the country.

Regarding the main motivation to carry out academic tourism, it is found that, due to student mobility, this tourist will be part of his university career within a university different from his or her origin. In this way, it should be noted that according to Cervera et al (2012), the image of the university is also an important aspect that should be considered capable of generating a competitive advantage in a student market with a lot of concurrence worldwide.

However, in order to eliminate these mistakes mentioned above and to adapt the definition of academic tourism to the concept of tourism proposed by the WTO (2010), Soares (2015) developed the definition of Pawlowska and Martínez (2009) considering these three aspects: activities not destination, duration of the stay and profile of the tourist. Therefore, the definition of academic tourism will be:

All trips carried out by people with stays of less than one year and more than one day, carried out in higher education centers in places other than their habitual environment, in order to carry out courses related to an academic career and / or attend specific courses organized by these centers.

But it is worth highlighting what is understood by the habitual environment of a person, which is being according to the WTO, a fundamental concept in tourism, and which is defined as the geographical area (although not necessarily contiguous) in which a person carries out their daily activities usual. That is to say, understanding the usual term in the proposal of definition of academic tourism has become a key to differentiating who is the academic tourist. For example, a student who completes his career in a university, even if he is in a different city from his home, will not be doing tourism, since this university is part of his usual environment.

To complete, it is necessary to delimit both the profile of the academic tourist (the one who conducts the academic tourism site), and the necessary attributes that characterize the destination for this type of tourism.

THE ATTRIBUTES NEEDED TO HAVE ACADEMIC TOURISM

As already mentioned above, the reasons that lead the individual to make a trip are very variable according to each tourist type. In order to have this type of tourism in particular, the academic tourism, the destinations (offer) must have characteristics able to attract the academic tourists (demand). According to Leiva (2012), the tourist that makes trips for reasons of studies, although the main motivation is the educational-academic offer, also has other secondary reasons that are not related to the academic. What can be identified is that they are also playful aspects, knowledge of new places, cultures and people that strongly motivate academic tourists (GARCÍA; COLLADO, 2007; MTUR, 2008; LEIVA, 2012).

What is understood from the problematic of this term is that the motivations that academic students take to make their journey are very varied, being influenced not only by academic aspects (libraries, university residences, university services) but also by tourist attributes of the destination (transportation, restoration) (PAWLOWSKA; MARTÍNEZ, 2009; PAWLOWSKA, 2011). Not only that, we must also consider the statement by Baloglu and McCleary (1999) that the segmentation must be such that the interest of different groups, in this case, the future student tourist. In addition, according to Gândara (2008) the image of the destiny must be in accordance with the reality, so that the satisfaction with this one is reached.

There are several components that influence the election of an academic tourism destination and the most important attributes are: access to the destination (transport routes available to reach the place); the elements that generate tourist flows, that is, the facilities that presuppose a complete system; and the tourist attractions, which are decisive in choosing a destination or another. It is also worth highlighting the ease of symbolic access, such as institutional agreements between universities, as well as between countries, related to visas for students (EMBRATUR, 2009; PLAYING…, 2012).

In the previous box, attributes of academic tourism destinations have been identified that generate interest in their target audience. In it, a review of the attributes commonly cited by the authors of the theories on the study trips, compiling the information and relating it to the academic tourism. Knowing the tourist attractions capable of influencing the choice of a tourist destination or another, it is finally possible to explore how the demand for this type of tourism. The next section is intended to define the profile of academic tourists.

Table 2. Attractions proposed to characterize academic tourism

Attractive	Authors
Higher education colleges and universities	García and Collado (2007); Pawlowska and Martínez (2009); Pawlowska (2011); Berdugo (2012); Leiva, (2012); Cervera et al (2012)
Cultural attractions	García and Collado (2007); Pawlowska and Martínez (2009); Berdugo (2012)
Linguistic aspects	Baralo (2006); García and Collado (2007); Embratur (2009)
Meet different people	MTUR (2008)
Tourist visits	Berdugo (2012)

Own elaboration

THE PROFILE OF ACADEMIC TOURIST

Based on the readings made for this research, and the contributions of the different types of tourism cited in previous sections, an academic tourist profile was attempted following some considerations: activities in the destination, duration of the stay and motivation of the trip. In relation to the activities carried out at destination, it is understood that the great difference capable of characterizing the academic tourist profile compared to that of other tourism related to study trips is that, in order to be considered as academic tourism, the main activity will have a primordial relationship with the academic training of tourist, that is, with his university career (PAWLOWSKA; MARTÍNEZ, 2009; PAWLOWSKA, 2011; LEIVA, 2012).

In destination, the academic tourist will eventually use tourist services such as restoration, accommodation, visits among others. It can not be overlooked that because of academic tourism, tourists must also have libraries, university residences, scientific laboratories among other activities related to their training. In addition, it should be emphasized that in order to be seen as tourism, the duration can not exceed the period of 1 year and may not be less than 1 day. Therefore, these academic tourists must do only part of their career in a university other than theirs, in their country of origin or abroad. Finally, the motivation of this tourist is the one to form in its university branch. That is, the student tourist will be part of his academic course in another university. It should be clarified that he may also have finished his graduation career and be in another destination doing postgraduate studies.

It seems logical to think that from there, surely, other secondary motivations may appear for the academic tourist, but, if they are seen as main reasons for the trip, they would then characterize another mode (language tourism, congress tourism, language stays ...). With that, the profile would be that of university students and post-graduate students stimulated to take part of their academic career in a place other than theirs; for a period less than one year; by personal motivation or development of their future professional careers; interested in knowing new cultures and people from different countries; who mostly use bilateral programs between their universities of origin (or countries) and universities at destination.

Finally, this chapter aims to preset the academic tourism segment as a rising trend that can improve indicators, both academic and marketing, of tourist destinations. On the one hand economistic arguments were presented, on the other the academic tourist can be highlighted as a source of reliable information about the destination. That is, returning to their place of origin, the individual will share their experience with other people, including students, commenting on their experiences at the university, and of course, on the receiving destination. At this time, both the power of attraction of their listeners to the place will increase, as will act as a paradiplomacy. However, both financial aspects (impacts of academic tourism) and marketing (influence on the image of the destination) are strong arguments for betting on this segment, both from the academic literature, as well as destinations with good universities.

Completely, we highlight here an economic importance of a tourism segment like this, which minimizes the effects of seasonality, as it can be used as a bridge to attract other tourists who visit them during their stay (family and friends). In a global way it should be noted that for a destination to achieve a position within a competitive space such as the current one, all those involved in the academic segment in question must work together. That is to say, university, public Administration, sectors of lodging or restoration, public and deprived beings must be united to obtain not only the attraction of the student tourist, but also their loyalty. It is thought that the experience in the destination will not be influenced only by the academic experience, but also by all the other services that contribute to the life of a citizen, native or foreign.

Finally, the last thing that emphasizes is the question of the language. That is, as was said in the literature review, language is a primary reason to be considered by the student who wants to be part of his career in another destination. That is, if the destination, apart from idiomatic tourism (such as studying the native language of the place), can also offer the possibility of researching, publishing, learning, communicating in a language similar to yours, that is an advantage that destinations They face countries that speak equal or similar languages.

REFERNCES

Asquerino, P. P. (2013). Turismo de estudios, una conexión diferente con el destino. *Revista Hosteltur, 228*, 46.

Azevedo, A., Magalhães, D., & Pereira, J. (2010). *City Marketing. Myplace in XXI*. Porto: Vida Económica.

Baloglu, S., & Mccleary, K. W. (1999). A model of destination image formation. *Annals of Tourism Research, 26*(4), 868–897. doi:10.1016/S0160-7383(99)00030-4

Baralo, M. (2006). Turismo lingüístico, más y mejor. Nexotur, 507, 23-29.

Berdugo, O. (2014). Español recurso económico: anatomía de un nuevo sector. *Cuadernos Cervantes, 2*(3). Disponible en: http://www.cuadernoscervantes.com/ele_30_esprececonom.html

Canalis, X. (2013). Turismo joven, de nicho a segmento estratégico. Revista Hosteltur, 224, 134-135.

Cervera, Schlesinger, W., Mesta, M. Á., & Sánchez, R. (2012). Medición de la imagen de la universidad y sus efectos sobre la identificación y lealtad del egresado: Una aproximación desde el modelo de Beerli y Díaz (2003). *Revista Española de Investigación de Marketing ESIC, 16*(2), 7–29. doi:10.1016/S1138-1442(14)60012-7

Chen, H. J., Chen, P. J., & Okumos, F. (2013). The relationship between travel constraints and destination image: A case study of Brunei. *Tourism Management, 35*, 198–208. doi:10.1016/j.tourman.2012.07.004

Embratur. (2009). *Estudo de inteligência de mercado para o segmento de estudos e intercâmbio*. Brasil, xun.

Gândara, J. M. G. (2008). A imagem dos destinos turísticos urbanos. *Revista Eletrônica de Turismo Cultural*, 1-22.

García, E. A., & Collado, A. M. (2007). La enseñanza del español como recurso turístico en Castilla-La Mancha. *Boletín Económico de ICE, 2923*, 33-40.

Gonçalves, A. R. (2010). Museus, Comunidade local e Turismo. In *Congresso Turismo Cultural, Territórios E Identidades, 2006* (pp. 81–105). Leiria: Instituto Politécnico de Leiria.

Hassan, S. S. (2000). Determinants of Market Competitiveness in an Environmentally Sustainable Tourism Industry. *Journal of Travel Research*, *38*(28), 239–245. doi:10.1177/004728750003800305

Hosteltur. (2013). Turismos de estudios contra la estacionalidad. *Hosteltur, 225*. Disponible en: http://www.hosteltur.com/139680_espana-recibio-936000-extranjeros-su-oferta-educativa.html

Leiva, F. S., (2012). La movilidad estudiantil internacional como turismo académico. Caracterización de la movilidad estudiantil y análisis de sus desplazamientos (flujos) turísticos durante su estadía en la Región Universitaria de Valparaíso, una oportunidad no gestionada. *Revista Geográfica Valparaíso, 46*, 54-68.

Limanond, T., Butsingkorn, T., & Chermkhunthod, C. (2011). Travel behavior of university students who live on campus: A case study of a rural university in Asia. *Transport Policy*, *18*(1), 163–171. doi:10.1016/j.tranpol.2010.07.006

Marques, C. P. (2011). Mapping Affective Image Of Destinations, Algarve. International Conference on Tourism & Management Studies, 2, 1040-1043.

Ministério de Turismo. (2008). Secretaria Nacional de Políticas do Turismo. Turismo de estudos e intercâmbio: Orientações Básicas.

Moiteiro, G. C. (2010). Turismo Cultural e patrimonio. Uma reflexão em torno do tópico da interpretação do patrimonio enquanto instrumento de valorização de bens culturais. In *Congresso Turismo Cultural, Territórios E Identidades* (pp. 141–158). Leiria: Instituto Politécnico de Leiria.

Park, S. H., Latkova, P., & Nicholls, S. (2006). Image of the united states as a travel destination: A case study of united kingdom college students, *In*: Northeastern Recreation Research Symposium, 2006, Boston. Anais: 2006. p. 8-15.

Pawlowska, E. (2011). *El turismo académico. Un análisis económico para el caso de galicia. 2011. 275f. Tese (Doutoramento en Economía Aplicada).* Santiago de Compostela: Universidade de Santiago de Compostela.

Pawlowska, E., & Martínez, F. (2009). Unha aproximación ao impacto económico directo do turismo académico: O caso dos intercambios Erasmus na Universidade de Santiago de Compostela. *Revista Galega de Economía*, *18*(2), 91–110.

Playing the Visa Card. (2012). *The Economist*. Disponible en http://www.economist.com/whichmba/playing-visa-card/print

Ramos, C., Suárez, F., & Urgorri, A. (2014, August 11). A la caza del universitario extranjero. *La Voz de Galicia*, p. 4.

Richards, G., & Wilson, J. (2003). *Today's Youth Travellers: Tomorrow's Global Nomads. New Horizons in Independent Youth and Student Travel*. Amsterdam: ISTC.

Soares, J. R. R. (2015). *Relación entre imagen turística construida y lealdad: Análisis de los estudiantes internacionales en Galicia* (PhD Thesis). Universidade da Coruña.

Soares, J. R. R. (2013). A imagem dos destinos de turismo acadêmico. Congreso En Línea De Administración, 10.

Valdés, J. A. (2003). *Marketing Estratégico e Estratégia Competitiva de Empresas Turísticas: Um estudo de caso da cadeia hoteleira Sol Meliá* (PhD thesis). Faculdade de Economia, Administração e Contabilidade, Universidade de São Paulo, São Paulo, Brazil.

Victer, P. P. (2009). *Marketing no turismo: um estudo descritivo sobre a imagem do intercâmbio de cursos de idiomas. 2009. 137f. Dissertação (Mestrado em Administração)*. Belo Horizonte: Faculdade de Ciências Empresariais, Universidade Fumec.

WTO Organización Mundial Del Turismo. (2010). *Introducción al turismo*. Madrid: Author.

ENDNOTES

[1] International organization that groups companies, associations and destinations interested in the young, student and educational market, with more than 500 members in 120 countries.

[2] This work refers to tourist student as that tourist who makes trips for the purpose of conducting studies in another destination that is not their origin.

[3] It is a mobility program aimed at students of Spanish universities that allows to take part of the degree in another Spanish university different from theirs, with immediate recognition in their academic record of the credits obtained at the university of destination.

Compilation of References

Aas, C., Ladkin, A., & Fletcher, J. (2005). Stakeholder collaboration and heritage management. *Annals of Tourism Research, 32*(1), 28–48. doi:10.1016/j.annals.2004.04.005

Abu Sharwar, B., & Atwell, E. (2007). Chatbots: Are they really useful. *LDV-Forum Journal for Computational Linguistics and Language Technology, 22*(1), 29-49.

Acar, D., Ömürbek, N., & Ömürbek, V. (2003). Bilgi Teknolojilerinin Gıda Sektöründe Kullanımının Analizi (Utilization of information technologies in food industry). *Süleyman Demirel Üniversitesi İktisadi ve İdari Bilimler Fakültesi Dergisi, 8*(2), 1–22.

African Travel Times. (2016). Synagogue Church: The vanguard of Nigeria as religious destination. *African Travel Times.* Retrieved from http://africantraveltimes.com/news/synagogue-church-the-vanguard-of-nigeria-as-religious-destination/

Akinto, O. A. (2017). How Nigeria will lose billions where Israel and Saudi Arabia gain. *Nairaland Forum.* Retrieved September 2017, from http://www.how-nigeria-will-lose-billions-where-israel-and-saudi-arabia-gain/nairalandforum.com.

Akyel, R. (2010). Türkiye'de İç Kontrol Kavramı, Unsurları ve Etkinliğinin Değerlendirilmesi. *Yönetim ve Ekonomi Dergisi, 17*(1).

Alberta Tourism. (2016). *Tourism development guide. A guide to help navigate the tourism development process.* Edmonton: Alberta Tourism.

Alberto, W. D., María del Pilar, D., María Valeria, A., Fabiana, P. S., Cecilia, H. A., & María de los Ángeles, B. (2001). Pattern Recognition Techniques for the Evaluation of Spatial and Temporal Variations in Water Quality. A Case Study. *Water Research, 35*(12), 2881–2894. doi:10.1016/S0043-1354(00)00592-3 PMID:11471688

Albuquerque, H., da Silva, A. M., Martins, F., & Costa, C. (2018). Wellness tourism as a complementary activity in saltpans regeneration. In I. Azara, E. Michopoulou, F. Niccolini, B. Taff, & A. Clarke (Eds.), *Tourism, Health, Wellbeing and Protected Areas* (pp. 56–67). Wallingford, UK: CAB International. doi:10.1079/9781786391315.0056

Alobaidy, A. H. M. J., Abid, H. S., & Maulood, B. K. (2010). Application of Water Quality Index for Assessment of Dokan Lake Ecosystem, Kurdistan Region, Iraq. *Journal of Water Resource and Protection, 2*(9), 792–798. doi:10.4236/jwarp.2010.29093

Ama, A. J. N. (2012). An Assessment Of Internal Control System On The Image Of The Hospitality Industries. In *Royal Mac – Dic Hotel And Capital View Hotels*. Kwame Nkrumah University of Science and Technology.

Amatya, P. H. (1997). Nepal's Experience with Ecotourism in Annapurna Conservation Area Project. In World Ecotour' 97 Abstracts Volume. Rio de Janiero, Brazil: BIOSFERA.

Amudo, A., & Inanga, E. L. (2009). Evaluation of Internal Control Systems: A case study from Uganda. *International Research Journal of Finance and Economics, 27*.

Anderson, N. (2016, March). *Blockchain Technology: A game changer in accounting?* Retrieved from Deloitte: https://www2.deloitte.com/content/dam/Deloitte/de/Documents/Innovation/Blockchain_A%20game-changer%20in%20accounting.pdf

Anderson, R., Benefield, J., & Hurst, M. (2015). Property-type diversification and REIT performance: an analysis of operating performance and abnormal returns. Journal of Economics & Finance, 39(1), 48-74.

Annual Report 2016-17 Ministry of Tourism Government of India. (n.d.). Retrieved from: http://tourism.gov.in/sites/default/files/annualreports/MoT%20Annual%20Report%20201617_English.pdf

Antara, M. & Prameswari, Y.A. (2018). Push and Pull Factors of Tourists Visit the Tourism Destination of Bali, Indonesia. *Journal of Tourism and Hospitality Management, 6*(1), 112-120. Doi:10.15640/jthm.v6n1a1

APHA/AWWA/WEF. (2012). Standard Methods for the Examination of Water and Wastewater. *Standard Methods, 541*.

Apollo, M. (2018). Ethics in tourism as a key to development, prosperity and well-being of all stakeholders: 3rd International Congress on Ethics and Tourism, Krakow, 27–28 April 2017. *International Journal of Environmental Studies, 75*(2), 361–365. doi:10.1080/00207233.2017.1383076

Appiah-Opoku, S. (2007). Indigenous beliefs and environmental stewardship: A rural Ghana experience. *Journal of Cultural Geography, 24*(2), 79–98. doi:10.1080/08873630709478212

Arend, R., Lévesque, M. (2010). *Is the Resource-Based View a Practical Organizational Theory?* Doi:10.1287/orsc.1090.0484

Arunotai, N. (2006). Moken traditional knowledge: An unrecognised form of natural resources management and conservation. *International Social Science Journal, 58*(187), 139–150. doi:10.1111/j.1468-2451.2006.00599.x

Ashiegbu, O. P., & Achunike, H. C. (2014). Religion and tourism in Nigeria. *Research on Humanities and Social Sciences, 4*(15), 130–139.

Asquerino, P. P. (2013). Turismo de estudios, una conexión diferente con el destino. *Revista Hosteltur, 228*, 46.

Atmaca, M. (2012). Muhasebe Skandallarının Önlenmesinde İç Kontrol Sisteminin Etkinleştirilmesi. *Afyon Kocatepe Üniversitesi İİBF Dergisi, 14*(1).

Auger, U. G. (1967). *Method and Apparatus for Coordinating Restaurant Operation.* U.S. Patent No. 3,310,797. Washington, DC: U.S. Patent and Trademark Office.

Awang, K. W., Wan, M. W. H., & Zahari, M. S. M. (2009). Tourism development: A geographical perspective. *Asian Social Science, 5*(5), 67–76. doi:10.5539/ass.v5n5p67

Axinte, G., & Spulbar, C. (2009). Critical Success Factors for Romanian Tourism. *Bulletin University of Agricultural Sciences and Veterinary Medicine (UASVM) - Horticulture, 66*(2), 22 – 28.

Azevedo, A., Magalhães, D., & Pereira, J. (2010). *City Marketing. Myplace in XXI.* Porto: Vida Económica.

Azuma, R. (1997). A survey of augmented reality. *In Presence. Presence (Cambridge, Mass.), 6*(4), 355–385. doi:10.1162/pres.1997.6.4.355

Baer, A. (1989). Maintaining biocultural diversity. *Conservation Biology, 3*(1), 97–98. doi:10.1111/j.1523-1739.1989.tb00233.x

Bagri, S. C. (2005). (Submitted to). Ecotourism in Kedarnath Musk Deer Sanctuary. *Major Research Project.*

Balint, P., & Mashinya, J. (2008). CAMPFIRE during Zimbabwe's national crisis: Local impacts and broader implications for community-based wildlife management. *Society & Natural Resources, 21*(9), 783–796. doi:10.1080/08941920701681961

Ballet, J., Sirven, N., & Requiers-Desjardins, M. (2007). Social capital and natural resource management. *Journal of Environment & Development, 16*(4), 355–374. doi:10.1177/1070496507310740

Baloglu, S., & Mccleary, K. W. (1999). A model of destination image formation. *Annals of Tourism Research, 26*(4), 868–897. doi:10.1016/S0160-7383(99)00030-4

Balsas, C. (2012). Sustainable development in Portugal: An analysis of Lisbon and Porto. I. Vojnovic (Ed.), Building Sustainable Communities: A Global Urban Perspective (pp.633–651). East Lansing, MI: Michigan State University Press.

Balsas, C. (2016). Mediterranean Saltscapes: The need to enhance fragile ecological and cultural resources in Portugal. ZARCH: Journal of Interdisciplinary Studies in Architecture and Urbanism, 7, 133 160. doi.org/. doi:10.26754/ojs_zarch/zarch.201671519

Balsas, C., Kotval, Z., & Mullin, J. (2001). Historic Preservation in Waterfront Communities in Portugal and the USA. *Portuguese Studies Review, 8*(1), 40–61.

Banerjee, S., Maiti, S. K., & Kumar, A. (2015). Metal contamination in water and bioaccumulation of metals in the planktons, molluscs and fishes in Jamshedpur stretch of Subarnarekha River of Chotanagpur plateau, India. *Water and Environment Journal: the Journal / the Chartered Institution of Water and Environmental Management, 29*(2), 207–213. doi:10.1111/wej.12108

Baralo, M. (2006). Turismo lingüístico, más y mejor. Nexotur, 507, 23-29.

Baskin, J. (1995). *Local economic development: Tourism - Good or Bad? In Tourism workshop proceedings: small, medium, micro enterprises.* Johannesburg: Land and Agriculture Policy Center.

Bateman, I., & Turner, R. K. (1993). Valuation of the Environment, Methods and Techniques: The Contingent Valuation Method. In R. K. Turner (Ed.), *Sustainable Environmental Economics and Management* (pp. 120–191). London: Belhaven.

Bateman, I., Willis, K., & Garrod, G. (1994). Consistency between Contingent Valuation Estimates. *Regional Studies, 28*(5), 457–474. doi:10.1080/00343409412331348396

Bates, B. C., Kundzewicz, Z. W., Wu, S., & Palutikof, J. P. (2008). *Climate Change and Water.* doi:10.1016/j.jmb.2010.08.039

Beatley, T. (2014). *Blue Urbanism: Exploring Connections between Cities and Oceans.* Washington, DC: Island Press. doi:10.5822/978-1-61091-564-9

Becerra, F. (2008). Las redes empresariales y la dinámica de la empresa: aproximación teórica. Revista Innovar: estrategia e innovaciones, 18(32).

Beck, J. A. (2012). A biocultural approach to development. *Terralingua,* 3. Retrieved from http://www.terralingua.org/bcdconservation/?p=1493

Becker, C. D., & Ghimire, K. (2003). Synergy between traditional ecological knowledge and conservation science supports forest preservation in Ecuador. *Ecology and Society, 8*(1).

Benedict, M. A., & McMahon, E. T. (2000). Green Infrastructure: Smart Conservation for the 21st Century. *Recreation,* (37), 4–7. doi:10.4135/9781412973816.n70

Berdugo, O. (2014). Español recurso económico: anatomía de un nuevo sector. *Cuadernos Cervantes, 2*(3). Disponible en: http://www.cuadernoscervantes.com/ele_30_esprececonom.html

Bergmann-Baker, U., Brotton, J., & Wall, G. (1995). Socio-economic impacts of fluctuating water levels on recreational boating in the great lakes. *Canadian Water Resources Journal, 20*(3), 185–194. doi:10.4296/cwrj2003185

Berkes, F. (1999). *Sacred ecology: Traditional ecological knowledge and resource management.* New York, NY: Taylor & Francis.

Berkes, F., & Berkes, M. K. (2009). Ecological complexity, fuzzy logic, and holism in indigenous knowledge. *Futures, 41*(1), 6–12. doi:10.1016/j.futures.2008.07.003

Berkes, F., Colding, J., & Folke, C. (2000). Rediscovery of traditional ecological knowledge as adaptive management. *Ecological Applications, 10*(5), 1251–1262. doi:10.1890/1051-0761(2000)010[1251:ROTEKA]2.0.CO;2

Berna, J. L., Moreno, A., & Ferrer, J. (1991). The behaviour of LAS in the environment. *Journal of Chemical Technology and Biotechnology (Oxford, Oxfordshire), 50*(3), 387–398. doi:10.1002/jctb.280500310

Bhat, S. A., & Pandit, A. K. (2014). Surface Water Quality Assessment of Wular Lake, A Ramsar Site in Kashmir Himalaya, Using Discriminant Analysis and WQI. *Journal of Ecosystem, 18.* doi:10.1155/2014/724728

Bianchi, G. & Chen, Y. (2015). CEO compensation and the performance of firms in the hospitality industry: a cross-industry comparison. *International Journal of Tourism Sciences, 15*(3 – 4), 121-138. Doi:10.1080/15980634.2016.1181320

Binder, W. (1994). Schutz der Binnengewässer [in German]. *Economía, 5*, 183.

Birau, R. (2015). International Tourism and Hospitality in the Digital Age. In *The Global Implications of Ecotourism in Emerging Economies.* IGI Global. Doi:10.4018/978-1-4666-8268-9

Biswas, J. (2017, December 13). Chennai Restaurant Becomes India's First To Hire Robots As Waiters. *Analytics India Magazine.* Retrieved from https://www.analyticsindiamag.com/robot-waiter-india-chennai/

Blaustein, R. J. (2007). Protected areas and equity concerns. *Bioscience, 57*(3), 216–221.

Blount, B. G. (2001). Indigenous peoples and the uses and abuses of ecotourism. In L. Maffi (Ed.), *On biocultural diversity: Linking language, knowledge, and the environment* (pp. 503–516). Washington, DC: Smithsonian Institution Press.

Boo, E. (1990). *Ecotourism, the Potential and Pitfalls. World Wild life Fund .*

BookDifferent. (2016). Retrieved from http://www.bookdifferent.com/en/

Borrini-Feyerabend, G., Dudley, N., Jaeger, T., Lassen, B., Broome, N. P., Phillips, A., & Sandwith, T. (2013). *Governance of protected areas: From understanding to action.* Retrieved from http://cmsdata.iucn.org/downloads/governance_of_protected_areas from_understanding_to_action.pdf

Bossel, H. (1999). *Indicators for sustainable development: Theory, method, applications.* Winnipeg, MB: International Institute for Sustainable Development.

Bourdieu, P. (1990). *The logic of practice*. Stanford, CA: Stanford University Press.

Boyacioglu, H., Boyacioglu, H., & Gunduz, O. (2005). Application of Factor Analysis in the Assessment of Surface Water Quality in Buyuk Menderes River Basin - EW_2005_9-10_05.pdf. *European Water*, 43–49. Retrieved from http://www.ewra.net/ew/pdf/EW_2005_9-10_05.pdf

Branco, M. (2007). *Revitalização e valorização económica do salgado de Aveiro – relatório final*. Aveiro: MultiAveiro.

Breaky, N., Ruhanen, L., & Shakeela, A. (2004). The Role of Employment in the Sustainable Development Paradigm—The Local Tourism Labor Market in Small Island Developing States". *Journal of Human Resources in Hospitality & Tourism*, *10*(4). doi:10.1080/15332845.2011.588493

Bridgewater, P. (2002). Biosphere reserves: Special places for people and nature. *Environmental Science & Policy*, *5*(1), 9–12.

Brockington, D. (2007). Forests, community conservation, and local government performance: The Village Forest Reserves of Tanzania. *Society & Natural Resources*, *20*(9), 835–848. doi:10.1080/08941920701460366

Brohman, J. (1996). New directions in tourism for third world development. *Annals of Tourism Research, 23*, 48–70. Available at: http://www.ansvarligturisme.org/CapeTown.html

Brohman, J. (n.d.). New Directions in Tourism for Third World Development. *Annals of Tourism Research, 23*.

Brohman, J. (1996). New Directions in Tourism for Third World Development. *Annals of Tourism Research, 23*.

Brosius, J., & Hitchner, S. L. (2010). Cultural diversity and conservation. *International Social Science Journal*, *61*(199), 141–168. doi:10.1111/j.1468-2451.2010.01753.x

Browning, B. (2017). *Human Space 2.0: Biophilic design in hospitality*. Retrieved from www.humanspaces.com

Brundiers, K., Wiek, A., & Redman, C. L. (2010). Real-world learning opportunities in sustainability: From classroom into the real world. *International Journal of Sustainability in Higher Education*, *11*(4), 308–324. doi:10.1108/14676371011077540

Burns, J. W., Berenschot, C. E., Calabrese, G., Kasper, C. D., & Lovell, R. (2013). *Restaurant Management System and Method*. U.S. Patent No. 8,620,753. Washington, DC: U.S. Patent and Trademark Office.

Busuioc, M.F., Simon, T., Niculescu, A.C., & Trifanescu, R. (2016). New Opportunities For Niche Tourism In Romania: Ethnographic Tourism. *Romanian Economic Business Review*, *11*(4.1), 35-43.

Cai, L. A. (1999). Relationship of household characteristics and lodging expenditure on leisure trips. *Journal of Hospitality & Leisure Marketing*, 6(2), 5–18. doi:10.1300/J150v06n02_02

Callender, E., & Rice, K. C. (1999). *The Urban Environmental Gradient: Anthropogenic Influences on the Spatial and Temporal Distributions of Lead and Zinc in Sediments*. doi:10.1021/ES990380S

Canalis, X. (2013). Turismo joven, de nicho a segmento estratégico. Revista Hosteltur, 224, 134-135.

Canavan, B. (2014). Sustainable tourism: Development, decline and de-growth. Management issues from the Isle of Man". *Journal of Sustainable Tourism*, 22(1), 127–147. doi:10.1080/09 669582.2013.819876

Candrea, A.N., Ispas, A., Untaru, E.N., & Nechita, F. (2016). Marketing the Count's way: how Dracula's myth can revive Romanian tourism. *Bulletin of the Transilvania University of Braşov*, 9(58), 83-90.

Can, E. N. (2014). *Hastane İşletmeciliğinde İç Kontrol Sisteminin Etkinliği. Yayımlanmamış Doktora Tezi*. İstanbul: Marmara Üniversitesi Sosyal Bilimler Enstitüsü.

Carlson, T. J., & Maffi, L. (2004). *Ethnobotany and conservation of biocultural diversity*. Bronx, NY: New York Botanical Garden Press.

Carpenter, S. R. (2008). Phosphorus control is critical to mitigating eutrophication. *Proceedings of the National Academy of Sciences of the United States of America*, 105(32), 11039–11040. doi:10.1073/pnas.0806112105 PMID:18685114

Carranza, M., & García, P. (2014). *Fideicomisos de infraestructura y bienes raíces (FIBRAS) para incrementar el rendimiento de la cartera de inversión de una sociedad de inversión especializada en fondos para el retiro (siefore)*. Monterrey: Universidad Panamericana.

Carroll, A. (1998). Corporate Social Responsibility. *Business & Society*, 3(38), 268–295. doi:10.1177/000765039903800303

Castellino, D. (2013). *Social inclusion & human rights: Implications for 2030 and beyond*. Retrieved from http://unsdsn.org/wp-content/uploads/2014/02/130114- Social-Exclusion-and-Human-Rights-Paper-for-HLP.pdf

Cater, E., & Lowman, G. (Eds.). (1994). *Ecotourism*. Chichester, UK: Wiley.

Catterall, M., Maclaran, P., & Stevens, L. (2010). Postmodern Paralysis: The Critical Impasse in Feminist Perspectives on Consumers. *Journal of Marketing Management*, 489–504.

Cavazos, M., Rodríguez, M., & Garza, H. (2015). *Análisis del desempeño financiero de portafolios de inversión en FIBRAs y acciones*. Monterrey: Universidad Autónoma de Nuevo León.

Central Pollution Control Board. (2010). Status of Water Quality in India- 2009. *Central Pollution Control Board, Monitoring Series: MINARS/ /2009-10*.

Central Pollution Control Board. (2013). *Status of Water Quality in India- 2011*. Central Pollution Control Board.

Cervera, Schlesinger, W., Mesta, M. Á., & Sánchez, R. (2012). Medición de la imagen de la universidad y sus efectos sobre la identificación y lealtad del egresado: Una aproximación desde el modelo de Beerli y Díaz (2003). *Revista Española de Investigación de Marketing ESIC*, *16*(2), 7–29. doi:10.1016/S1138-1442(14)60012-7

Chan Li, M. F., Mc Vay, S. E., & Skaife, H. (2015). Does Ineffective Internal Control over Financial Reportind affect Firm's Operations? Evidence from Firms' Inventory Management. *The Accounting Review*, *90*(2).

Chan, E. S. W., & Hsu, C. H. C. (2016). Environmental management research in hospitality, *International Journal of Contemporary Hospitality Management*, *28*(5), 886–923. doi:10.1108/IJCHM-02-2015-0076

Chapman. (1992). Water Quality Assessments -A Guide to Use of Biota, Sediments and Water in Environmental Monitoring - Second Edition. Unesco/Who/Unep, 6(5), 419.

Chen, H. J., Chen, P. J., & Okumos, F. (2013). The relationship between travel constraints and destination image: A case study of Brunei. *Tourism Management*, *35*, 198–208. doi:10.1016/j.tourman.2012.07.004

Chen, Y., & Hu, H. (2013). Internet of intelligent things and robot as a service. *Simulation Modelling Practice and Theory*, *34*, 159–171. doi:10.1016/j.simpat.2012.03.006

Cheong, S. N., Chiew, W. W., & Yap, W. J. (2010, December). *Design and development of multi-touchable e-restaurant management system*. Paper presented at the meeting of the 2010 International Conference on Science and Social Research (CSSR 2010), Kuala Lumpur, Malaysia. 10.1109/CSSR.2010.5773867

Chow, M. F., Shiah, F. K., Lai, C. C., Kuo, H. Y., Wang, K. W., Lin, C. H., ... Ko, C. Y. (2016). Evaluation of surface water quality using multivariate statistical techniques: A case study of Fei-Tsui Reservoir basin, Taiwan. *Environmental Earth Sciences*, *75*(1), 1–15. doi:10.100712665-015-4922-5

Çiftçi, Y., & Köroğlu, Ç. (2008). Otel İşletmelerinde Yiyecek İçecek Kontrol Yöntemlerinin İncelenmesi (Marmaris İlçesi Örneği). *Manas Üniversitesi Sosyal Bilimler Dergisi, 19*.

Coelho, R., Hilário, M., Silva, F., & Silva, S. (2014). Peixe Rei Solar Salt Works Project: Ecotourism and tourism experience as complementary activities. In European Salt Producers Association (EuSalt) (Eds.), *Solar Salt Works & The Economic Value of Biodiversity – Proceedings of the International Conference* (pp.155–186). Trapani, Sicily: EuSalt.

Coelho, C. (2008). Os muros (motas) das marinhas de sal de Aveiro. In I. Amorim (Ed.), *A Articulação do Sal Português aos Circuitos Mundiais: Antigos e novos Consumos* (pp. 279–289). Porto: Instituto de História Moderna – Universidade do Porto.

Cohen, S., Higham, J.E., Peeters, P., & Gossling, S. (2014). Why tourism mobility behaviours must change. In *Understanding and Governing Sustainable Tourism Mobility: Psychological and Behavioural Approaches*. Academic Press.

Cohen, S., Higham, J., & Cavaliere, C. (2011). Binge flying: Behavioural addiction and climate change. *Annals of Tourism Research*, *38*(3), 1070–1089. doi:10.1016/j.annals.2011.01.013

Cole, D. N. (2000). *Dispersed Recreation*. Retrieved from http://winapps.umt.edu/winapps/media2/leopold/pubs/421.pdf

Coleman, J. H. (1998). *Restaurant Management System*. U.S. Patent No. 5,839,115. Washington, DC: U.S. Patent and Trademark Office.

Coleman, J. H., Davis, J. C., & Morgan, R. L. (1997). *Restaurant Management System*. U.S. Patent No. 5,602,730. Washington, DC: U.S. Patent and Trademark Office.

Collis, D. (1994). How valuable are organizational capabilities? *Strategic Management Journal*, *15*(S1), 143–152. doi:10.1002mj.4250150910

Cordeiro, A. R., & Paredes, L. C. (2013). Valorização turística da ilha da Morraceira (Município da Figueira da Foz): Novas utilizações do potencial endógeno do estuário do Mondego. *Caderno de Geografia*, *32*, 229–238. doi:10.14195/0871-1623_32_18

Cosma, S., Pop, C., & Negrusa, A. (2007). Should Dracula Myth be a Brand to Promote Romania as a Tourist Destination? Interdisciplinary Management Research, Josip Juraj Strossmayer University of Osijek, Faculty of Economics.

COSO. (1992). *Internal Control Integrated Framework*. Retrieved from www.coso.org

Costa, S., Azeiteiro, U., & Pardal, M. (2013a). The contribution of scientific research for integrated coastal management: The mondego estuary as a study case. *Journal of Integrated Coastal Zone Management*, *13*(2), 229–241. doi:10.5894/rgci391

Costa, S., Pardal, M., & Azeiteiro, U. (2013b). The use of an estuarine system (Mondego estuary, Portugal) as a didactic tool to incorporate education for sustainable development into school curricula. *Journal of Integrated Coastal Zone Management*, *13*(2), 243–251. doi:10.5894/rgci417

CPCB-ENVIS. (2013). *Inclusion of Biological Parameters for Bio-Mapping CPCB Initiative for Bio-Mapping of River Basins in India*. Retrieved from http://cpcbenvis.nic.in/newsletter/bio-mapping-march1999/march1999.htm

Crisman, T. L. (1999). Conservation of Mediterranean coastal saline ecosystems: The private sector role in maintaining ecological function. In: N. A. Korovessis & T. D. Lekkas (Eds.), *Proceedings of the Post Conference Symposium Salworks: Preserving Saline Coastal Ecosystems* (pp.39–47). Academic Press.

Crisman, T. L., Takavakoglou, V., Alexandridis, T., Antonopoulos, V., & Zalidis, G. (2009). Rehabilitation of abandoned saltworks to maximize conservation, ecotourism and water treatment potential. *Global NEST Journal, 11*(1), 24–31. doi:10.30955/gnj.000614

Croall, J. (1995). *Preserve or Destroy: Tourism and the Environment*. London: Calouste Gulbenkian Foundation.

Cruz, T., Neves, R., Pacheco, C., Fonseca, C., & Martins, F. (2014). A avifauna aquática das salinas estuarinas da Ria de Aveiro e da Foz do Rio Mondego. *Revista Captar: Ciência e Ambiente para Todos, 3*(2). Retrieved July 27, 2017 from <http://revistas.ua.pt/index.php/captar/article/view/2900>

Dahm, H. (2004). Salt museums. In R. Neves, T. Petanidou, R. Rufino & P. Pinto (Eds.), ALAS – All About Salt: Salt and salinas in the Mediterranean (pp. 104–107). Figueira da Foz: Intermezzo.

Dalgar, H. (2012). İşletmelerin Muhasebe Departmanlarında Hata ve Hileleri Önlemeye Yönelik İç Kontrol Sisteminin Oluşturulması: Bir Vaka Çalışması. *Muhasebe Öğretim Üyeleri Bilim ve Dayanışma Vakfı Dergisi, 3*.

Dallen, J. T., & Olsen, H. D. (2006). *Tourism, religion and spiritual journeys*. London: Routledge.

Darwish, M. A. G. (2013). Geochemistry of the High Dam Lake sediments, south Egypt: Implications for environmental significance. *International Journal of Sediment Research, 28*(4), 544–559. doi:10.1016/S1001-6279(14)60012-3

Davidson, S., De Fillipi, P., & Potts, J. (2016). *Disrupting Governance: The New Institutional Economics of Distributed Ledger Technology*. Retrieved from http://ssrn.com/abstract=2811995

Davies, T., Davies, T., & Cahill, S. (2000). *Environmental Implications of the Tourism Industry*. Academic Press.

Davis, B., Lockwood, A., Alcott, P., & Pantelidis, I. S. (2018). *Food and beverage management* (6th ed.). London: Routledge. doi:10.4324/9781315563374

Davis, P. (1999). *Ecomuseum, A sense of place*. London: Leicester University Press.

De León, P. (2015). *Más allá de las tasas, los factores detrás del bajo rendimiento de FIBRAS en 2015*. DF, México: Reporte Actinver.

Demirel, Y. (2007). Bilgi ve Bilgi Paylaşımının İşletme Performansı Etkisi Üzerine Bir Araştırma. *Yönetim Bilimleri Dergisi, 5*(2).

Di Maggio, P., & Powell, W. (1991) *El nuevo institucionalismo en el análisis organizacional*. Laboratorio de Análisis Institucional del Sistema Universitario Mexicano. Recuperado de http://laisumedu.org

Dickman, M., & Dorais, M. (1977). The impact of human trampling on phosphorus loading to a small lake in Gatineau Park, Quebec, Canada. *Journal of Environmental Management, 5*(4), 335–344. Retrieved from https://www.cabdirect.org/cabdirect/abstract/19781940757

Dineshkumar, S., & Kogalacumar, P. (2013). Internal Control System and its impact on the Performance of the Sri Lanka Telecom limited in Jaffna District. *International Journal of Advancements in Computing Technology, 2*(6).

Ding, J., Jiang, Y., Fu, L., Liu, Q., Peng, Q., & Kang, M. (2015). Impacts of Land Use on Surface Water Quality in a Subtropical River Basin: A Case Study of the Dongjiang River Basin, Southeastern China. *Water (Basel), 7*(12), 4427–4445. doi:10.3390/w7084427

District Statistical Handbook. (2011). Govt. of West Bengal Economic Review of West Bengal.

Dolnicar, S., Crouch, G. I., & Long, P. (2008). Environment-friendly tourists: What do we really know about them? *Journal of Sustainable Tourism, 16*(2), 197–210. doi:10.2167/jost738.0

Dorr, J. A. (1985). *Restaurant Management Information and Control Method and Apparatus*. U.S. Patent No. 4,530,067. Washington, DC: U.S. Patent and Trademark Office.

Dowling, R. K. (1998) *The Growth of Australian Ecotourism*. Paper presented at the NZ Tourism and Hospitality Research Conference, Third Biennial Conference, Akaroa, Canterbury, NZ.

Doyle, J. T., Ge, W., & McVay, S. (2007). Accruals Quality and Internal Control Over Financial Reporting. *The Accounting Review, 82*(5), 1141–1170. doi:10.2308/accr.2007.82.5.1141

Dragin, A. S., Jovičić, D., & Lukić, T. (2010). Cruising along the river Danube: Contemporary tourism trend in Serbia. *Geographica Pannonica, 14*(3), 98–108. doi:10.5937/GeoPan1003098D

Drake, S. (1991). *Local Participation in ecotourism project. In Nature Tourism* (p. 132). Washington, DC: Island Press.

Edward, S. N., Mehaughliu, W. J., & Ham, S. H. (1998). *Comparative Study of Ecotourism Policy in the Americas*. University of Idaho, Organisation of American States.

Edwards, J. S. A. (2013). The food service industry: Eating out is more than just a meal. *Food Quality and Preference, 27*(2), 223–229. doi:10.1016/j.foodqual.2012.02.003

Edwards, J. S. A., & Hartwell, H. J. (2009). Institutional meals. In H. L. Meiselman (Ed.), *Meals in science and practice. Interdisciplinary research and business applications* (pp. 102–127). Oxford, UK: CRC Press, Woodhead Publishing.

Ehrhard, M., & Brigham, E. (2007). *Finanzas corporativas*. DF, México: Cengage Learning.

Ejoh, N., & Ejom, P. (2014). The Impact Of Internal Control Activities on Financial Performance of Tertiary Institutions in Nigeria. *Journal Of Economics and Sustainable Development, 5*(16).

Elbannan, M. A. (2009). Quality of Internal Control Over Financial Reporting, Corporate Governance And Credit Ratings. *International Journal of Disclosure and Governance, 6*(2), 127–149. doi:10.1057/jdg.2008.32

Ele, C. O., & Anicher, A. (2017). Religious tourism in Nigeria: The economic perspective. *OJAMSS: Online Journal of Arts. Management and Social Sciences, 2*(1), 220–232.

Elkins, K. (2015, December 30). *This restaurant has a new secret weapon: a robot that slices the perfect noodle faster than any human.* Retrieved from Businessinsider.com: http://www.businessinsider.com/noodle-slicing-robot-could-revolutionize-the-restaurant-industry-2015-5

Embratur. (2009). *Estudo de inteligência de mercado para o segmento de estudos e intercâmbio.* Brasil, xun.

Emelike, O. (2011, September 12). Osun-Osogbo festival: Heritage beyond religion and race. Gateway Nigeria, 11-14.

Epler Wood, M. (1991). Global Solutions: on ecotourism society. In *Nature Tourism* (p. 204). Washington, DC: Island Press.

Evaristo, V., & Botequilha-Leitão, A. (2008). *Multifunctional planning and design for the Castro Marim and Vila Real de Santo António Salt-Marshes Natural Reserve.* In *1st WSEAS International Conference on Landscape Architecture (LA '08)*, Algarve, Portugal.

Eyoboka, S., & Latona, O. (2016, December 8). Holy Ghost Congress: RCCG turns forest to city. *Vanguard*, 32-35.

Federal Republic of Nigeria. (2006). Nigeria tourism development master plan. Institutional capacity strengthening to the tourism sector in Nigeria. Abuja: Federal Republic of Nigeria & World Tourism Organization (WTO).

Feng, Li., & McKay. (2009). Analysis of the Relationship Between Listed Companies' Earnings Quality and Internal Control Information Disclosure. *Modern Economy, 2009*, 2.

Filloon, W. (2016, December 30). *Bratwurst-Cooking Robot is a feat of German Engineering.* Retrieved from eater.com: http://www.eater.com/2016/7/19/12227128/bratwurst-robot-sausage-cooking-germany

FINN. (2016). *Reporte trimestral Enero-Marzo 2016 FIBRA Inn.* Recuperado de http://www.FIBRAinn.mx

Fitzsimmons, J. A., & Maurer, G. B. (1991). A walk-through audit to improve restaurant performance. *The Cornell Hotel and Restaurant Administration Quarterly, 31*(4), 95–100. doi:10.1177/001088049103100422

Fowler, G. (2017). Robot baristas serve up the future of coffee at Cafe X. *The Wall Street Journal.* Retrieved from https://www.wsj.com/articles/robot-baristas-serve-up-the-future-of-coffee-at-cafe-x-1485781201

Friedman, M. (1962). *Capitalism and Freedom.* Chicago: University of Chicago Press.

Gadiyar, A. (2017). *The Chatbot Imperative: Intelligence, Personalization and Utilitarian Design.* Retrieved from https://www.cognizant.com/whitepapers/the-chatbot-imperative-intelligence-personalization-and-utilitarian-design-codex2469.pdf

Gândara, J. M. G. (2008). A imagem dos destinos turísticos urbanos. *Revista Eletrônica de Turismo Cultural*, 1-22.

Gandotroa, N. (2000). *Sustainable Tourism in Vaishno Devi Hills*. WWF Jammu.

García, E. A., & Collado, A. M. (2007). La enseñanza del español como recurso turístico en Castilla-La Mancha. *Boletín Económico de ICE, 2923*, 33-40.

Garcia-Esteves, J., Ludwig, W., Kerhervé, P., Probst, J. L., & Lespinas, F. (2007). Predicting the impact of land use on the major element and nutrient fluxes in coastal Mediterranean rivers: The case of the Têt River (Southern France). *Applied Geochemistry, 22*(1), 230–248. doi:10.1016/j.apgeochem.2006.09.013

Garizi, Z., Sheikh, V., & Sadoddin, A. (2011). Assessment of seasonal variations of chemical characteristics in surface water using multivariate statistical methods. *International Journal of Environmental Science and Technology, 8*(3), 581–592. doi:10.1007/BF03326244

Garrod, G. D., Willis, K. G., & Saunders, C. M. (1994). The Benefits and Costs of the Somerset Levels and Moors ESA. *Journal of Rural Studies, 10*(2), 131–145. doi:10.1016/0743-0167(94)90025-6

Gauci, R., Schembri, J. A., & Inkpen, R. (2017). Traditional use of shore platforms: A study of the artisanal management of salinas on the Maltese Islands (Central Mediterranean). *SAGE Open, 7*(2), 2158244017706597. doi:10.1177/2158244017706597

Gboyega, A. (2013). Religious tourists experience Nigeria in rundown Lagos suburbs. *The Nation*. Retrieved September 29, 2017 from http://thenationonlineng.net/religious-tourists-experience-nigeria-in-rundown-lagos-suburb/

Ge, L., Yang, C., & Ge, R. (2003). Electronic Restaurant Service Management System. *U.S. Patent Application No. 10/104,187*.

Gedecho, E. K. (2014). Challenges of religious tourism development: The case the Gishen Mariam, Ethiopia. *American Journal of Tourism Research, 3*(2), 42–57. doi:10.11634/216837861403567

Geiser, L. H., Ingersoll, A. R., Bytnerowicz, A., & Copeland, S. A. (2008). Evidence of Enhanced Atmospheric Ammoniacal Nitrogen in Hells Canyon National Recreation Area: Implications for Natural and Cultural Resources. *Journal of the Air & Waste Management Association, 58*(9), 1223–1234. doi:10.3155/1047-3289.58.9.1223 PMID:18817115

Ge, W., & Mc Vay, S. (2005). The Disclosure of Material Weaknesses in Internal Control after the Sarbanes-Oxley Act. *Accounting Horizons, 19*(3), 137–158. doi:10.2308/acch.2005.19.3.137

Glasson, J., Godfrey, K., Goodey, B., Absalom, H., & Van Der Borg, J. (1995). *Towards Visitor Impact Management*. Aldershot, UK: Avebury.

Gokovali, U., & Bahar, O. (2006). Contribution of Tourism to Economic Growth: A Panel Data Approach. *Anatolia: An International Journal of Tourism and Hospitality Research, 17*(2), 1–13. doi:10.1080/13032917.2006.9687184

Gomes, P., & Veiga, A. (2002). *Figueira da Foz – Memória, Conhecimento, e Inovação...* Paços de Ferreira: Néstia Editores.

Gomes, A., & Marques, G. (2008). Ecomuseu Marinha da Troncalhada – Centro Interpretativo: Impulsionador das Salinas de Aveiro. In I. Amorim (Ed.), *A Articulação do Sal Português aos Circuitos Mundiais: Antigos e novos Consumos* (pp. 329–338). Porto: Instituto de História Moderna – Universidade do Porto.

Gonçalves, A. R. (2010). Museus, Comunidade local e Turismo. In *Congresso Turismo Cultural, Territórios E Identidades, 2006* (pp. 81–105). Leiria: Instituto Politécnico de Leiria.

Gorbaneff, Y. (2003). *Teoría del agente principal y el mercadeo.* Revista Universitaria EAFIT.

Gössling, S., Ceron, J. P., Dubois, G., Hall, C. M., Gössling, I. S., Upham, P., & Earthscan, L. (2009). Hypermobile travellers Archived 2010-06-19 at the Wayback Machine. In Climate Change and Aviation: Issues, Challenges and Solutions. Academic Press.

Gössling, S. (2002). Global environmental consequences of tourism. *Global Environmental Change, 12*(4), 283–302. doi:10.1016/S0959-3780(02)00044-4

Gossling, S., Hall, M., Peeters, P., & Scott, D. (2010). The future of tourism: Can tourism growth and climate policy be reconciled? A mitigation perspective. *Tourism Recreation Research, 35*(2), 119–130. doi:10.1080/02508281.2010.11081628

Gössling, S., Peeters, P., Hall, C. M., Ceron, J. P., Dubois, G., Lehmann, L. V., & Scott, D. (2012). Tourism and water use: Supply, demand, and security. An international review. *Tourism Management, 33*(1), 1–15. doi:10.1016/j.tourman.2011.03.015

Grosclaude, P., & Soguel, N. C. (1994). Valuing Damage to Historic Buildings Using a Contingent Market. *Journal of Environmental Planning and Management, 37*(3), 279–288. doi:10.1080/09640569408711976

Grove, A., & Rackham, O. (2001). *The Nature of Mediterranean Europe: An ecological history.* New Haven, CT: Yale University Press.

Gupta, M. (2017). *Blockchain for dummies.* Hoboken, NJ: John Wiley & Sons.

Hadwen, W. L., Arthington, A. H., & Mosisch, T. D. (2003). The impact of tourism on dune lakes on Fraser Island, Australia. *Lakes and Reservoirs: Research and Management, 8*(1), 15–26. doi:10.1046/j.1440-1770.2003.00205.x

Hall, D. R. (1993). ECotourism in the Danube Delta. *The Tourist Review, 48*(3), 11-13. doi:10.1108/eb058125

Hall, C. M., Baird, T., James, M., & Ram, Y. (2016). Climate change and cultural heritage: Conservation and heritage tourism in the Anthropocene. *Journal of Heritage Tourism, 11*(1), 10–24. doi:10.1080/1743873X.2015.1082573

Hall, C. M., & Lew, A. (2009). *Understanding and Managing Tourism Impacts: An Integrated Approach*. London: Routledge. doi:10.4324/9780203875872

Hammitt, W. E., Cole, D. N., & Monz, C. (2015). *Wildland Recreation: Ecology and Management*. John Wiley & Sons, Inc. Retrieved from http://download.e-bookshelf.de/download/0003/2464/78/L-G-0003246478-0006240746.pdf

Hammitt, W. E., Cole, D., & Monz, C. (2015). Recreation Ecology. In Recreation Ecology (pp. 121–180). Academic Press.

Handicrafts of Burdwan District. (2008). Ministry of Textiles, Govt. of India.

Hanley, N. D. (1989). Valuing Rural Recreation Benefits: An Empirical Comparison of Two Approaches. *Journal of Agricultural Economics*, *40*(3), 361–374. doi:10.1111/j.1477-9552.1989.tb01117.x

Haque, M. Z., Rahim, S. A., Abdullah, M. P., Embi, A. F., Elfithri, R., Lihan, T., ... Mokhtar, M. (2016). Multivariate chemometric approach on the surface water quality in langat upstream tributaries, peninsular Malaysia. *Journal of Environmental Science and Technology*, *9*(3), 277–284. doi:10.3923/jest.2016.277.284

Haque, S. M., & Dar, S. A. (2007). Sustainable Approach to Ecotourism. In S. P. Bansal & ... (Eds.), *Cutting Edge Research in Tourism - Emerging Issues and Challenges* (pp. 249–261). Chandigarh: Aman Publication.

Harrison, D. (1997). Ecotourism in the South Pacific: The case of Fiji. In World Ecotour' 97 Abstracts Volume. Rio de Janiero, Brazil: BIOSFERA.

Harrison, D. (1992). *International Tourism in the less developed countries*. Chichester, UK: Wiley.

Harrison, S. S. C., Pretty, J. L., Shepherd, D., Hildrew, A. G., Smith, C., Hey, R. D., & Harrison, S. (2004). The effect of instream rehabilitation structures on macroinvertebrates in lowland rivers. *Journal of Applied Ecology Journal of Applied Ecology Journal of Applied Ecology*, *41*(6), 1140–1154. Retrieved from https://besjournals.onlinelibrary.wiley.com/doi/pdf/10.1111/j.0021-8901.2004.00958.x

Harun, S., Dambul, R., Abdullah, M. H., & Mohamed, M. (2014). Spatial and seasonal variations in surface water quality of the Lower Kinabatangan River Catchment, Sabah, Malaysia. Academic Press.

Hassan, S. S. (2000). Determinants of Market Competitiveness in an Environmentally Sustainable Tourism Industry. *Journal of Travel Research*, *38*(28), 239–245. doi:10.1177/004728750003800305

Hein, T., Schwarz, U., Habersack, H., Nichersu, I., Preiner, S., Willby, N., & Weigelhofer, G. (2016). Current status and restoration options for floodplains along the Danube River. *Science of The Total Environment*, *543*(Part A), 778-790.

Helena, B., Pardo, R., Vega, M., Barrado, E., Fernandez, J. M., & Fernandez, L. (2000). Temporal evolution of groundwater composition in an alluvial aquifer (Pisuerga River, Spain) by principal component analysis. *Water Research*, *34*(3), 807–816. doi:10.1016/S0043-1354(99)00225-0

Henama, U. (2017). T.B. Josua emigrating to Isreal: Lesson for South Africa on religious tourism. *The Cable*. Retrieved September 20, from https://www.thecable.ng/tb-joshua-emigrating-israel-lessons-south-africa-religious-tourism

Henriques, F. (2017, July 1). Vidas de sal. *Público*.

Herbert, R. J., Broderick, L. G., Ross, K., Moody, C., Cruz, T., Clarke, L., & Stillman, R. A. (2018). Artificial coastal lagoons at solar salt-working sites: A network of habitats for specialised, protected and alien biodiversity. *Estuarine, Coastal and Shelf Science*, *203*, 1–16. doi:10.1016/j.ecss.2018.01.015

Hermanson, D. R., & Hermanson, H. M. (1994, Winter). The Internal Control Paradox: What Every Manager Should Know. *Review of Business*, 29–32.

Hermanson, D. R., Smith, J. L., & Nathaniel, M. S. (2012). How Effective are Organizastions' Internal Controls? Insights into Specific Internal Control Elements. *Current Issues in Auditing*, *6*(1), 31–50. doi:10.2308/ciia-50146

Hilton. (2016, February 3). *Hilton and IBM pilot "Connie" the world;s first Watson- enabled hotel concierge.* Retrieved from http://news.hiltonworldwide.com/index.cfm/news/hilton-and-ibm-pilot-connie-theworlds-first-watsoneabled-hotel-concierge

Hodges, J. (2015). *Restaurant Management System.* 3rd Year Project Report. The University of Manchester School of Computer Science. Retrieved from http://studentnet.cs.manchester.ac.uk/resources/library/3rd-year-projects/2015/jonathan.hodges-2.pdf

Hogan, J. (2008, September 19). *Hotel Online.* Retrieved from My definition of hospitality. What's yours?: http://www.hotel-online.com/News/PR2008_3rd/Sept08_HospitalityDefined.html

Hosteltur. (2013). Turismos de estudios contra la estacionalidad. *Hosteltur, 225*. Disponible en: http://www.hosteltur.com/139680_espana-recibio-936000-extranjeros-su-oferta-educativa.html

Hotelogix. (2018, February 7). Retrieved from https://www.hotelogix.com/blog/2018/02/07/top-hospitality-industry-technology-trends-2018/

Howton, S., Howton, S., Lee, J., & Mi, L. (2012). REIT Ownership and Property Performance: Evidence from the Lodging Industry. Journal of Real Estate Portfolio Management, 18(2), 169-185.

Høyer, K. G. (2000). Sustainable tourism or sustainable mobility? The Norwegian case. *Journal of Sustainable Tourism*, *8*(2), 147–160. doi:10.1080/09669580008667354

Hueso, K., & Petanidou, T. (2011). Cultural aspects of Mediterranean salinas. In T. Papayannis & D. Pritchard (Eds.), *Culture and wetlands in the Mediterranean: An evolving story* (pp. 213–226). Athens: Med-INA.

Ibagere, E., & Adeseye, B. O. (2016). *Aesthetic of indigenous faith tourism in Nigeria.* Retrieved September 21, 2017, from http:www.ojs.mona.uwi.edu/index.php/cjp/article/view/4374/3336

Iheanacho, N. (2015). Nigerian praxis of religious tourism and pilgrimage motivations in a globalizing world. *Ciencias da Religiao: Historia e Sociadade, 13*(1), 259–284.

IndiaTourismStatistics. (2003). Retrieved from: http://tourism. gov.in/sites/default/files/Other/INDIA%20TOURISM%20STATISTICS%202003.pdf

IndiaTourismStatistics. (2007). Retrieved from: http://tourism. gov.in/sites/default/files/Other/INDIA%20TOURISM%20STATISTICS%202007.pdf

IndiaTourismStatistics. (2014) Retrieved from: http://tourism.gov. in/sites/default/files/ Other/INDIA%20TOURISM%20STATISTICS%202014.pdf

IndiaTourismStatistics. (2017) Retrieved from: http://tourism. gov.in/sites/default/files/ Other/INDIA%20TOURISM%20STATISTICS%202017.pdf

Inskeep, E. (1999). *Tourism Planning: An Integrated and Sustainable Development Approach.* New York: Van Nostrand Reinhold.

INTOSAI. (2006). *International Organizastion of Supreme Audit Institutions.* Retrieved from www.intosai.org

Iorga, A. (2015). Tourism and Protected Areas: Political Ecology of The Rural Tourism in Romanian Danube Delta. *Journal of Tourism – Studies and Research in Tourism, 20,* 34-41.

IPCC. (2007). *Climate Change 2007: impacts, adaptation and vulnerability: contribution of Working Group II to the fourth assessment report of the Intergovernmental Panel.* IPCC. doi:10.1256/004316502320517344

Ivanov, S., Webster, C., & Berezina, K. (2017). Adoption of robots and service automation by tourism and hospitality companies. *Revista Turismo & Desenvolvimento,* 1501-1517.

Jagels, M. G., & Ralston, C. E. (2007). *Hospitality Management Accounting.* Wiley&Sons Inc.

Jahan, S., & Strezov, V. (2017). Water quality assessment of Australian ports using water quality evaluation indices. *PLoS One, 12*(12), 1–16. doi:10.1371/journal.pone.0189284 PMID:29244876

Jarvie, H. P., Whitton, B. A., & Neal, C. (1998). Nitrogen and phosphorus in east coast British rivers: Speciation, sources and biological significance. *The Science of the Total Environment, 210–211,* 79–109. doi:10.1016/S0048-9697(98)00109-0

Jayasekara, D. N. R. (2016). *Restaurant Management System* (Unpublished Doctoral dissertation).

Jha, B. R., Waidbacher, H., Sharma, S., & Straif, M. (2010). Study of agricultural impacts through fish base variables in different rivers. *International Journal of Environmental Science and Technology, 7*(3), 609–615. doi:10.1007/BF03326170

Jiang, Y. (2009). Evaluating eco-sustainability and its spatial variability in tourism areas: A case study in Lijiang County, China. *International Journal of Sustainable Development and World Ecology*, *16*(2), 117–126. doi:10.1080/13504500902808628

Jogaratnam, G., McCleary, K. W., Mena, M. M., & Yoo, J. J. E. (2005). An Analysis of Hospitality and Tourism Research: Institutional Contributions. *Journal of Hospitality & Tourism Research (Washington, D.C.)*, *29*(3), 356–371. doi:10.1177/1096348005276929

Jokipii, A. (2010). Determinants And Consequences Of Internal Control In Firms: A Contingency Theory Based Analysis. *The Journal of Management and Governance*, 14.

Joye, Y. (2007). Architectural Lessons From Environmental Psychology: The Case of Biophilic Architecture. *Review of General Psychology*, *11*(4), 305–328. doi:10.1037/1089-2680.11.4.305

Juahir, H., Zain, S. M., Yusoff, M. K., Hanidza, T. I. T., Armi, A. S. M., Toriman, M. E., & Mokhtar, M. (2011). Spatial water quality assessment of Langat River Basin (Malaysia) using environmetric techniques. *Environmental Monitoring and Assessment*, *173*(1–4), 625–641. doi:10.100710661-010-1411-x PMID:20339961

Juang, D. F., Lee, C. H., & Hsueh, S. C. (2009). Chlorinated volatile organic compounds found near the water surface of heavily polluted rivers. *International Journal of Environmental Science and Technology*, *6*(4), 545–556. doi:10.1007/BF03326094

Judeh, A,. Sheikh, I., & Sbugh, S. (2009). The Application Of Accounting Responsibility In The Jordanian Hotels: A Case Study. *Alzarqa Journal For Humanities Research, 9*(9).

Kamra, K. K. (n.d.). *Managing Tourist Destination: Development, Planning, Marketing, Policies*. Kanishka Publication.

Kanaan, K. (2018). Balanced Performance Evaluation in the Light of the Digital Hotels Era. *Journal of Tourism and Hospitality Management*, *6*(1), 100-111. Doi:10.15640/jthm.v6n1a10

Kannel, P. R., Lee, S., Kanel, S. R., & Khan, S. P. (2007). Chemometric application in classification and assessment of monitoring locations of an urban river system. *Analytica Chimica Acta*, *582*(2), 390–399. doi:10.1016/j.aca.2006.09.006 PMID:17386518

Kant, A. K., & Graubard, B. I. (2004). Eatingout in America, 1987–2000: Trends and nutritional correlates. *Preventive Medicine*, *38*(2), 243–249. doi:10.1016/j.ypmed.2003.10.004 PMID:14715218

Karbassi, A. R., Nouri, J., Mehrdadi, N., & Ayaz, G. O. (2008). Flocculation of heavy metals during mixing of freshwater with Caspian Sea water. *Environmental Geology*, *53*(8), 1811–1816. doi:10.100700254-007-0786-7

Katircioglu, S., Katircioğlu, S., & Altinay, M. (2018). Interactions between tourism and financial sector development: Evidence from Turkey. *Service Industries Journal*, *38*(9-10), 9–10, 519–542. doi:10.1080/02642069.2017.1406479

Kaushik, A., Kansal, A., Santosh, Meena, Kumari, S., & Kaushik, C. P. (2009). Heavy metal contamination of river Yamuna, Haryana, India: Assessment by Metal Enrichment Factor of the Sediments. *Journal of Hazardous Materials, 164*(1), 265–270. doi:10.1016/j.jhazmat.2008.08.031 PMID:18809251

Kay, D., Wyer, M. D., Crowther, J., & Fewtrell, L. (1998). Faecal indicator impacts on recreational waters: Budget studies and diffuse source modelling. *Journal of Applied Microbiology, 85*(S1), 70S–82S. doi:10.1111/j.1365-2672.1998.tb05285.x PMID:21182695

Kelkar, O. P. (2002). Ecotourism and Green Productivity in India. In T. Hundloe (Ed.), *Linking Green Productivity to Ecotourism-Experiences in the Asia Pacific Region*. Printery, Australia: University of Queensland.

Khamis, H. A. (2013). *Contribution of Internal Control System to the Financial Performance of Financial Institution. A Case of People's Bank of Zanzibar Ltd.* Mzumbe University Accounting and Finance Institute.

Khan, E. A., Khaled, M., & Shambour, Y. (2018). An analytical study of mobile applications for Hajj and Umrah services. *Applied Computing and Informatics, 14*(1), 37–47. doi:10.1016/j.aci.2017.05.004

Kinyua, J. K, Gakure, R., Gekara, M., & Orwa, G. (2015). Effect of Internal Control Environment on the Financial Performance of Companies Quoted in the Nairobi Securities Exchange. *International Journal of Innovative Finance and Economics Research, 3*.

Kirshenblatt-Gimblett, B. (1998). *Destination Culture – Tourism, Museums and Heritage*. Berkeley, CA: University of California Press.

Kortekaas, K. H. (2004). Sustainable tourism initiatives in European saltscapes. In F. Pineda, C. A. Brebbia, & M. Mugica (Eds.), *Sustainable Tourism: First International conference on sustainable tourism* (pp. 199–207). Southampton, UK: WIT Press.

Kowalewski, D., McLaughlin, J., & Hill, A. (2017). Blockchain will transform loyalty programs. *Harvard Business Review*. Retrieved from http://hbr.org/2017/03/blockchain-will-transform-customer-loyalty-programs

Krishna, A. K., Satyanarayanan, M., & Govil, P. K. (2009). Assessment of heavy metal pollution in water using multivariate statistical techniques in an industrial area: A case study from Patancheru, Medak District, Andhra Pradesh, India. *Journal of Hazardous Materials, 167*(1–3), 366–373. doi:10.1016/j.jhazmat.2008.12.131 PMID:19304387

Kukoyi, I. A., & Iwuagwu, C. (2015). Service delivery and customer satisfaction in hospitality industry: A study of the Divine Fountain Hotels Limited, Lagos, Nigeria, *Journal of Hospitality Management and Tourism. Academic Journals, 6*(1), 1–7. doi:10.5897/JHMT2015.0139

Kurlansky, M. (2003). *Salt: A world history*. New York: Penguin Books.

Lachat, C., Nago, E., Verstraeten, R., Roberfroid, D., Van Camp, J., & Kolsteren, P. (2012). Eating out of home and its association with dietary intake: A systematic review of the evidence. *Obesity Reviews*, *13*(4), 329–346. doi:10.1111/j.1467-789X.2011.00953.x PMID:22106948

Larsen, G. R., & Guiver, J. W. (2013). Understanding tourists' perceptions of distance: A key to reducing the environmental impacts of tourism mobility. *Journal of Sustainable Tourism*, *21*(7), 968–981. doi:10.1080/09669582.2013.819878

Lascurain, H. C. (1996). *Tourism, Ecotourism and Protected Area*. Gland, Switzerland: IUCN.

Lea, J. P. (1988). *Tourism and Development in the Third World*. London: Routledge.

Lee, C.-M., Miller, W. F., & Hancock, M. G. (2000). *The Silicon Valley Edge: A Habitat for Innovation and Entrepreneurship | Stanford Graduate School of Business*. Stanford University Press. Retrieved from https://www.gsb.stanford.edu/faculty-research/books/silicon-valley-edge-habitat-innovation-entrepreneurship

Leifer, R. (2003). Restaurant Management System. *U.S. Patent Application No. 10/195,336*.

Leiva, F. S., (2012). La movilidad estudiantil internacional como turismo académico. Caracterización de la movilidad estudiantil y análisis de sus desplazamientos (flujos) turísticos durante su estadía en la Región Universitaria de Valparaíso, una oportunidad no gestionada. *Revista Geográfica Valparaíso, 46*, 54-68.

Li, Y., & Singal, M. (2018). Firm Performance in the Hospitality Industry: Do CEO Attributes and Compensation Matter? *Journal of Hospitality & Tourism Research*. doi:10.1177/1096348018776453

Li, C., Yang, J., Wang, X., Wang, E., Li, B., He, R., & Yuan, H. (2015). Removal of nitrogen by heterotrophic nitrification-aerobic denitrification of a phosphate accumulating bacterium Pseudomonas stutzeri YG-24. *Bioresource Technology*, *182*, 18–25. doi:10.1016/j.biortech.2015.01.100 PMID:25668754

Liddle, M. J., & Scorgie, H. R. A. (1980). The effects of recreation on freshwater plants and animals: A review. *Biological Conservation*, *17*(3), 183–206. doi:10.1016/0006-3207(80)90055-5

Light, D. (2007). Dracula Tourism in Romania. Cultural Identity and the State. *Annals of Tourism Research, Elsevier Ltd.*, *34*(3), 746–765. doi:10.1016/j.annals.2007.03.004

Limanond, T., Butsingkorn, T., & Chermkhunthod, C. (2011). Travel behavior of university students who live on campus: A case study of a rural university in Asia. *Transport Policy*, *18*(1), 163–171. doi:10.1016/j.tranpol.2010.07.006

Linneman, P. (2013). Outlook for Mexican FIBRAs: A call for educating investors and raising standards. Retail Property Insights, 20(3).

Li, S., Gu, S., Tan, X., & Zhang, Q. (2009). Water quality in the upper Han River basin, China: The impacts of land use/land cover in riparian buffer zone. *Journal of Hazardous Materials*, *165*(1–3), 317–324. doi:10.1016/j.jhazmat.2008.09.123 PMID:19019532

Liu, C.-W., Lin, K.-H., & Kuo, Y.-M. (2003). Application of factor analysis in the assessment of groundwater quality in a blackfoot disease area in Taiwan. *The Science of the Total Environment, 313*(1–3), 77–89. doi:10.1016/S0048-9697(02)00683-6 PMID:12922062

López, E., Aguilera, P. A., Schmitz, M. F., Castro, H., & Pineda, F. D. (2010). Selection of ecological indicators for the conservation, management and monitoring of Mediterranean coastal salinas. *Environmental Monitoring and Assessment, 166*(1–4), 241–256. doi:10.100710661-009-0998-2 PMID:19479329

Lusa. (2018, February 21). Museus de Aveiro ultrapassaram os 100 mil visitants. *Diário de Noticias*.

Lu, Y., Yuan, J., Lu, X., Su, C., Zhang, Y., Wang, C. C. X., ... Garbutt, R. A. (2018). Major threats of pollution and climate change to global coastal ecosystems and enhanced management for sustainability. *Environmental Pollution, 239*, 670–680. doi:10.1016/j.envpol.2018.04.016 PMID:29709838

Mahoney, J. (2012). *Economic Foundations of Strategy*. Thousand Oaks, CA: Sage Publishing.

Makinde, D. O. (2011). Potentialities of the Egungun festival as a tool for tourism development in Ogbomoso, Nigeria. *WIT: Transaction on Ecology and the Environment, 148*, 583–593. doi:10.2495/RAV110531

Makino, S., Isobe, T., & Chan, C. (2004). Does country matter? *Strategic Management Journal, 25*(10), 1027–1043. doi:10.1002mj.412

Malhado A., de Araujo L., Rothfuss R. (2014). The attitude-behaviour gap and the role of information in influencing sustainable mobility in mega-events. In *Understanding and Governing Sustainable Tourism Mobility: Psychological and Behavioural Approaches*. Academic Press.

Mallin, M. A., Williams, K. E., Esham, E. C., & Lowe, R. P. (2000). Effect of human development on bacteriological water quality in coastal watersheds. *Ecological Applications, 10*(4), 1047–1056. doi:10.1890/1051-0761(2000)010[1047:EOHDOB]2.0.CO;2

Mark, M. (2013, September 1). Lagos business cash in on lure of super pastor TB Joshua. *The Guardian*, 37-40.

Markides, C., & Williamson, P. (1994). Related Diversification, Core Competencies and Corporate Performance. *Strategic Management Journal*. doi:10.1002mj.4250151010

Marques, C. P. (2011). Mapping Affective Image Of Destinations, Algarve. International Conference on Tourism & Management Studies, 2, 1040-1043.

Marques, J., Marques, C., Mota, J., Pinto, S., & Garcia, A. (2017). *Avaliação integrada, ecológica e sociocultural – o salgado da Figueira da Foz na perspectiva do desenvolvimento sustentável*. Figueira da Foz: Câmara Municipal da Figueira da Foz.

Martin, H. (2016, June 18). Robots Deliver Fun with Hotel Room Service Orders, and they don't expect a tip. *The Los Angeles Times*.

Martins, F., Albuquerque, H., & Silva, M. (2013). Learning about natural places – Santiago da Fonte saltpan visitor model. In *Proceedings of the 7th WEEC*. Fondation Mohammed VI Pour La Protection de L'Environnement.

Martins, F., Albuquerque, H., & Silva, A. M. (2014). Salinas acessíveis – um projeto para todos: O caso da Marinha Santiago da Fonte em Aveiro, Portugal. *Revista Turismo & Desenvolvimento, 4*(21–22), 377–392.

Mathieson, A., & Wall, G. (1982). *Tourism: Economic, Physical and Social Impacts*. Harlow: Longman.

Mawanda, S. P. (2008). *Effects of Internal Control System on Financial Performance in Uganda's Institution of Higher Learning*. Dissertation for award of MBA in Uganda Martyrs University.

Mbanefo, S. U. (2016). *Accountability now*. Abuja: Nigerian Tourism Development Corporation.

McKenna, J. E. (2003). An enhanced cluster analysis program with bootstrap significance testing for ecological community analysis. *Environmental Modelling & Software, 18*(3), 205–220. doi:10.1016/S1364-8152(02)00094-4

Medlik, S. (1993). *Dictionary of Travel, Tourism and Hospitality*. Oxford, UK: Butterworth Heinemann.

Mehmetoglu, M. (2007). Nature-based tourists: The relationship between their trip expenditures and activities. *Journal of Sustainable Tourism, 15*(2), 200–215. doi:10.2167/jost642.0

Memis Kocaman, E., & Kocaman, M. (2014). Yiyecek ve içecek işletmelerinde otomasyon sistemleri kullanımının yönetim sürecine etkileri [The effects of the use of automation systems in food and beverage business on the management process]. *Standard, 53*(625), 28–33.

Middleton, V. T. C. (1991). *Whither the package tour? Tourism Management*. Butterworth Heinemann.

Middleton, V. T. C., & Clarke, J. (2000). *Marketing in Travel and Tourism*. New Delhi: Butterworth Heinemann.

Middleton, V. T. C., & Hawkins, R. (1988). *Sustainable Tourism: A Marketing Perspective*. Butterworth Heinemann.

Mill, R. C., & Morrison, A. M. (1992). *The Tourism System: An Introductory Text*. Englewood Cliffs, NJ: Prentice Hall Publication.

Ministério de Turismo. (2008). Secretaria Nacional de Políticas do Turismo. Turismo de estudos e intercâmbio: Orientações Básicas.

Mishra, J. M. (2005). *Ecotourism Planning in the Garhwal Himalaya - A case study of Chomoli district of Uttarakhand State* (Unpublished PhD Thesis). HNB Garhwal University, Srinagar Garhwal.

Mittal, A., Agarwal, A., Chuksey, A., Shriwas, R., & Agarwal, S. (2016). A comparative study of chatbots and humans. *International Journal of Advanced Research in Computer and Communication Engineering*, 5(3).

Modeste, N. C. (1995). The Impact of Growth in the Tourism Sector On Economic Development: The Experience Of Selected Caribbean Countries. *Economic International*, *48*, 375–385.

Moeller, R. R. (2009). *Brink's Modern Internal Auditing*. John Wiley&Sons.

Mohanlal, K. G. (2002). Ecotourism in Kerala. In T. Hundloe (Ed.), *Linking Green Productivity to Ecotourism-Experiences in the Asia Pacific Region*. Printery, Australia: University of Queensland.

Moisey, R. N. (2008). Tourism, recreation, and sustainability: linking culture and the environment (2nd ed.). Wallingford, UK: CABI.

Moiteiro, G. C. (2010). Turismo Cultural e patrimonio. Uma reflexão em torno do tópico da interpretação do patrimonio enquanto instrumento de valorização de bens culturais. In *Congresso Turismo Cultural, Territórios E Identidades* (pp. 141–158). Leiria: Instituto Politécnico de Leiria.

Monbiot, G. (1994). *No Man's Land*. London: Macmillan.

Morais, J. P. (2012). La eficacia de las actividades de educacion e interpretacion ambiental en contextos de ecoturismo. El caso de la Ruta de las Salinas de Figueira da Foz, Portugal. In L. Muñoz, M. Pubill, J. Álamo, & P. Cartea (Eds.), *Nuevas Investigaciones Iberoamericanas en Educación Ambiental* (pp. 68–85). Madrid: Ministerio de Agricultura, Alimentación y Medio Ambiente.

Moreira, C., & Santos, N. (2010). New opportunities for water environments. River tourism and water leisure activities. In E. Brito-Henriques, J. Sarmento, & M. Lousada (Eds.), *Water and Tourism – resources management, planning and sustainability* (pp. 147–168). Lisbon: CEG.

Mowforth, M., & Munt, I. (1998). *Tourism and Sustainability: New Tourism in the Third World*. London: Routledge. doi:10.4324/9780203437292

Mueller, R. J. (1992). *Customer Operable System for a Retail Store or Fast-Food Restaurant Having Plural Ordering Stations*. U.S. Patent No. 5,128,862. Washington, DC: U.S. Patent and Trademark Office.

Mueller, R. J., Neimeister, C. K., Counter, J. R., & Marcus, M. P. (1993). *Customer self-ordering system using information displayed on a screen*. U.S. Patent No. 5,235,509. Retrieved from http://patents.com/us-5235509.html

Muraleetharan, P. (2010). *Internal Control and Impact of Financial Performance of The Organizations*. Academic Press.

Murphy, J., Hofacker, C., & Gretzel, U. (2017). Dawning of the Age of Robotics in Hospitality and Tourism: Challenges for Teaching and Research. *European Journal for Teaching and Research*, *15*, 104–111.

Murphy, P., & Prichard, M. (1997). Destination Price-Value Perceptions: An Examination of Origin and Seasonal Influences. *Journal of Travel Research, 35*(3), 16–22. doi:10.1177/004728759703500303

Mwakimasinde, M., Odhiambo, A., & Byaruhanga, J. (2014). Effects of Internal Control Systems on Financial Performance of Sugarcane outgrowercompanies in Kenya. *Journal of Business and Management, 16*(12).

Mycoo, M. (2014). Sustainable tourism, climate change and sea level rise adaptation policies in Barbados". *Natural Resources Forum, 38*.

National Water Development Agency. (2006). *Feasibility Report of Ken Betwa Link Project DPRs Phase I and II Completed*. Retrieved March 26, 2018, from http://www.nwda.gov.in/content/innerpage/FRof-DPR-Phase-I-and-II-Completed.php

Nayyar, A., Mahapatra, B., Le, D., & Suseendran, G. (2018). Virtual Reality (VR) & Augmented Reality (AR) technologies for tourism and hospitality industry. *IACSIT International Journal of Engineering and Technology, 7*(2.21), 156–160. doi:10.14419/ijet.v7i2.21.11858

Nedelec, L. (2008). Les Marais Salants Portugais, Vers Une Gestion Intégrée? In I. Amorim (Ed.), *A Articulação do Sal Português aos Circuitos Mundiais: Antigos e novos Consumos* (pp. 305–319). Porto: Instituto de História Moderna – Universidade do Porto.

Negi, J. S. (2007). *Rural Tourism and Economic Growth*. New Delhi: Cyber Tech Publications.

Neves, R. (2004a). Figueira saltworks: Geography and salt history. In R. Neves, T. Petanidou, R. Rufino, & P. Pinto (Eds.), ALAS – All About Salt: Salt and salinas in the Mediterranean (pp. 19–21). Figueira da Foz: Intermezzo.

Neves, R. (2004b). Figueira da Foz – Organization and evolution of salinas on the Mondego estuary. In R. Neves, T. Petanidou, R. Rufino & P. Pinto (Eds.), ALAS – All About Salt: Salt and salinas in the Mediterranean (pp. 45–47). Figueira da Foz: Intermezzo.

Neves, R. (2004c). Local actions – Figueira da Foz. In R. Neves, T. Petanidou, R. Rufino & P. Pinto (Eds.), ALAS – All About Salt: Salt and salinas in the Mediterranean (pp. 94–96). Figueira da Foz: Intermezzo.

Neves, R. (2005). *Os salgados portugueses no séc. XX – que perspectivas para as salinas portuguesas no séc. XXI? In I Seminário Internacional Sobre o Sal Português* (pp. 129–133). Porto: Instituto de História Moderna, Universidade do Porto.

Njeri, K. C. (2014). *Effect of Internal Controls on The Financial Performance of Manufacturing Firms in Kenya*. University of Nairobi.

Number of Domestic Tourist Visits in India. (1991 to 2015). Retrieved from: http:// www.indiastat. com/ tourism/29/stats.aspx

Nweze, C. C. (2016). *Awhum monastery or tourism destination*. Enugu: Fountain of Reason. Retrieved September 25, 2017, from https://fountainheadrepository.com/2017/06/11/awhum-monastery-or-tourism-destination/

O'Connell, M. J. (2003). Detecting, measuring and reversing changes to wetlands. *Wetlands Ecology and Management, 11*(6), 397–401. doi:10.1023/B:WETL.0000007191.77103.53

O'Dell, T. (2005). Experiencescapes. In T. O'Dell & P. Billing (Eds.), *Experiencescapes: Tourism, culture and economy* (pp. 1–31). Copenhagen: Copenhagen Business School Press.

Obasola, K. E. (2014). Religious tourism and sustainable development: A study of Eyo festival in Lagos, Nigeria. *International Journal of Social Sciences and Education, 4*(2), 524–534.

Obiora, J.N.P., & Nwokorie, E.C. (2018). Impediments to Rural Youth Entrepreneurship towards the Hospitality Sector in Nigeria: The Case of Ihitte-Uboma, Imo State. *Journal of Tourism and Hospitality Management, 6*(1), 81-91. Doi:10.15640/jthm.v6n1a8

Ojewusi, S. (2015, March 23). T.B. Joshua and Synagogue tragedy: Another perspective. *The Authority*, 17-21.

Okonkwo, E. E., & Nzeh, C. A. (2016). Faith-based activities and their tourism potentials in Nigeria. *International Journal of Research in Arts and Social Sciences, 1*(1), 286–298.

Okutmuş, E., & Uyar, S. (2014). *Yiyecek İçecek Departmanında Yapılan Bir Hilenin Tespiti: Vaka Analizi*. Mali Çözüm Dergisi, Ocak-Şubat.

Olalı, H., & Korzay, M. (1993). *Otel İşletmeciliği*. İstanbul: Beta Basım Yayım Dağıtım.

Oluwa, A. O. (2016). *How Nigeria will lose billions where Israel and Saudi*. Retrieved September 18, 2017 from http://www.nairaland.com/3800455/how-nigeria-lose-billions-where

Opara, C., & Onoriode, L. G. (2017). *Tourism: Impact of churches' December crusade rush in Nigeria. In African travel times* (pp. 1–16). Lagos: ATT.

Oredola, A. (2016). Aokpe Pilgrimage Centre thrives as a tourist product. *Business Hallmarknews*. Retrieved September 30, from http://hallmarknews.com/aokpe-pilgrimage-centre-thrives-as-a-tourist-product/

Organización de las Naciones Unidas. (2011). *Situación y perspectivas para la economía mundial 2011*. Recuperado de http://www.un.org

Ouyang, Y., Nkedi-Kizza, P., Wu, Q. T., Shinde, D., & Huang, C. H. (2006). Assessment of seasonal variations in surface water quality. *Water Research, 40*(20), 3800–3810. doi:10.1016/j.watres.2006.08.030 PMID:17069873

Pacitto, J. L., & Jacquemin, O. (2017). Salt Solar Wastelands: To new "saltscapes" resilient in the Mediterranean. In A. Kallel, M. Ksibi, & H. Dhia (Eds.), *Euro-Mediterranean Conference for Environmental Integration* (pp. 1005–1008). Cham: Springer.

Palma, P., Alvarenga, P., Palma, V. L., Fernandes, R. M., Soares, A. M. V. M., & Barbosa, I. R. (2010). Assessment of anthropogenic sources of water pollution using multivariate statistical techniques: A case study of the Alqueva's reservoir, Portugal. *Environmental Monitoring and Assessment*, *165*(1–4), 539–552. doi:10.100710661-009-0965-y PMID:19444629

Pandey, P. K., Kass, P. H., Soupir, M. L., Biswas, S., & Singh, V. P. (2014). Contamination of water resources by pathogenic bacteria. *AMB Express*, *4*(1), 51. doi:10.118613568-014-0051-x PMID:25006540

Paredes, L., Rochette, A., & Marques, D. (2013). Environmental area applied to strategic projects: From education and training towards sustainable development based on territorial competitiveness. In *Proceedings 19th Congress of APDR – Resilient Territories: Innovation and creativity for new modes of regional development* (pp.1116–1126). Faro: APDR.

Park, S. H., Latkova, P., & Nicholls, S. (2006). Image of the united states as a travel destination: A case study of united kingdom college students, *In*: Northeastern Recreation Research Symposium, 2006, Boston. Anais: 2006. p. 8-15.

Parry, M., Arnell, N., Berry, P., Dodman, D., Fankhauser, S., Hope, C., … Wheeler, T. (2009). Assessing the costs of adaptation to climate change: A review of the UNFCCC and other recent estimates. *IIED*, *3*. doi:10.1641/0006-3568(2001)051[0723:CCAFD]2.0.CO;2

Parsa, H. G., Harrington, R., & Ottenbacher, M. (2009). Defining the Hospitality Discipline: a Discussion of Pedagogical and Research Implications. *Journal of Hospitality & Tourism Research*, *33*(3), 263-283. doi:10.1177/1096348009338675

Patrichi, I.C. (2013). Dark Tourism – A Niche Segment For The Romanian Tourism. *Romanian Economic Business Review*, *8*(4.1), 351-358.

Pawlowska, E. (2011). *El turismo académico. Un análisis económico para el caso de galicia. 2011. 275f. Tese (Doutoramento en Economía Aplicada)*. Santiago de Compostela: Universidade de Santiago de Compostela.

Pawlowska, E., & Martínez, F. (2009). Unha aproximación ao impacto económico directo do turismo académico: O caso dos intercambios Erasmus na Universidade de Santiago de Compostela. *Revista Galega de Economía*, *18*(2), 91–110.

Peeters P., Gössling S., Ceron J.P., Dubois G., Patterson T., Richardson R.B., & Studies E. (2004). *The Eco-efficiency of Tourism*. Academic Press.

Peeters, P., & Dubois, G. (2010). Tourism travel under climate change mitigation constraints. *Journal of Transport Geography*, *18*(3), 447–457. doi:10.1016/j.jtrangeo.2009.09.003

Peng, M. (2012). *Estrategia global*. México: D.F. Cengage Learning.

Pereira, R., Soares, A. M. V. M., Ribeiro, R., & Goncalves, F. (2005). Public attitudes towards the restoration and management of Lake Vela (Central Portugal). *Fresenius Environmental Bulletin*, *14*(4), 273–281.

Petanidou, T., & Vayanni, L. (2004). Salinas and Tourism. In R. Neves, T. Petanidou, R. Rufino & P. Pinto (Eds.), ALAS – All About Salt: Salt and salinas in the Mediterranean (pp. 107–109). Figueira da Foz: Intermezzo.

Peters, G., & Panayi, E. (2016). Understanding modern banking ledgers through blockchain technologies: Future of transaction processing and smart contracts on the internet of money. *Banking Beyond Banks and Monet*, 239-278.

Phiri, O., Mumba, P., Moyo, B. H. Z., & Kadewa, W. (2005). Assessment of the impact of industrial effluents on water quality of receiving rivers in urban areas of Malawi. *International Journal of Environmental Science and Technology*, 2(3), 237–244. doi:10.1007/BF03325882

Phung, D., Huang, C., Rutherford, S., Dwirahmadi, F., Chu, C., Wang, X., ... Dinh, T. A. D. (2015). Temporal and spatial assessment of river surface water quality using multivariate statistical techniques: A study in Can Tho City, a Mekong Delta area, Vietnam. *Environmental Monitoring and Assessment*, 187(5), 229. doi:10.100710661-015-4474-x PMID:25847419

Pinto, R., Patrício, J., Neto, J., Salas, F., & Marques, J. (2010). Assessing estuarine quality under the ecosystem services scope: Ecological and socioeconomic aspects. *Ecological Complexity*, 7(3), 389–402. doi:10.1016/j.ecocom.2010.05.001

Pizam, A. (2009). Editorial: Green hotels: A fad, ploy or fact of life? *International Journal of Hospitality Management*, 1(28). doi:10.1016/j.ijhm.2008.09.001

Playing the Visa Card. (2012). *The Economist*. Disponible en http://www.economist.com/whichmba/playing-visa-card/print

Queiroz, R., Guerreiro, J., & Ventura, M. A. (2014). Demand of the tourists visiting protected areas in small oceanic islands: The Azores case-study (Portugal). *Environment, Development and Sustainability*, 16(5), 1119–1135. doi:10.100710668-014-9516-y

Rai, V., Shinde, S., Mhatre, B., & Mahadik, P. (2014). Restaurant management system. *International Journal of Research in Information Technology*, 2(3), 284–288.

Ramos, C., Suárez, F., & Urgorri, A. (2014, August 11). A la caza del universitario extranjero. *La Voz de Galicia*, p. 4.

Randall, A. (1994). A Difficulty with the Travel Cost Method. *Land Economics*, 70(1), 88–96. doi:10.2307/3146443

Rashid, I., & Romshoo, S. A. (2013). Impact of anthropogenic activities on water quality of Lidder River in Kashmir Himalayas. *Environmental Monitoring and Assessment*, 185(6), 4705–4719. doi:10.100710661-012-2898-0 PMID:23001554

Razak, N. A., & Ibrahim, J. A. (2017). From names of places to Mahsuri's curse: exploring the roles of myths and legends in tourism. *International Journal of Business, Economics and Law*, 14(2), 10 - 17.

Razmkhah, H., Abrishamchi, A., & Torkian, A. (2010). Evaluation of spatial and temporal variation in water quality by pattern recognition techniques: A case study on Jajrood River (Tehran, Iran). *Journal of Environmental Management*, *91*(4), 852–860. doi:10.1016/j.jenvman.2009.11.001 PMID:20056527

Reay, D. S. (2004). New Directions: Flying in the face of the climate change convention. *Atmospheric Environment*, *38*(5), 793–794. doi:10.1016/j.atmosenv.2003.10.026

Ribeiro, A., & Fidalgo, V. (2015). O Turismo da Discórdia – Boom turístico em Lisboa e no Porto está longe de agradar a gregos e a troianos. *CM Jornal.* Retrieved December 18, 2017 from <http://www.cmjornal.pt/exclusivos/imprimir/o_turismo_da_discordia>

Richard, P. (2005). Cultural Landscape Tourism: Facilitating Meaning. In S. Wahab & J. J. Pigram (Eds.), *Tourism Development and Growth: The Challenges of Sustainability* (pp. 190–216). London: Routledge.

Richards, G., & Wilson, J. (2003). *Today's Youth Travellers: Tomorrow's Global Nomads. New Horizons in Independent Youth and Student Travel.* Amsterdam: ISTC.

Robinson, V., & McCarroll, D. (Eds.). (1990). *The Isle of Man: Celebrating a Sense of Place.* Liverpool, UK: Liverpool University Press.

Rodrigues, C., Bio, A., Amat, F., & Vieira, N. (2011). Artisal salt production in Aveiro/Portugal – an ecofriendly process. *Saline Systems*, *7*(1), 3. doi:10.1186/1746-1448-7-3 PMID:22053788

Rose, S. (2002). Comparative major ion geochemistry of Piedmont streams in the Atlanta, Georgia region: Possible effects of urbanization. *Environmental Geology*, *42*(1), 102–113. doi:10.100700254-002-0545-8

Ross & Geoffery. (1999). Ecotourism Toward Congruence between Theory and Practice. *Tourism Management, 20*, 123 – 133.

Rufino, R. (2004a). Ecological features of the Mondego estuary and its salinas. In R. Neves, T. Petanidou, R. Rufino, & P. Pinto (Eds.), ALAS – All About Salt: Salt and salinas in the Mediterranean (pp.70–71). Figueira da Foz: Intermezzo.

Rufino, R. (2004b). Salinas and nature conservation. In R. Neves, T. Petanidou, R. Rufino & P. Pinto (Eds.), ALAS – All About Salt: Salt and salinas in the Mediterranean (pp. 77–81). Figueira da Foz: Intermezzo.

Sahu, B. K., Begum, M., Khadanga, M. K., Jha, D. K., Vinithkumar, N. V., & Kirubagaran, R. (2013). Evaluation of significant sources influencing the variation of physico-chemical parameters in Port Blair Bay, South Andaman, India by using multivariate statistics. *Marine Pollution Bulletin*, *66*(1–2), 246–251. doi:10.1016/j.marpolbul.2012.09.021 PMID:23107366

Sainz-López, N. (2017). Comparative analysis of traditional solar saltworks and other economic activities in a Portuguese protected estuary. *Boletin de Investigaciones Marinas y Costeras*, *46*(1), 171–189.

Sandstedt, G. O. (1983). *Restaurant or retail vending facility.* U.S. Patent No.4,415,065. Retrieved from http://patents.com/us-4415065.html

Sârbu, C., & Pop, H. F. (2005). Principal component analysis versus fuzzy principal component analysis: A case study: The quality of danube water (1985-1996). *Talanta, 65*(5), 1215–1220. doi:10.1016/j.talanta.2004.08.047 PMID:18969934

Saurí-Pujol, D., & Llurdés-Coit, J. (1995). Embellishing nature: The case of the salt mountain project of Cardona, Catalonia, Spain. *Geoforum, 26*(1), 35–48. doi:10.1016/0016-7185(95)00016-E

Schachat, R., Fisher, M., & Lowy, J. (2010). Real Estate Investment Trust Corner. Journal of Passthrough Entities, 31(6), 39–42. Retrieved from http://www.sectur.gob.mx

Scheyvens, R. (1999). Ecotourism and the Empowerment of Local Communities. *Tourism Management, 20*(2), 245–249. doi:10.1016/S0261-5177(98)00069-7

Scheyvens, R. (2002). Backpacker tourism and third world development. *Annals of Tourism Research, 1*(29), 144–164. doi:10.1016/S0160-7383(01)00030-5

Schmidt, L., Nave, J., O'riordan, T., & Guerra, J. (2011). Trends and dilemmas facing environmental education in Portugal: From environmental problem assessment to citizenship involvement. *Journal of Environmental Policy and Planning, 13*(2), 159–177. doi:10.1080/1523908X.2011.576167

Schneider, A., & Church, B. K. (2008). The Effects of Auditors' Internal Control Opinions on Loan Decisions. *Journal of Accounting and Public Policy, 27*(1), 1–18. doi:10.1016/j.jaccpubpol.2007.11.004

Schulz, L. (1981). Nährstoffeintrag in Seen durch Badegäste. (in German). *Zbl. Bakt. Hyg. I. Abt. Orig.B., 173*, 528–548.

Sciolino, E. (2009, January 27). From a Portuguese marsh, salt the traditional way. *New York Times*, p. A12.

SCOAN. (2016). *Synagogue Church of All Nations*. Retrieved May 15, 2017, fromhttps://www.revolvy.com/main/index.php?s=Synagogue%20Church%20Of%20All%20Nations&item_type=topic

Sebilcioğlu, F., Karaağaoğlu, S., & Karacacay, G. (2013). *Kurumsal Yönetim İlkeleri Işığında Aile Şirketleri Rehberi.* İstanbul: Türkiye Kurumsal Yönetim Derneği.

Sharari. (2006). *The Relationship Between Internal Control and Performance of Staff In The PPA in the Kingdom of Saudi Arabia: Attitude of the staff* (Unpublished Master's Thesis). University of Jordan, Amman, Jordan.

Sharma, J. K. (Ed.). (2008). Tourism Planning and Development, A New Perspective. New Delhi: Kanishka Publishers.

Shrestha, S., & Kazama, F. (2007). Assessment of surface water quality using multivariate statistical techniques: A case study of the Fuji river basin, Japan. *Environmental Modelling & Software*, *22*(4), 464–475. doi:10.1016/j.envsoft.2006.02.001

Silva, J. D., Srinivasalu, S., Roy, P. D., & Jonathan, M. P. (2014). Environmental conditions inferred from multi-element concentrations in sediments off Cauvery delta, Southeast India. *Environmental Earth Sciences*, *71*(5), 2043–2058. doi:10.100712665-013-2606-6

Simeonov, V., Stratis, J. A., Samara, C., Zachariadis, G., Voutsa, D., Anthemidis, A., ... Kouimtzis, T. (2003). Assessment of the surface water quality in Northern Greece. *Water Research*, *37*(17), 4119–4124. doi:10.1016/S0043-1354(03)00398-1 PMID:12946893

Singh, K. P., Malik, A., Mohan, D., & Sinha, S. (2004). Multivariate statistical techniques for the evaluation of spatial and temporal variations in water quality of Gomti River (India)—A case study. *Water Research*, *38*(18), 3980–3992. doi:10.1016/j.watres.2004.06.011 PMID:15380988

Singh, K. P., Malik, A., & Sinha, S. (2005). Water quality assessment and apportionment of pollution sources of Gomti river (India) using multivariate statistical techniques - A case study. *Analytica Chimica Acta*, *538*(1–2), 355–374. doi:10.1016/j.aca.2005.02.006

Singh, M., Ansari, A. A., Müller, G., & Singh, I. B. (1997). Heavy metals in freshly deposited sediments of the Gomati River (a tributary of the Ganga River): Effects of human activities. *Environmental Geology*, *29*(3–4), 246–252. doi:10.1007002540050123

Sloan, G. (2017, February 4). Robot bartenders? This new cruise ship has them. *USA Today*. Retrieved from USA Today: http://www.usatoday.com/story/cruiselog/2014/11/01/quantum-robot-bar-cruise/18308319/

Soares, J. R. R. (2013). A imagem dos destinos de turismo acadêmico. Congreso En Línea De Administración, 10.

Soares, J. R. R. (2015). *Relación entre imagen turística construida y lealdad: Análisis de los estudiantes internacionales en Galicia* (PhD Thesis). Universidade da Coruña.

Soodanian, S., Navid, B. J., & Kheirollahi, F. (2013). The Relationship Between Firm Characteristics and Internal Control Weaknesses in the Financial Reporting Environment of Companies Listed on the Tehran Stock Exchange. *Journal of Applied Environmental and Biological Sciences*, *3*(11), 68–74.

Sophie, W. (2016, March 9). *Rise of the machines: Robots could be staffing hotels by 2020*. Retrieved from Big Hospitality: https://www.bighospitality.co.uk/Article/2016/03/09/Rise-of-the-machines-Robots-could-be-staffing-hotels-by-2020

Spulbar, C., & Niţoi, M. (2012). *Comparative analysis of banking systems*. SITECH Publishing House Craiova.

Spulbar, C., & Nitoi, M. (2015). An Examination of Banks' Cost Efficiency in Central and Eastern Europe. *Procedia Economics and Finance, 22,* 544–551. doi:10.1016/S2212-5671(15)00256-7

Spulbar, C., & Nitoi, M. (2016). The relationship between bank efficiency and risk and productivity patterns in Romanian banking system. *Romanian Journal of Economic Forecasting, 19*(1), 39–53.

Stausberg, M. (2011). *Religion and tourism: crossroads, destinations and encounters.* London: Routledge.

Steiner, C. (2006). Tourism, Poverty Reduction and the Political Economy: Egyptian Perspectives on Tourism's Economic Benefits in a Semi-Rentier State. *Tourism Hospitality Planning and Development, 3*(3), 161–177. doi:10.1080/14790530601132286

Suk, T. J., Sorenson, S. K., & Dileanis, P. D. (1987). The relation between human presence and occurrence of Giardia cysts in streams in the Sierra Nevada, California. *Journal of Freshwater Ecology, 4*(1), 71–75. doi:10.1080/02705060.1987.9665163

Sun, D., & Walsh, D. (1998). Review of studies on environmental impacts of recreation and tourism in Australia. *Journal of Environmental Management, 53*(4), 323–338. doi:10.1006/jema.1998.0200

Suresh, S. (2016). Big data and predictive analytics. *Pediatrics Clinics, 63*(2), 357–366. doi:10.1016/j.pcl.2015.12.007 PMID:27017041

Sushirobo. (2016, December 30). *Sushi machines.* Retrieved from Sushirobo: http://www.sushirobo.com/#machines

Suthar, S., Sharma, J., Chabukdhara, M., & Nema, A. K. (2009). Water quality assessment of river Hindon at Ghaziabad, India: Impact of industrial and urban wastewater. *Environmental Monitoring and Assessment.* doi:10.100710661-009-0930-9 PMID:19418235

Tang, A., & Xu, L. (2007). *Institutional Ownership, Internal Control Material Weakness and Firm Performance.* Working paper, Morgan State University.

Tan, N., Mohan, R., & Watanbe, A. (2016). Toward a framework for robot-inclusive environments. *Automation in Construction, 69,* 68–78. doi:10.1016/j.autcon.2016.06.001

Teixeira, Z., Marques, C., Mota, J., & Garcia, C. (2018). Identification of potential aquaculture sites in solar saltscapes via the Analytic Hierarchy process. *Ecological Indicators, 93,* 231–242. doi:10.1016/j.ecolind.2018.05.003

Termorshuizen, J., & Opdam, P. (2009). Landscape services as a bridge between landscape ecology and sustainable development. *Landscape Ecology, 24*(8), 1037–1052. doi:10.100710980-008-9314-8

The European Network for Historic Places of Worship. (2013). *World – Growth of religious tourism*. Retrieved September 20th, 2017 from http://www.frh-europe.org/world-growth-of-religious-tourism/

The Maravi Post. (2014, October 12). SCOAN update: Tourism hard-hit by Synagogue building collapse, say airport transport operators. *The Malavi Post*, 21-22.

Thompson, I. B. (1999). The role of artisanal technology and indigenous knowledge transfer in the survival of a classic cultural landscape: The marais salants of Guerande, Loire-Atlantique, France. *Journal of Historical Geography*, *25*(2), 216–234. doi:10.1006/jhge.1999.0115

Thrane, C. (2002). Jazz Festival Visitors and Their Expenditures: Linking Spending Patterns to Musical Interest. *Journal of Travel Research*, *40*(3), 281–286. doi:10.1177/0047287502040003006

Thrun, S. (2004). Toward a Framework for Human-Robot Interaction. *Human-Computer Interaction*, *19*(1), 9–24. doi:10.120715327051hci1901&2_2

Thuot, L., Vaugeois, N., & Maher, P. (2010). Fostering innovation in sustainable tourism. *Journal of Rural and Community Development, 5*, 76–89. doi:10.25316/ir-138

Tong, J., & Chen, Y. (2009). Recovery of nitrogen and phosphorus from alkaline fermentation liquid of waste activated sludge and application of the fermentation liquid to promote biological municipal wastewater treatment. *Water Research*, *43*(12), 2969–2976. doi:10.1016/j.watres.2009.04.015 PMID:19443007

Tong, S. T. Y., & Chen, W. (2002). Modeling the relationship between land use and surface water quality. *Journal of Environmental Management*, *66*(4), 377–393. doi:10.1006/jema.2002.0593 PMID:12503494

Tourism Policy of West Bengal. (1996). The Government of West Bengal.

Trejos, B., & Chiang, L. H. N. (2009). Local economic linkages to community-based tourism in rural Costa Rica". *Singapore Journal of Tropical Geography*, *30*(3), 373–387. doi:10.1111/j.1467-9493.2009.00375.x

Tripp, T., & Vaszary, M. (2006). Restaurant Management Using Network With Customer-Operated Computing Devices. *U.S. Patent Application No. 11/024,105*.

Tunstall, S. M., & Coker, A. (1995). Survey-based Valuation Methods. In A. Coker & C. Richards (Eds.), *Valuing the Environment: Economic Approaches to Environmental Evaluation* (pp. 104–126). Chichester, UK: Wiley.

Tutunea, M., & Rus, R.V. (2011). Mobile-Tourism in Romania. *Journal Studia Universitatis Babeş-Bolyai Negotia, 56*(1), 76-88.

Tutunea, M.F. (2016). Mobile applications for tourism. Study regarding their use by Romanians. *Annals of "Constantin Brancusi" University of Targu-Jiu, 4*, 78-84.

Twinning-Ward, L., & Butler, R. (2002). Implementing STD on a Small Island: Development and Use of Sustainable Tourism Development Indicators in Samoa". *Journal of Sustainable Tourism*, *10*(5), 363–387. doi:10.1080/09669580208667174

Uchenna, H. O., & Okpoko, P. U. (2017). Impact of religious tourism in southeastern Nigeria. *Journal of Tourism and Heritage Studies*, *6*(1), 99–112.

Understanding Internal Controls. A References Guide for Managing University Business Practices. (n.d.). Retrieved from http://www.ucop.edu/ctlacct/under-ic.pdf

UNWTO. (2002). *Tourism and Poverty Alleviation*. Madrid: United Nations World Tourism Organization.

UNWTO. (2007). *World Tourism Barometer*. Madrid: World Tourism Organisation.

Urry, J. (1990). *The Tourist Gaze: Leisure and travel in contemporary societies*. London: Sage.

Usul, H. (2013). *Bağımsız Denetim*. Ankara: Detay Yayıncılık.

Valdés, J. A. (2003). *Marketing Estratégico e Estratégia Competitiva de Empresas Turísticas: Um estudo de caso da cadeia hoteleira Sol Meliá* (PhD thesis). Faculdade de Economia, Administração e Contabilidade, Universidade de São Paulo, São Paulo, Brazil.

Vargas, J. G., Guerra, E., Bojórquez, A., & Bojórquez, F. (2014). *Gestión estratégica de organizaciones. Ciudad Autónoma de Buenos Aires*. Elaleph.

Varol, M., & Şen, B. (2009). Assessment of surface water quality using multivariate statistical techniques: A case study of Behrimaz Stream, Turkey. *Environmental Monitoring and Assessment*, *159*(1–4), 543–553. doi:10.100710661-008-0650-6 PMID:19051048

Varol, M., & Şen, B. (2012). Assessment of nutrient and heavy metal contamination in surface water and sediments of the upper Tigris River, Turkey. *Catena*, *92*, 1–10. doi:10.1016/j.catena.2011.11.011

Vaugeois, N. (2000). Tourism in Developing Countries: Refining a Useful Tool for Economic Development. *Proceedings of 6th World Leisure Congress*.

Vega, M., Pardo, R., Barrado, E., & Debán, L. (1998). Assessment of seasonal and polluting effects on the quality of river water by exploratory data analysis. *Water Research*, *32*(12), 3581–3592. doi:10.1016/S0043-1354(98)00138-9

Victer, P. P. (2009). *Marketing no turismo: um estudo descritivo sobre a imagem do intercâmbio de cursos de idiomas. 2009. 137f. Dissertação (Mestrado em Administração)*. Belo Horizonte: Faculdade de Ciências Empresariais, Universidade Fumec.

Vieira, N., & Bio, A. (2004). Artisanal Salina – Unique wetland habitats worth preserving. *Marine Science Research & Development*, 4-125. doi: . doi:10.4172/2155-9910.1000e125

Vukonic, B. (1998). Religious tourism: Economic value or an empty box? *Zagreb International Review of Economic and Business, 1*(1), 83–94.

Vutukuru, S. S. (2003). Chromium induced alterations in some biochemical profiles of the Indian major carp, Labeo rohita (Hamilton). *Bulletin of Environmental Contamination and Toxicology, 70*(1), 118–123. doi:10.100700128-002-0164-9 PMID:12478433

Walker, J. (2010). *Introduction to Hospitality Management*. London: Pearson Education.

Walmsley, J. G. (1999). The ecological importance of Mediterranean salinas. In: N. A. Korovessis & T. D. Lekkas (Eds.), *Proceedings of the Post Conference Symposium Salworks: Preserving Saline Coastal Ecosystems* (pp.81–95). Academic Press.

Wang, Y., Rompf, P., Severt, D., & Peerapatdit, N. (2006). Examining and Identifying the Determinants of Travel Expenditure Patterns. *International Journal of Tourism Research, 8*(5), 333–346. doi:10.1002/jtr.583

Weyel, P. (2011). *Portfolio Theory and the Financial Crisis*. Norderstedt. Grin Verlag.

Willis, K. G. (1994). Taying for Heritage: What Price for Durham Cathedral? *Journal of Environmental Planning and Management, 37*(3), 267–278. doi:10.1080/09640569408711975

Wolf, J. D. (1967). *Business Order Control System andApparatus*. U.S. Patent No. 3,304,416. Washington, DC: U.S. Patent and Trademark Office.

Wood, E., Gatz, M. F., & Lindberg, K. (1995). Ecotourism Society: An action Agenda. In J. Kusler (Ed.), *Ecotourism and Resource Conservation* (pp. 75–79). Madison, WI: Omnipress.

World Travel & Tourism Council (WTTC). (2015). *Travel & Tourism Economic Impact 2016*. Retrieved from: Https://Www.Wttc.Org//Media/Files/Reports/Economic%20impac t%20research/Regions%202016/World2016.Pdf

Wright, A., & De Filippi, P. (2015). *Decentralized Blockchain Technology and the Rise of Lex Cryptographia*. SSRN. doi:10.2139srn.2580664

WTO Organización Mundial Del Turismo. (2010). *Introducción al turismo*. Madrid: Author.

WTTC, WTO & Earth Council. (1995). Agenda 21 for the travel and tourism industry: Towards Environmentally Sustainable Development. London: WTTC.

Wu, T. C., Xie, P. F., & Tsai, M. C. (2015). Perceptions of attractiveness for salt heritage tourism: A tourist perspective. *Tourism Management, 51*, 201–209. doi:10.1016/j.tourman.2015.05.026

Yeung, I. M. H. (1999). Multivariate analysis of the Hong Kong Victoria Harbour water quality data. *Environmental Monitoring and Assessment, 59*(3), 331–342. doi:10.1023/A:1006177824327

Zhang, H., & Lei, S. (2012). A structural model of residents' intention to participate in ecotourism: The case of a wetland community. *Tourism Management, 33*(4), 916–925. doi:10.1016/j.tourman.2011.09.012

Zhao, W., Wang, Y., Lin, X., Zhou, D., Pan, M., & Yang, J. (2014). Identification of the salinity effect on N2O production pathway during nitrification: Using stepwise inhibition and15N isotope labeling methods. *Chemical Engineering Journal*, *253*, 418–426. doi:10.1016/j.cej.2014.05.052

Zhou, Q., Zhang, J., Fu, J., Shi, J., & Jiang, G. (2008). Biomonitoring : An appealing tool for assessment of metal pollution in the aquatic ecosystem. *Analytica Chimica Acta*, *606*(2), 135–150. doi:10.1016/j.aca.2007.11.018 PMID:18082645

Related References

To continue our tradition of advancing information science and technology research, we have compiled a list of recommended IGI Global readings. These references will provide additional information and guidance to further enrich your knowledge and assist you with your own research and future publications.

Abtahi, M. S., Behboudi, L., & Hasanabad, H. M. (2017). Factors Affecting Internet Advertising Adoption in Ad Agencies. *International Journal of Innovation in the Digital Economy*, 8(4), 18–29. doi:10.4018/IJIDE.2017100102

Agrawal, S. (2017). The Impact of Emerging Technologies and Social Media on Different Business(es): Marketing and Management. In O. Rishi & A. Sharma (Eds.), *Maximizing Business Performance and Efficiency Through Intelligent Systems* (pp. 37–49). Hershey, PA: IGI Global. doi:10.4018/978-1-5225-2234-8.ch002

Alnoukari, M., Razouk, R., & Hanano, A. (2016). BSC-SI: A Framework for Integrating Strategic Intelligence in Corporate Strategic Management. *International Journal of Social and Organizational Dynamics in IT*, 5(2), 1–14. doi:10.4018/IJSODIT.2016070101

Alnoukari, M., Razouk, R., & Hanano, A. (2016). BSC-SI, A Framework for Integrating Strategic Intelligence in Corporate Strategic Management. *International Journal of Strategic Information Technology and Applications*, 7(1), 32–44. doi:10.4018/IJSITA.2016010103

Altındağ, E. (2016). Current Approaches in Change Management. In A. Goksoy (Ed.), *Organizational Change Management Strategies in Modern Business* (pp. 24–51). Hershey, PA: IGI Global. doi:10.4018/978-1-4666-9533-7.ch002

Alvarez-Dionisi, L. E., Turner, R., & Mittra, M. (2016). Global Project Management Trends. *International Journal of Information Technology Project Management*, 7(3), 54–73. doi:10.4018/IJITPM.2016070104

Anantharaman, R. N., Rajeswari, K. S., Angusamy, A., & Kuppusamy, J. (2017). Role of Self-Efficacy and Collective Efficacy as Moderators of Occupational Stress Among Software Development Professionals. *International Journal of Human Capital and Information Technology Professionals*, 8(2), 45–58. doi:10.4018/IJHCITP.2017040103

Aninze, F., El-Gohary, H., & Hussain, J. (2018). The Role of Microfinance to Empower Women: The Case of Developing Countries. *International Journal of Customer Relationship Marketing and Management*, 9(1), 54–78. doi:10.4018/IJCRMM.2018010104

Arsenijević, O. M., Orčić, D., & Kastratović, E. (2017). Development of an Optimization Tool for Intangibles in SMEs: A Case Study from Serbia with a Pilot Research in the Prestige by Milka Company. In M. Vemić (Ed.), *Optimal Management Strategies in Small and Medium Enterprises* (pp. 320–347). Hershey, PA: IGI Global. doi:10.4018/978-1-5225-1949-2.ch015

Aryanto, V. D., Wismantoro, Y., & Widyatmoko, K. (2018). Implementing Eco-Innovation by Utilizing the Internet to Enhance Firm's Marketing Performance: Study of Green Batik Small and Medium Enterprises in Indonesia. *International Journal of E-Business Research*, 14(1), 21–36. doi:10.4018/IJEBR.2018010102

Atiku, S. O., & Fields, Z. (2017). Multicultural Orientations for 21st Century Global Leadership. In N. Baporikar (Ed.), *Management Education for Global Leadership* (pp. 28–51). Hershey, PA: IGI Global. doi:10.4018/978-1-5225-1013-0.ch002

Atiku, S. O., & Fields, Z. (2018). Organisational Learning Dimensions and Talent Retention Strategies for the Service Industries. In N. Baporikar (Ed.), *Global Practices in Knowledge Management for Societal and Organizational Development* (pp. 358–381). Hershey, PA: IGI Global. doi:10.4018/978-1-5225-3009-1.ch017

Ávila, L., & Teixeira, L. (2018). The Main Concepts Behind the Dematerialization of Business Processes. In M. Khosrow-Pour, D.B.A. (Ed.), Encyclopedia of Information Science and Technology, Fourth Edition (pp. 888-898). Hershey, PA: IGI Global. doi:10.4018/978-1-5225-2255-3.ch076

Bartens, Y., Chunpir, H. I., Schulte, F., & Voß, S. (2017). Business/IT Alignment in Two-Sided Markets: A COBIT 5 Analysis for Media Streaming Business Models. In S. De Haes & W. Van Grembergen (Eds.), *Strategic IT Governance and Alignment in Business Settings* (pp. 82–111). Hershey, PA: IGI Global. doi:10.4018/978-1-5225-0861-8.ch004

Bashayreh, A. M. (2018). Organizational Culture and Organizational Performance. In W. Lee & F. Sabetzadeh (Eds.), *Contemporary Knowledge and Systems Science* (pp. 50–69). Hershey, PA: IGI Global. doi:10.4018/978-1-5225-5655-8.ch003

Bedford, D. A. (2018). Sustainable Knowledge Management Strategies: Aligning Business Capabilities and Knowledge Management Goals. In N. Baporikar (Ed.), *Global Practices in Knowledge Management for Societal and Organizational Development* (pp. 46–73). Hershey, PA: IGI Global. doi:10.4018/978-1-5225-3009-1.ch003

Benmoussa, F., Nakara, W. A., & Jaouen, A. (2016). The Use of Social Media by SMEs in the Tourism Industry. In I. Lee (Ed.), *Encyclopedia of E-Commerce Development, Implementation, and Management* (pp. 2159–2170). Hershey, PA: IGI Global. doi:10.4018/978-1-4666-9787-4.ch155

Berger, R. (2016). Indigenous Management and Bottom of Pyramid Countries: The Role of National Institutions. In U. Aung & P. Ordoñez de Pablos (Eds.), *Managerial Strategies and Practice in the Asian Business Sector* (pp. 107–123). Hershey, PA: IGI Global. doi:10.4018/978-1-4666-9758-4.ch007

Bharwani, S., & Musunuri, D. (2018). Reflection as a Process From Theory to Practice. In M. Khosrow-Pour, D.B.A. (Ed.), Encyclopedia of Information Science and Technology, Fourth Edition (pp. 1529-1539). Hershey, PA: IGI Global. doi:10.4018/978-1-5225-2255-3.ch132

Bhatt, G. D., Wang, Z., & Rodger, J. A. (2017). Information Systems Capabilities and Their Effects on Competitive Advantages: A Study of Chinese Companies. *Information Resources Management Journal*, *30*(3), 41–57. doi:10.4018/IRMJ.2017070103

Bhushan, M., & Yadav, A. (2017). Concept of Cloud Computing in ESB. In R. Bhadoria, N. Chaudhari, G. Tomar, & S. Singh (Eds.), *Exploring Enterprise Service Bus in the Service-Oriented Architecture Paradigm* (pp. 116–127). Hershey, PA: IGI Global. doi:10.4018/978-1-5225-2157-0.ch008

Bhushan, S. (2017). System Dynamics Base-Model of Humanitarian Supply Chain (HSCM) in Disaster Prone Eco-Communities of India: A Discussion on Simulation and Scenario Results. *International Journal of System Dynamics Applications, 6*(3), 20–37. doi:10.4018/IJSDA.2017070102

Biswas, A., & De, A. K. (2017). On Development of a Fuzzy Stochastic Programming Model with Its Application to Business Management. In S. Trivedi, S. Dey, A. Kumar, & T. Panda (Eds.), *Handbook of Research on Advanced Data Mining Techniques and Applications for Business Intelligence* (pp. 353–378). Hershey, PA: IGI Global. doi:10.4018/978-1-5225-2031-3.ch021

Bücker, J., & Ernste, K. (2018). Use of Brand Heroes in Strategic Reputation Management: The Case of Bacardi, Adidas, and Daimler. In A. Erdemir (Ed.), *Reputation Management Techniques in Public Relations* (pp. 126–150). Hershey, PA: IGI Global. doi:10.4018/978-1-5225-3619-2.ch007

Bureš, V. (2018). Industry 4.0 From the Systems Engineering Perspective: Alternative Holistic Framework Development. In R. Brunet-Thornton & F. Martinez (Eds.), *Analyzing the Impacts of Industry 4.0 in Modern Business Environments* (pp. 199–223). Hershey, PA: IGI Global. doi:10.4018/978-1-5225-3468-6.ch011

Buzady, Z. (2017). Resolving the Magic Cube of Effective Case Teaching: Benchmarking Case Teaching Practices in Emerging Markets – Insights from the Central European University Business School, Hungary. In D. Latusek (Ed.), *Case Studies as a Teaching Tool in Management Education* (pp. 79–103). Hershey, PA: IGI Global. doi:10.4018/978-1-5225-0770-3.ch005

Campatelli, G., Richter, A., & Stocker, A. (2016). Participative Knowledge Management to Empower Manufacturing Workers. *International Journal of Knowledge Management, 12*(4), 37–50. doi:10.4018/IJKM.2016100103

Căpusneanu, S., & Topor, D. I. (2018). Business Ethics and Cost Management in SMEs: Theories of Business Ethics and Cost Management Ethos. In I. Oncioiu (Ed.), *Ethics and Decision-Making for Sustainable Business Practices* (pp. 109–127). Hershey, PA: IGI Global. doi:10.4018/978-1-5225-3773-1.ch007

Carneiro, A. (2016). Maturity in Health Organization Information Systems: Metrics and Privacy Perspectives. *International Journal of Privacy and Health Information Management, 4*(2), 1–18. doi:10.4018/IJPHIM.2016070101

Chan, R. L., Mo, P. L., & Moon, K. K. (2018). Strategic and Tactical Measures in Managing Enterprise Risks: A Study of the Textile and Apparel Industry. In K. Strang, M. Korstanje, & N. Vajjhala (Eds.), *Research, Practices, and Innovations in Global Risk and Contingency Management* (pp. 1–19). Hershey, PA: IGI Global. doi:10.4018/978-1-5225-4754-9.ch001

Chandan, H. C. (2016). Motivations and Challenges of Female Entrepreneurship in Developed and Developing Economies. In N. Baporikar (Ed.), *Handbook of Research on Entrepreneurship in the Contemporary Knowledge-Based Global Economy* (pp. 260–286). Hershey, PA: IGI Global. doi:10.4018/978-1-4666-8798-1.ch012

Charlier, S. D., Burke-Smalley, L. A., & Fisher, S. L. (2018). Undergraduate Programs in the U.S: A Contextual and Content-Based Analysis. In J. Mendy (Ed.), *Teaching Human Resources and Organizational Behavior at the College Level* (pp. 26–57). Hershey, PA: IGI Global. doi:10.4018/978-1-5225-2820-3.ch002

Chaudhuri, S. (2016). Application of Web-Based Geographical Information System (GIS) in E-Business. In U. Panwar, R. Kumar, & N. Ray (Eds.), *Handbook of Research on Promotional Strategies and Consumer Influence in the Service Sector* (pp. 389–405). Hershey, PA: IGI Global. doi:10.4018/978-1-5225-0143-5.ch023

Choudhuri, P. S. (2016). An Empirical Study on the Quality of Services Offered by the Private Life Insurers in Burdwan. In U. Panwar, R. Kumar, & N. Ray (Eds.), *Handbook of Research on Promotional Strategies and Consumer Influence in the Service Sector* (pp. 31–55). Hershey, PA: IGI Global. doi:10.4018/978-1-5225-0143-5.ch002

Dahlberg, T., Kivijärvi, H., & Saarinen, T. (2017). IT Investment Consistency and Other Factors Influencing the Success of IT Performance. In S. De Haes & W. Van Grembergen (Eds.), *Strategic IT Governance and Alignment in Business Settings* (pp. 176–208). Hershey, PA: IGI Global. doi:10.4018/978-1-5225-0861-8.ch007

Damnjanović, A. M. (2017). Knowledge Management Optimization through IT and E-Business Utilization: A Qualitative Study on Serbian SMEs. In M. Vemić (Ed.), *Optimal Management Strategies in Small and Medium Enterprises* (pp. 249–267). Hershey, PA: IGI Global. doi:10.4018/978-1-5225-1949-2.ch012

Daneshpour, H. (2017). Integrating Sustainable Development into Project Portfolio Management through Application of Open Innovation. In M. Vemić (Ed.), *Optimal Management Strategies in Small and Medium Enterprises* (pp. 370–387). Hershey, PA: IGI Global. doi:10.4018/978-1-5225-1949-2.ch017

Daniel, A. D., & Reis de Castro, V. (2018). Entrepreneurship Education: How to Measure the Impact on Nascent Entrepreneurs. In A. Carrizo Moreira, J. Guilherme Leitão Dantas, & F. Manuel Valente (Eds.), *Nascent Entrepreneurship and Successful New Venture Creation* (pp. 85–110). Hershey, PA: IGI Global. doi:10.4018/978-1-5225-2936-1.ch004

David, F., van der Sijde, P., & van den Besselaar, P. (2016). Enterpreneurial Incentives, Obstacles, and Management in University-Business Co-Operation: The Case of Indonesia. In J. Saiz-Álvarez (Ed.), *Handbook of Research on Social Entrepreneurship and Solidarity Economics* (pp. 499–518). Hershey, PA: IGI Global. doi:10.4018/978-1-5225-0097-1.ch024

David, R., Swami, B. N., & Tangirala, S. (2018). Ethics Impact on Knowledge Management in Organizational Development: A Case Study. In N. Baporikar (Ed.), *Global Practices in Knowledge Management for Societal and Organizational Development* (pp. 19–45). Hershey, PA: IGI Global. doi:10.4018/978-1-5225-3009-1.ch002

Delias, P., & Lakiotaki, K. (2018). Discovering Process Horizontal Boundaries to Facilitate Process Comprehension. *International Journal of Operations Research and Information Systems*, 9(2), 1–31. doi:10.4018/IJORIS.2018040101

Denholm, J., & Lee-Davies, L. (2018). Success Factors for Games in Business and Project Management. In *Enhancing Education and Training Initiatives Through Serious Games* (pp. 34–68). Hershey, PA: IGI Global. doi:10.4018/978-1-5225-3689-5.ch002

Deshpande, M. (2017). Best Practices in Management Institutions for Global Leadership: Policy Aspects. In N. Baporikar (Ed.), *Management Education for Global Leadership* (pp. 1–27). Hershey, PA: IGI Global. doi:10.4018/978-1-5225-1013-0.ch001

Deshpande, M. (2018). Policy Perspectives for SMEs Knowledge Management. In N. Baporikar (Ed.), *Knowledge Integration Strategies for Entrepreneurship and Sustainability* (pp. 23–46). Hershey, PA: IGI Global. doi:10.4018/978-1-5225-5115-7.ch002

Dezdar, S. (2017). ERP Implementation Projects in Asian Countries: A Comparative Study on Iran and China. *International Journal of Information Technology Project Management*, 8(3), 52–68. doi:10.4018/IJITPM.2017070104

Domingos, D., Martinho, R., & Varajão, J. (2016). Controlled Flexibility in Healthcare Processes: A BPMN-Extension Approach. In M. Cruz-Cunha, I. Miranda, R. Martinho, & R. Rijo (Eds.), *Encyclopedia of E-Health and Telemedicine* (pp. 521–535). Hershey, PA: IGI Global. doi:10.4018/978-1-4666-9978-6.ch040

Domingos, D., Respício, A., & Martinho, R. (2017). Reliability of IoT-Aware BPMN Healthcare Processes. In C. Reis & M. Maximiano (Eds.), *Internet of Things and Advanced Application in Healthcare* (pp. 214–248). Hershey, PA: IGI Global. doi:10.4018/978-1-5225-1820-4.ch008

Dosumu, O., Hussain, J., & El-Gohary, H. (2017). An Exploratory Study of the Impact of Government Policies on the Development of Small and Medium Enterprises in Developing Countries: The Case of Nigeria. *International Journal of Customer Relationship Marketing and Management*, 8(4), 51–62. doi:10.4018/IJCRMM.2017100104

Durst, S., Bruns, G., & Edvardsson, I. R. (2017). Retaining Knowledge in Smaller Building and Construction Firms. *International Journal of Knowledge and Systems Science*, 8(3), 1–12. doi:10.4018/IJKSS.2017070101

Edvardsson, I. R., & Durst, S. (2017). Outsourcing, Knowledge, and Learning: A Critical Review. *International Journal of Knowledge-Based Organizations*, 7(2), 13–26. doi:10.4018/IJKBO.2017040102

Edwards, J. S. (2018). Integrating Knowledge Management and Business Processes. In M. Khosrow-Pour, D.B.A. (Ed.), Encyclopedia of Information Science and Technology, Fourth Edition (pp. 5046-5055). Hershey, PA: IGI Global. doi:10.4018/978-1-5225-2255-3.ch437

Ejiogu, A. O. (2018). Economics of Farm Management. In *Agricultural Finance and Opportunities for Investment and Expansion* (pp. 56–72). Hershey, PA: IGI Global. doi:10.4018/978-1-5225-3059-6.ch003

Ekanem, I., & Abiade, G. E. (2018). Factors Influencing the Use of E-Commerce by Small Enterprises in Nigeria. *International Journal of ICT Research in Africa and the Middle East*, 7(1), 37–53. doi:10.4018/IJICTRAME.2018010103

Ekanem, I., & Alrossais, L. A. (2017). Succession Challenges Facing Family Businesses in Saudi Arabia. In P. Zgheib (Ed.), *Entrepreneurship and Business Innovation in the Middle East* (pp. 122–146). Hershey, PA: IGI Global. doi:10.4018/978-1-5225-2066-5.ch007

El Faquih, L., & Fredj, M. (2017). Ontology-Based Framework for Quality in Configurable Process Models. *Journal of Electronic Commerce in Organizations*, *15*(2), 48–60. doi:10.4018/JECO.2017040104

El-Gohary, H., & El-Gohary, Z. (2016). An Attempt to Explore Electronic Marketing Adoption and Implementation Aspects in Developing Countries: The Case of Egypt. *International Journal of Customer Relationship Marketing and Management*, *7*(4), 1–26. doi:10.4018/IJCRMM.2016100101

Entico, G. J. (2016). Knowledge Management and the Medical Health Librarians: A Perception Study. In J. Yap, M. Perez, M. Ayson, & G. Entico (Eds.), *Special Library Administration, Standardization and Technological Integration* (pp. 52–77). Hershey, PA: IGI Global. doi:10.4018/978-1-4666-9542-9.ch003

Faisal, M. N., & Talib, F. (2017). Building Ambidextrous Supply Chains in SMEs: How to Tackle the Barriers? *International Journal of Information Systems and Supply Chain Management*, *10*(4), 80–100. doi:10.4018/IJISSCM.2017100105

Fernandes, T. M., Gomes, J., & Romão, M. (2017). Investments in E-Government: A Benefit Management Case Study. *International Journal of Electronic Government Research*, *13*(3), 1–17. doi:10.4018/IJEGR.2017070101

Fouda, F. A. (2016). A Suggested Curriculum in Career Education to Develop Business Secondary Schools Students' Career Knowledge Management Domains and Professional Thinking. *International Journal of Technology Diffusion*, *7*(2), 42–62. doi:10.4018/IJTD.2016040103

Gallardo-Vázquez, D., & Pajuelo-Moreno, M. L. (2016). How Spanish Universities are Promoting Entrepreneurship through Your Own Lines of Teaching and Research? In L. Carvalho (Ed.), *Handbook of Research on Entrepreneurial Success and its Impact on Regional Development* (pp. 431–454). Hershey, PA: IGI Global. doi:10.4018/978-1-4666-9567-2.ch019

Gao, S. S., Oreal, S., & Zhang, J. (2018). Contemporary Financial Risk Management Perceptions and Practices of Small-Sized Chinese Businesses. In I. Management Association (Ed.), Global Business Expansion: Concepts, Methodologies, Tools, and Applications (pp. 917-931). Hershey, PA: IGI Global. doi:10.4018/978-1-5225-5481-3.ch041

Garg, R., & Berning, S. C. (2017). Indigenous Chinese Management Philosophies: Key Concepts and Relevance for Modern Chinese Firms. In B. Christiansen & G. Koc (Eds.), *Transcontinental Strategies for Industrial Development and Economic Growth* (pp. 43–57). Hershey, PA: IGI Global. doi:10.4018/978-1-5225-2160-0.ch003

Gencer, Y. G. (2017). Supply Chain Management in Retailing Business. In U. Akkucuk (Ed.), *Ethics and Sustainability in Global Supply Chain Management* (pp. 197–210). Hershey, PA: IGI Global. doi:10.4018/978-1-5225-2036-8.ch011

Giacosa, E. (2016). Innovation in Luxury Fashion Businesses as a Means for the Regional Development. In L. Carvalho (Ed.), *Handbook of Research on Entrepreneurial Success and its Impact on Regional Development* (pp. 206–222). Hershey, PA: IGI Global. doi:10.4018/978-1-4666-9567-2.ch010

Giacosa, E. (2018). The Increasing of the Regional Development Thanks to the Luxury Business Innovation. In L. Carvalho (Ed.), *Handbook of Research on Entrepreneurial Ecosystems and Social Dynamics in a Globalized World* (pp. 260–273). Hershey, PA: IGI Global. doi:10.4018/978-1-5225-3525-6.ch011

Gianni, M., & Gotzamani, K. (2016). Integrated Management Systems and Information Management Systems: Common Threads. In P. Papajorgji, F. Pinet, A. Guimarães, & J. Papathanasiou (Eds.), *Automated Enterprise Systems for Maximizing Business Performance* (pp. 195–214). Hershey, PA: IGI Global. doi:10.4018/978-1-4666-8841-4.ch011

Gianni, M., Gotzamani, K., & Linden, I. (2016). How a BI-wise Responsible Integrated Management System May Support Food Traceability. *International Journal of Decision Support System Technology*, 8(2), 1–17. doi:10.4018/IJDSST.2016040101

Glykas, M., & George, J. (2017). Quality and Process Management Systems in the UAE Maritime Industry. *International Journal of Productivity Management and Assessment Technologies*, 5(1), 20–39. doi:10.4018/IJPMAT.2017010102

Glykas, M., Valiris, G., Kokkinaki, A., & Koutsoukou, Z. (2018). Banking Business Process Management Implementation. *International Journal of Productivity Management and Assessment Technologies*, 6(1), 50–69. doi:10.4018/IJPMAT.2018010104

Gomes, J., & Romão, M. (2017). The Balanced Scorecard: Keeping Updated and Aligned with Today's Business Trends. *International Journal of Productivity Management and Assessment Technologies*, 5(2), 1–15. doi:10.4018/IJPMAT.2017070101

Gomes, J., & Romão, M. (2017). Aligning Information Systems and Technology with Benefit Management and Balanced Scorecard. In S. De Haes & W. Van Grembergen (Eds.), *Strategic IT Governance and Alignment in Business Settings* (pp. 112–131). Hershey, PA: IGI Global. doi:10.4018/978-1-5225-0861-8.ch005

Grefen, P., & Turetken, O. (2017). Advanced Business Process Management in Networked E-Business Scenarios. *International Journal of E-Business Research*, *13*(4), 70–104. doi:10.4018/IJEBR.2017100105

Haider, A., & Saetang, S. (2017). Strategic IT Alignment in Service Sector. In S. Rozenes & Y. Cohen (Eds.), *Handbook of Research on Strategic Alliances and Value Co-Creation in the Service Industry* (pp. 231–258). Hershey, PA: IGI Global. doi:10.4018/978-1-5225-2084-9.ch012

Haider, A., & Tang, S. S. (2016). Maximising Value Through IT and Business Alignment: A Case of IT Governance Institutionalisation at a Thai Bank. *International Journal of Technology Diffusion*, *7*(3), 33–58. doi:10.4018/IJTD.2016070104

Hajilari, A. B., Ghadaksaz, M., & Fasghandis, G. S. (2017). Assessing Organizational Readiness for Implementing ERP System Using Fuzzy Expert System Approach. *International Journal of Enterprise Information Systems*, *13*(1), 67–85. doi:10.4018/IJEIS.2017010105

Haldorai, A., Ramu, A., & Murugan, S. (2018). Social Aware Cognitive Radio Networks: Effectiveness of Social Networks as a Strategic Tool for Organizational Business Management. In H. Bansal, G. Shrivastava, G. Nguyen, & L. Stanciu (Eds.), *Social Network Analytics for Contemporary Business Organizations* (pp. 188–202). Hershey, PA: IGI Global. doi:10.4018/978-1-5225-5097-6.ch010

Hall, O. P. Jr. (2017). Social Media Driven Management Education. *International Journal of Knowledge-Based Organizations*, *7*(2), 43–59. doi:10.4018/IJKBO.2017040104

Hanifah, H., Halim, H. A., Ahmad, N. H., & Vafaei-Zadeh, A. (2017). Innovation Culture as a Mediator Between Specific Human Capital and Innovation Performance Among Bumiputera SMEs in Malaysia. In N. Ahmad, T. Ramayah, H. Halim, & S. Rahman (Eds.), *Handbook of Research on Small and Medium Enterprises in Developing Countries* (pp. 261–279). Hershey, PA: IGI Global. doi:10.4018/978-1-5225-2165-5.ch012

Hartlieb, S., & Silvius, G. (2017). Handling Uncertainty in Project Management and Business Development: Similarities and Differences. In Y. Raydugin (Ed.), *Handbook of Research on Leveraging Risk and Uncertainties for Effective Project Management* (pp. 337–362). Hershey, PA: IGI Global. doi:10.4018/978-1-5225-1790-0.ch016

Hass, K. B. (2017). Living on the Edge: Managing Project Complexity. In Y. Raydugin (Ed.), *Handbook of Research on Leveraging Risk and Uncertainties for Effective Project Management* (pp. 177–201). Hershey, PA: IGI Global. doi:10.4018/978-1-5225-1790-0.ch009

Related References

Hassan, A., & Privitera, D. S. (2016). Google AdSense as a Mobile Technology in Education. In J. Holland (Ed.), *Wearable Technology and Mobile Innovations for Next-Generation Education* (pp. 200–223). Hershey, PA: IGI Global. doi:10.4018/978-1-5225-0069-8.ch011

Hassan, A., & Rahimi, R. (2016). Consuming "Innovation" in Tourism: Augmented Reality as an Innovation Tool in Digital Tourism Marketing. In N. Pappas & I. Bregoli (Eds.), *Global Dynamics in Travel, Tourism, and Hospitality* (pp. 130–147). Hershey, PA: IGI Global. doi:10.4018/978-1-5225-0201-2.ch008

Hawking, P., & Carmine Sellitto, C. (2017). Developing an Effective Strategy for Organizational Business Intelligence. In M. Tavana (Ed.), *Enterprise Information Systems and the Digitalization of Business Functions* (pp. 222–237). Hershey, PA: IGI Global. doi:10.4018/978-1-5225-2382-6.ch010

Hawking, P., & Sellitto, C. (2017). A Fast-Moving Consumer Goods Company and Business Intelligence Strategy Development. *International Journal of Enterprise Information Systems*, *13*(2), 22–33. doi:10.4018/IJEIS.2017040102

Hawking, P., & Sellitto, C. (2017). Business Intelligence Strategy: Two Case Studies. *International Journal of Business Intelligence Research*, *8*(2), 17–30. doi:10.4018/IJBIR.2017070102

Haynes, J. D., Arockiasamy, S., Al Rashdi, M., & Al Rashdi, S. (2016). Business and E Business Strategies for Coopetition and Thematic Management as a Sustained Basis for Ethics and Social Responsibility in Emerging Markets. In M. Al-Shammari & H. Masri (Eds.), *Ethical and Social Perspectives on Global Business Interaction in Emerging Markets* (pp. 25–39). Hershey, PA: IGI Global. doi:10.4018/978-1-4666-9864-2.ch002

Hee, W. J., Jalleh, G., Lai, H., & Lin, C. (2017). E-Commerce and IT Projects: Evaluation and Management Issues in Australian and Taiwanese Hospitals. *International Journal of Public Health Management and Ethics*, *2*(1), 69–90. doi:10.4018/IJPHME.2017010104

Hernandez, A. A. (2018). Exploring the Factors to Green IT Adoption of SMEs in the Philippines. *Journal of Cases on Information Technology*, *20*(2), 49–66. doi:10.4018/JCIT.2018040104

Hernandez, A. A., & Ona, S. E. (2016). Green IT Adoption: Lessons from the Philippines Business Process Outsourcing Industry. *International Journal of Social Ecology and Sustainable Development*, *7*(1), 1–34. doi:10.4018/IJSESD.2016010101

Hollman, A., Bickford, S., & Hollman, T. (2017). Cyber InSecurity: A Post-Mortem Attempt to Assess Cyber Problems from IT and Business Management Perspectives. *Journal of Cases on Information Technology, 19*(3), 42–70. doi:10.4018/JCIT.2017070104

Igbinakhase, I. (2017). Responsible and Sustainable Management Practices in Developing and Developed Business Environments. In Z. Fields (Ed.), *Collective Creativity for Responsible and Sustainable Business Practice* (pp. 180–207). Hershey, PA: IGI Global. doi:10.4018/978-1-5225-1823-5.ch010

Ilahi, L., Ghannouchi, S. A., & Martinho, R. (2016). A Business Process Management Approach to Home Healthcare Processes: On the Gap between Intention and Reality. In M. Cruz-Cunha, I. Miranda, R. Martinho, & R. Rijo (Eds.), *Encyclopedia of E-Health and Telemedicine* (pp. 439–457). Hershey, PA: IGI Global. doi:10.4018/978-1-4666-9978-6.ch035

Iwata, J. J., & Hoskins, R. G. (2017). Managing Indigenous Knowledge in Tanzania: A Business Perspective. In P. Jain & N. Mnjama (Eds.), *Managing Knowledge Resources and Records in Modern Organizations* (pp. 198–214). Hershey, PA: IGI Global. doi:10.4018/978-1-5225-1965-2.ch012

Jabeen, F., Ahmad, S. Z., & Alkaabi, S. (2016). The Internationalization Decision-Making of United Arab Emirates Family Businesses. In N. Zakaria, A. Abdul-Talib, & N. Osman (Eds.), *Handbook of Research on Impacts of International Business and Political Affairs on the Global Economy* (pp. 1–22). Hershey, PA: IGI Global. doi:10.4018/978-1-4666-9806-2.ch001

Jain, P. (2017). Ethical and Legal Issues in Knowledge Management Life-Cycle in Business. In P. Jain & N. Mnjama (Eds.), *Managing Knowledge Resources and Records in Modern Organizations* (pp. 82–101). Hershey, PA: IGI Global. doi:10.4018/978-1-5225-1965-2.ch006

Jamali, D., Abdallah, H., & Matar, F. (2016). Opportunities and Challenges for CSR Mainstreaming in Business Schools. *International Journal of Technology and Educational Marketing, 6*(2), 1–29. doi:10.4018/IJTEM.2016070101

James, S., & Hauli, E. (2017). Holistic Management Education at Tanzanian Rural Development Planning Institute. In N. Baporikar (Ed.), *Management Education for Global Leadership* (pp. 112–136). Hershey, PA: IGI Global. doi:10.4018/978-1-5225-1013-0.ch006

Janošková, M., Csikósová, A., & Čulková, K. (2018). Measurement of Company Performance as Part of Its Strategic Management. In R. Leon (Ed.), *Managerial Strategies for Business Sustainability During Turbulent Times* (pp. 309–335). Hershey, PA: IGI Global. doi:10.4018/978-1-5225-2716-9.ch017

Jean-Vasile, A., & Alecu, A. (2017). Theoretical and Practical Approaches in Understanding the Influences of Cost-Productivity-Profit Trinomial in Contemporary Enterprises. In A. Jean Vasile & D. Nicolò (Eds.), *Sustainable Entrepreneurship and Investments in the Green Economy* (pp. 28–62). Hershey, PA: IGI Global. doi:10.4018/978-1-5225-2075-7.ch002

Jha, D. G. (2016). Preparing for Information Technology Driven Changes. In S. Tiwari & L. Nafees (Eds.), *Innovative Management Education Pedagogies for Preparing Next-Generation Leaders* (pp. 258–274). Hershey, PA: IGI Global. doi:10.4018/978-1-4666-9691-4.ch015

Joia, L. A., & Correia, J. C. (2018). CIO Competencies From the IT Professional Perspective: Insights From Brazil. *Journal of Global Information Management*, 26(2), 74–103. doi:10.4018/JGIM.2018040104

Juma, A., & Mzera, N. (2017). Knowledge Management and Records Management and Competitive Advantage in Business. In P. Jain & N. Mnjama (Eds.), *Managing Knowledge Resources and Records in Modern Organizations* (pp. 15–28). Hershey, PA: IGI Global. doi:10.4018/978-1-5225-1965-2.ch002

K., I., & A, V. (2018). Monitoring and Auditing in the Cloud. In K. Munir (Ed.), *Cloud Computing Technologies for Green Enterprises* (pp. 318-350). Hershey, PA: IGI Global. doi:10.4018/978-1-5225-3038-1.ch013

Kabra, G., Ghosh, V., & Ramesh, A. (2018). Enterprise Integrated Business Process Management and Business Intelligence Framework for Business Process Sustainability. In A. Paul, D. Bhattacharyya, & S. Anand (Eds.), *Green Initiatives for Business Sustainability and Value Creation* (pp. 228–238). Hershey, PA: IGI Global. doi:10.4018/978-1-5225-2662-9.ch010

Kaoud, M. (2017). Investigation of Customer Knowledge Management: A Case Study Research. *International Journal of Service Science, Management, Engineering, and Technology*, 8(2), 12–22. doi:10.4018/IJSSMET.2017040102

Kara, M. E., & Fırat, S. Ü. (2016). Sustainability, Risk, and Business Intelligence in Supply Chains. In M. Erdoğdu, T. Arun, & I. Ahmad (Eds.), *Handbook of Research on Green Economic Development Initiatives and Strategies* (pp. 501–538). Hershey, PA: IGI Global. doi:10.4018/978-1-5225-0440-5.ch022

Katuu, S. (2018). A Comparative Assessment of Enterprise Content Management Maturity Models. In N. Gwangwava & M. Mutingi (Eds.), *E-Manufacturing and E-Service Strategies in Contemporary Organizations* (pp. 93–118). Hershey, PA: IGI Global. doi:10.4018/978-1-5225-3628-4.ch005

Khan, M. A. (2016). MNEs Management Strategies in Developing Countries: Establishing the Context. In M. Khan (Ed.), *Multinational Enterprise Management Strategies in Developing Countries* (pp. 1–33). Hershey, PA: IGI Global. doi:10.4018/978-1-5225-0276-0.ch001

Khan, M. A. (2016). Operational Approaches in Organizational Structure: A Case for MNEs in Developing Countries. In M. Khan (Ed.), *Multinational Enterprise Management Strategies in Developing Countries* (pp. 129–151). Hershey, PA: IGI Global. doi:10.4018/978-1-5225-0276-0.ch007

Kinnunen, S., Ylä-Kujala, A., Marttonen-Arola, S., Kärri, T., & Baglee, D. (2018). Internet of Things in Asset Management: Insights from Industrial Professionals and Academia. *International Journal of Service Science, Management, Engineering, and Technology*, 9(2), 104–119. doi:10.4018/IJSSMET.2018040105

Klein, A. Z., Sabino de Freitas, A., Machado, L., Freitas, J. C. Jr, Graziola, P. G. Jr, & Schlemmer, E. (2017). Virtual Worlds Applications for Management Education. In L. Tomei (Ed.), *Exploring the New Era of Technology-Infused Education* (pp. 279–299). Hershey, PA: IGI Global. doi:10.4018/978-1-5225-1709-2.ch017

Kożuch, B., & Jabłoński, A. (2017). Adopting the Concept of Business Models in Public Management. In M. Lewandowski & B. Kożuch (Eds.), *Public Sector Entrepreneurship and the Integration of Innovative Business Models* (pp. 10–46). Hershey, PA: IGI Global. doi:10.4018/978-1-5225-2215-7.ch002

Kumar, J., Adhikary, A., & Jha, A. (2017). Small Active Investors' Perceptions and Preferences Towards Tax Saving Mutual Fund Schemes in Eastern India: An Empirical Note. *International Journal of Asian Business and Information Management*, 8(2), 35–45. doi:10.4018/IJABIM.2017040103

Lassoued, Y., Bouzguenda, L., & Mahmoud, T. (2016). Context-Aware Business Process Versions Management. *International Journal of e-Collaboration*, *12*(3), 7–33. doi:10.4018/IJeC.2016070102

Lavassani, K. M., & Movahedi, B. (2017). Applications Driven Information Systems: Beyond Networks toward Business Ecosystems. *International Journal of Innovation in the Digital Economy*, 8(1), 61–75. doi:10.4018/IJIDE.2017010104

Lazzareschi, V. H., & Brito, M. S. (2017). Strategic Information Management: Proposal of Business Project Model. In G. Jamil, A. Soares, & C. Pessoa (Eds.), *Handbook of Research on Information Management for Effective Logistics and Supply Chains* (pp. 59–88). Hershey, PA: IGI Global. doi:10.4018/978-1-5225-0973-8.ch004

Lederer, M., Kurz, M., & Lazarov, P. (2017). Usage and Suitability of Methods for Strategic Business Process Initiatives: A Multi Case Study Research. *International Journal of Productivity Management and Assessment Technologies*, 5(1), 40–51. doi:10.4018/IJPMAT.2017010103

Lee, I. (2017). A Social Enterprise Business Model and a Case Study of Pacific Community Ventures (PCV). In V. Potocan, M. Üngan, & Z. Nedelko (Eds.), *Handbook of Research on Managerial Solutions in Non-Profit Organizations* (pp. 182–204). Hershey, PA: IGI Global. doi:10.4018/978-1-5225-0731-4.ch009

Lee, L. J., & Leu, J. (2016). Exploring the Effectiveness of IT Application and Value Method in the Innovation Performance of Enterprise. *International Journal of Enterprise Information Systems*, 12(2), 47–65. doi:10.4018/IJEIS.2016040104

Lee, Y. (2016). Alignment Effect of Entrepreneurial Orientation and Marketing Orientation on Firm Performance. *International Journal of Customer Relationship Marketing and Management*, 7(4), 58–69. doi:10.4018/IJCRMM.2016100104

Leon, L. A., Seal, K. C., Przasnyski, Z. H., & Wiedenman, I. (2017). Skills and Competencies Required for Jobs in Business Analytics: A Content Analysis of Job Advertisements Using Text Mining. *International Journal of Business Intelligence Research*, 8(1), 1–25. doi:10.4018/IJBIR.2017010101

Leu, J., Lee, L. J., & Krischke, A. (2016). Value Engineering-Based Method for Implementing the ISO14001 System in the Green Supply Chains. *International Journal of Strategic Decision Sciences*, 7(4), 1–20. doi:10.4018/IJSDS.2016100101

Levy, C. L., & Elias, N. I. (2017). SOHO Users' Perceptions of Reliability and Continuity of Cloud-Based Services. In M. Moore (Ed.), *Cybersecurity Breaches and Issues Surrounding Online Threat Protection* (pp. 248–287). Hershey, PA: IGI Global. doi:10.4018/978-1-5225-1941-6.ch011

Levy, M. (2018). Change Management Serving Knowledge Management and Organizational Development: Reflections and Review. In N. Baporikar (Ed.), *Global Practices in Knowledge Management for Societal and Organizational Development* (pp. 256–270). Hershey, PA: IGI Global. doi:10.4018/978-1-5225-3009-1.ch012

Lewandowski, M. (2017). Public Organizations and Business Model Innovation: The Role of Public Service Design. In M. Lewandowski & B. Kożuch (Eds.), *Public Sector Entrepreneurship and the Integration of Innovative Business Models* (pp. 47–72). Hershey, PA: IGI Global. doi:10.4018/978-1-5225-2215-7.ch003

Lhannaoui, H., Kabbaj, M. I., & Bakkoury, Z. (2017). A Survey of Risk-Aware Business Process Modelling. *International Journal of Risk and Contingency Management, 6*(3), 14–26. doi:10.4018/IJRCM.2017070102

Li, J., Sun, W., Jiang, W., Yang, H., & Zhang, L. (2017). How the Nature of Exogenous Shocks and Crises Impact Company Performance?: The Effects of Industry Characteristics. *International Journal of Risk and Contingency Management, 6*(4), 40–55. doi:10.4018/IJRCM.2017100103

Lu, C., & Liu, S. (2016). Cultural Tourism O2O Business Model Innovation-A Case Study of CTrip. *Journal of Electronic Commerce in Organizations, 14*(2), 16–31. doi:10.4018/JECO.2016040102

Machen, B., Hosseini, M. R., Wood, A., & Bakhshi, J. (2016). An Investigation into using SAP-PS as a Multidimensional Project Control System (MPCS). *International Journal of Enterprise Information Systems, 12*(2), 66–81. doi:10.4018/IJEIS.2016040105

Malega, P. (2017). Small and Medium Enterprises in the Slovak Republic: Status and Competitiveness of SMEs in the Global Markets and Possibilities of Optimization. In M. Vemić (Ed.), *Optimal Management Strategies in Small and Medium Enterprises* (pp. 102–124). Hershey, PA: IGI Global. doi:10.4018/978-1-5225-1949-2.ch006

Malewska, K. M. (2017). Intuition in Decision-Making on the Example of a Non-Profit Organization. In V. Potocan, M. Üngan, & Z. Nedelko (Eds.), *Handbook of Research on Managerial Solutions in Non-Profit Organizations* (pp. 378–399). Hershey, PA: IGI Global. doi:10.4018/978-1-5225-0731-4.ch018

Maroofi, F. (2017). Entrepreneurial Orientation and Organizational Learning Ability Analysis for Innovation and Firm Performance. In N. Baporikar (Ed.), *Innovation and Shifting Perspectives in Management Education* (pp. 144–165). Hershey, PA: IGI Global. doi:10.4018/978-1-5225-1019-2.ch007

Martins, P. V., & Zacarias, M. (2017). A Web-based Tool for Business Process Improvement. *International Journal of Web Portals*, *9*(2), 68–84. doi:10.4018/IJWP.2017070104

Matthies, B., & Coners, A. (2017). Exploring the Conceptual Nature of e-Business Projects. *Journal of Electronic Commerce in Organizations*, *15*(3), 33–63. doi:10.4018/JECO.2017070103

McKee, J. (2018). Architecture as a Tool to Solve Business Planning Problems. In M. Khosrow-Pour, D.B.A. (Ed.), Encyclopedia of Information Science and Technology, Fourth Edition (pp. 573-586). Hershey, PA: IGI Global. doi:10.4018/978-1-5225-2255-3.ch050

McMurray, A. J., Cross, J., & Caponecchia, C. (2018). The Risk Management Profession in Australia: Business Continuity Plan Practices. In N. Bajgoric (Ed.), *Always-On Enterprise Information Systems for Modern Organizations* (pp. 112–129). Hershey, PA: IGI Global. doi:10.4018/978-1-5225-3704-5.ch006

Meddah, I. H., & Belkadi, K. (2018). Mining Patterns Using Business Process Management. In R. Hamou (Ed.), *Handbook of Research on Biomimicry in Information Retrieval and Knowledge Management* (pp. 78–89). Hershey, PA: IGI Global. doi:10.4018/978-1-5225-3004-6.ch005

Mendes, L. (2017). TQM and Knowledge Management: An Integrated Approach Towards Tacit Knowledge Management. In D. Jaziri-Bouagina & G. Jamil (Eds.), *Handbook of Research on Tacit Knowledge Management for Organizational Success* (pp. 236–263). Hershey, PA: IGI Global. doi:10.4018/978-1-5225-2394-9.ch009

Mnjama, N. M. (2017). Preservation of Recorded Information in Public and Private Sector Organizations. In P. Jain & N. Mnjama (Eds.), *Managing Knowledge Resources and Records in Modern Organizations* (pp. 149–167). Hershey, PA: IGI Global. doi:10.4018/978-1-5225-1965-2.ch009

Mokoqama, M., & Fields, Z. (2017). Principles of Responsible Management Education (PRME): Call for Responsible Management Education. In Z. Fields (Ed.), *Collective Creativity for Responsible and Sustainable Business Practice* (pp. 229–241). Hershey, PA: IGI Global. doi:10.4018/978-1-5225-1823-5.ch012

Muniapan, B. (2017). Philosophy and Management: The Relevance of Vedanta in Management. In P. Ordóñez de Pablos (Ed.), *Managerial Strategies and Solutions for Business Success in Asia* (pp. 124–139). Hershey, PA: IGI Global. doi:10.4018/978-1-5225-1886-0.ch007

Muniapan, B., Gregory, M. L., & Ling, L. A. (2016). Marketing Education in Sarawak: Looking at It from the Employers' Viewpoint. In B. Smith & A. Porath (Eds.), *Global Perspectives on Contemporary Marketing Education* (pp. 112–130). Hershey, PA: IGI Global. doi:10.4018/978-1-4666-9784-3.ch008

Murad, S. E., & Dowaji, S. (2017). Using Value-Based Approach for Managing Cloud-Based Services. In A. Turuk, B. Sahoo, & S. Addya (Eds.), *Resource Management and Efficiency in Cloud Computing Environments* (pp. 33–60). Hershey, PA: IGI Global. doi:10.4018/978-1-5225-1721-4.ch002

Mutahar, A. M., Daud, N. M., Thurasamy, R., Isaac, O., & Abdulsalam, R. (2018). The Mediating of Perceived Usefulness and Perceived Ease of Use: The Case of Mobile Banking in Yemen. *International Journal of Technology Diffusion*, *9*(2), 21–40. doi:10.4018/IJTD.2018040102

Naidoo, V. (2017). E-Learning and Management Education at African Universities. In N. Baporikar (Ed.), *Management Education for Global Leadership* (pp. 181–201). Hershey, PA: IGI Global. doi:10.4018/978-1-5225-1013-0.ch009

Naidoo, V., & Igbinakhase, I. (2018). Opportunities and Challenges of Knowledge Retention in SMEs. In N. Baporikar (Ed.), *Knowledge Integration Strategies for Entrepreneurship and Sustainability* (pp. 70–94). Hershey, PA: IGI Global. doi:10.4018/978-1-5225-5115-7.ch004

Nayak, S., & Prabhu, N. (2017). Paradigm Shift in Management Education: Need for a Cross Functional Perspective. In N. Baporikar (Ed.), *Management Education for Global Leadership* (pp. 241–255). Hershey, PA: IGI Global. doi:10.4018/978-1-5225-1013-0.ch012

Ndede-Amadi, A. A. (2016). Student Interest in the IS Specialization as Predictor of the Success Potential of New Information Systems Programmes within the Schools of Business in Kenyan Public Universities. *International Journal of Information Systems and Social Change*, *7*(2), 63–79. doi:10.4018/IJISSC.2016040104

Nedelko, Z., & Potocan, V. (2016). Management Practices for Processes Optimization: Case of Slovenia. In G. Alor-Hernández, C. Sánchez-Ramírez, & J. García-Alcaraz (Eds.), *Handbook of Research on Managerial Strategies for Achieving Optimal Performance in Industrial Processes* (pp. 545–561). Hershey, PA: IGI Global. doi:10.4018/978-1-5225-0130-5.ch025

Nedelko, Z., & Potocan, V. (2017). Management Solutions in Non-Profit Organizations: Case of Slovenia. In V. Potocan, M. Üngan, & Z. Nedelko (Eds.), *Handbook of Research on Managerial Solutions in Non-Profit Organizations* (pp. 1–22). Hershey, PA: IGI Global. doi:10.4018/978-1-5225-0731-4.ch001

Nedelko, Z., & Potocan, V. (2017). Priority of Management Tools Utilization among Managers: International Comparison. In V. Wang (Ed.), *Encyclopedia of Strategic Leadership and Management* (pp. 1083–1094). Hershey, PA: IGI Global. doi:10.4018/978-1-5225-1049-9.ch075

Nedelko, Z., Raudeliūnienė, J., & Črešnar, R. (2018). Knowledge Dynamics in Supply Chain Management. In N. Baporikar (Ed.), *Knowledge Integration Strategies for Entrepreneurship and Sustainability* (pp. 150–166). Hershey, PA: IGI Global. doi:10.4018/978-1-5225-5115-7.ch008

Nguyen, H. T., & Hipsher, S. A. (2018). Innovation and Creativity Used by Private Sector Firms in a Resources-Constrained Environment. In S. Hipsher (Ed.), *Examining the Private Sector's Role in Wealth Creation and Poverty Reduction* (pp. 219–238). Hershey, PA: IGI Global. doi:10.4018/978-1-5225-3117-3.ch010

Nycz, M., & Pólkowski, Z. (2016). Business Intelligence as a Modern IT Supporting Management of Local Government Units in Poland. *International Journal of Knowledge and Systems Science, 7*(4), 1–18. doi:10.4018/IJKSS.2016100101

Obaji, N. O., Senin, A. A., & Olugu, M. U. (2016). Supportive Government Policy as a Mechanism for Business Incubation Performance in Nigeria. *International Journal of Information Systems and Social Change, 7*(4), 52–66. doi:10.4018/IJISSC.2016100103

Obicci, P. A. (2017). Risk Sharing in a Partnership. In *Risk Management Strategies in Public-Private Partnerships* (pp. 115–152). Hershey, PA: IGI Global. doi:10.4018/978-1-5225-2503-5.ch004

Obidallah, W. J., & Raahemi, B. (2017). Managing Changes in Service Oriented Virtual Organizations: A Structural and Procedural Framework to Facilitate the Process of Change. *Journal of Electronic Commerce in Organizations, 15*(1), 59–83. doi:10.4018/JECO.2017010104

Ojasalo, J., & Ojasalo, K. (2016). Service Logic Business Model Canvas for Lean Development of SMEs and Start-Ups. In N. Baporikar (Ed.), *Handbook of Research on Entrepreneurship in the Contemporary Knowledge-Based Global Economy* (pp. 217–243). Hershey, PA: IGI Global. doi:10.4018/978-1-4666-8798-1.ch010

Ojo, O. (2017). Impact of Innovation on the Entrepreneurial Success in Selected Business Enterprises in South-West Nigeria. *International Journal of Innovation in the Digital Economy*, 8(2), 29–38. doi:10.4018/IJIDE.2017040103

Okdinawati, L., Simatupang, T. M., & Sunitiyoso, Y. (2017). Multi-Agent Reinforcement Learning for Value Co-Creation of Collaborative Transportation Management (CTM). *International Journal of Information Systems and Supply Chain Management*, 10(3), 84–95. doi:10.4018/IJISSCM.2017070105

Ortner, E., Mevius, M., Wiedmann, P., & Kurz, F. (2016). Design of Interactional Decision Support Applications for E-Participation in Smart Cities. *International Journal of Electronic Government Research*, 12(2), 18–38. doi:10.4018/IJEGR.2016040102

Pal, K. (2018). Building High Quality Big Data-Based Applications in Supply Chains. In A. Kumar & S. Saurav (Eds.), *Supply Chain Management Strategies and Risk Assessment in Retail Environments* (pp. 1–24). Hershey, PA: IGI Global. doi:10.4018/978-1-5225-3056-5.ch001

Palos-Sanchez, P. R., & Correia, M. B. (2018). Perspectives of the Adoption of Cloud Computing in the Tourism Sector. In J. Rodrigues, C. Ramos, P. Cardoso, & C. Henriques (Eds.), *Handbook of Research on Technological Developments for Cultural Heritage and eTourism Applications* (pp. 377–400). Hershey, PA: IGI Global. doi:10.4018/978-1-5225-2927-9.ch018

Parry, V. K., & Lind, M. L. (2016). Alignment of Business Strategy and Information Technology Considering Information Technology Governance, Project Portfolio Control, and Risk Management. *International Journal of Information Technology Project Management*, 7(4), 21–37. doi:10.4018/IJITPM.2016100102

Pashkova, N., Trujillo-Barrera, A., Apostolakis, G., Van Dijk, G., Drakos, P. D., & Baourakis, G. (2016). Business Management Models of Microfinance Institutions (MFIs) in Africa: A Study into Their Enabling Environments. *International Journal of Food and Beverage Manufacturing and Business Models*, 1(2), 63–82. doi:10.4018/IJFBMBM.2016070105

Patiño, B. E. (2017). New Generation Management by Convergence and Individual Identity: A Systemic and Human-Oriented Approach. In N. Baporikar (Ed.), *Innovation and Shifting Perspectives in Management Education* (pp. 119–143). Hershey, PA: IGI Global. doi:10.4018/978-1-5225-1019-2.ch006

Pawliczek, A., & Rössler, M. (2017). Knowledge of Management Tools and Systems in SMEs: Knowledge Transfer in Management. In A. Bencsik (Ed.), *Knowledge Management Initiatives and Strategies in Small and Medium Enterprises* (pp. 180–203). Hershey, PA: IGI Global. doi:10.4018/978-1-5225-1642-2.ch009

Pejic-Bach, M., Omazic, M. A., Aleksic, A., & Zoroja, J. (2018). Knowledge-Based Decision Making: A Multi-Case Analysis. In R. Leon (Ed.), *Managerial Strategies for Business Sustainability During Turbulent Times* (pp. 160–184). Hershey, PA: IGI Global. doi:10.4018/978-1-5225-2716-9.ch009

Perano, M., Hysa, X., & Calabrese, M. (2018). Strategic Planning, Cultural Context, and Business Continuity Management: Business Cases in the City of Shkoder. In A. Presenza & L. Sheehan (Eds.), *Geopolitics and Strategic Management in the Global Economy* (pp. 57–77). Hershey, PA: IGI Global. doi:10.4018/978-1-5225-2673-5.ch004

Pereira, R., Mira da Silva, M., & Lapão, L. V. (2017). IT Governance Maturity Patterns in Portuguese Healthcare. In S. De Haes & W. Van Grembergen (Eds.), *Strategic IT Governance and Alignment in Business Settings* (pp. 24–52). Hershey, PA: IGI Global. doi:10.4018/978-1-5225-0861-8.ch002

Perez-Uribe, R., & Ocampo-Guzman, D. (2016). Conflict within Colombian Family Owned SMEs: An Explosive Blend between Feelings and Business. In J. Saiz-Álvarez (Ed.), *Handbook of Research on Social Entrepreneurship and Solidarity Economics* (pp. 329–354). Hershey, PA: IGI Global. doi:10.4018/978-1-5225-0097-1.ch017

Pérez-Uribe, R. I., Torres, D. A., Jurado, S. P., & Prada, D. M. (2018). Cloud Tools for the Development of Project Management in SMEs. In R. Perez-Uribe, C. Salcedo-Perez, & D. Ocampo-Guzman (Eds.), *Handbook of Research on Intrapreneurship and Organizational Sustainability in SMEs* (pp. 95–120). Hershey, PA: IGI Global. doi:10.4018/978-1-5225-3543-0.ch005

Petrisor, I., & Cozmiuc, D. (2017). Global Supply Chain Management Organization at Siemens in the Advent of Industry 4.0. In L. Saglietto & C. Cezanne (Eds.), *Global Intermediation and Logistics Service Providers* (pp. 123–142). Hershey, PA: IGI Global. doi:10.4018/978-1-5225-2133-4.ch007

Pierce, J. M., Velliaris, D. M., & Edwards, J. (2017). A Living Case Study: A Journey Not a Destination. In N. Silton (Ed.), *Exploring the Benefits of Creativity in Education, Media, and the Arts* (pp. 158–178). Hershey, PA: IGI Global. doi:10.4018/978-1-5225-0504-4.ch008

Radosavljevic, M., & Andjelkovic, A. (2017). Multi-Criteria Decision Making Approach for Choosing Business Process for the Improvement: Upgrading of the Six Sigma Methodology. In J. Stanković, P. Delias, S. Marinković, & S. Rochhia (Eds.), *Tools and Techniques for Economic Decision Analysis* (pp. 225–247). Hershey, PA: IGI Global. doi:10.4018/978-1-5225-0959-2.ch011

Radovic, V. M. (2017). Corporate Sustainability and Responsibility and Disaster Risk Reduction: A Serbian Overview. In M. Camilleri (Ed.), *CSR 2.0 and the New Era of Corporate Citizenship* (pp. 147–164). Hershey, PA: IGI Global. doi:10.4018/978-1-5225-1842-6.ch008

Raghunath, K. M., Devi, S. L., & Patro, C. S. (2018). Impact of Risk Assessment Models on Risk Factors: A Holistic Outlook. In K. Strang, M. Korstanje, & N. Vajjhala (Eds.), *Research, Practices, and Innovations in Global Risk and Contingency Management* (pp. 134–153). Hershey, PA: IGI Global. doi:10.4018/978-1-5225-4754-9.ch008

Raman, A., & Goyal, D. P. (2017). Extending IMPLEMENT Framework for Enterprise Information Systems Implementation to Information System Innovation. In M. Tavana (Ed.), *Enterprise Information Systems and the Digitalization of Business Functions* (pp. 137–177). Hershey, PA: IGI Global. doi:10.4018/978-1-5225-2382-6.ch007

Rao, Y., & Zhang, Y. (2017). The Construction and Development of Academic Library Digital Special Subject Databases. In L. Ruan, Q. Zhu, & Y. Ye (Eds.), *Academic Library Development and Administration in China* (pp. 163–183). Hershey, PA: IGI Global. doi:10.4018/978-1-5225-0550-1.ch010

Ravasan, A. Z., Mohammadi, M. M., & Hamidi, H. (2018). An Investigation Into the Critical Success Factors of Implementing Information Technology Service Management Frameworks. In K. Jakobs (Ed.), *Corporate and Global Standardization Initiatives in Contemporary Society* (pp. 200–218). Hershey, PA: IGI Global. doi:10.4018/978-1-5225-5320-5.ch009

Renna, P., Izzo, C., & Romaniello, T. (2016). The Business Process Management Systems to Support Continuous Improvements. In W. Nuninger & J. Châtelet (Eds.), *Handbook of Research on Quality Assurance and Value Management in Higher Education* (pp. 237–256). Hershey, PA: IGI Global. doi:10.4018/978-1-5225-0024-7.ch009

Rezaie, S., Mirabedini, S. J., & Abtahi, A. (2018). Designing a Model for Implementation of Business Intelligence in the Banking Industry. *International Journal of Enterprise Information Systems*, *14*(1), 77–103. doi:10.4018/IJEIS.2018010105

Riccò, R. (2016). Diversity Management: Bringing Equality, Equity, and Inclusion in the Workplace. In J. Prescott (Ed.), *Handbook of Research on Race, Gender, and the Fight for Equality* (pp. 335–359). Hershey, PA: IGI Global. doi:10.4018/978-1-5225-0047-6.ch015

Romano, L., Grimaldi, R., & Colasuonno, F. S. (2017). Demand Management as a Success Factor in Project Portfolio Management. In L. Romano (Ed.), *Project Portfolio Management Strategies for Effective Organizational Operations* (pp. 202–219). Hershey, PA: IGI Global. doi:10.4018/978-1-5225-2151-8.ch008

Rostek, K. B. (2016). Risk Management: Role and Importance in Business Organization. In D. Jakóbczak (Ed.), *Analyzing Risk through Probabilistic Modeling in Operations Research* (pp. 149–178). Hershey, PA: IGI Global. doi:10.4018/978-1-4666-9458-3.ch007

Rouhani, S., & Savoji, S. R. (2016). A Success Assessment Model for BI Tools Implementation: An Empirical Study of Banking Industry. *International Journal of Business Intelligence Research*, 7(1), 25–44. doi:10.4018/IJBIR.2016010103

Ruan, Z. (2016). A Corpus-Based Functional Analysis of Complex Nominal Groups in Written Business Discourse: The Case of "Business". *International Journal of Computer-Assisted Language Learning and Teaching*, 6(2), 74–90. doi:10.4018/IJCALLT.2016040105

Ruhi, U. (2018). Towards an Interdisciplinary Socio-Technical Definition of Virtual Communities. In M. Khosrow-Pour, D.B.A. (Ed.), Encyclopedia of Information Science and Technology, Fourth Edition (pp. 4278-4295). Hershey, PA: IGI Global. doi:10.4018/978-1-5225-2255-3.ch371

Ryan, J., Doster, B., Daily, S., & Lewis, C. (2016). A Case Study Perspective for Balanced Perioperative Workflow Achievement through Data-Driven Process Improvement. *International Journal of Healthcare Information Systems and Informatics*, 11(3), 19–41. doi:10.4018/IJHISI.2016070102

Safari, M. R., & Jiang, Q. (2018). The Theory and Practice of IT Governance Maturity and Strategies Alignment: Evidence From Banking Industry. *Journal of Global Information Management*, 26(2), 127–146. doi:10.4018/JGIM.2018040106

Sahoo, J., Pati, B., & Mohanty, B. (2017). Knowledge Management as an Academic Discipline: An Assessment. In B. Gunjal (Ed.), *Managing Knowledge and Scholarly Assets in Academic Libraries* (pp. 99–126). Hershey, PA: IGI Global. doi:10.4018/978-1-5225-1741-2.ch005

Saini, D. (2017). Relevance of Teaching Values and Ethics in Management Education. In N. Baporikar (Ed.), *Management Education for Global Leadership* (pp. 90–111). Hershey, PA: IGI Global. doi:10.4018/978-1-5225-1013-0.ch005

Sambhanthan, A. (2017). Assessing and Benchmarking Sustainability in Organisations: An Integrated Conceptual Model. *International Journal of Systems and Service-Oriented Engineering*, 7(4), 22–43. doi:10.4018/IJSSOE.2017100102

Sambhanthan, A., & Potdar, V. (2017). A Study of the Parameters Impacting Sustainability in Information Technology Organizations. *International Journal of Knowledge-Based Organizations*, 7(3), 27–39. doi:10.4018/IJKBO.2017070103

Sánchez-Fernández, M. D., & Manríquez, M. R. (2018). The Entrepreneurial Spirit Based on Social Values: The Digital Generation. In P. Isaias & L. Carvalho (Eds.), *User Innovation and the Entrepreneurship Phenomenon in the Digital Economy* (pp. 173–193). Hershey, PA: IGI Global. doi:10.4018/978-1-5225-2826-5.ch009

Sanchez-Ruiz, L., & Blanco, B. (2017). Process Management for SMEs: Barriers, Enablers, and Benefits. In M. Vemić (Ed.), *Optimal Management Strategies in Small and Medium Enterprises* (pp. 293–319). Hershey, PA: IGI Global. doi:10.4018/978-1-5225-1949-2.ch014

Sanz, L. F., Gómez-Pérez, J., & Castillo-Martinez, A. (2018). Analysis of the European ICT Competence Frameworks. In V. Ahuja & S. Rathore (Eds.), *Multidisciplinary Perspectives on Human Capital and Information Technology Professionals* (pp. 225–245). Hershey, PA: IGI Global. doi:10.4018/978-1-5225-5297-0.ch012

Sarvepalli, A., & Godin, J. (2017). Business Process Management in the Classroom. *Journal of Cases on Information Technology*, 19(2), 17–28. doi:10.4018/JCIT.2017040102

Satpathy, B., & Muniapan, B. (2016). Ancient Wisdom for Transformational Leadership and Its Insights from the Bhagavad-Gita. In U. Aung & P. Ordoñez de Pablos (Eds.), *Managerial Strategies and Practice in the Asian Business Sector* (pp. 1–10). Hershey, PA: IGI Global. doi:10.4018/978-1-4666-9758-4.ch001

Saygili, E. E., Ozturkoglu, Y., & Kocakulah, M. C. (2017). End Users' Perceptions of Critical Success Factors in ERP Applications. *International Journal of Enterprise Information Systems*, 13(4), 58–75. doi:10.4018/IJEIS.2017100104

Saygili, E. E., & Saygili, A. T. (2017). Contemporary Issues in Enterprise Information Systems: A Critical Review of CSFs in ERP Implementations. In M. Tavana (Ed.), *Enterprise Information Systems and the Digitalization of Business Functions* (pp. 120–136). Hershey, PA: IGI Global. doi:10.4018/978-1-5225-2382-6.ch006

Seidenstricker, S., & Antonino, A. (2018). Business Model Innovation-Oriented Technology Management for Emergent Technologies. In M. Khosrow-Pour, D.B.A. (Ed.), Encyclopedia of Information Science and Technology, Fourth Edition (pp. 4560-4569). Hershey, PA: IGI Global. doi:10.4018/978-1-5225-2255-3.ch396

Senaratne, S., & Gunarathne, A. D. (2017). Excellence Perspective for Management Education from a Global Accountants' Hub in Asia. In N. Baporikar (Ed.), *Management Education for Global Leadership* (pp. 158–180). Hershey, PA: IGI Global. doi:10.4018/978-1-5225-1013-0.ch008

Sensuse, D. I., & Cahyaningsih, E. (2018). Knowledge Management Models: A Summative Review. *International Journal of Information Systems in the Service Sector*, *10*(1), 71–100. doi:10.4018/IJISSS.2018010105

Sensuse, D. I., Wibowo, W. C., & Cahyaningsih, E. (2016). Indonesian Government Knowledge Management Model: A Theoretical Model. *Information Resources Management Journal*, *29*(1), 91–108. doi:10.4018/irmj.2016010106

Seth, M., Goyal, D., & Kiran, R. (2017). Diminution of Impediments in Implementation of Supply Chain Management Information System for Enhancing its Effectiveness in Indian Automobile Industry. *Journal of Global Information Management*, *25*(3), 1–20. doi:10.4018/JGIM.2017070101

Seyal, A. H., & Rahman, M. N. (2017). Investigating Impact of Inter-Organizational Factors in Measuring ERP Systems Success: Bruneian Perspectives. In M. Tavana (Ed.), *Enterprise Information Systems and the Digitalization of Business Functions* (pp. 178–204). Hershey, PA: IGI Global. doi:10.4018/978-1-5225-2382-6.ch008

Shaikh, A. A., & Karjaluoto, H. (2016). On Some Misconceptions Concerning Digital Banking and Alternative Delivery Channels. *International Journal of E-Business Research*, *12*(3), 1–16. doi:10.4018/IJEBR.2016070101

Shams, S. M. (2016). Stakeholder Relationship Management in Online Business and Competitive Value Propositions: Evidence from the Sports Industry. *International Journal of Online Marketing*, *6*(2), 1–17. doi:10.4018/IJOM.2016040101

Shamsuzzoha, A. (2016). Management of Risk and Resilience within Collaborative Business Network. In R. Addo-Tenkorang, J. Kantola, P. Helo, & A. Shamsuzzoha (Eds.), *Supply Chain Strategies and the Engineer-to-Order Approach* (pp. 143–159). Hershey, PA: IGI Global. doi:10.4018/978-1-5225-0021-6.ch008

Shaqrah, A. A. (2018). Analyzing Business Intelligence Systems Based on 7s Model of McKinsey. *International Journal of Business Intelligence Research*, *9*(1), 53–63. doi:10.4018/IJBIR.2018010104

Sharma, A. J. (2017). Enhancing Sustainability through Experiential Learning in Management Education. In N. Baporikar (Ed.), *Management Education for Global Leadership* (pp. 256–274). Hershey, PA: IGI Global. doi:10.4018/978-1-5225-1013-0.ch013

Shetty, K. P. (2017). Responsible Global Leadership: Ethical Challenges in Management Education. In N. Baporikar (Ed.), *Innovation and Shifting Perspectives in Management Education* (pp. 194–223). Hershey, PA: IGI Global. doi:10.4018/978-1-5225-1019-2.ch009

Sinthupundaja, J., & Kohda, Y. (2017). Effects of Corporate Social Responsibility and Creating Shared Value on Sustainability. *International Journal of Sustainable Entrepreneurship and Corporate Social Responsibility*, 2(1), 27–38. doi:10.4018/IJSECSR.2017010103

Škarica, I., & Hrgović, A. V. (2018). Implementation of Total Quality Management Principles in Public Health Institutes in the Republic of Croatia. *International Journal of Productivity Management and Assessment Technologies*, 6(1), 1–16. doi:10.4018/IJPMAT.2018010101

Smuts, H., Kotzé, P., Van der Merwe, A., & Loock, M. (2017). Framework for Managing Shared Knowledge in an Information Systems Outsourcing Context. *International Journal of Knowledge Management*, 13(4), 1–30. doi:10.4018/IJKM.2017100101

Soares, E. R., & Zaidan, F. H. (2016). Information Architecture and Business Modeling in Modern Organizations of Information Technology: Professional Career Plan in Organizations IT. In G. Jamil, J. Poças Rascão, F. Ribeiro, & A. Malheiro da Silva (Eds.), *Handbook of Research on Information Architecture and Management in Modern Organizations* (pp. 439–457). Hershey, PA: IGI Global. doi:10.4018/978-1-4666-8637-3.ch020

Sousa, M. J., Cruz, R., Dias, I., & Caracol, C. (2017). Information Management Systems in the Supply Chain. In G. Jamil, A. Soares, & C. Pessoa (Eds.), *Handbook of Research on Information Management for Effective Logistics and Supply Chains* (pp. 469–485). Hershey, PA: IGI Global. doi:10.4018/978-1-5225-0973-8.ch025

Spremic, M., Turulja, L., & Bajgoric, N. (2018). Two Approaches in Assessing Business Continuity Management Attitudes in the Organizational Context. In N. Bajgoric (Ed.), *Always-On Enterprise Information Systems for Modern Organizations* (pp. 159–183). Hershey, PA: IGI Global. doi:10.4018/978-1-5225-3704-5.ch008

Steenkamp, A. L. (2018). Some Insights in Computer Science and Information Technology. In *Examining the Changing Role of Supervision in Doctoral Research Projects: Emerging Research and Opportunities* (pp. 113–133). Hershey, PA: IGI Global. doi:10.4018/978-1-5225-2610-0.ch005

Studdard, N., Dawson, M., Burton, S. L., Jackson, N., Leonard, B., Quisenberry, W., & Rahim, E. (2016). Nurturing Social Entrepreneurship and Building Social Entrepreneurial Self-Efficacy: Focusing on Primary and Secondary Schooling to Develop Future Social Entrepreneurs. In Z. Fields (Ed.), *Incorporating Business Models and Strategies into Social Entrepreneurship* (pp. 154–175). Hershey, PA: IGI Global. doi:10.4018/978-1-4666-8748-6.ch010

Sun, Z. (2016). A Framework for Developing Management Intelligent Systems. *International Journal of Systems and Service-Oriented Engineering, 6*(1), 37–53. doi:10.4018/IJSSOE.2016010103

Swami, B., & Mphele, G. T. (2016). Problems Preventing Growth of Small Entrepreneurs: A Case Study of a Few Small Entrepreneurs in Botswana Sub-Urban Areas. In N. Baporikar (Ed.), *Handbook of Research on Entrepreneurship in the Contemporary Knowledge-Based Global Economy* (pp. 479–508). Hershey, PA: IGI Global. doi:10.4018/978-1-4666-8798-1.ch020

Tabach, A., & Croteau, A. (2017). Configurations of Information Technology Governance Practices and Business Unit Performance. *International Journal of IT/Business Alignment and Governance, 8*(2), 1–27. doi:10.4018/IJITBAG.2017070101

Talaue, G. M., & Iqbal, T. (2017). Assessment of e-Business Mode of Selected Private Universities in the Philippines and Pakistan. *International Journal of Online Marketing, 7*(4), 63–77. doi:10.4018/IJOM.2017100105

Tam, G. C. (2017). Project Manager Sustainability Competence. In *Managerial Strategies and Green Solutions for Project Sustainability* (pp. 178–207). Hershey, PA: IGI Global. doi:10.4018/978-1-5225-2371-0.ch008

Tambo, T. (2018). Fashion Retail Innovation: About Context, Antecedents, and Outcome in Technological Change Projects. In I. Management Association (Ed.), Fashion and Textiles: Breakthroughs in Research and Practice (pp. 233-260). Hershey, PA: IGI Global. doi:10.4018/978-1-5225-3432-7.ch010

Tambo, T., & Mikkelsen, O. E. (2016). Fashion Supply Chain Optimization: Linking Make-to-Order Purchasing and B2B E-Commerce. In S. Joshi & R. Joshi (Eds.), *Designing and Implementing Global Supply Chain Management* (pp. 1–21). Hershey, PA: IGI Global. doi:10.4018/978-1-4666-9720-1.ch001

Tandon, K. (2016). Innovative Andragogy: The Paradigm Shift to Heutagogy. In S. Tiwari & L. Nafees (Eds.), *Innovative Management Education Pedagogies for Preparing Next-Generation Leaders* (pp. 238–257). Hershey, PA: IGI Global. doi:10.4018/978-1-4666-9691-4.ch014

Tantau, A. D., & Frățilă, L. C. (2018). Information and Management System for Renewable Energy Business. In *Entrepreneurship and Business Development in the Renewable Energy Sector* (pp. 200–244). Hershey, PA: IGI Global. doi:10.4018/978-1-5225-3625-3.ch006

Teixeira, N., Pardal, P. N., & Rafael, B. G. (2018). Internationalization, Financial Performance, and Organizational Challenges: A Success Case in Portugal. In L. Carvalho (Ed.), *Handbook of Research on Entrepreneurial Ecosystems and Social Dynamics in a Globalized World* (pp. 379–423). Hershey, PA: IGI Global. doi:10.4018/978-1-5225-3525-6.ch017

Trad, A., & Kalpić, D. (2016). The E-Business Transformation Framework for E-Commerce Architecture-Modeling Projects. In I. Lee (Ed.), *Encyclopedia of E-Commerce Development, Implementation, and Management* (pp. 733–753). Hershey, PA: IGI Global. doi:10.4018/978-1-4666-9787-4.ch052

Trad, A., & Kalpić, D. (2016). The E-Business Transformation Framework for E-Commerce Control and Monitoring Pattern. In I. Lee (Ed.), *Encyclopedia of E-Commerce Development, Implementation, and Management* (pp. 754–777). Hershey, PA: IGI Global. doi:10.4018/978-1-4666-9787-4.ch053

Trad, A., & Kalpić, D. (2018). The Business Transformation Framework, Agile Project and Change Management. In M. Khosrow-Pour, D.B.A. (Ed.), Encyclopedia of Information Science and Technology, Fourth Edition (pp. 620-635). Hershey, PA: IGI Global. doi:10.4018/978-1-5225-2255-3.ch054

Trad, A., & Kalpić, D. (2018). The Business Transformation and Enterprise Architecture Framework: The Financial Engineering E-Risk Management and E-Law Integration. In B. Sergi, F. Fidanoski, M. Ziolo, & V. Naumovski (Eds.), *Regaining Global Stability After the Financial Crisis* (pp. 46–65). Hershey, PA: IGI Global. doi:10.4018/978-1-5225-4026-7.ch003

Turulja, L., & Bajgoric, N. (2018). Business Continuity and Information Systems: A Systematic Literature Review. In N. Bajgoric (Ed.), *Always-On Enterprise Information Systems for Modern Organizations* (pp. 60–87). Hershey, PA: IGI Global. doi:10.4018/978-1-5225-3704-5.ch004 van Wessel, R. M., de Vries, H. J., & Ribbers, P. M. (2016). Business Benefits through Company IT Standardization. In K. Jakobs (Ed.), *Effective Standardization Management in Corporate Settings* (pp. 34–53). Hershey, PA: IGI Global. doi:10.4018/978-1-4666-9737-9.ch003

Vargas-Hernández, J. G. (2017). Professional Integrity in Business Management Education. In N. Baporikar (Ed.), *Management Education for Global Leadership* (pp. 70–89). Hershey, PA: IGI Global. doi:10.4018/978-1-5225-1013-0.ch004

Vasista, T. G., & AlAbdullatif, A. M. (2017). Role of Electronic Customer Relationship Management in Demand Chain Management: A Predictive Analytic Approach. *International Journal of Information Systems and Supply Chain Management, 10*(1), 53–67. doi:10.4018/IJISSCM.2017010104

Vergidis, K. (2016). Rediscovering Business Processes: Definitions, Patterns, and Modelling Approaches. In P. Papajorgji, F. Pinet, A. Guimarães, & J. Papathanasiou (Eds.), *Automated Enterprise Systems for Maximizing Business Performance* (pp. 97–122). Hershey, PA: IGI Global. doi:10.4018/978-1-4666-8841-4.ch007

Vieru, D., & Bourdeau, S. (2017). Survival in the Digital Era: A Digital Competence-Based Multi-Case Study in the Canadian SME Clothing Industry. *International Journal of Social and Organizational Dynamics in IT, 6*(1), 17–34. doi:10.4018/IJSODIT.2017010102

Vijayan, G., & Kamarulzaman, N. H. (2017). An Introduction to Sustainable Supply Chain Management and Business Implications. In M. Khan, M. Hussain, & M. Ajmal (Eds.), *Green Supply Chain Management for Sustainable Business Practice* (pp. 27–50). Hershey, PA: IGI Global. doi:10.4018/978-1-5225-0635-5.ch002

Vlachvei, A., & Notta, O. (2017). Firm Competitiveness: Theories, Evidence, and Measurement. In A. Vlachvei, O. Notta, K. Karantininis, & N. Tsounis (Eds.), *Factors Affecting Firm Competitiveness and Performance in the Modern Business World* (pp. 1–42). Hershey, PA: IGI Global. doi:10.4018/978-1-5225-0843-4.ch001

von Rosing, M., Fullington, N., & Walker, J. (2016). Using the Business Ontology and Enterprise Standards to Transform Three Leading Organizations. *International Journal of Conceptual Structures and Smart Applications, 4*(1), 71–99. doi:10.4018/IJCSSA.2016010104

von Rosing, M., & von Scheel, H. (2016). Using the Business Ontology to Develop Enterprise Standards. *International Journal of Conceptual Structures and Smart Applications, 4*(1), 48–70. doi:10.4018/IJCSSA.2016010103

Walczak, S. (2016). Artificial Neural Networks and other AI Applications for Business Management Decision Support. *International Journal of Sociotechnology and Knowledge Development*, 8(4), 1–20. doi:10.4018/IJSKD.2016100101

Wamba, S. F., Akter, S., Kang, H., Bhattacharya, M., & Upal, M. (2016). The Primer of Social Media Analytics. *Journal of Organizational and End User Computing*, 28(2), 1–12. doi:10.4018/JOEUC.2016040101

Wang, C., Schofield, M., Li, X., & Ou, X. (2017). Do Chinese Students in Public and Private Higher Education Institutes Perform at Different Level in One of the Leadership Skills: Critical Thinking?: An Exploratory Comparison. In V. Wang (Ed.), *Encyclopedia of Strategic Leadership and Management* (pp. 160–181). Hershey, PA: IGI Global. doi:10.4018/978-1-5225-1049-9.ch013

Wang, F., Raisinghani, M. S., Mora, M., & Wang, X. (2016). Strategic E-Business Management through a Balanced Scored Card Approach. In I. Lee (Ed.), *Encyclopedia of E-Commerce Development, Implementation, and Management* (pp. 361–386). Hershey, PA: IGI Global. doi:10.4018/978-1-4666-9787-4.ch027

Wang, J. (2017). Multi-Agent based Production Management Decision System Modelling for the Textile Enterprise. *Journal of Global Information Management*, 25(4), 1–15. doi:10.4018/JGIM.2017100101

Wiedemann, A., & Gewald, H. (2017). Examining Cross-Domain Alignment: The Correlation of Business Strategy, IT Management, and IT Business Value. *International Journal of IT/Business Alignment and Governance*, 8(1), 17–31. doi:10.4018/IJITBAG.2017010102

Wolf, R., & Thiel, M. (2018). Advancing Global Business Ethics in China: Reducing Poverty Through Human and Social Welfare. In S. Hipsher (Ed.), *Examining the Private Sector's Role in Wealth Creation and Poverty Reduction* (pp. 67–84). Hershey, PA: IGI Global. doi:10.4018/978-1-5225-3117-3.ch004

Wu, J., Ding, F., Xu, M., Mo, Z., & Jin, A. (2016). Investigating the Determinants of Decision-Making on Adoption of Public Cloud Computing in E-government. *Journal of Global Information Management*, 24(3), 71–89. doi:10.4018/JGIM.2016070104

Xu, L., & de Vrieze, P. (2016). Building Situational Applications for Virtual Enterprises. In I. Lee (Ed.), *Encyclopedia of E-Commerce Development, Implementation, and Management* (pp. 715–724). Hershey, PA: IGI Global. doi:10.4018/978-1-4666-9787-4.ch050

Related References

Yablonsky, S. (2018). Innovation Platforms: Data and Analytics Platforms. In *Multi-Sided Platforms (MSPs) and Sharing Strategies in the Digital Economy: Emerging Research and Opportunities* (pp. 72–95). Hershey, PA: IGI Global. doi:10.4018/978-1-5225-5457-8.ch003

Yusoff, A., Ahmad, N. H., & Halim, H. A. (2017). Agropreneurship among Gen Y in Malaysia: The Role of Academic Institutions. In N. Ahmad, T. Ramayah, H. Halim, & S. Rahman (Eds.), *Handbook of Research on Small and Medium Enterprises in Developing Countries* (pp. 23–47). Hershey, PA: IGI Global. doi:10.4018/978-1-5225-2165-5.ch002

Zanin, F., Comuzzi, E., & Costantini, A. (2018). The Effect of Business Strategy and Stock Market Listing on the Use of Risk Assessment Tools. In *Management Control Systems in Complex Settings: Emerging Research and Opportunities* (pp. 145–168). Hershey, PA: IGI Global. doi:10.4018/978-1-5225-3987-2.ch007

Zgheib, P. W. (2017). Corporate Innovation and Intrapreneurship in the Middle East. In P. Zgheib (Ed.), *Entrepreneurship and Business Innovation in the Middle East* (pp. 37–56). Hershey, PA: IGI Global. doi:10.4018/978-1-5225-2066-5.ch003

About the Contributors

Debasish Batabyal, Ph.D., M.Com, MBA (Tourism), is an Assistant Professor in Amity Institute of Travel & Tourism, Amity University, Kolkata with a teaching experience of eleven years. He started his career in a Swiss MNC (SOTC, Kolkata) in 2003 as an Assistant Documentation Officer and switched over to academics thereafter. He has 35 publications in international and national journals of repute and edited two books with international publishers. He presents research papers in international and national conferences and designs short term training programs for industry and academics. Besides, he is associated with the Board of Studies of two universities offering post graduate and undergraduate programs in India. He was the member of the prestigious committees responsible for UNDP report, Gazettes, etc.

Dillip Kumar Das is currently working as an Associate Professor in the Department of Tourism, Sikkim Central University. He has been awarded PhD in the year 2008 in Tourism from Utkal University, Bhubaneswar, Orissa on the topic "Economic, Socio Cultural and Environmental Impact of Tourism: A case Study on Puri, Konark and Bhubaneswar". He has Completed Masters in Tourism Management (MTM) from IGNOU, and also Two times Qualified UGC- NET (National Eligibility test for Lectureship) in December 2003and in 2004. He has Completed Master Degree in Economics, from Ravenshaw University, Cuttack, and also Completed Diploma in Tourism Management, from Indian Institute of Tourism and Travel Management, Bhubaneswar, Orissa. The author's areas of research interest are Eco-Tourism, Tourism Impact Studies and Travel Agency Management. He has altogether 15 years of Academic experience in tourism education. The author is now currently associated with different university and institute of repute in India including I.G.N.O.U, IITTM, Magadh University, Utkal University, etc.

* * *

Carlos J. L. Balsas, Ph.D., AICP, is an assistant professor in the Geography and Planning Department at the University at Albany in New York (SUNY). His major publications include Commercial Urbanism in Portugal (1999) and Commercial Urbanism and Public-Private Partnerships (2002), both books were published by the Office of Economic and Prospective Studies (GEPE) – Portuguese Ministry of Economy, Lisbon, and Walkable Cities – Revitalization, Vibrancy and Sustainable Consumption across the Atlantic Ocean (2019) forthcoming by SUNY Press. Before joining the University at Albany in 2014 he was an assistant professor at Arizona State University (ASU) (2004–2011). His research interests include Comparative Urban Revitalization, Sustainable Transportation Planning, and Planning Pedagogy.

Floribert Patrick C. Endong, Ph.D. is a research consultant in the humanities and social sciences. He is a reviewer and editor with many scientific journals in the social sciences. His current research interest focuses on religious communications, religious tourism, international communication, gender studies, digital media, media laws, international relations and culture. He is author of more than 100 peer-reviewed articles and book chapters in the above mentioned areas of interest. He recently edited a book titled "Exploring the Role of Social Media in Transnational Advocacy" published by IGI Global (Hershey, USA).

Murat Erdoğan is Assistant Professor in Akdeniz University, Faculty of Economics and Administrative Sciences, Department of Business Administration, Turkey. His research interests generally focused on internal control, internal audit, occupational fraud and business performance.

Mehmet Kocaman is a lecturer at Zile Dinçerler School of Tourism and Hotel Management, Tokat Gaziosmanpasa University, Turkey. He obtained his master degree from Ahmet Yesevi University in 2005 and another his master degree Karadeniz Technical University in 2008. He has teaching experience on the accounting, finance, economics, business.

Emel Memis Kocaman obtained her PhD degree from Gazi University in 2009. She is an associate professor and head of the department of food and beverage management at Tokat Gaziosmanpasa University, Turkey. Her research interests are food & beverage management, gastronomy, traditional foods, menu, food safety, nutrition.

Abhijit Pandit, Ph.D., M.B.A., M.Sc., MIMA, has more than 11 years of full-time teaching and research experience, areas of interest are Services Marketing, Hospitality Management, Consumer Behavior, Operations Research, Econometrics, Quantitative Techniques, etc.

Natisha Saqib is Assistant Professor, Department of Management Studies, University of Kashmir. She has eight years of experience in teaching, research and management training. Her work has been published in many leading international journals. Her research interests include strategic marketing, advertising, consumer behavior and tourism marketing.

Partho Pratim Seal is an Assistant Professor at Welcomgroup Graduate School of Hotel Administration (WGSHA), Manipal Academy of Higher Education, Manipal. Currently pursuing (PhD) in Hotel and Tourism Management, has published articles in reputed journals and has authored three books Computers in Hotels: Concepts and Application, Food and Beverage Management and How to Succeed in Hotel Management Job Interviews.

Ravi Sharma is currently working as an Assistant Professor in the Department of Energy and Environment with Symbiosis Institute of International Business (SIIB) under Symbiosis International University, Pune, India. Masters of Science in Zoology with Environmental Sciences and Toxicology as specialization and Ph.D. in Forestry under discipline Forest Ecology and Environment from Forest Research Institute University (FRIU), Dehradun, India. He was also awarded Junior Research Fellowship (2003-2005) from University Grants Commission (UGC) during his research tenure with Indian Institute of Forest Management (IIFM), Bhopal. Academic area of interest is in subjects of Zoology, Environmental Sciences, GIS, and Ecology. The academic experience at higher education level is more than 8+ years. His research focus is Environmental Impact Assessment, Ecotourism and Sustainability, Ecological Risk Assessment and Environmental Monitoring. He is engaged in research and academic activities at University level. IRCA approved Lead Auditor for ISO- 14001:2015.

José G. Vargas-Hernández, M.B.A., Ph.D., Member of the National System of Researchers of Mexico and a research professor at University Center for Economic and Managerial Sciences, University of Guadalajara. Professor Vargas-Hernández has a Ph. D. in Public Administration and a Ph.D. in Organizational Economics. He has undertaken studies in Organisational Behaviour and has a Master of Business Administration, published four books and more than 200 papers in international journals and reviews (some translated to English, French, German, Portuguese, Farsi, Chinese, etc.) and more than 300 essays in national journals and reviews. He has obtained several international Awards and recognition.

Index

Ensure Quality Research is Introduced to the Academic Community

Become an IGI Global Reviewer for Authored Book Projects

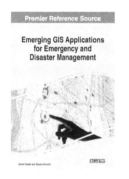

Premier Reference Source

Emerging GIS Applications for Emergency and Disaster Management

Premier Reference Source

Managerial Strategies and Green Solutions for Project Sustainability

Premier Reference Source

Comparative Approaches to Using R and Python for Statistical Data Analysis

Premier Reference Source

Solutions for High-Touch Communications in a High-Tech World

The overall success of an authored book project is dependent on quality and timely reviews.

In this competitive age of scholarly publishing, constructive and timely feedback significantly expedites the turnaround time of manuscripts from submission to acceptance, allowing the publication and discovery of forward-thinking research at a much more expeditious rate. Several IGI Global authored book projects are currently seeking highly qualified experts in the field to fill vacancies on their respective editorial review boards:

Applications may be sent to:
development@igi-global.com

Applicants must have a doctorate (or an equivalent degree) as well as publishing and reviewing experience. Reviewers are asked to write reviews in a timely, collegial, and constructive manner. All reviewers will begin their role on an ad-hoc basis for a period of one year, and upon successful completion of this term can be considered for full editorial review board status, with the potential for a subsequent promotion to Associate Editor.

If you have a colleague that may be interested in this opportunity, we encourage you to share this information with them.

Ingram Content Group UK Ltd.
Milton Keynes UK
UKHW031813210323
418905UK00012B/845